Author:	Gokurakuin Sakurako
Translator:	Lindsey Johnston
Editors:	Kevin P. Croall
	Michiko Nakayama
Production Artist:	Eileen Ho
US Cover Design:	Eileen Ho
Marketing:	Shawn Sander
V.P of Operation:	Yuki Chung
President:	Jennifer Chen

Category Freaks

Publisher
DrMaster Publications, Inc.
4044 Clipper Ct.
Fremont, CA 94538
www.DrMasterbooks.com

First Edition: June 2005
ISBN 1-58899-300-0

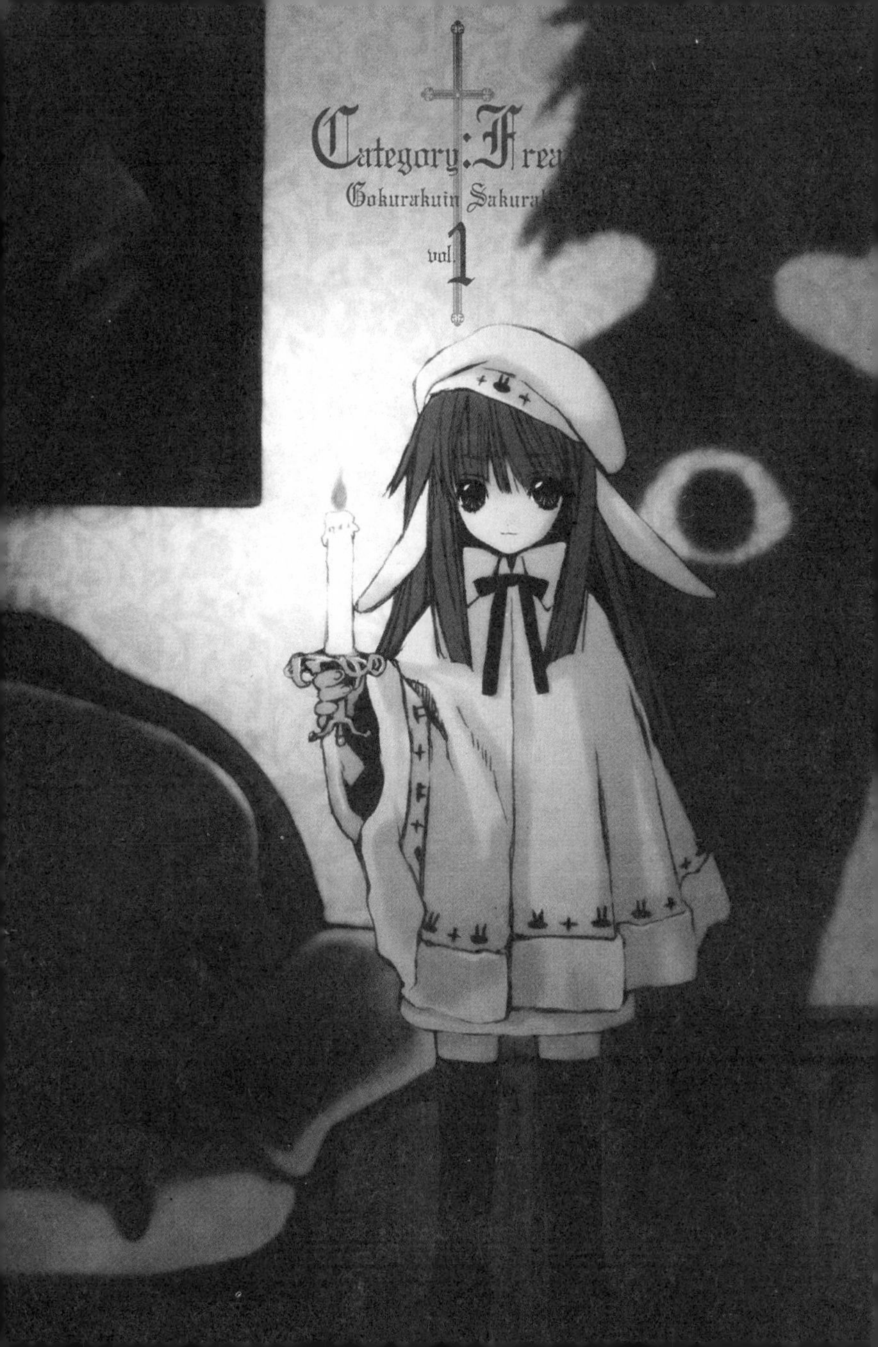

Category:Frea
Gokurakuin Sakura
vol.1

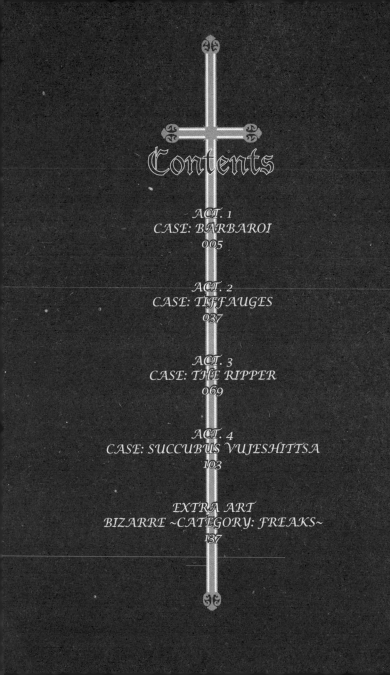

Contents

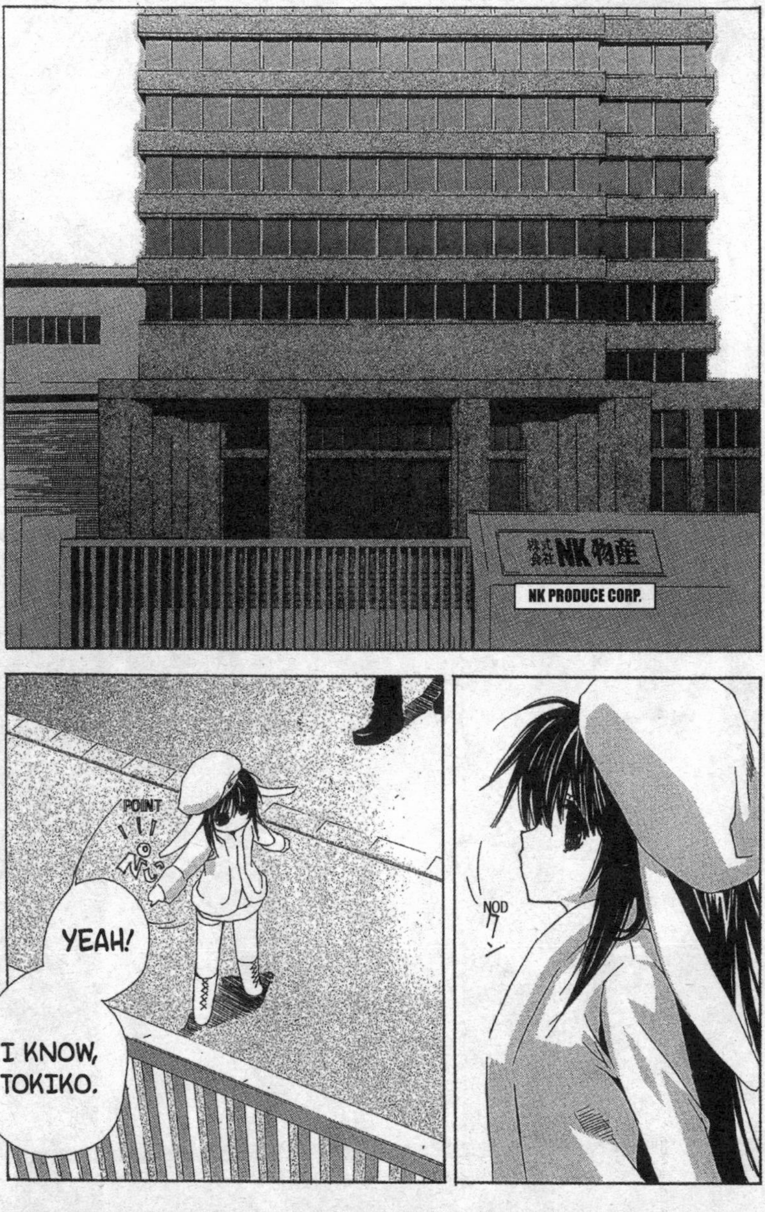
株式会社NK物産
NK PRODUCE CORP.
NOD
POINT
YEAH!
I KNOW, TOKIKO.

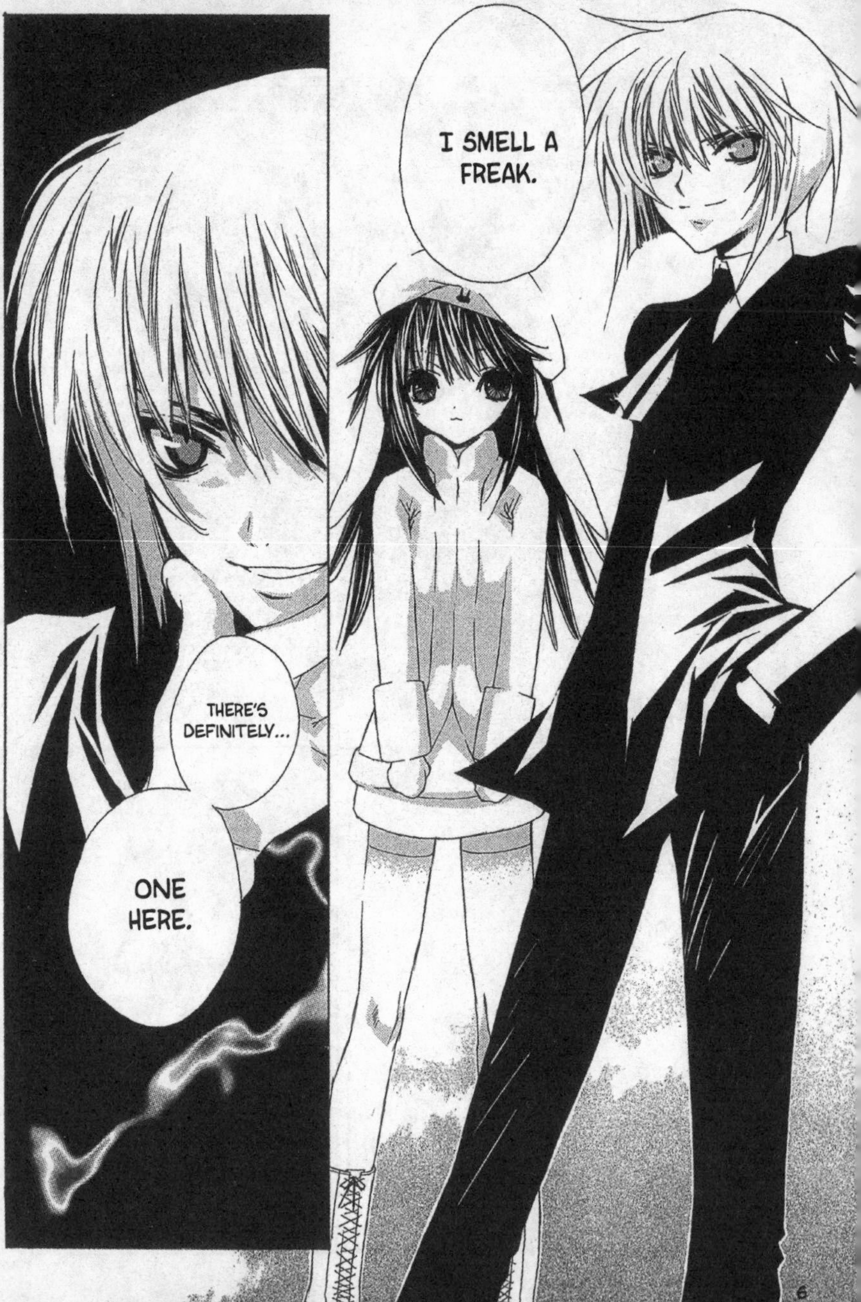
I SMELL A FREAK.
THERE'S DEFINITELY...
ONE HERE.

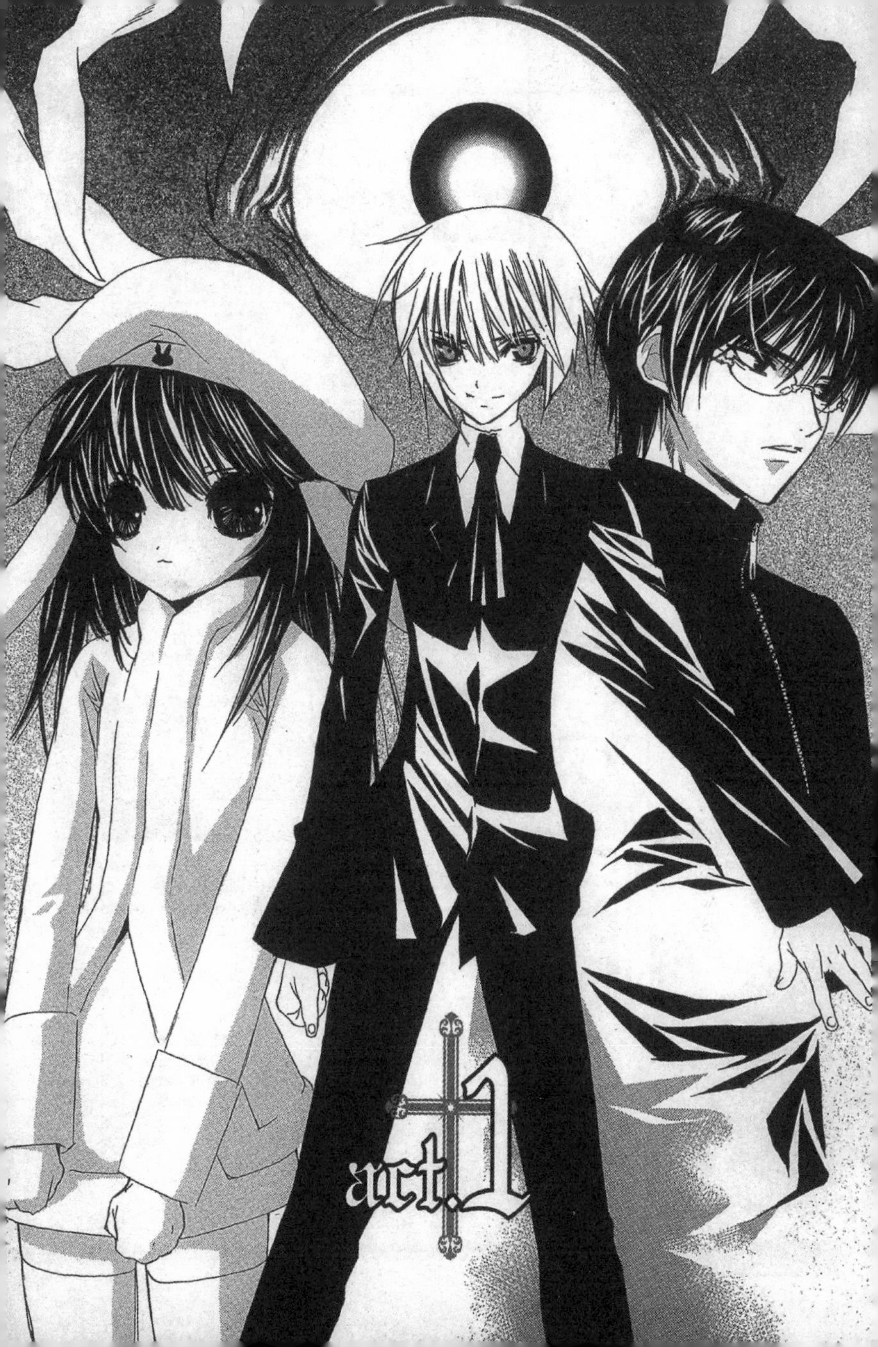
act. 1

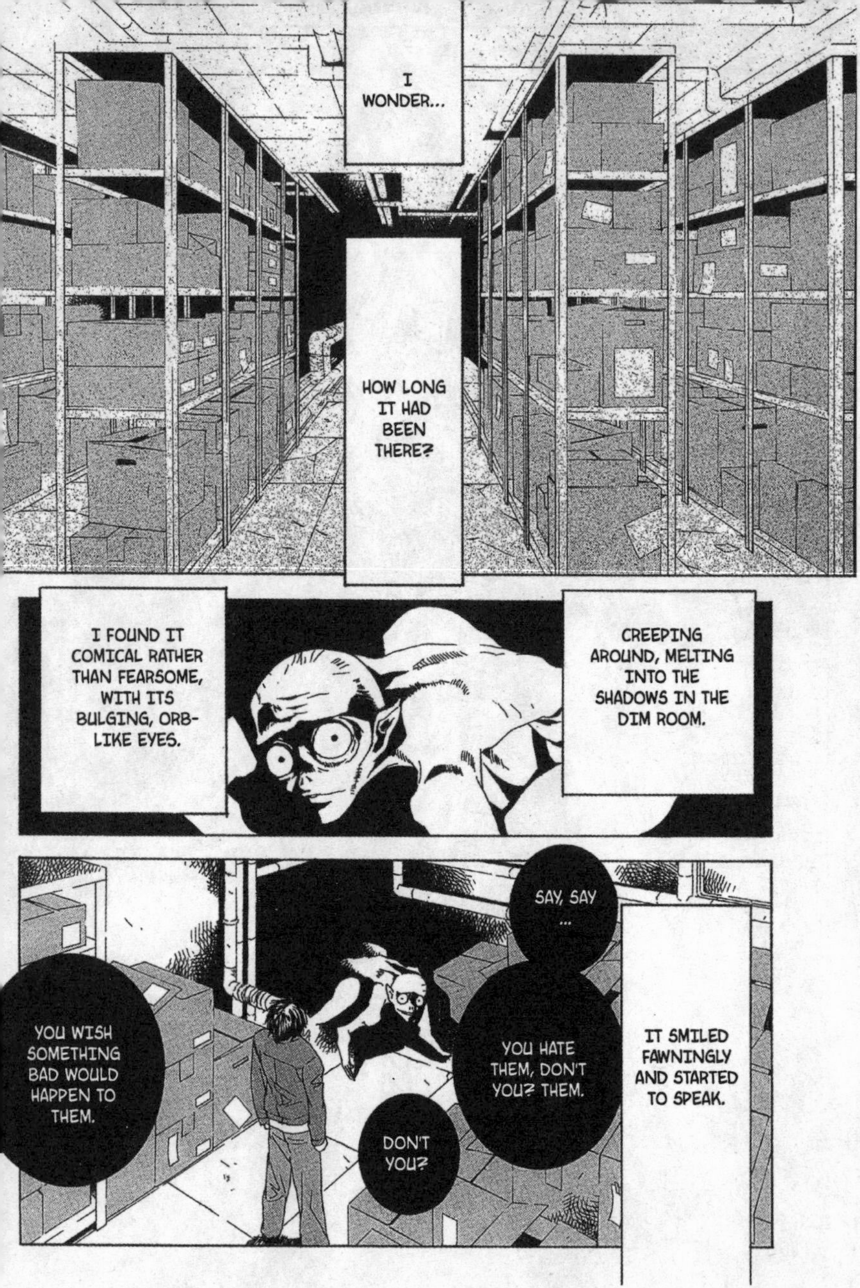
I WONDER...
HOW LONG IT HAD BEEN THERE?
CREEPING AROUND, MELTING INTO THE SHADOWS IN THE DIM ROOM.
I FOUND IT COMICAL RATHER THAN FEARSOME, WITH ITS BULGING, ORB-LIKE EYES.
IT SMILED FAWNINGLY AND STARTED TO SPEAK.
SAY, SAY ...
YOU HATE THEM, DON'T YOU? THEM.
DON'T YOU?
YOU WISH SOMETHING BAD WOULD HAPPEN TO THEM.

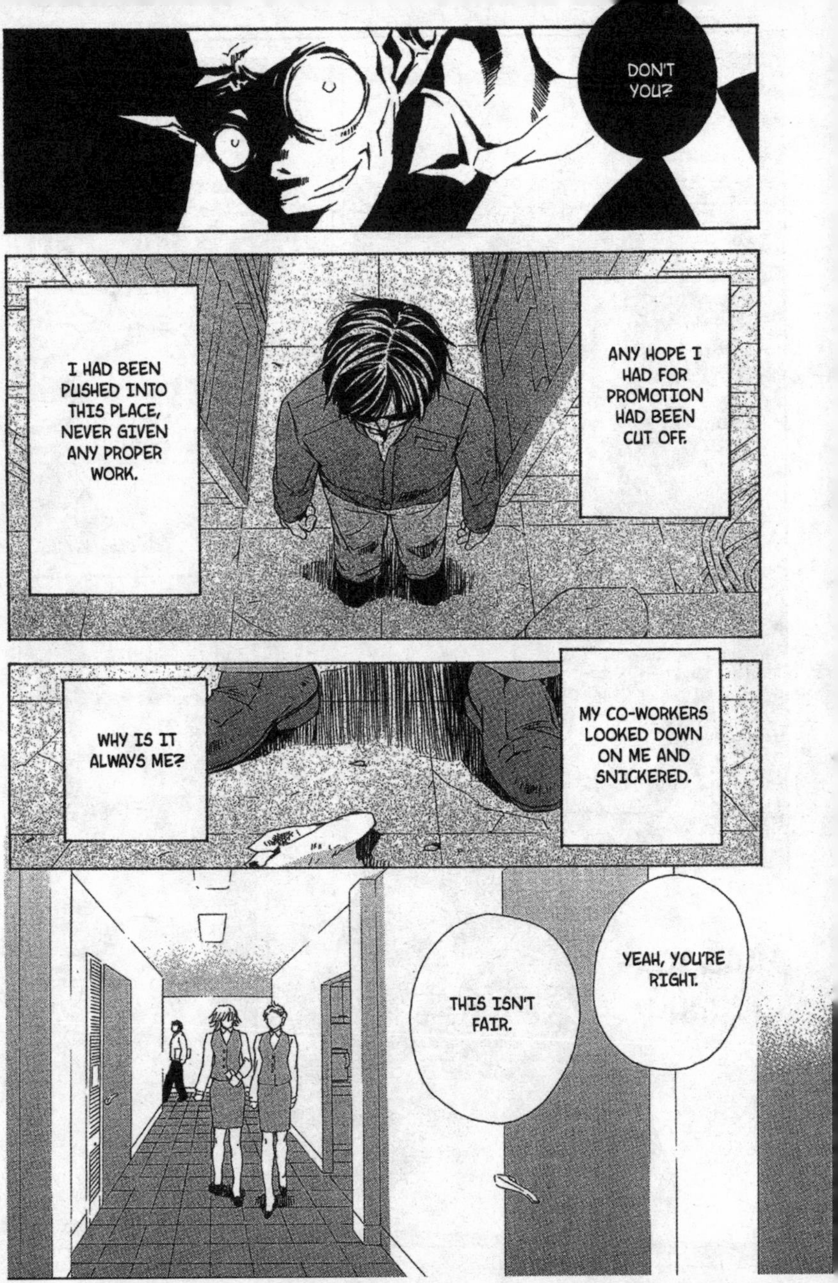
DON'T YOU?
I HAD BEEN PUSHED INTO THIS PLACE, NEVER GIVEN ANY PROPER WORK.
ANY HOPE I HAD FOR PROMOTION HAD BEEN CUT OFF.
WHY IS IT ALWAYS ME?
MY CO-WORKERS LOOKED DOWN ON ME AND SNICKERED.
YEAH, YOU'RE RIGHT.
THIS ISN'T FAIR.

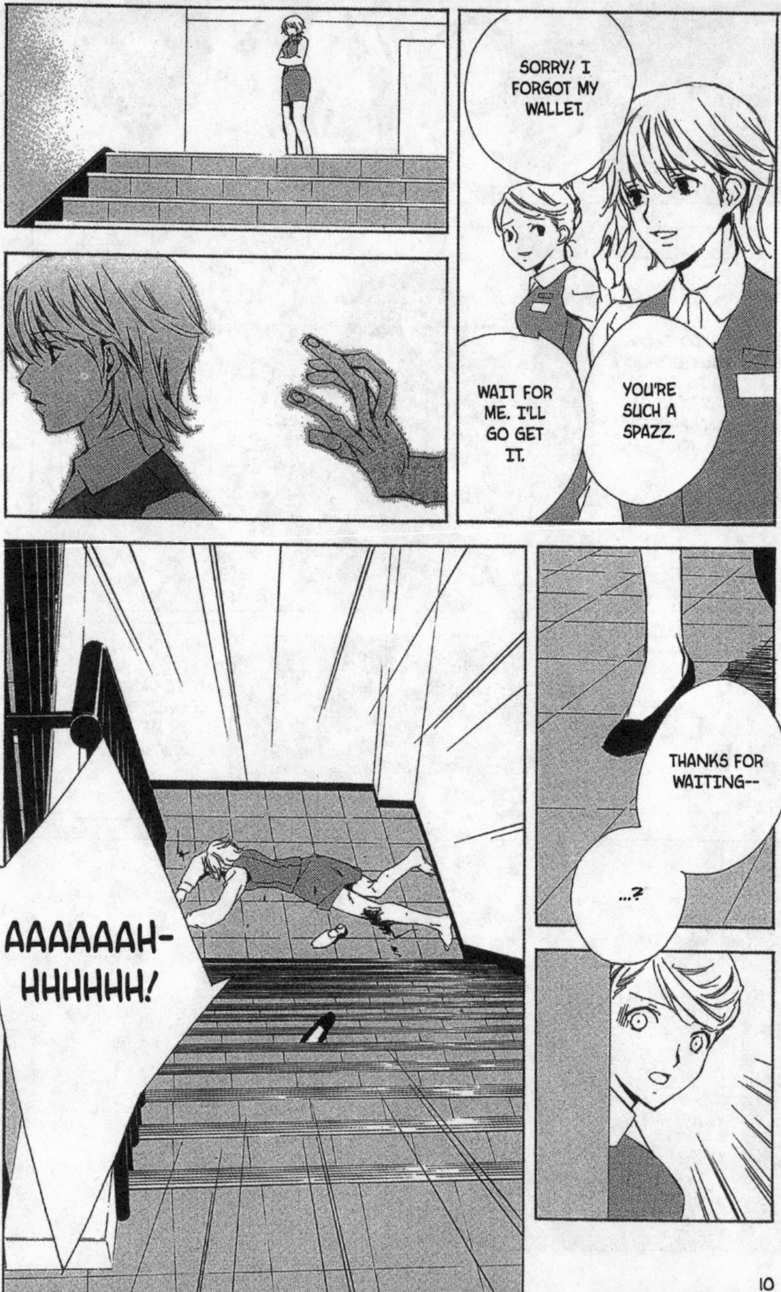
SORRY! I FORGOT MY WALLET.
YOU'RE SUCH A SPAZZ.
WAIT FOR ME. I'LL GO GET IT.
THANKS FOR WAITING--
...?
AAAAAH-HHHHHH!

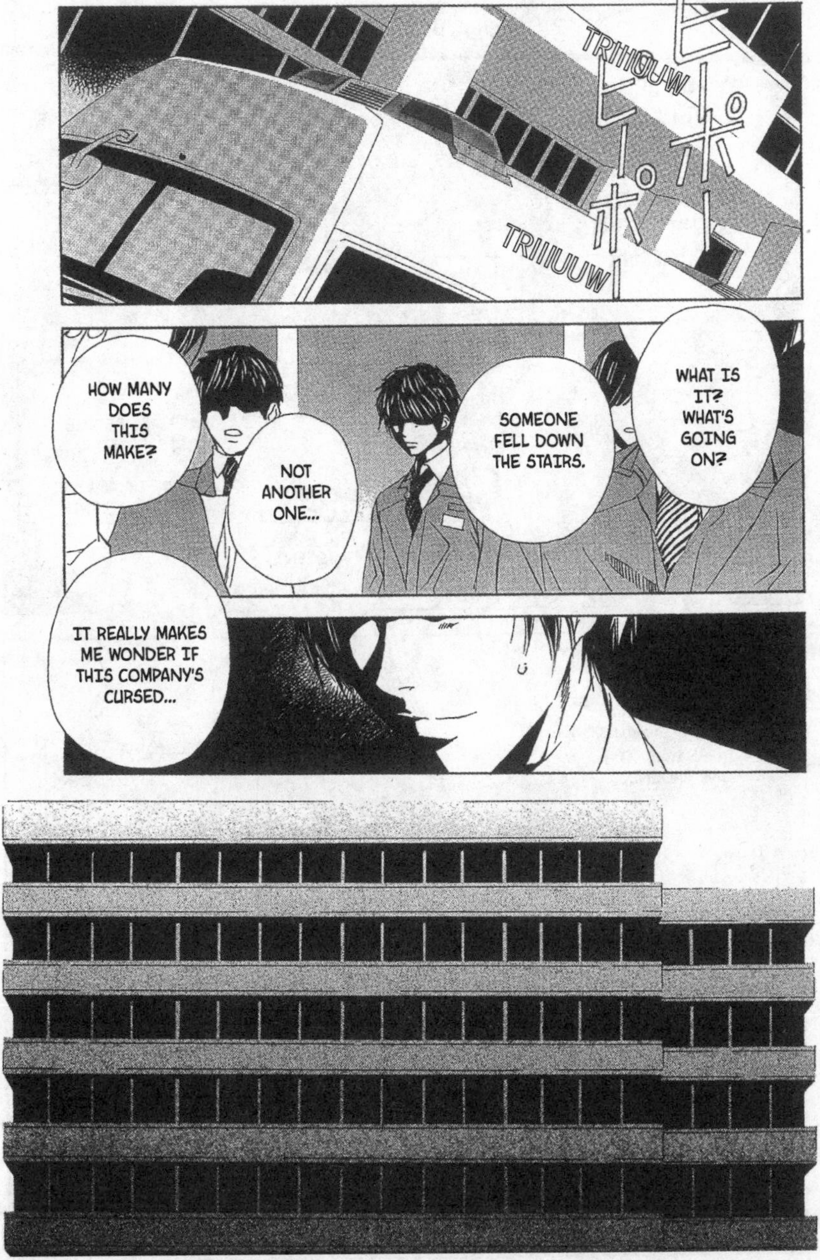
TRIIIUUW
ピーポーピーポー
TRIIIUUW
WHAT IS IT? WHAT'S GOING ON?
SOMEONE FELL DOWN THE STAIRS.
NOT ANOTHER ONE...
HOW MANY DOES THIS MAKE?
IT REALLY MAKES ME WONDER IF THIS COMPANY'S CURSED...

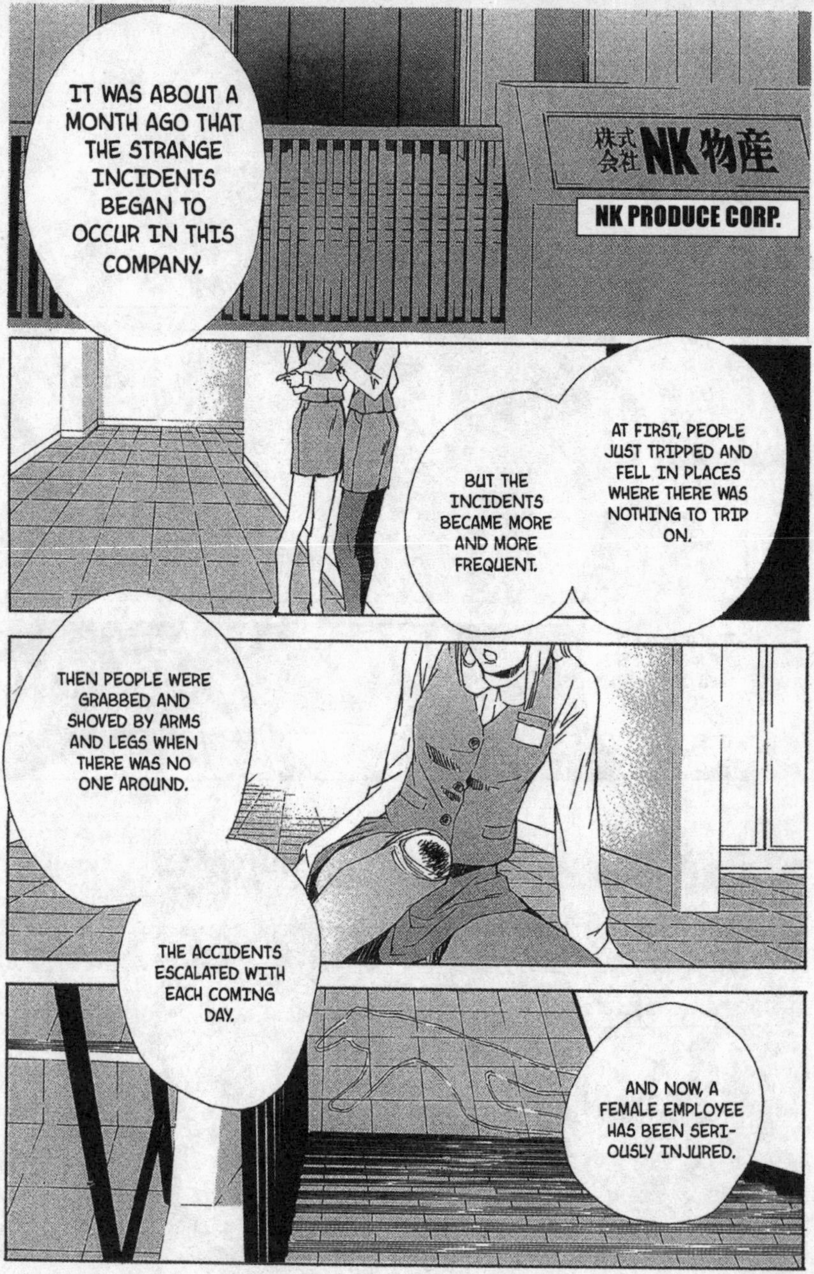
IT WAS ABOUT A MONTH AGO THAT THE STRANGE INCIDENTS BEGAN TO OCCUR IN THIS COMPANY.
株式会社 NK物産
NK PRODUCE CORP.
AT FIRST, PEOPLE JUST TRIPPED AND FELL IN PLACES WHERE THERE WAS NOTHING TO TRIP ON.
BUT THE INCIDENTS BECAME MORE AND MORE FREQUENT.
THEN PEOPLE WERE GRABBED AND SHOVED BY ARMS AND LEGS WHEN THERE WAS NO ONE AROUND.
THE ACCIDENTS ESCALATED WITH EACH COMING DAY.
AND NOW, A FEMALE EMPLOYEE HAS BEEN SERI-OUSLY INJURED.

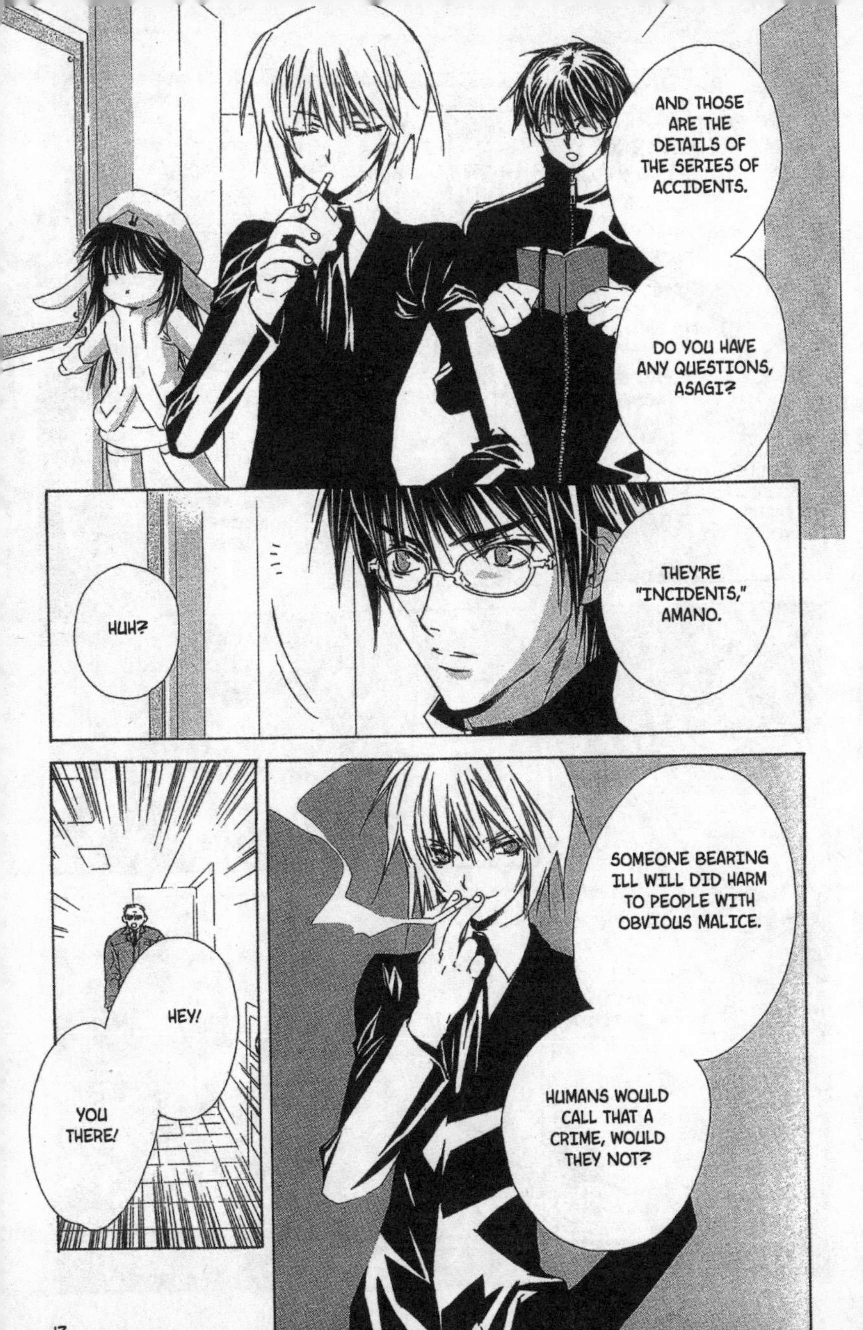
AND THOSE ARE THE DETAILS OF THE SERIES OF ACCIDENTS.
DO YOU HAVE ANY QUESTIONS, ASAGI?
THEY'RE "INCIDENTS," AMANO.
HUH?
SOMEONE BEARING ILL WILL DID HARM TO PEOPLE WITH OBVIOUS MALICE.
HUMANS WOULD CALL THAT A CRIME, WOULD THEY NOT?
HEY!
YOU THERE!

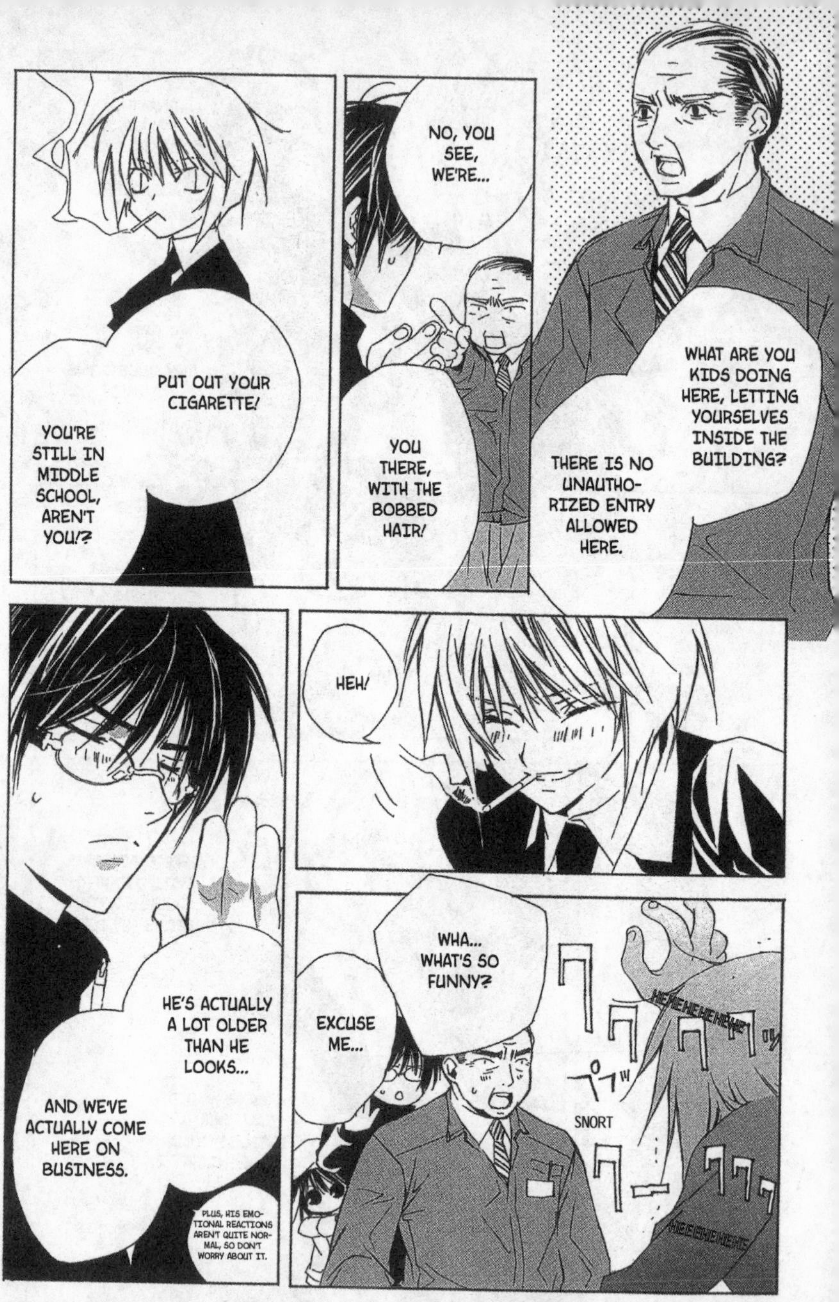
WHAT ARE YOU KIDS DOING HERE, LETTING YOURSELVES INSIDE THE BUILDING?
THERE IS NO UNAUTHO-RIZED ENTRY ALLOWED HERE.
NO, YOU SEE, WE'RE...
YOU THERE, WITH THE BOBBED HAIR!
PUT OUT YOUR CIGARETTE!
YOU'RE STILL IN MIDDLE SCHOOL, AREN'T YOU!?
HEH!
WHA... WHAT'S SO FUNNY?
SNORT
EXCUSE ME...
HE'S ACTUALLY A LOT OLDER THAN HE LOOKS...
AND WE'VE ACTUALLY COME HERE ON BUSINESS.
PLUS, HIS EMO-TIONAL REACTIONS AREN'T QUITE NOR-MAL, SO DON'T WORRY ABOUT IT.

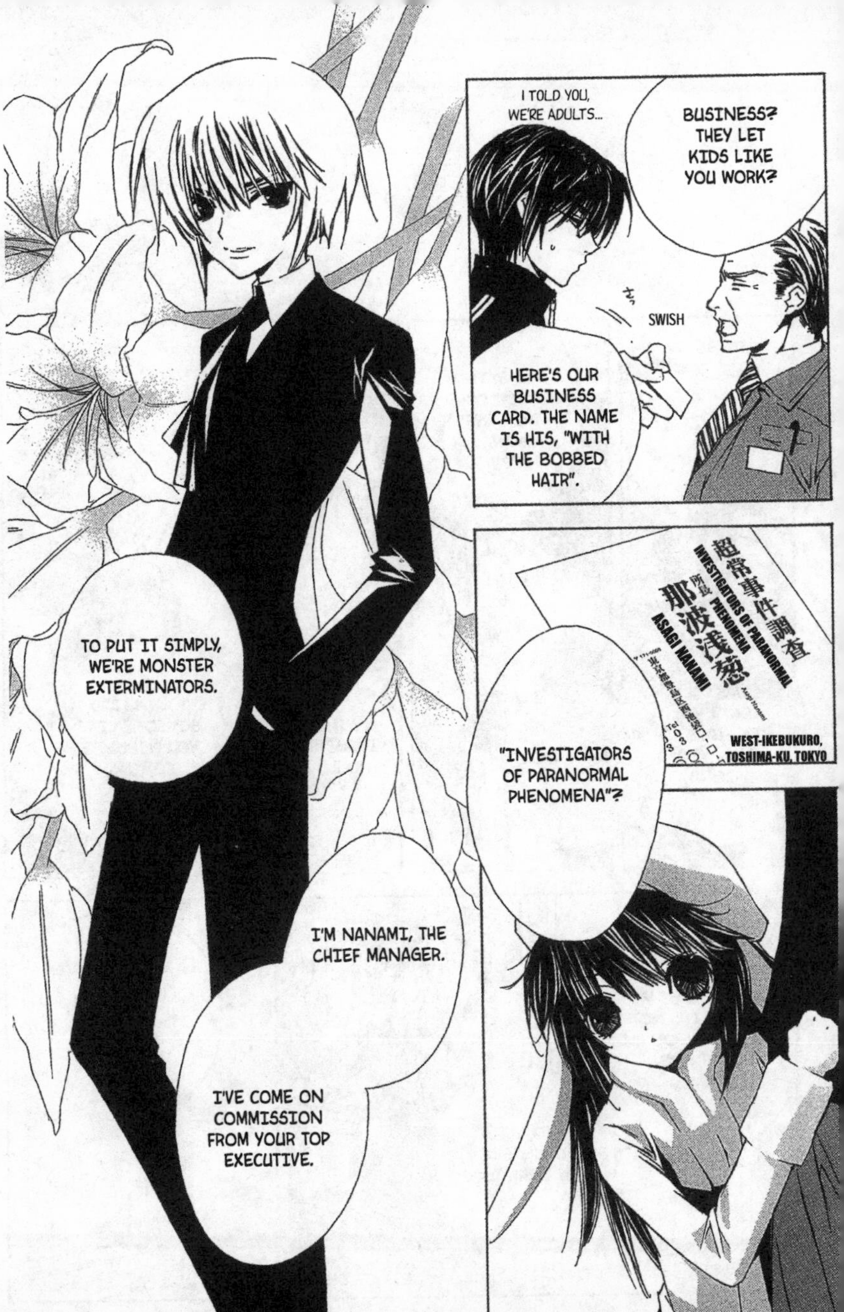
BUSINESS? THEY LET KIDS LIKE YOU WORK?
I TOLD YOU, WE'RE ADULTS...
SWISH
HERE'S OUR BUSINESS CARD. THE NAME IS HIS, "WITH THE BOBBED HAIR".
超常事件調査
INVESTIGATORS OF PARANORMAL PHENOMENA
所長 那波浅葱
ASAGI NANAMI
WEST-IKEBUKURO, TOSHIMA-KU, TOKYO
"INVESTIGATORS OF PARANORMAL PHENOMENA"?
I'M NANAMI, THE CHIEF MANAGER.
I'VE COME ON COMMISSION FROM YOUR TOP EXECUTIVE.
TO PUT IT SIMPLY, WE'RE MONSTER EXTERMINATORS.

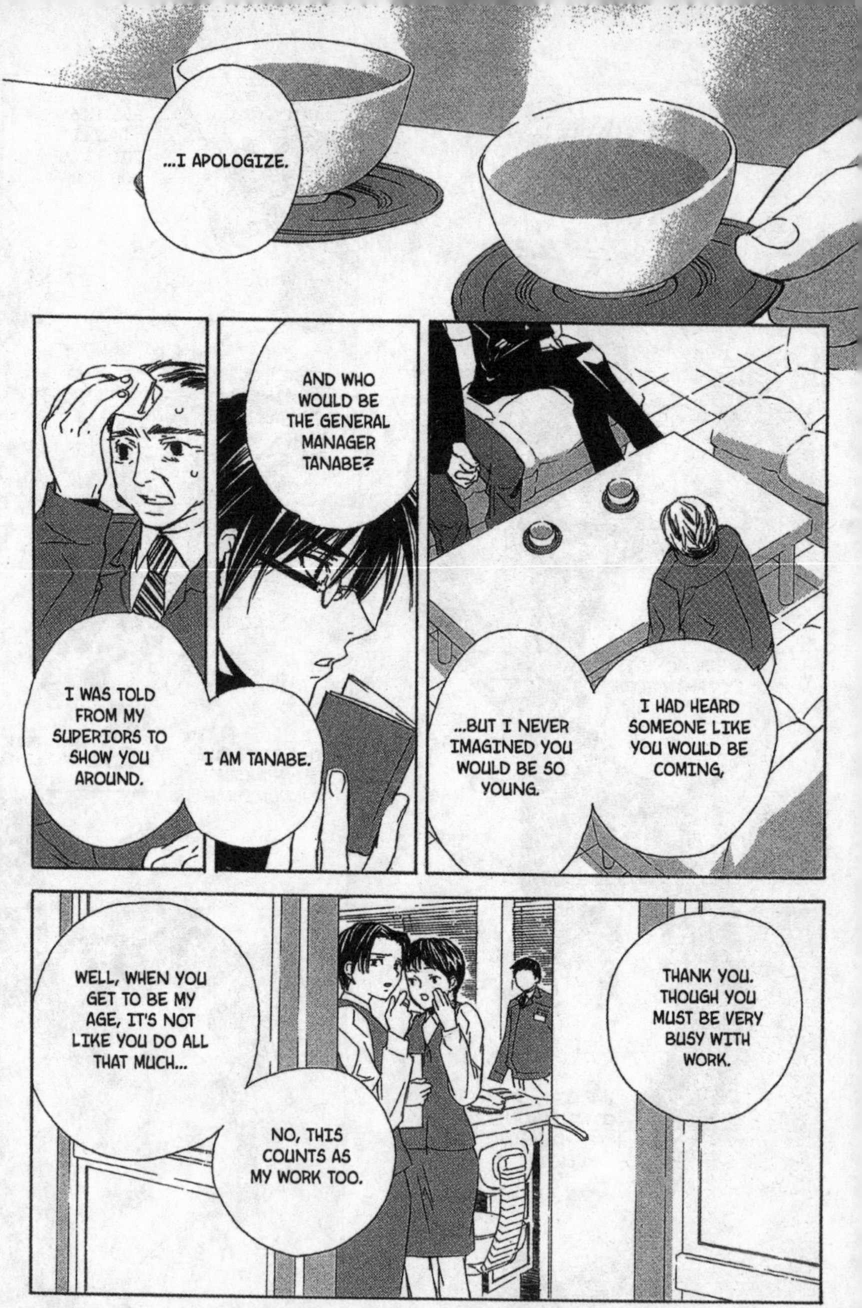
...I APOLOGIZE.
I HAD HEARD SOMEONE LIKE YOU WOULD BE COMING,
...BUT I NEVER IMAGINED YOU WOULD BE SO YOUNG.
AND WHO WOULD BE THE GENERAL MANAGER TANABE?
I AM TANABE.
I WAS TOLD FROM MY SUPERIORS TO SHOW YOU AROUND.
THANK YOU. THOUGH YOU MUST BE VERY BUSY WITH WORK.
WELL, WHEN YOU GET TO BE MY AGE, IT'S NOT LIKE YOU DO ALL THAT MUCH...
NO, THIS COUNTS AS MY WORK TOO.

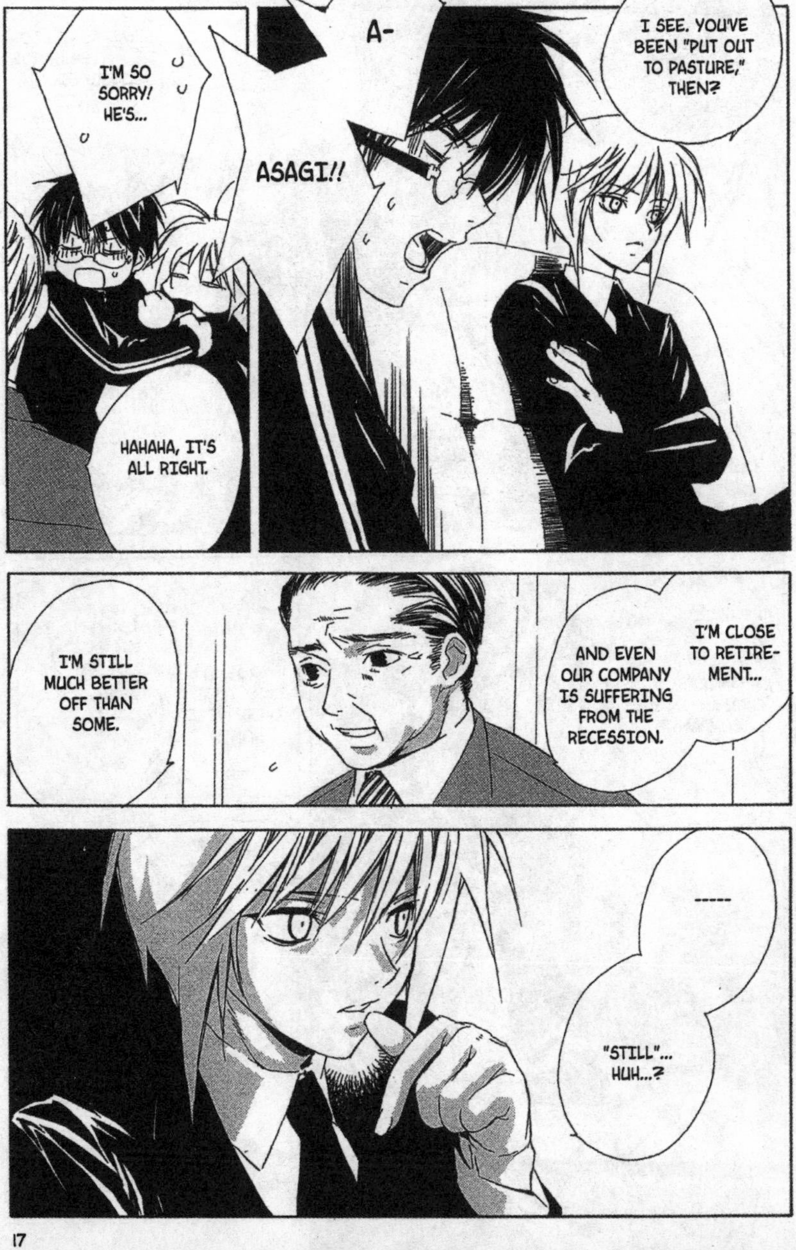
I SEE. YOU'VE BEEN "PUT OUT TO PASTURE," THEN?
A-
ASAGI!!
I'M SO SORRY! HE'S...
HAHAHA, IT'S ALL RIGHT.
I'M CLOSE TO RETIRE-MENT...
AND EVEN OUR COMPANY IS SUFFERING FROM THE RECESSION.
I'M STILL MUCH BETTER OFF THAN SOME.

"STILL"... HUH...?

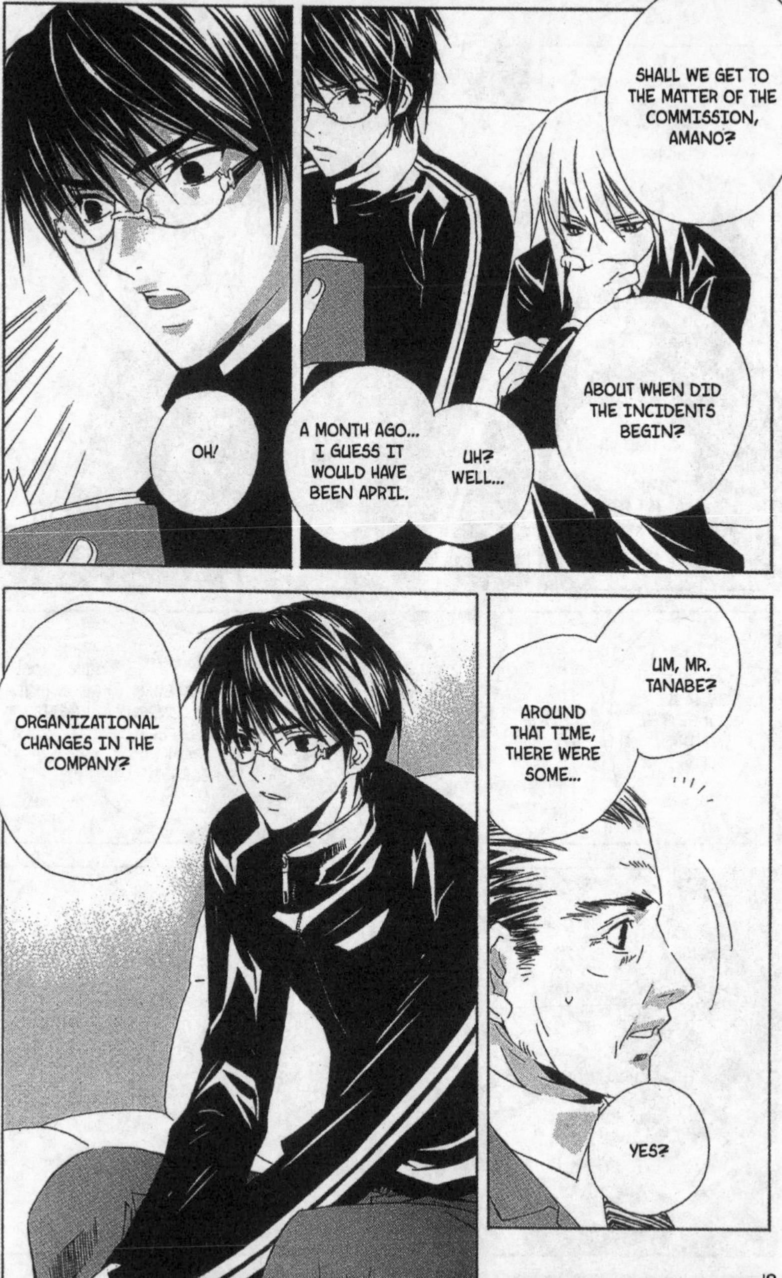
SHALL WE GET TO THE MATTER OF THE COMMISSION, AMANO?
ABOUT WHEN DID THE INCIDENTS BEGIN?
UH? WELL...
A MONTH AGO... I GUESS IT WOULD HAVE BEEN APRIL.
OH!
UM, MR. TANABE?
AROUND THAT TIME, THERE WERE SOME...
YES?
ORGANIZATIONAL CHANGES IN THE COMPANY?

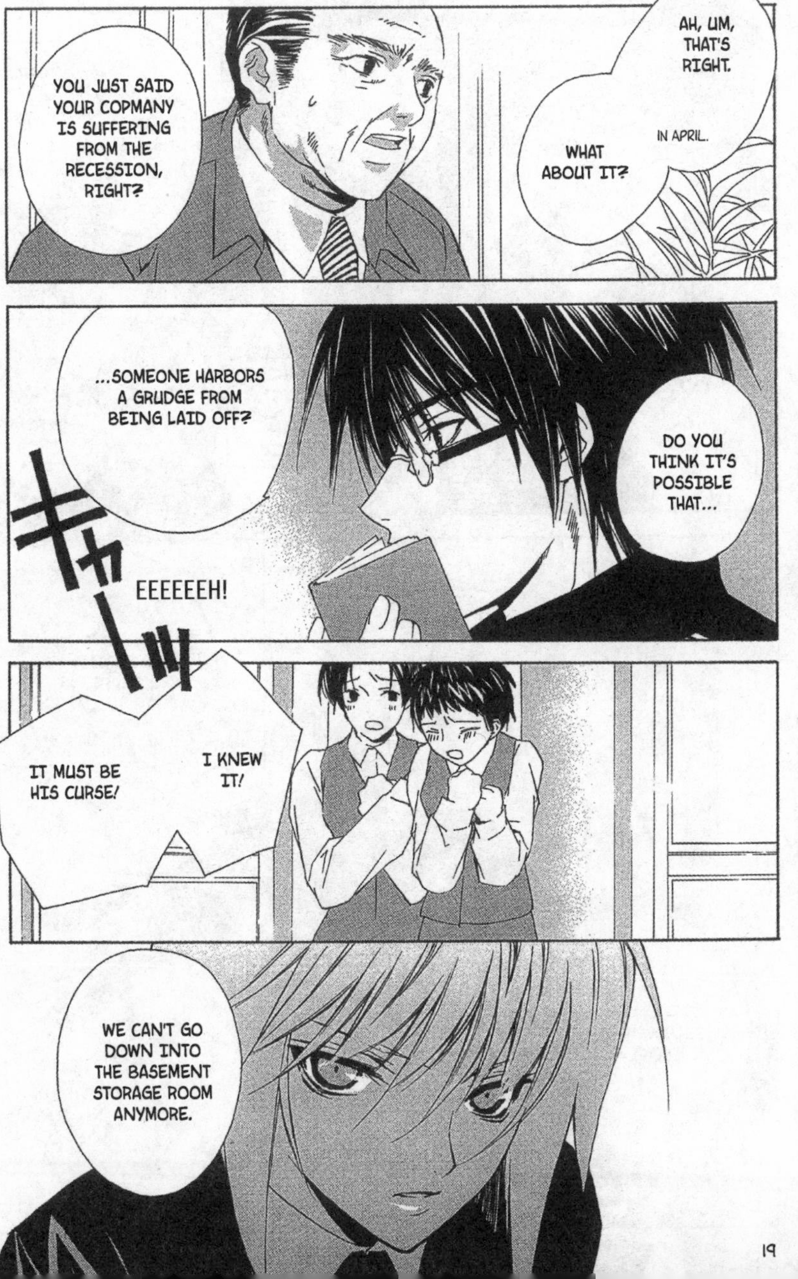
AH, UM, THAT'S RIGHT.
IN APRIL.
WHAT ABOUT IT?
YOU JUST SAID YOUR COPMANY IS SUFFERING FROM THE RECESSION, RIGHT?
DO YOU THINK IT'S POSSIBLE THAT...
...SOMEONE HARBORS A GRUDGE FROM BEING LAID OFF?
キャー
EEEEEEH!
I KNEW IT!
IT MUST BE HIS CURSE!
WE CAN'T GO DOWN INTO THE BASEMENT STORAGE ROOM ANYMORE.

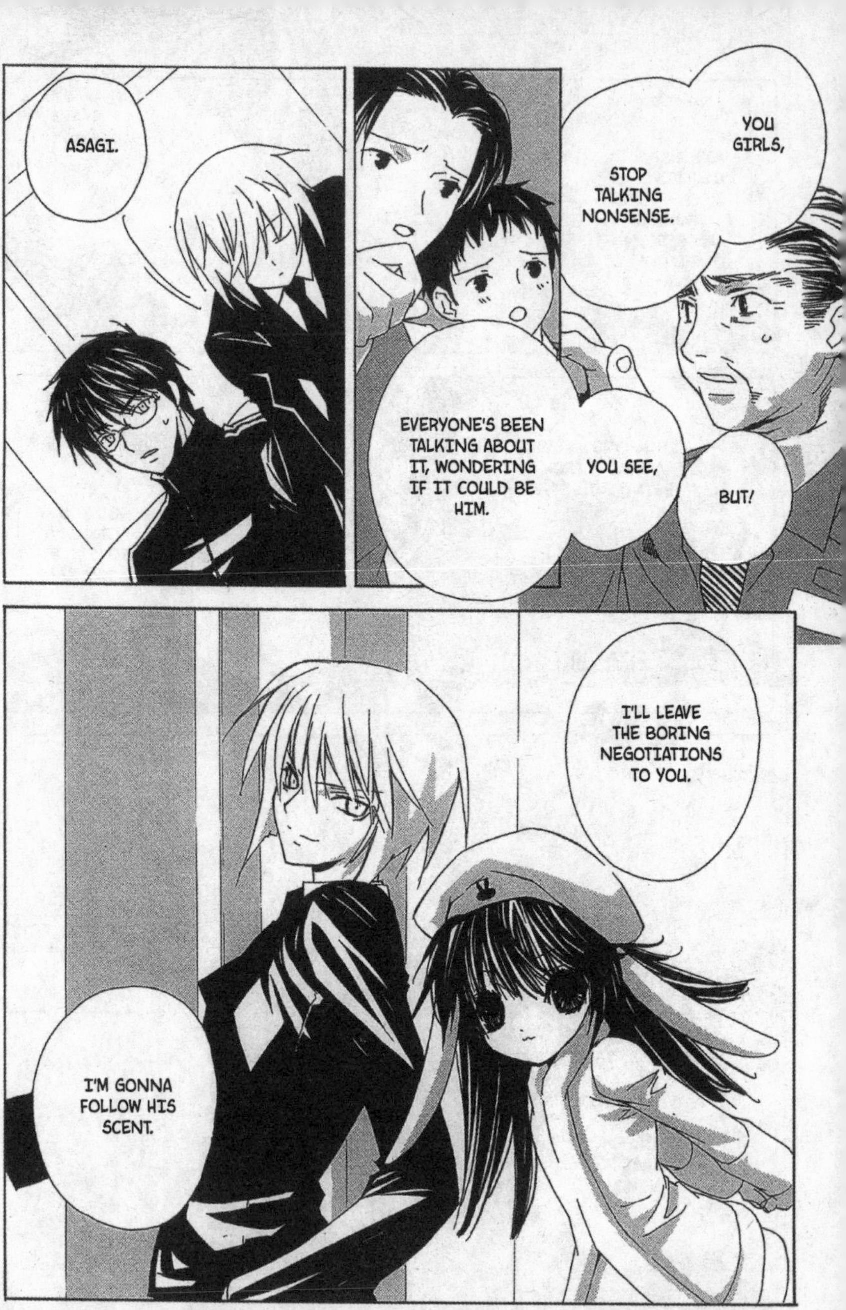
YOU GIRLS,
STOP TALKING NONSENSE.
BUT!
YOU SEE,
EVERYONE'S BEEN TALKING ABOUT IT, WONDERING IF IT COULD BE HIM.
ASAGI.
I'LL LEAVE THE BORING NEGOTIATIONS TO YOU.
I'M GONNA FOLLOW HIS SCENT.

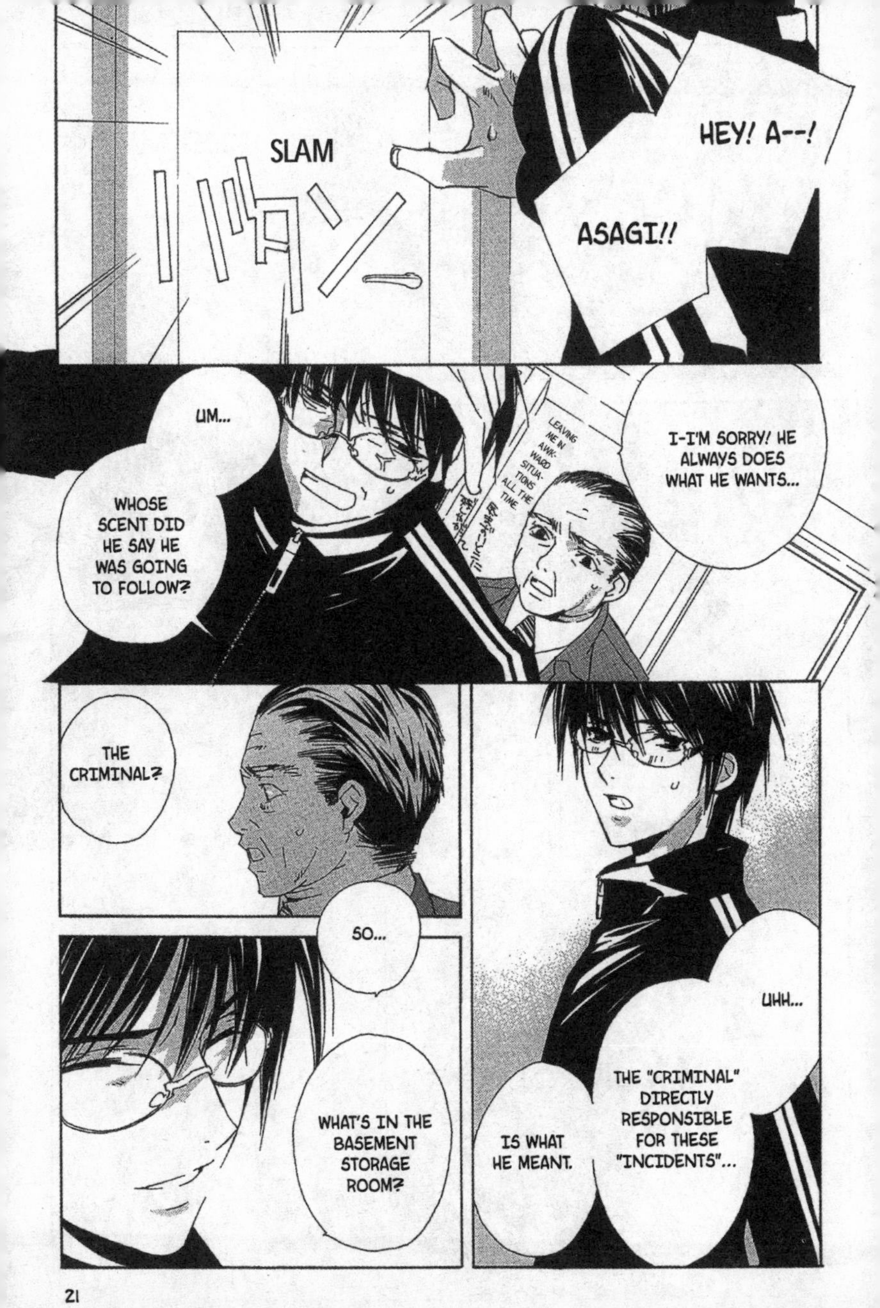
HEY! A--!
ASAGI!!
SLAM
I-I'M SORRY! HE ALWAYS DOES WHAT HE WANTS...
LEAVING ME IN AWK-WARD SITUA-TIONS ALL THE TIME
UM...
WHOSE SCENT DID HE SAY HE WAS GOING TO FOLLOW?
THE CRIMINAL?
UHH...
THE "CRIMINAL" DIRECTLY RESPONSIBLE FOR THESE "INCIDENTS"...
IS WHAT HE MEANT.
SO...
WHAT'S IN THE BASEMENT STORAGE ROOM?

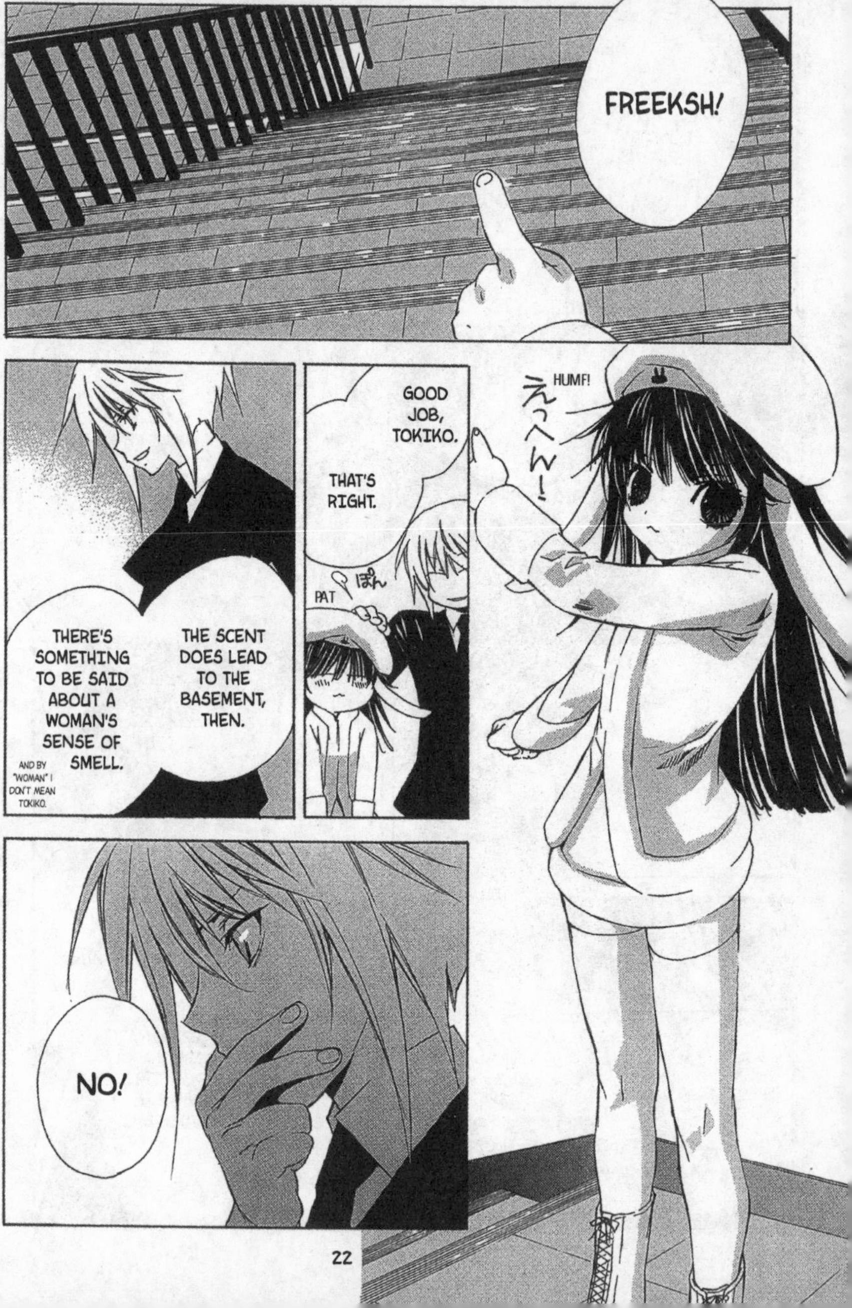
FREEKSH!
HUMF!
えっへん!
GOOD JOB, TOKIKO.
THAT'S RIGHT.
PAT
ぽん
THE SCENT DOES LEAD TO THE BASEMENT, THEN.
THERE'S SOMETHING TO BE SAID ABOUT A WOMAN'S SENSE OF SMELL.
AND BY "WOMAN" I DON'T MEAN TOKIKO.
NO!

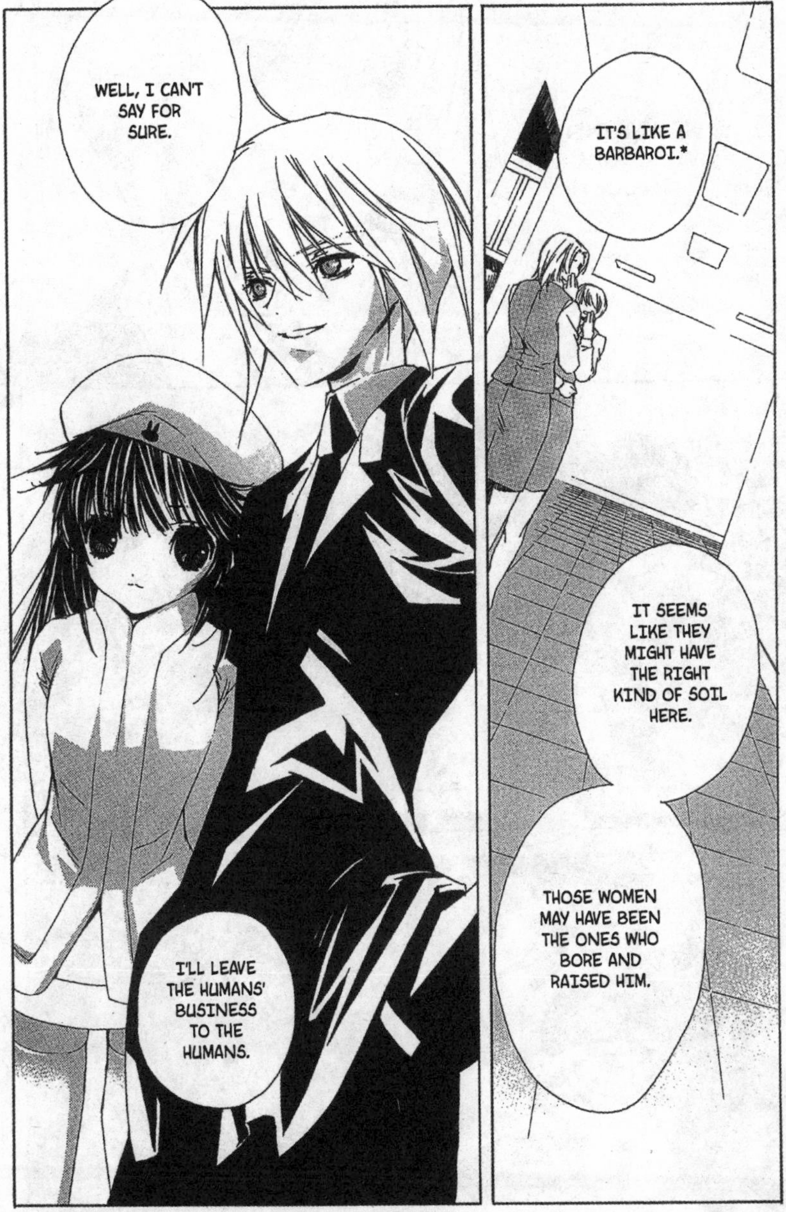
IT'S LIKE A BARBAROI.*
IT SEEMS LIKE THEY MIGHT HAVE THE RIGHT KIND OF SOIL HERE.
THOSE WOMEN MAY HAVE BEEN THE ONES WHO BORE AND RAISED HIM.
WELL, I CAN'T SAY FOR SURE.
I'LL LEAVE THE HUMANS' BUSINESS TO THE HUMANS.

*GREEK TERM FOR A NON-GREEK SPEAKER; A "BABBLER"

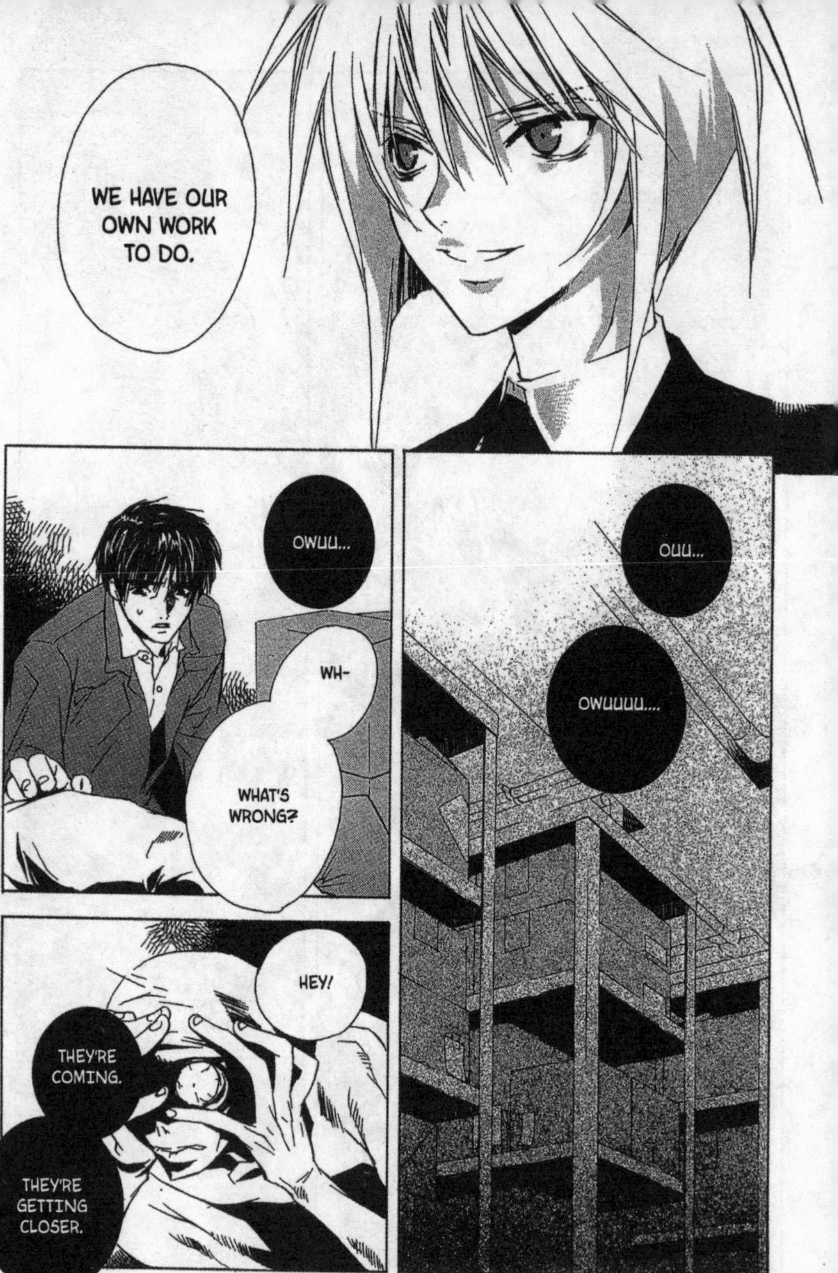
WE HAVE OUR OWN WORK TO DO.
OUU...
OWUUUU....
OWUU...
WH-
WHAT'S WRONG?
HEY!
THEY'RE COMING.
THEY'RE GETTING CLOSER.

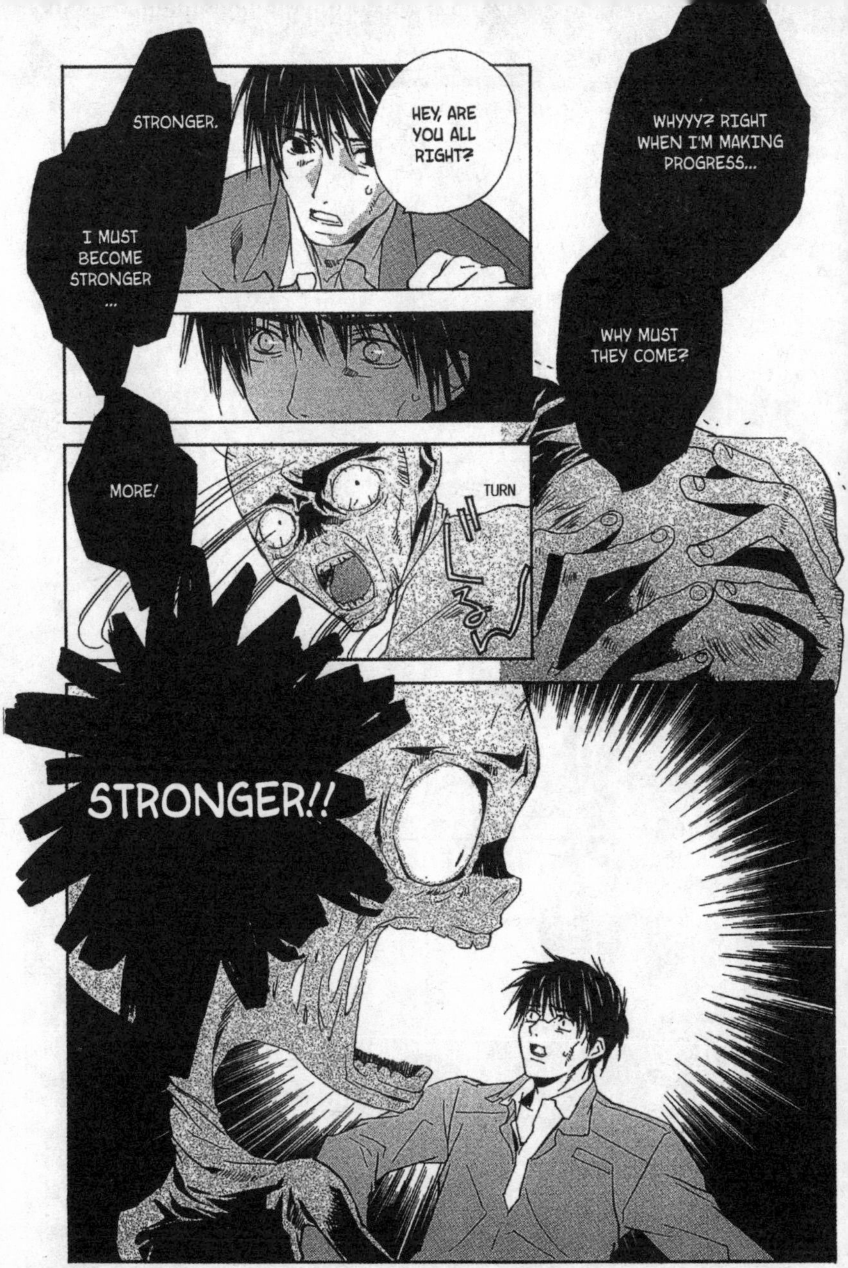
WHYYY? RIGHT WHEN I'M MAKING PROGRESS...
HEY, ARE YOU ALL RIGHT?
STRONGER.
I MUST BECOME STRONGER ...
WHY MUST THEY COME?
TURN
MORE!
STRONGER!!

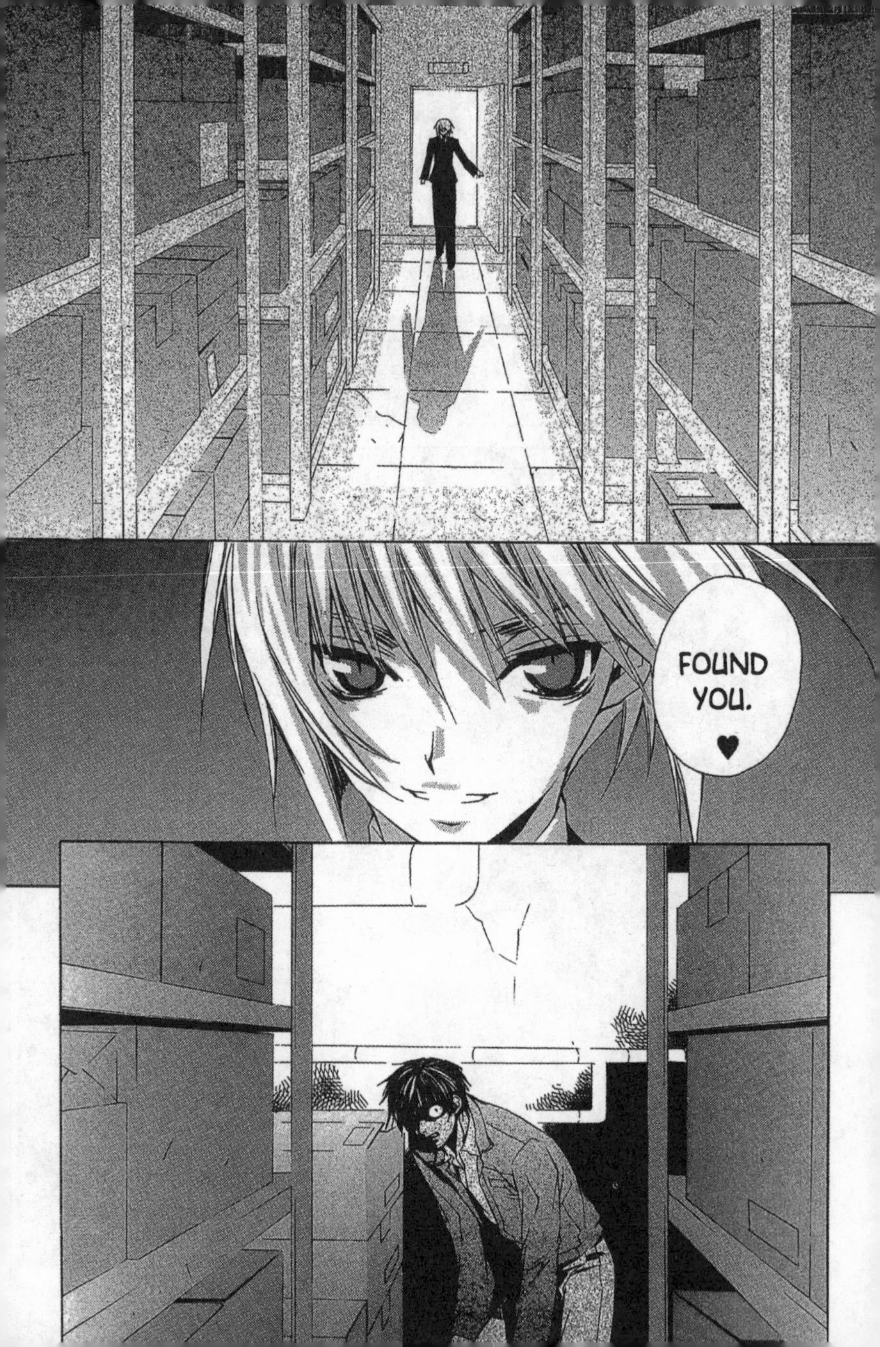
FOUND YOU. ♥

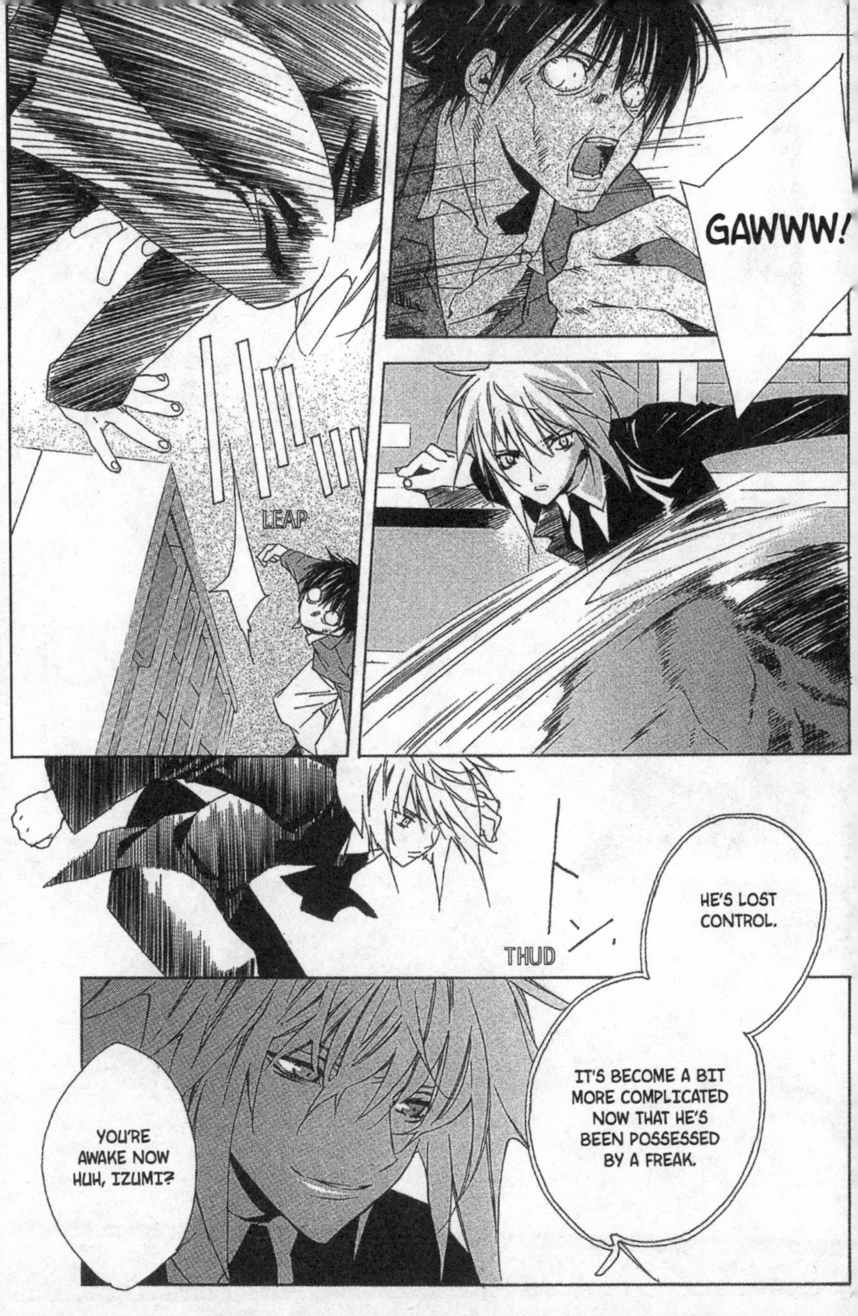
GAWWW!
LEAP
THUD
HE'S LOST CONTROL.
IT'S BECOME A BIT MORE COMPLICATED NOW THAT HE'S BEEN POSSESSED BY A FREAK.
YOU'RE AWAKE NOW HUH, IZUMI?

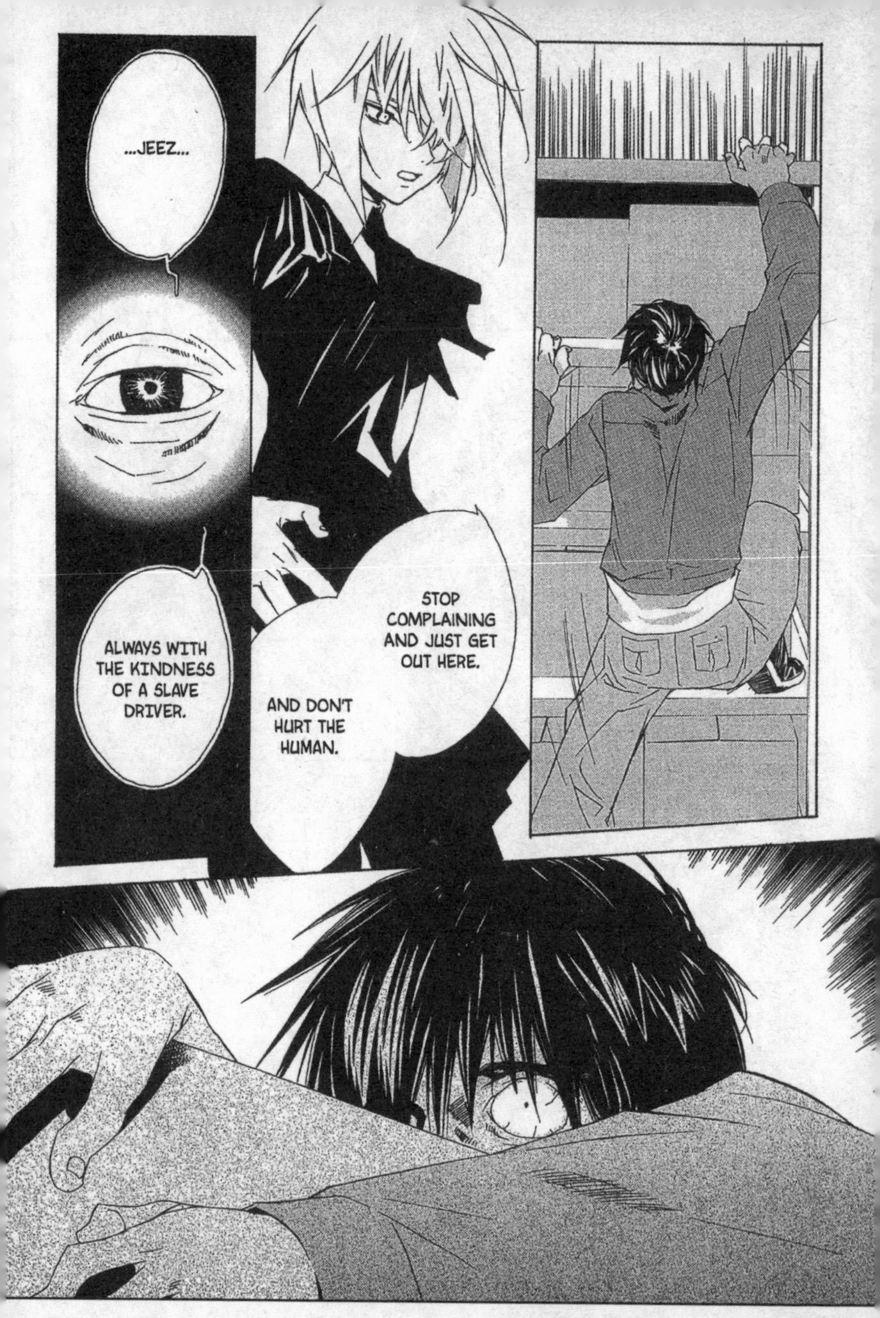
STOP COMPLAINING AND JUST GET OUT HERE.
AND DON'T HURT THE HUMAN.
...JEEZ...
ALWAYS WITH THE KINDNESS OF A SLAVE DRIVER.

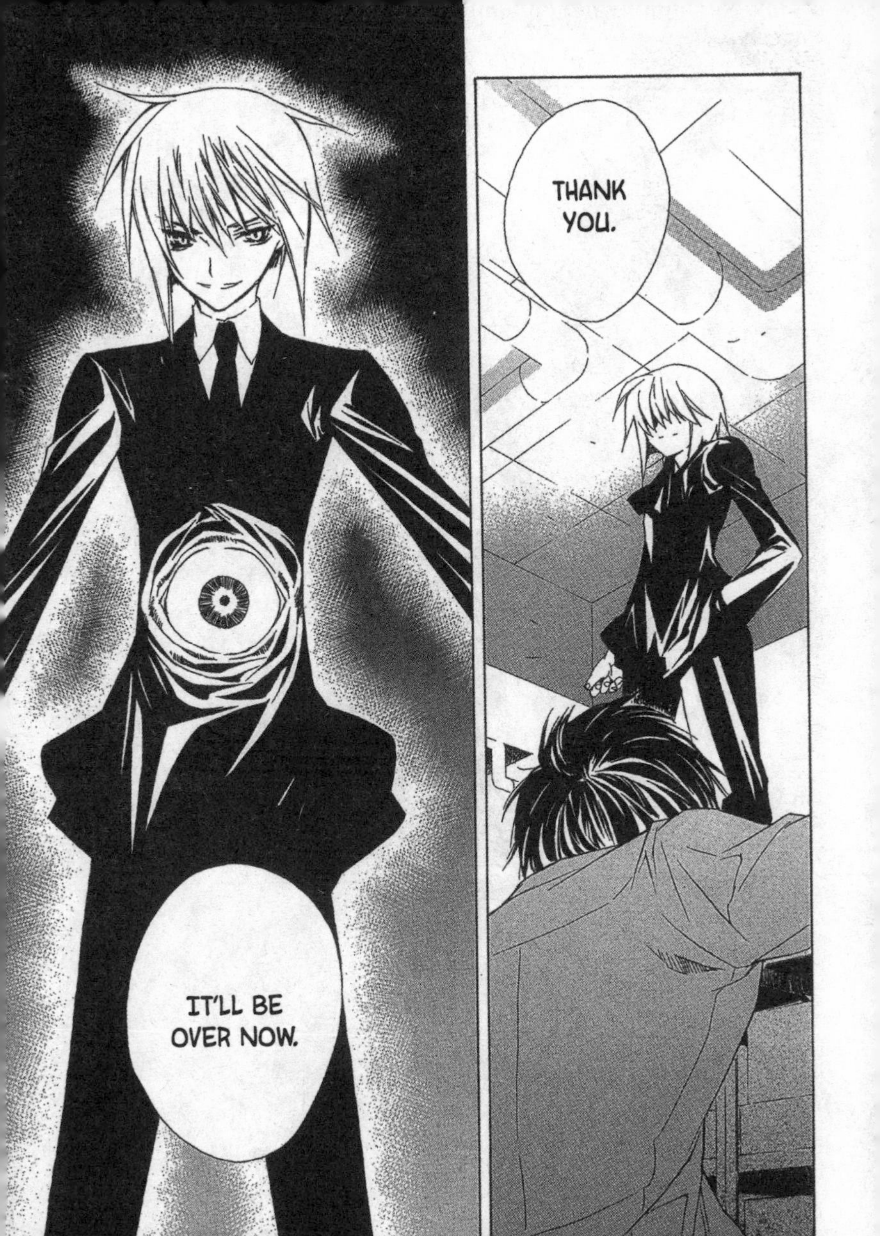
THANK YOU.
IT'LL BE OVER NOW.

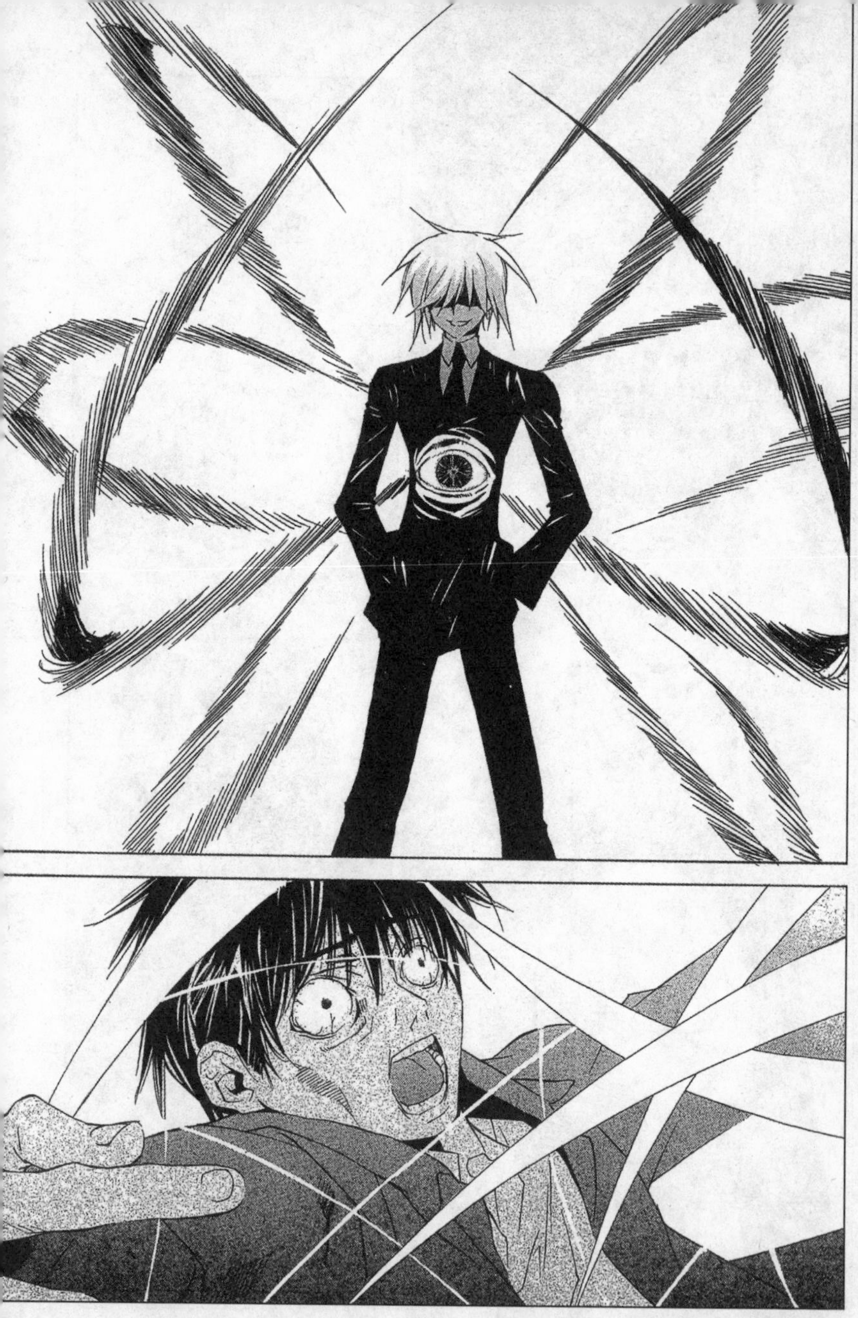

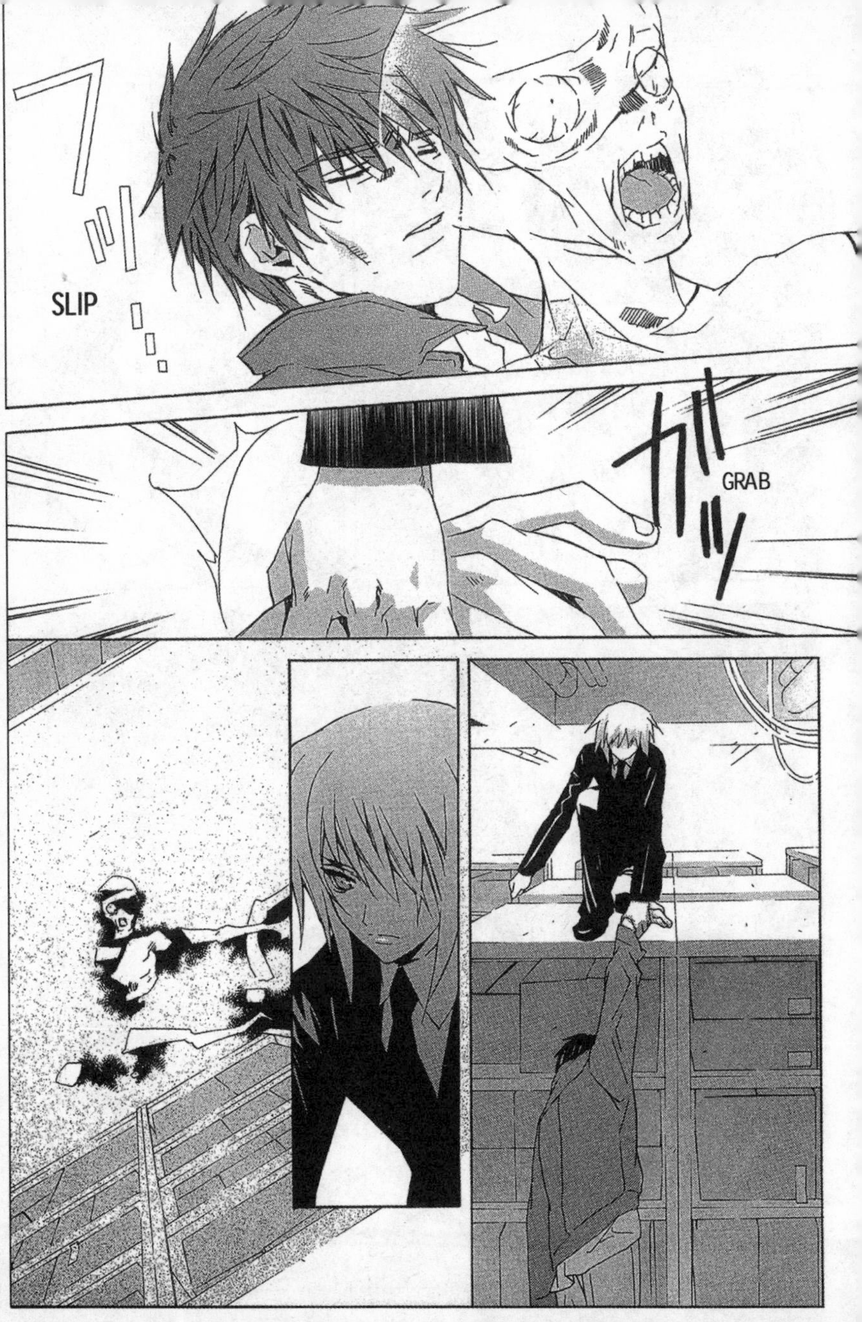
SLIP
ガッ
GRAB

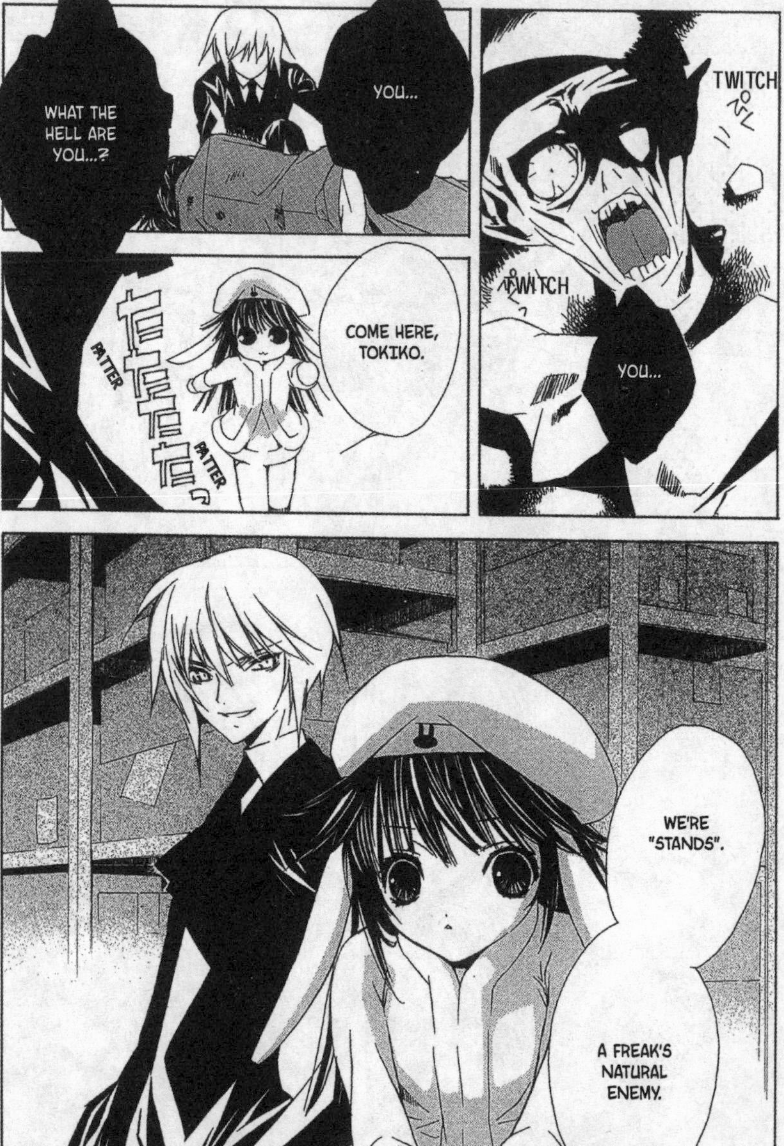
TWITCH
TWITCH
YOU...
YOU...
WHAT THE HELL ARE YOU...?
COME HERE, TOKIKO.
PATTER
PATTER
WE'RE "STANDS".
A FREAK'S NATURAL ENEMY.

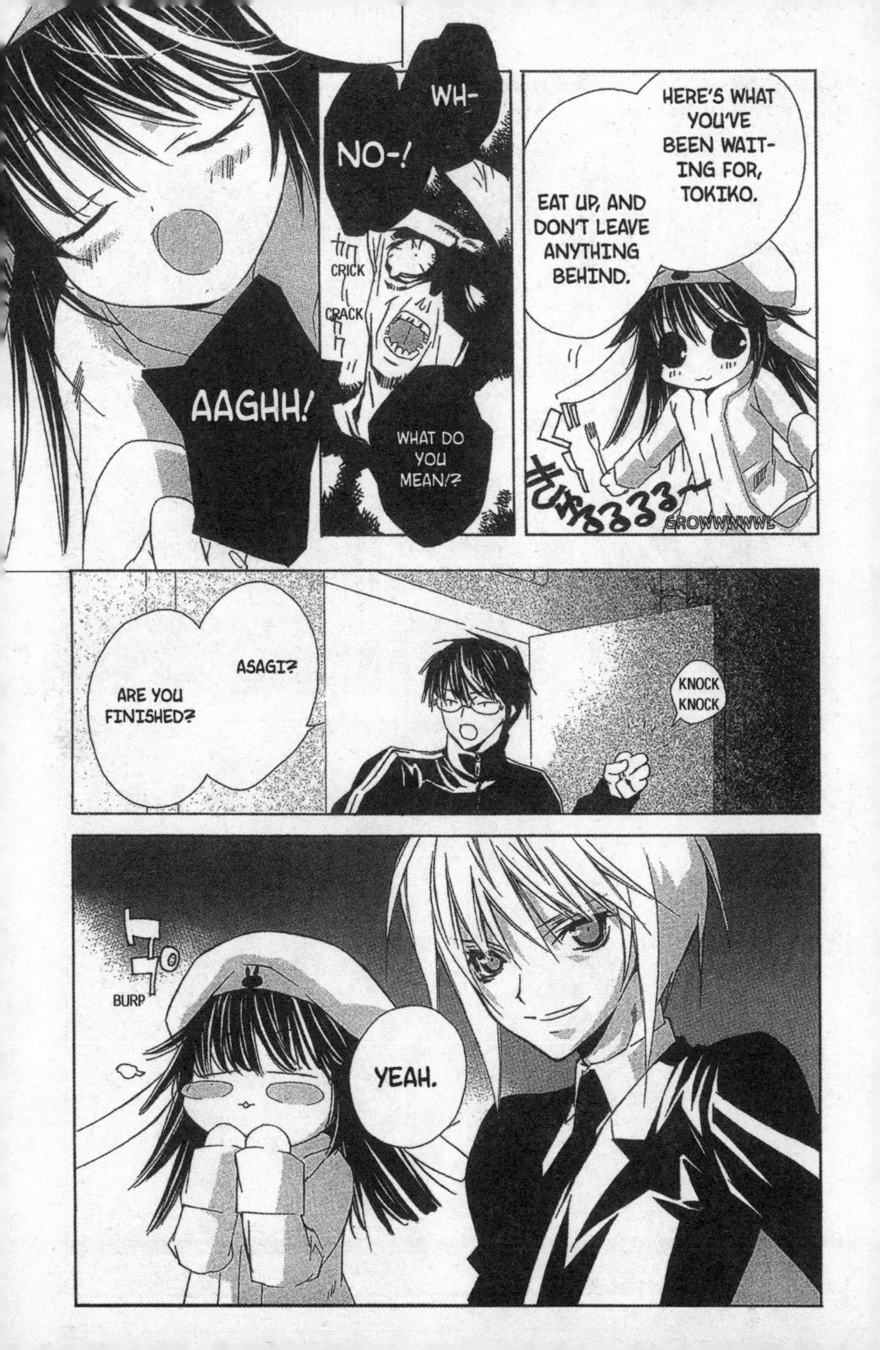
HERE'S WHAT YOU'VE BEEN WAIT-ING FOR, TOKIKO.
EAT UP, AND DON'T LEAVE ANYTHING BEHIND.
GROWWWWWL
WH-
NO-!
CRICK
CRACK
WHAT DO YOU MEAN!?
AAGHH!
KNOCK KNOCK
ASAGI?
ARE YOU FINISHED?
BURP
YEAH.

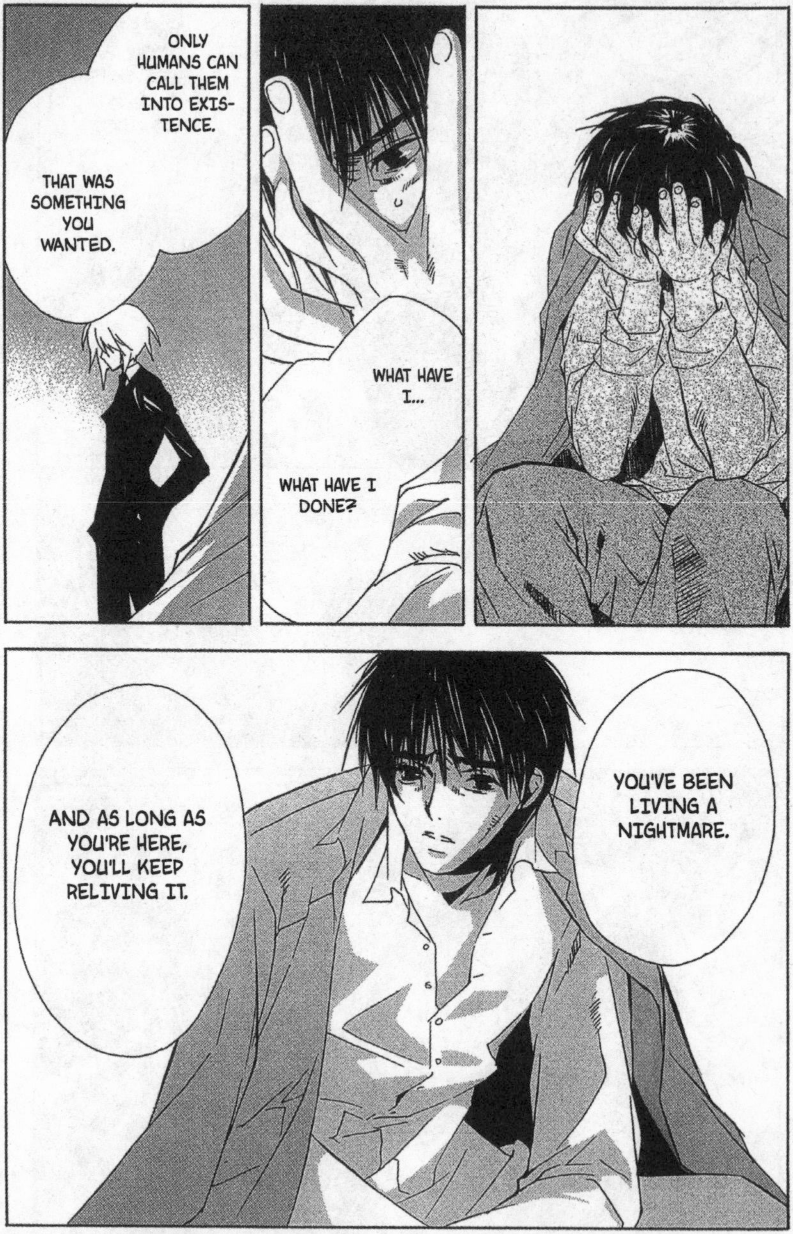
WHAT HAVE I...
WHAT HAVE I DONE?
ONLY HUMANS CAN CALL THEM INTO EXIS-TENCE.
THAT WAS SOMETHING YOU WANTED.
YOU'VE BEEN LIVING A NIGHTMARE.
AND AS LONG AS YOU'RE HERE, YOU'LL KEEP RELIVING IT.

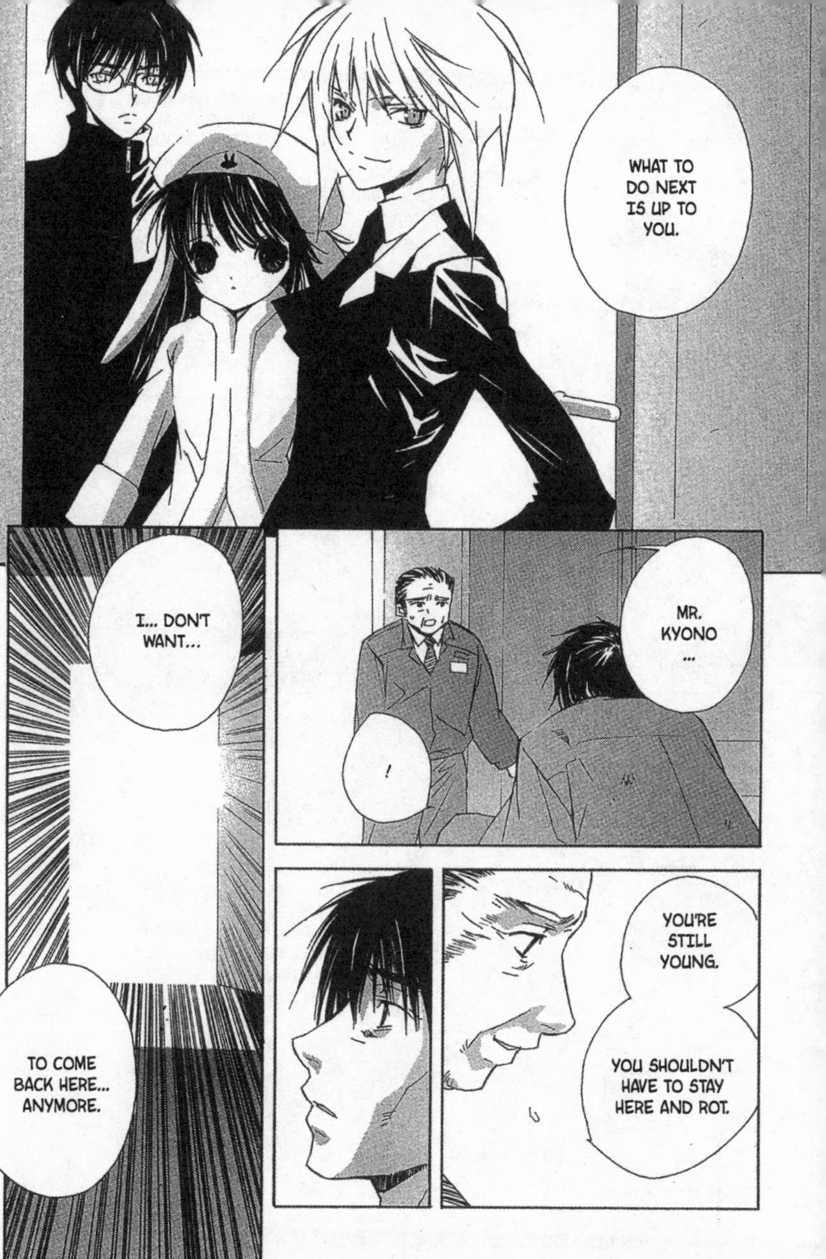
WHAT TO DO NEXT IS UP TO YOU.
MR. KYONO ...
!
YOU'RE STILL YOUNG.
YOU SHOULDN'T HAVE TO STAY HERE AND ROT.
I... DON'T WANT...
TO COME BACK HERE... ANYMORE.

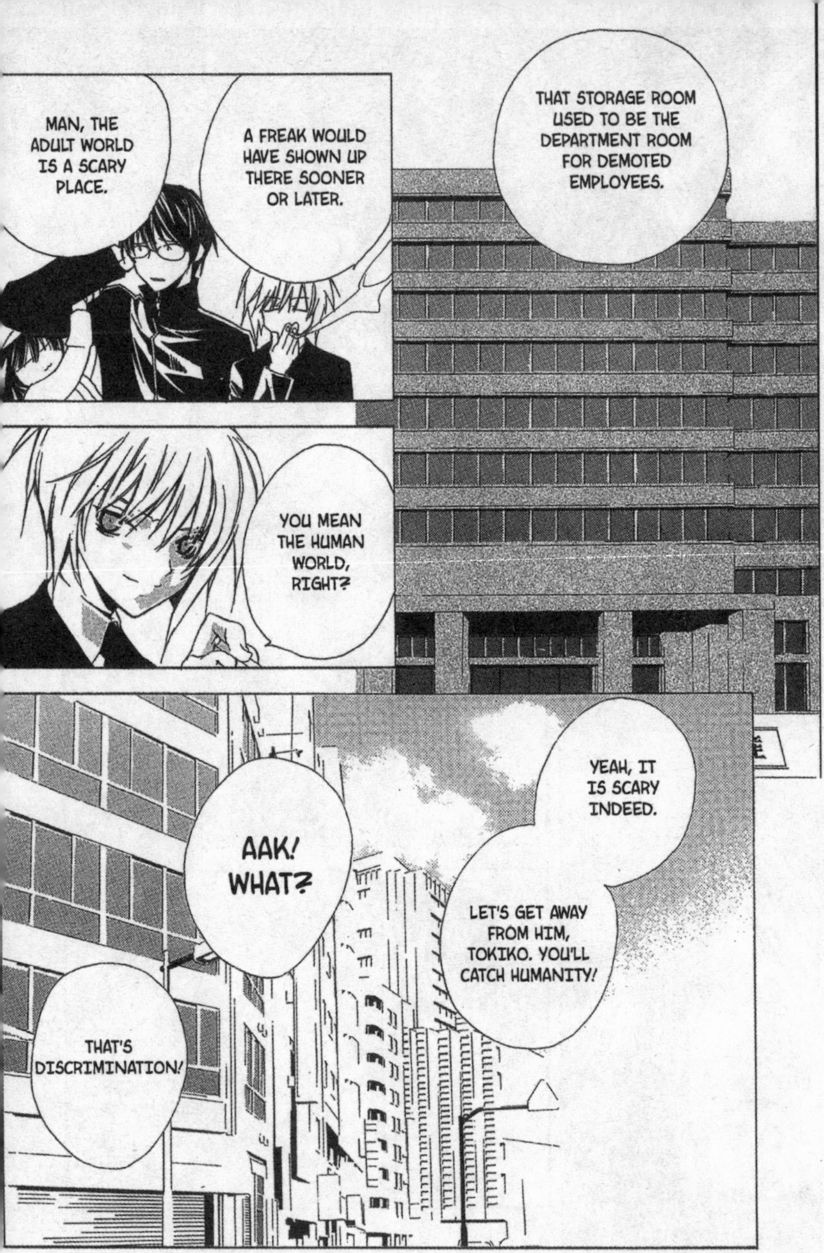
THAT STORAGE ROOM USED TO BE THE DEPARTMENT ROOM FOR DEMOTED EMPLOYEES.
A FREAK WOULD HAVE SHOWN UP THERE SOONER OR LATER.
MAN, THE ADULT WORLD IS A SCARY PLACE.
YOU MEAN THE HUMAN WORLD, RIGHT?
YEAH, IT IS SCARY INDEED.
LET'S GET AWAY FROM HIM, TOKIKO. YOU'LL CATCH HUMANITY!
AAK! WHAT?
THAT'S DISCRIMINATION!

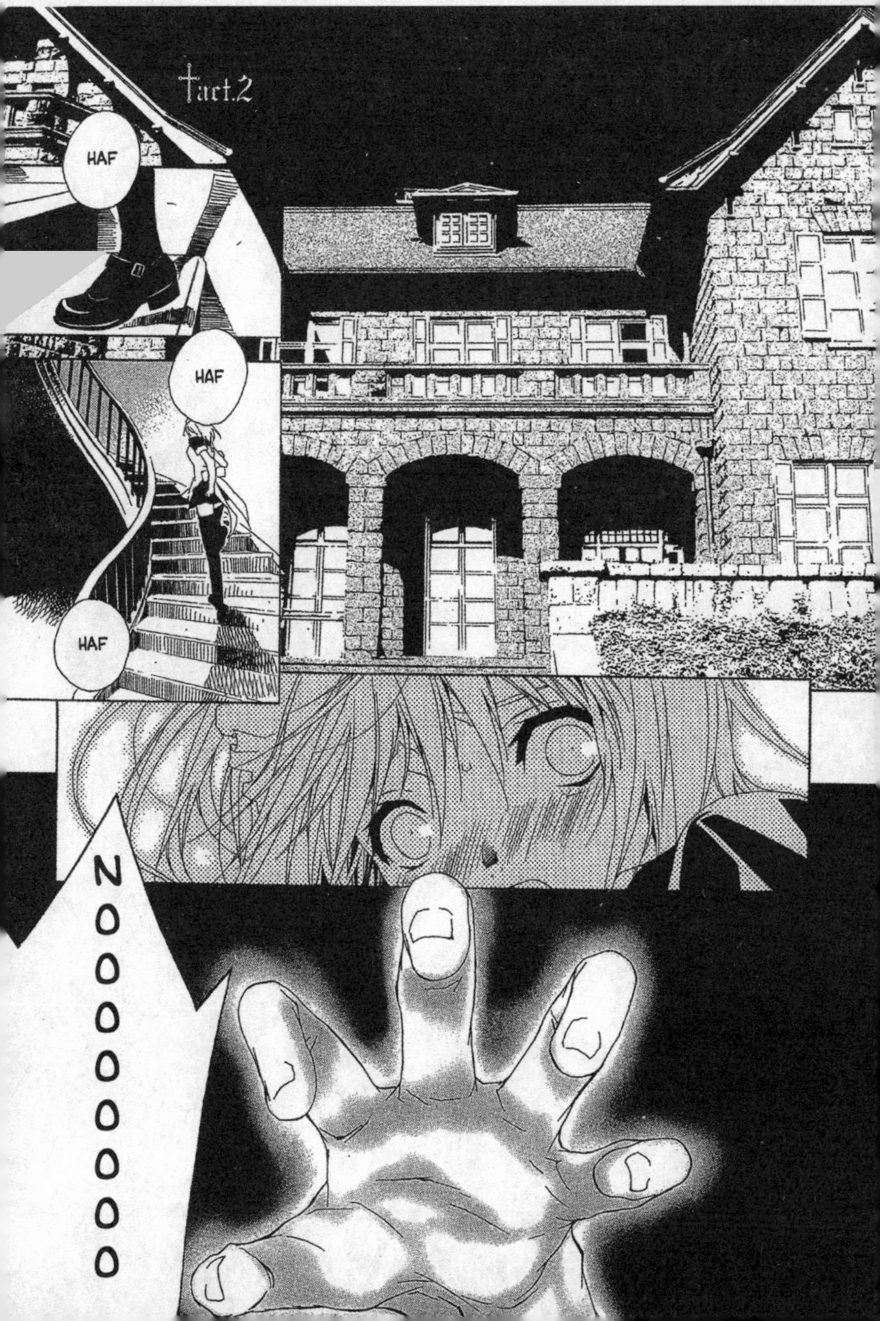
†act.2
HAF
HAF
HAF
NOOOOOOOO

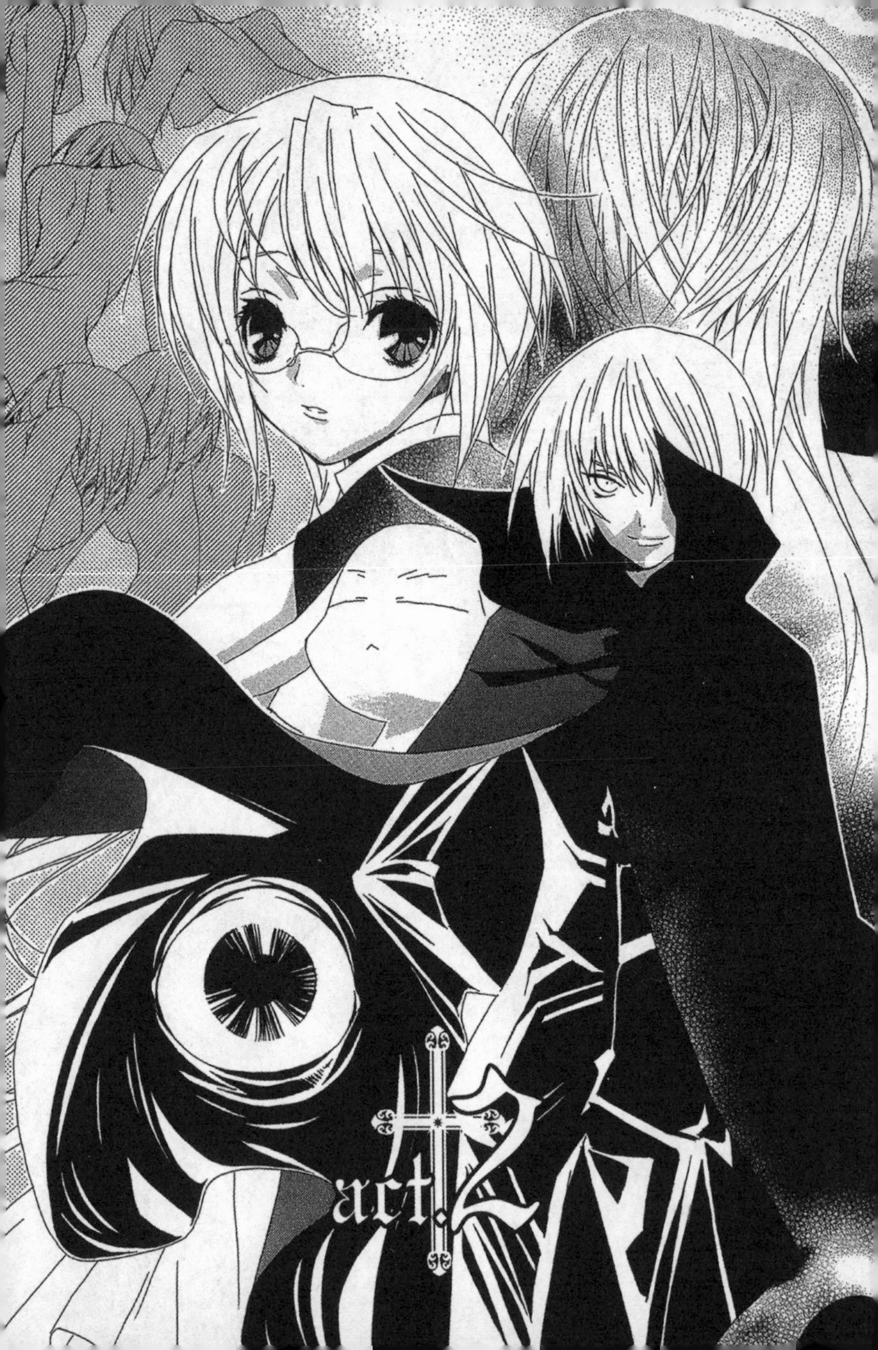
act.2

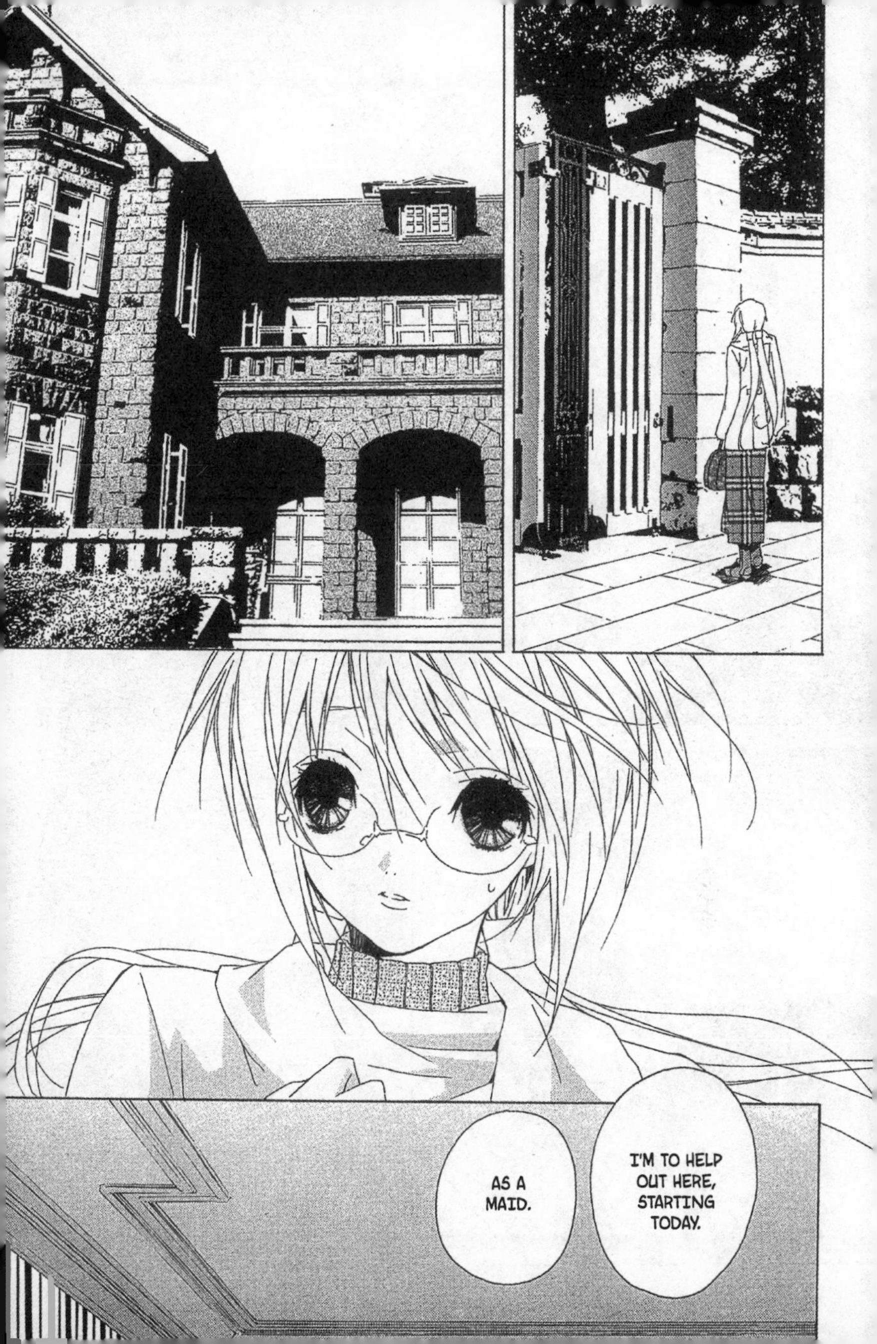
I'M TO HELP OUT HERE, STARTING TODAY.
AS A MAID.

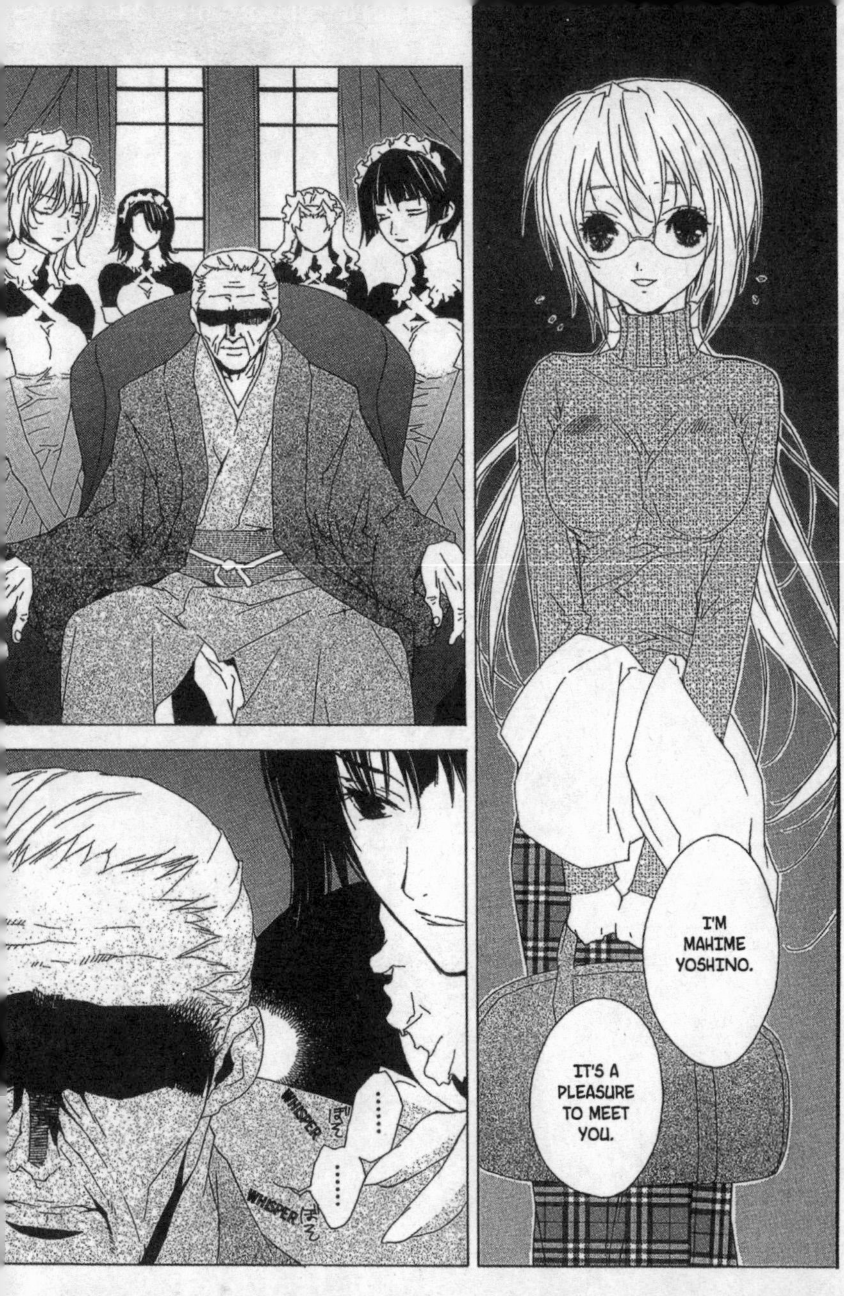
I'M MAHIME YOSHINO.
IT'S A PLEASURE TO MEET YOU.
......
WHISPER
......
WHISPER

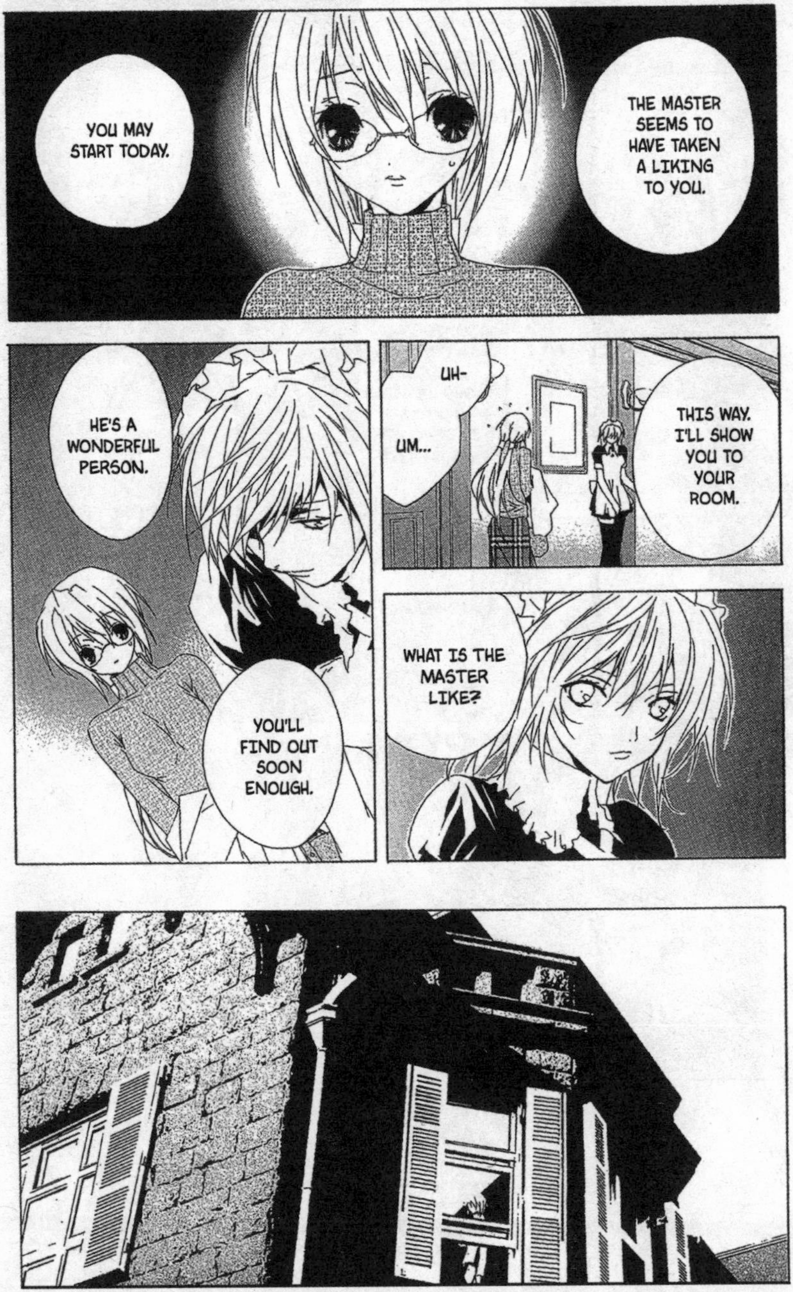
THE MASTER SEEMS TO HAVE TAKEN A LIKING TO YOU.
YOU MAY START TODAY.
THIS WAY. I'LL SHOW YOU TO YOUR ROOM.
UH-
UM...
WHAT IS THE MASTER LIKE?
HE'S A WONDERFUL PERSON.
YOU'LL FIND OUT SOON ENOUGH.

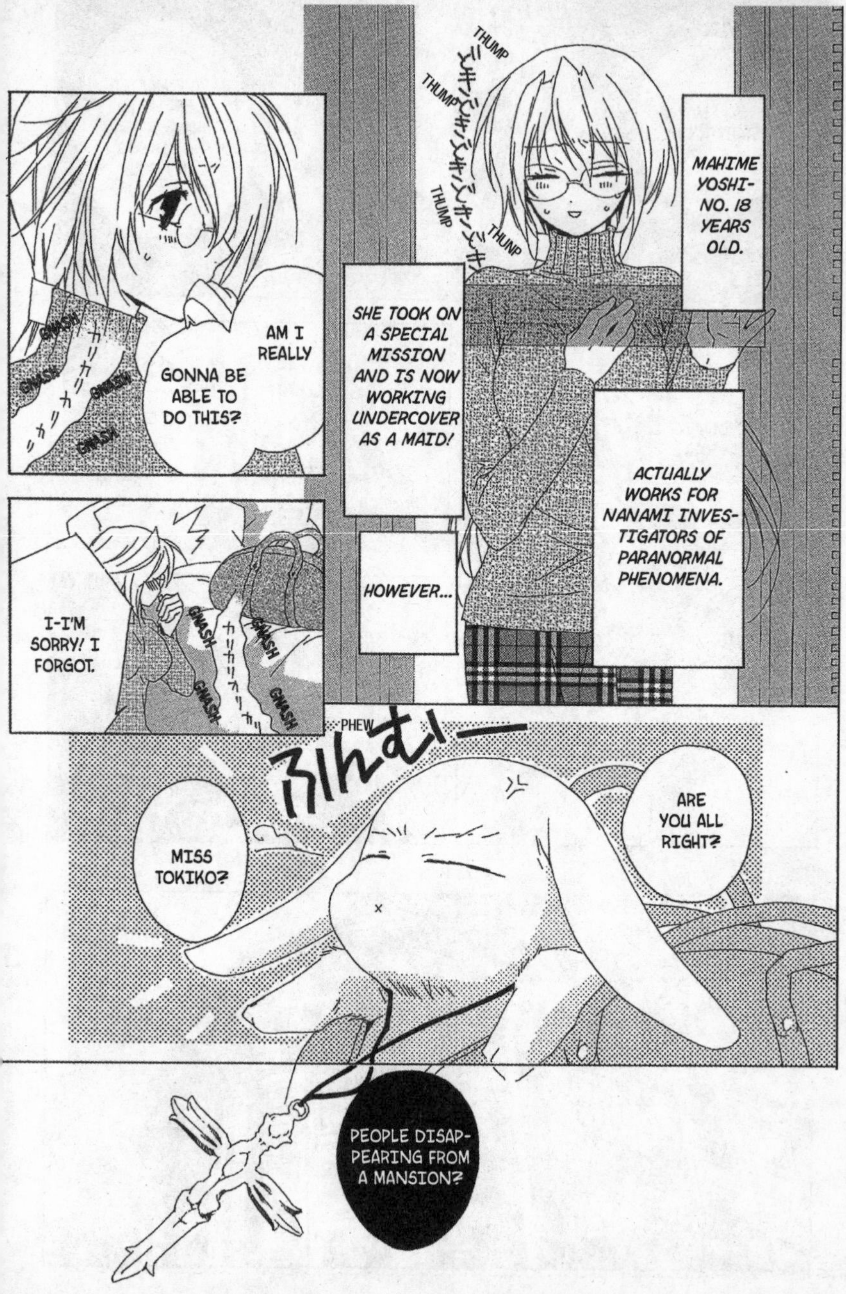
THUMP
THUMP
THUMP
THUMP
MAHIME YOSHINO. 18 YEARS OLD.
ACTUALLY WORKS FOR NANAMI INVESTIGATORS OF PARANORMAL PHENOMENA.
SHE TOOK ON A SPECIAL MISSION AND IS NOW WORKING UNDERCOVER AS A MAID!
HOWEVER...
GNASH
GNASH
GNASH
GNASH
AM I REALLY GONNA BE ABLE TO DO THIS?
GNASH
GNASH
GNASH
GNASH
I-I'M SORRY! I FORGOT.
PHEW
ARE YOU ALL RIGHT?
MISS TOKIKO?
PEOPLE DISAPPEARING FROM A MANSION?

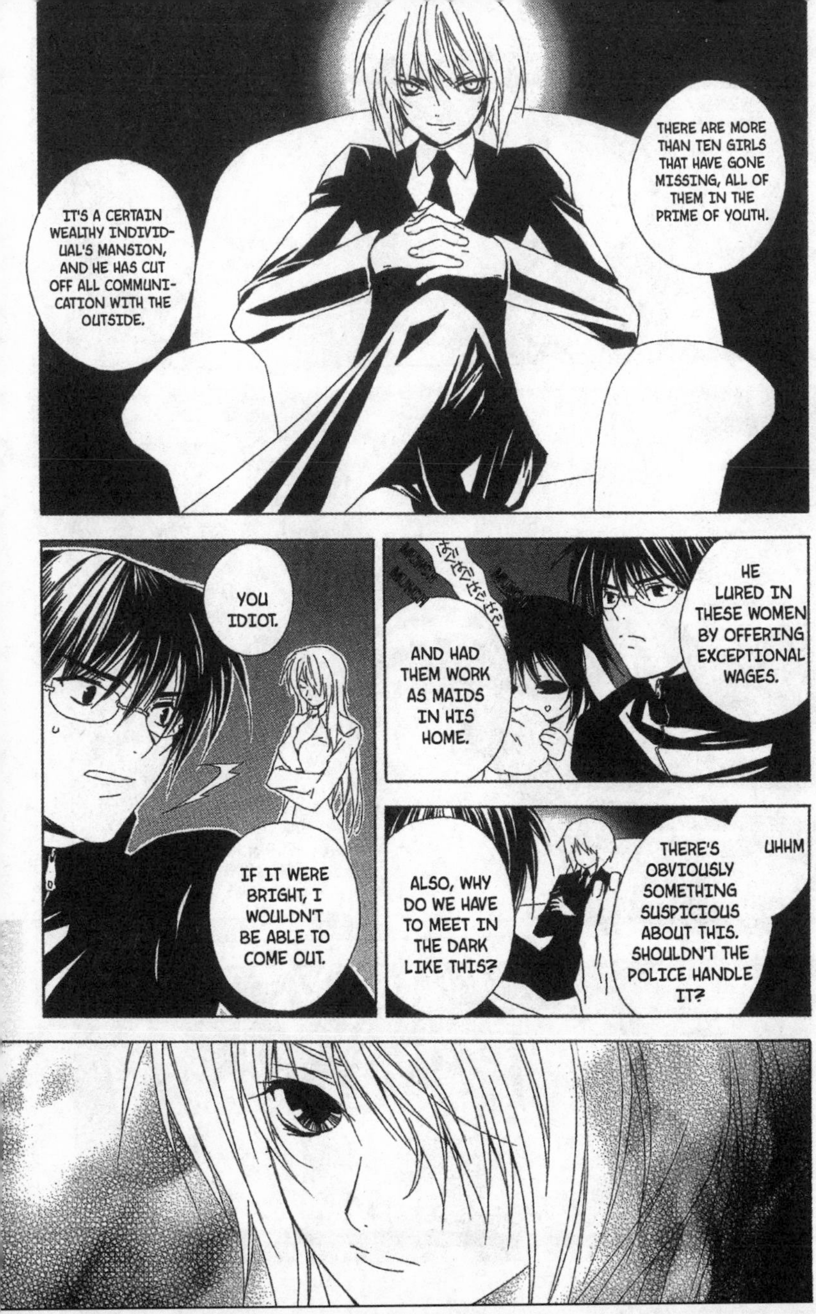

THERE ARE MORE THAN TEN GIRLS THAT HAVE GONE MISSING, ALL OF THEM IN THE PRIME OF YOUTH.
IT'S A CERTAIN WEALTHY INDIVIDUAL'S MANSION, AND HE HAS CUT OFF ALL COMMUNICATION WITH THE OUTSIDE.
HE LURED IN THESE WOMEN BY OFFERING EXCEPTIONAL WAGES.
AND HAD THEM WORK AS MAIDS IN HIS HOME.
MUNCH MUNCH
UHHM
THERE'S OBVIOUSLY SOMETHING SUSPICIOUS ABOUT THIS. SHOULDN'T THE POLICE HANDLE IT?
ALSO, WHY DO WE HAVE TO MEET IN THE DARK LIKE THIS?
YOU IDIOT.
IF IT WERE BRIGHT, I WOULDN'T BE ABLE TO COME OUT.

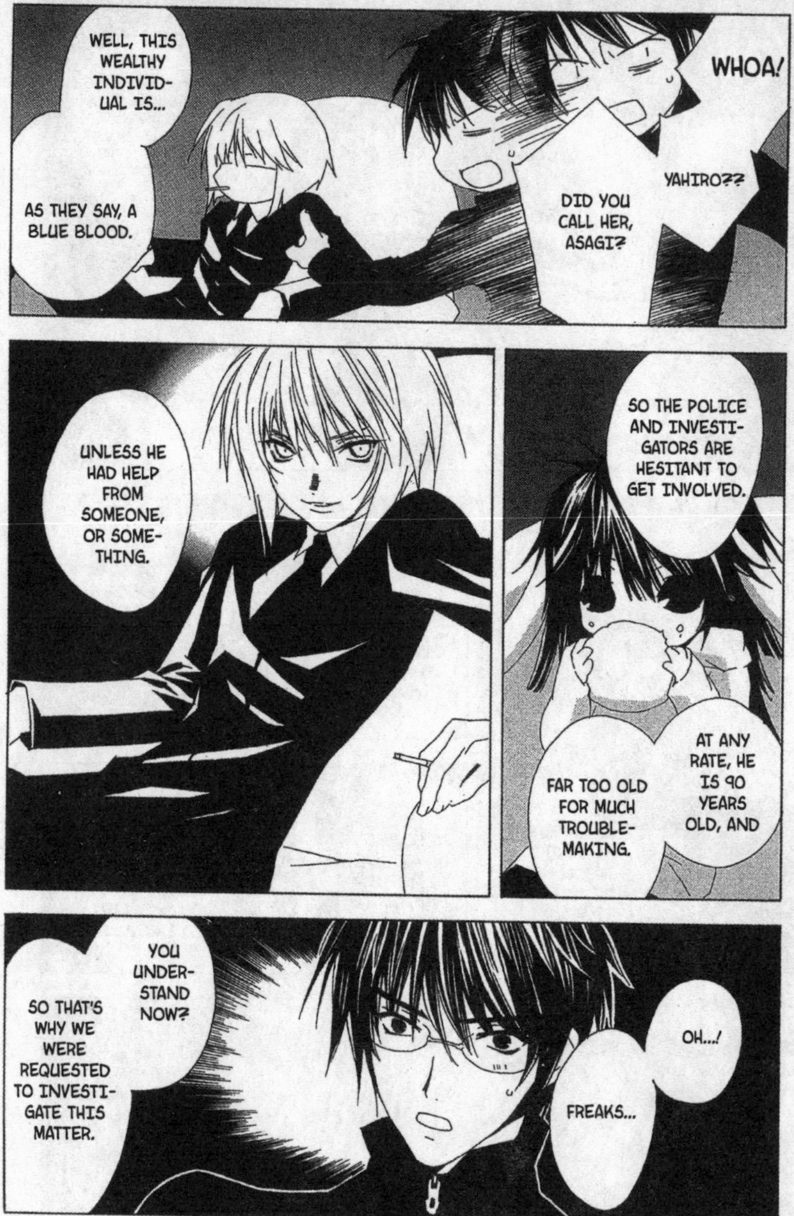
WHOA!
YAHIRO??
DID YOU CALL HER, ASAGI?
WELL, THIS WEALTHY INDIVIDUAL IS...
AS THEY SAY, A BLUE BLOOD.
AT ANY RATE, HE IS 90 YEARS OLD, AND
FAR TOO OLD FOR MUCH TROUBLE-MAKING.
SO THE POLICE AND INVESTI-GATORS ARE HESITANT TO GET INVOLVED.
UNLESS HE HAD HELP FROM SOMEONE, OR SOME-THING.
OH...!
FREAKS...
YOU UNDER-STAND NOW?
SO THAT'S WHY WE WERE REQUESTED TO INVESTI-GATE THIS MATTER.

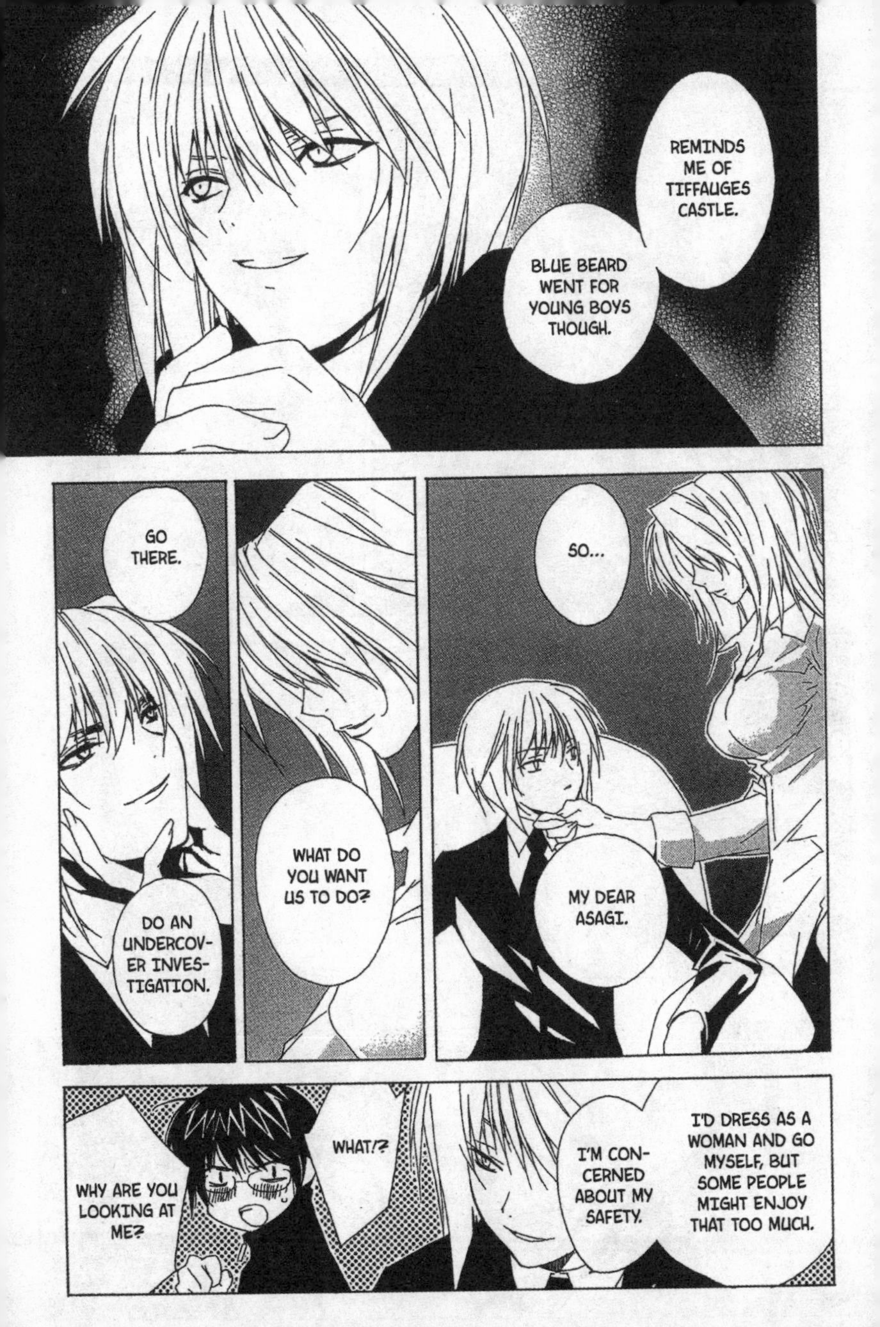
REMINDS ME OF TIFFAUGES CASTLE.
BLUE BEARD WENT FOR YOUNG BOYS THOUGH.
SO...
MY DEAR ASAGI.
WHAT DO YOU WANT US TO DO?
GO THERE.
DO AN UNDERCOVER INVESTIGATION.
I'D DRESS AS A WOMAN AND GO MYSELF, BUT SOME PEOPLE MIGHT ENJOY THAT TOO MUCH.
I'M CONCERNED ABOUT MY SAFETY.
WHAT!?
WHY ARE YOU LOOKING AT ME?

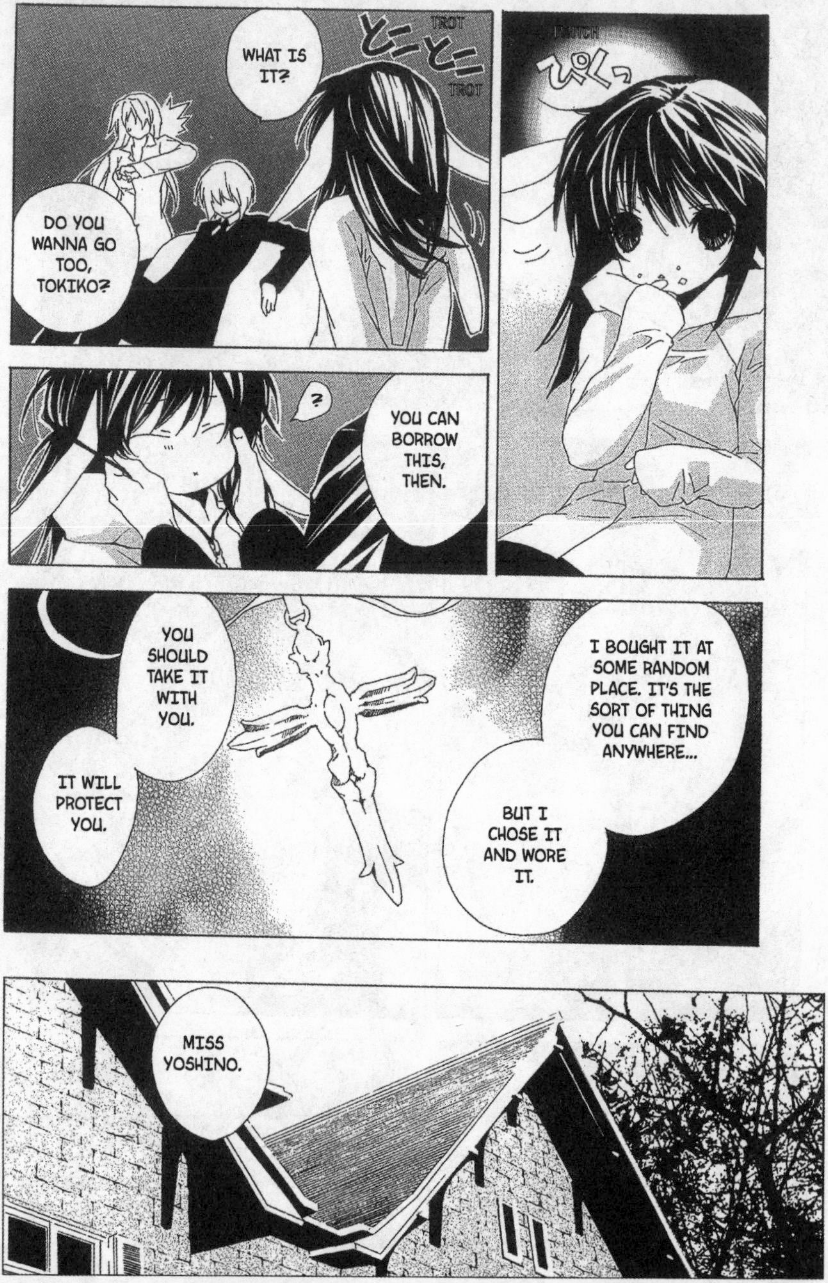
TWITCH
TROT
TROT
WHAT IS IT?
DO YOU WANNA GO TOO, TOKIKO?
?
YOU CAN BORROW THIS, THEN.
I BOUGHT IT AT SOME RANDOM PLACE. IT'S THE SORT OF THING YOU CAN FIND ANYWHERE...
BUT I CHOSE IT AND WORE IT.
YOU SHOULD TAKE IT WITH YOU.
IT WILL PROTECT YOU.
MISS YOSHINO.

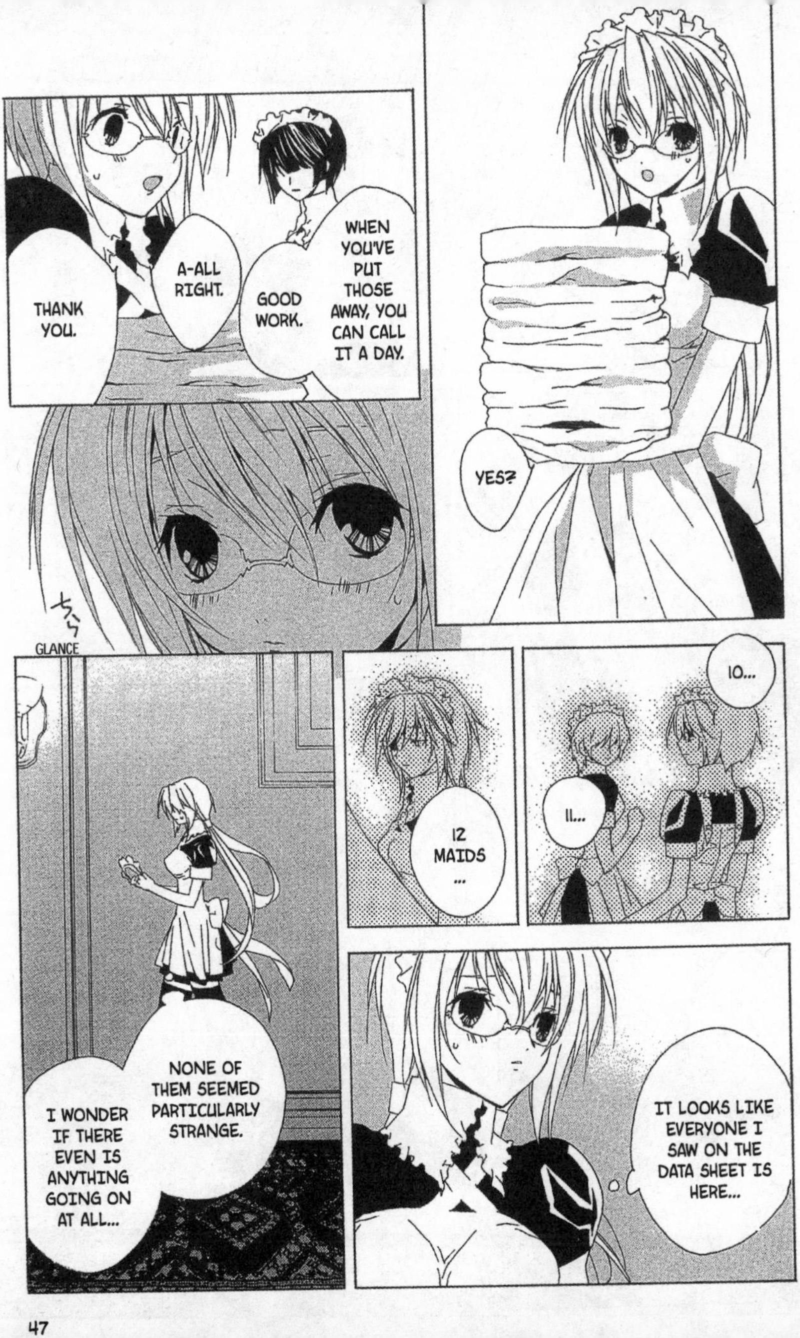
YES?
WHEN YOU'VE PUT THOSE AWAY, YOU CAN CALL IT A DAY.
GOOD WORK.
A-ALL RIGHT.
THANK YOU.
ちら
GLANCE
10...
11...
12 MAIDS ...
IT LOOKS LIKE EVERYONE I SAW ON THE DATA SHEET IS HERE...
NONE OF THEM SEEMED PARTICULARLY STRANGE.
I WONDER IF THERE EVEN IS ANYTHING GOING ON AT ALL...

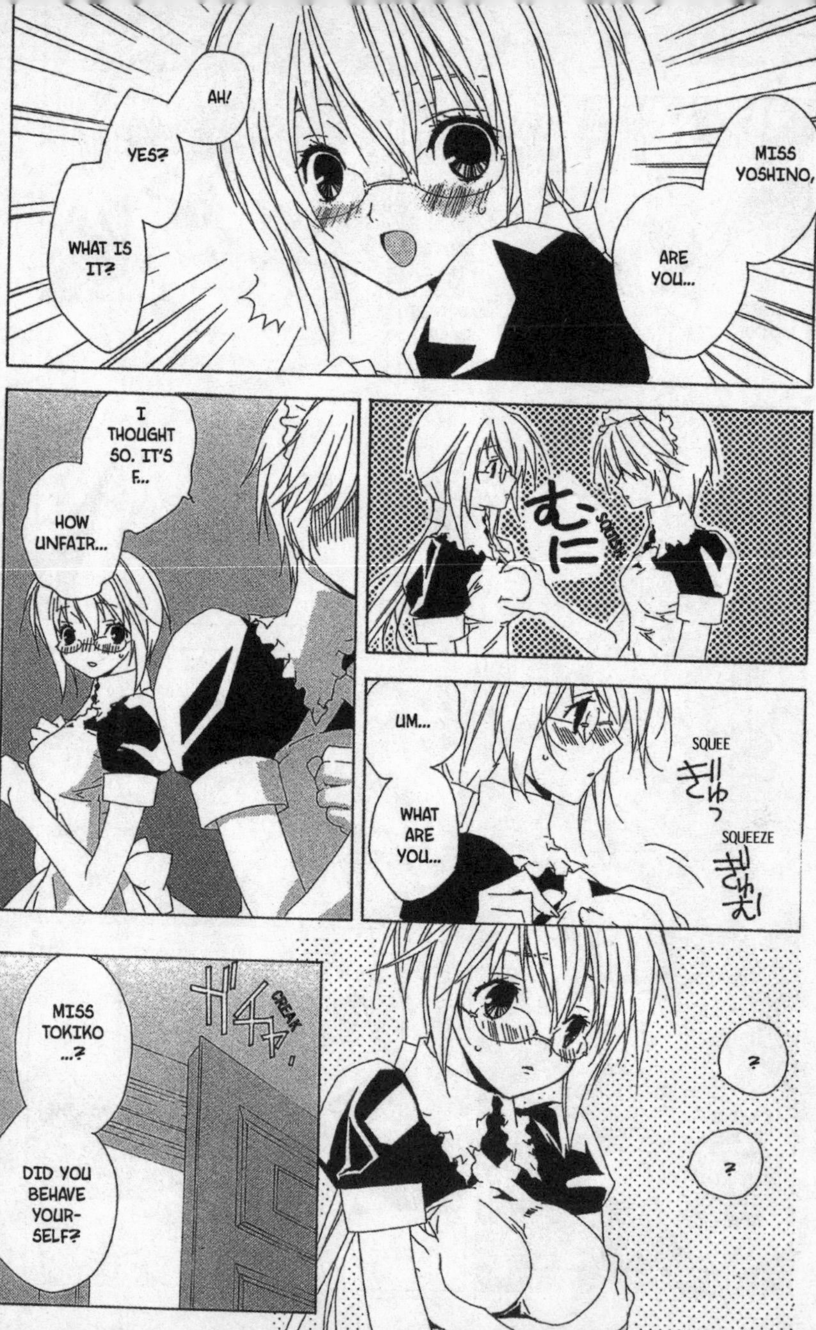

MISS YOSHINO,
ARE YOU...
AH!
YES?
WHAT IS IT?
むに
SQUISH
SQUEE
きゅっ
SQUEEZE
UM...
WHAT ARE YOU...
I THOUGHT SO. IT'S F...
HOW UNFAIR...
?
?
ガチャ
CREAK
MISS TOKIKO ...?
DID YOU BEHAVE YOURSELF?

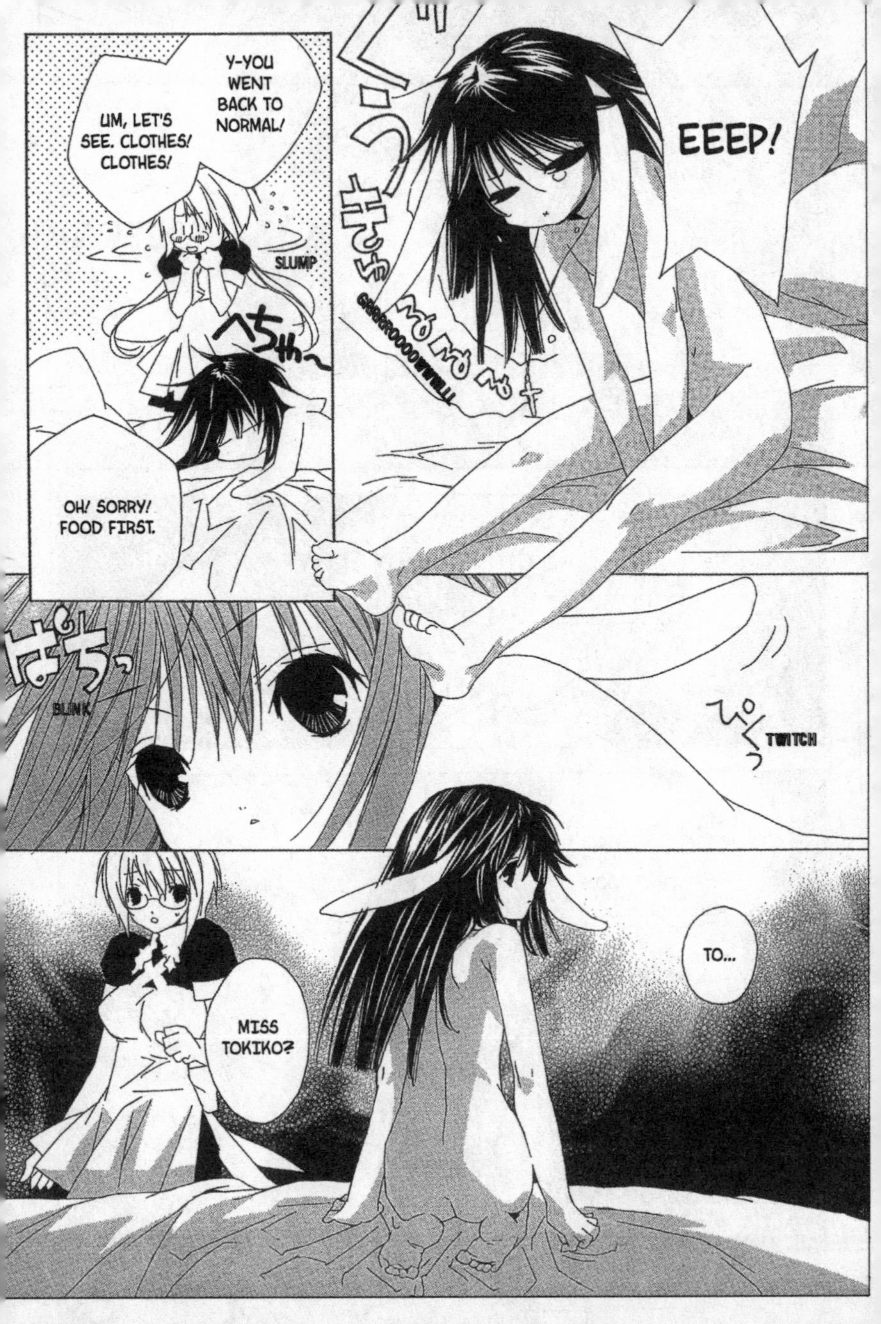
EEEP!
GRRRROOOOWWLLL
Y-YOU WENT BACK TO NORMAL!
UM, LET'S SEE. CLOTHES! CLOTHES!
SLUMP
OH! SORRY! FOOD FIRST.
ぴくっ
TWITCH
ぱちっ
BLINK
TO...
MISS TOKIKO?

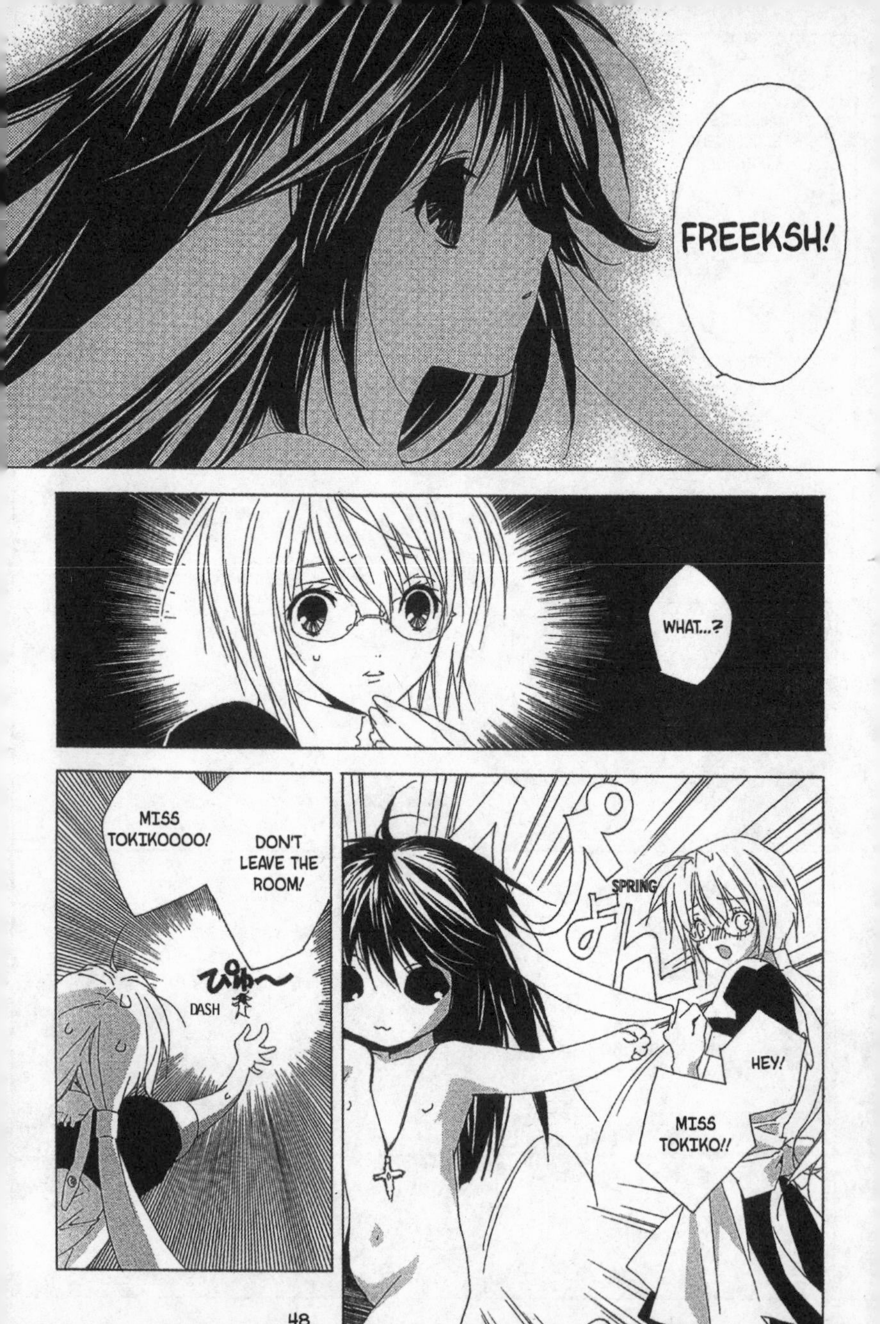
FREEKSH!
WHAT...?
SPRING
HEY!
MISS TOKIKO!!
MISS TOKIKOOOO!
DON'T LEAVE THE ROOM!
ぴゅ～
DASH

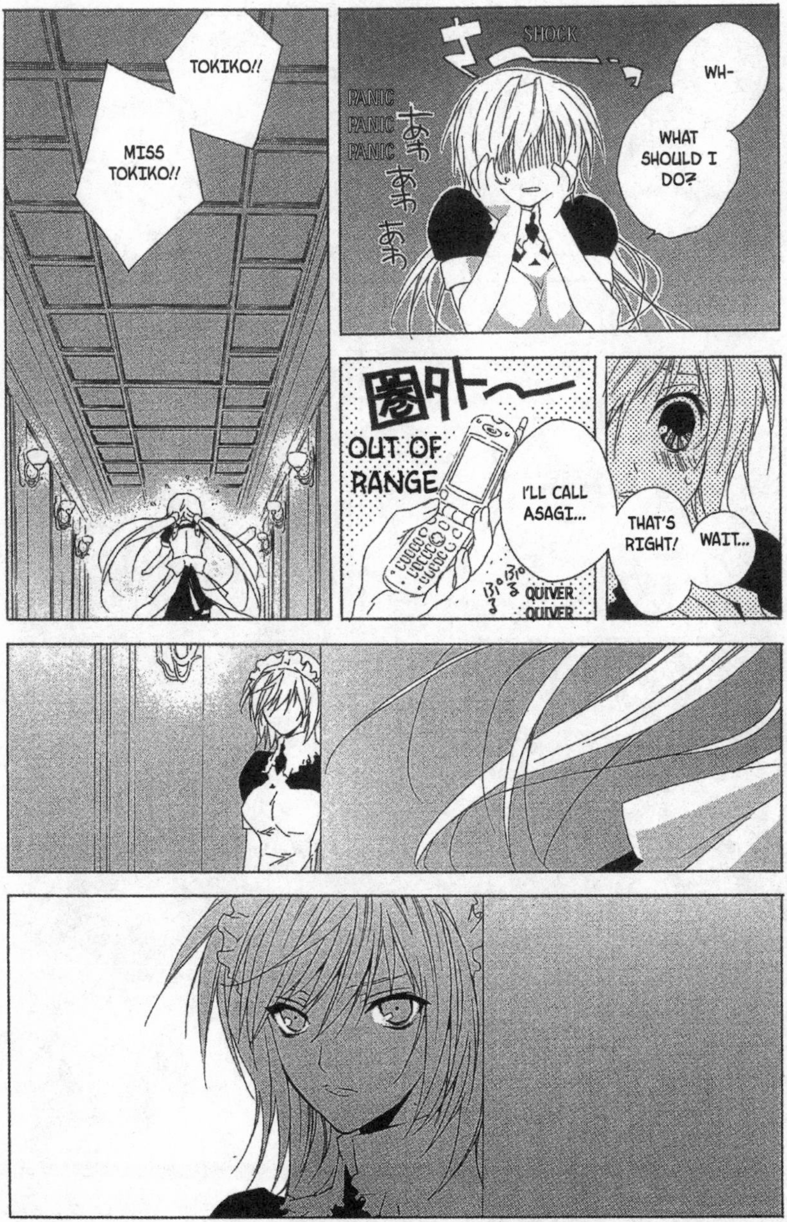

SHOCK
PANIC
PANIC
PANIC
WH-
WHAT SHOULD I DO?
WAIT...
THAT'S RIGHT!
I'LL CALL ASAGI...
圏外〜
OUT OF RANGE
QUIVER
QUIVER
TOKIKO!!
MISS TOKIKO!!

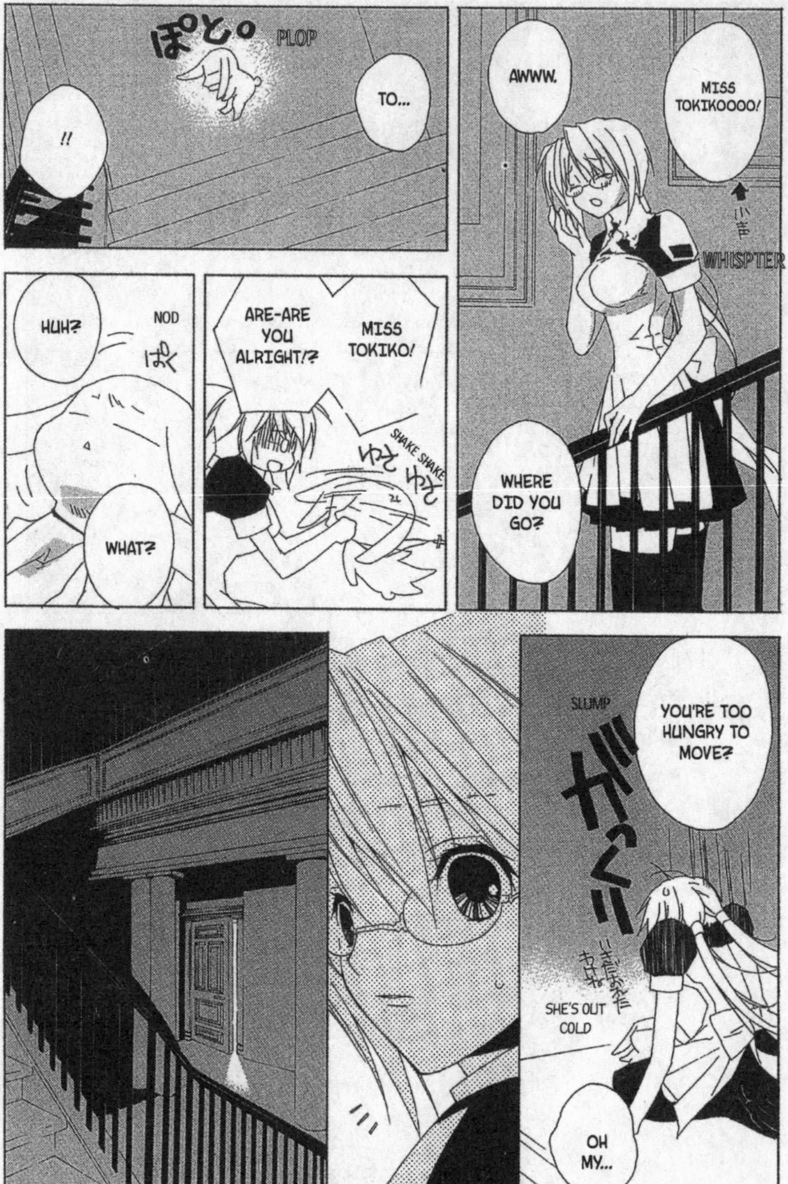
MISS TOKIKOOOO!
WHISPTER
AWWW.
WHERE DID YOU GO?
TO...
PLOP
!!
MISS TOKIKO!
ARE-ARE YOU ALRIGHT!?
SHAKE SHAKE
NOD
HUH?
WHAT?
YOU'RE TOO HUNGRY TO MOVE?
SLUMP
SHE'S OUT COLD
OH MY...

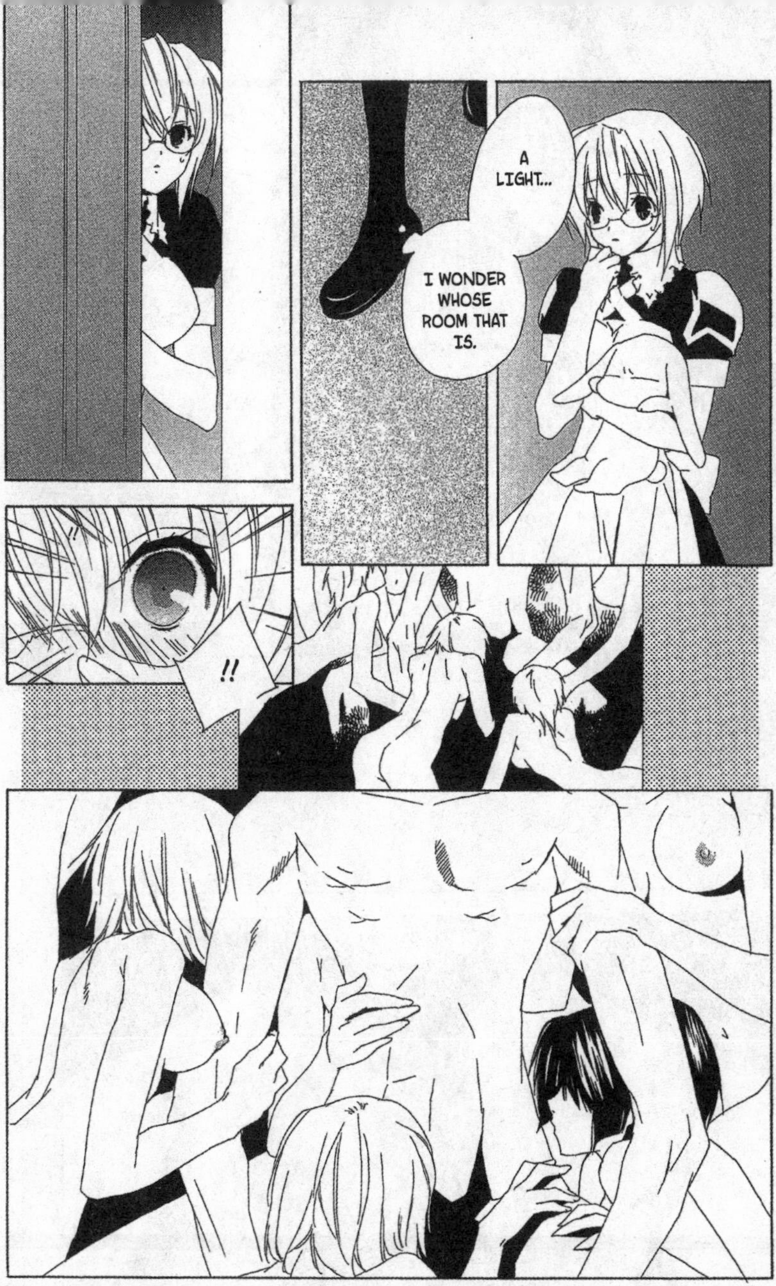
A LIGHT...
I WONDER WHOSE ROOM THAT IS.
!!
!!

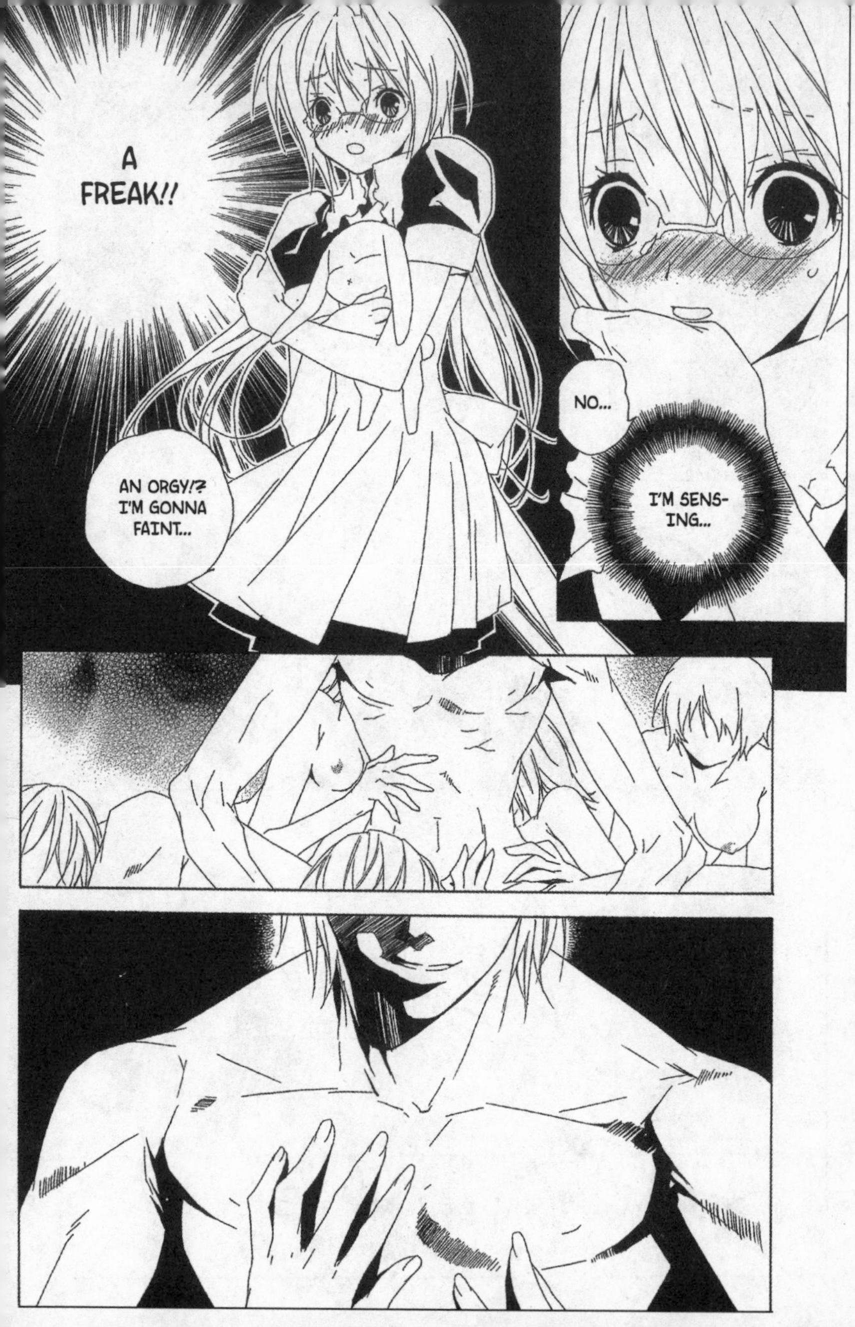
NO...
I'M SENSING...
A FREAK!!
AN ORGY!? I'M GONNA FAINT...

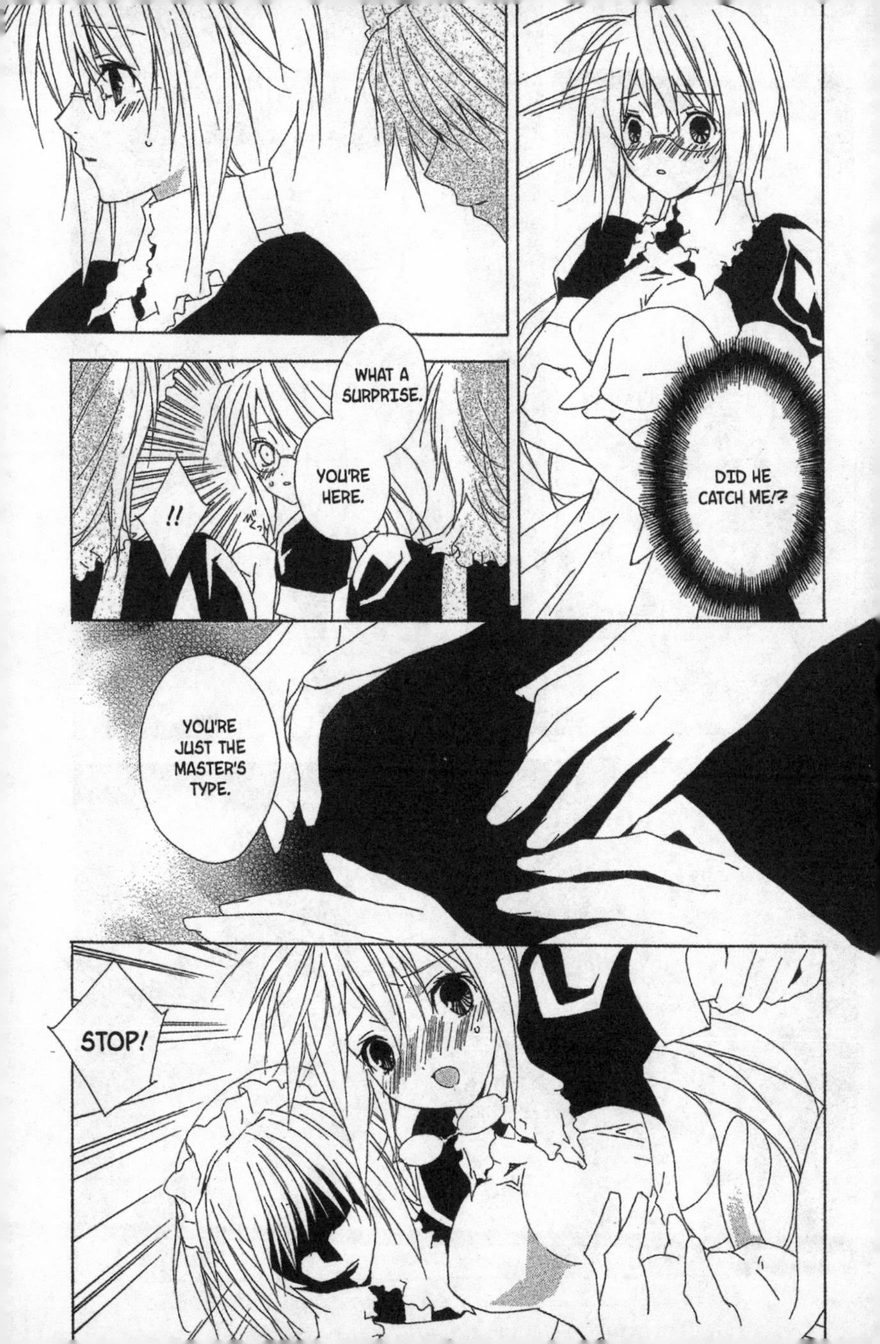

WHAT A SURPRISE.
YOU'RE HERE.
DID HE CATCH ME!?
!!
YOU'RE JUST THE MASTER'S TYPE.
STOP!

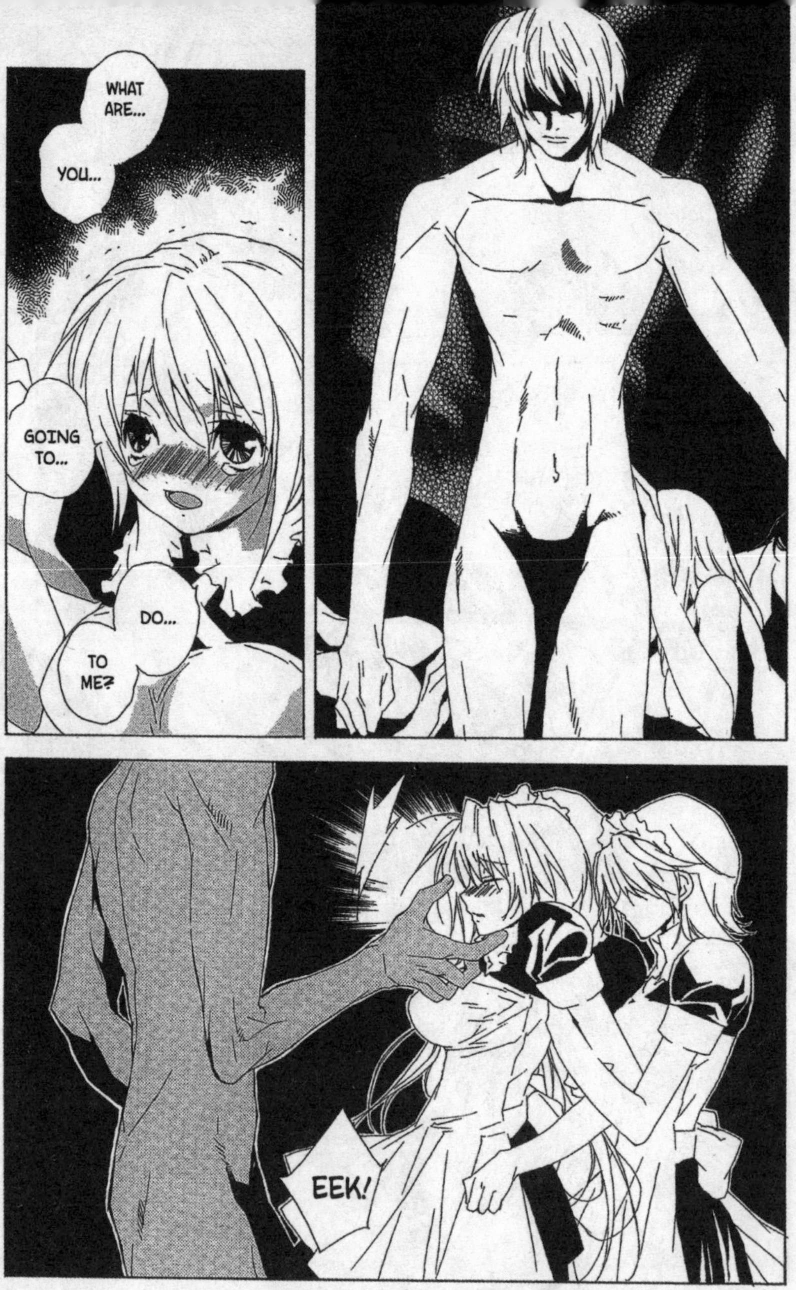
WHAT ARE...
YOU...
GOING TO...
DO...
TO ME?
EEK!

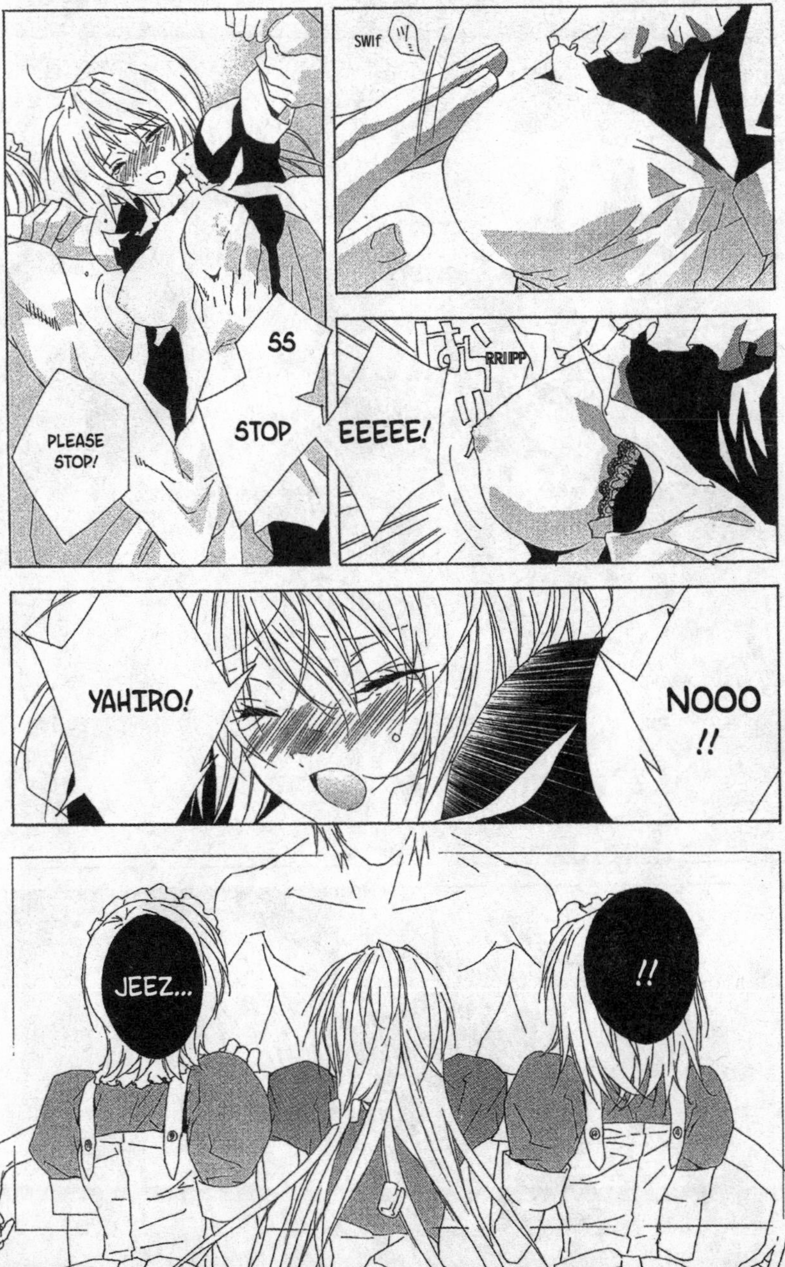
SWIf
RRIPP
SS
STOP
EEEEE!
PLEASE STOP!
NOOO !!
YAHIRO!
!!
JEEZ...

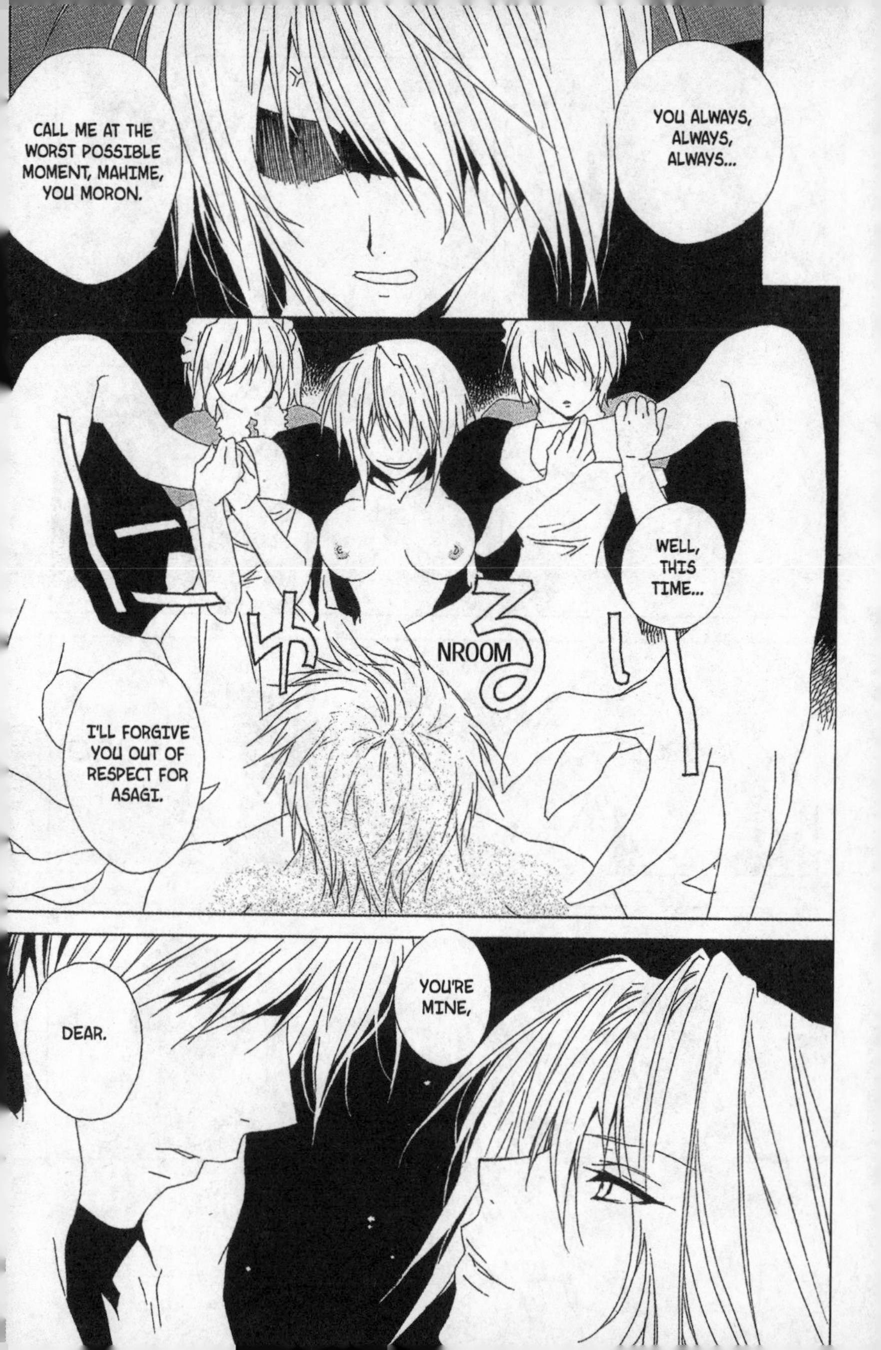
YOU ALWAYS, ALWAYS, ALWAYS...
CALL ME AT THE WORST POSSIBLE MOMENT, MAHIME, YOU MORON.
WELL, THIS TIME...
NROOM
I'LL FORGIVE YOU OUT OF RESPECT FOR ASAGI.
YOU'RE MINE,
DEAR.

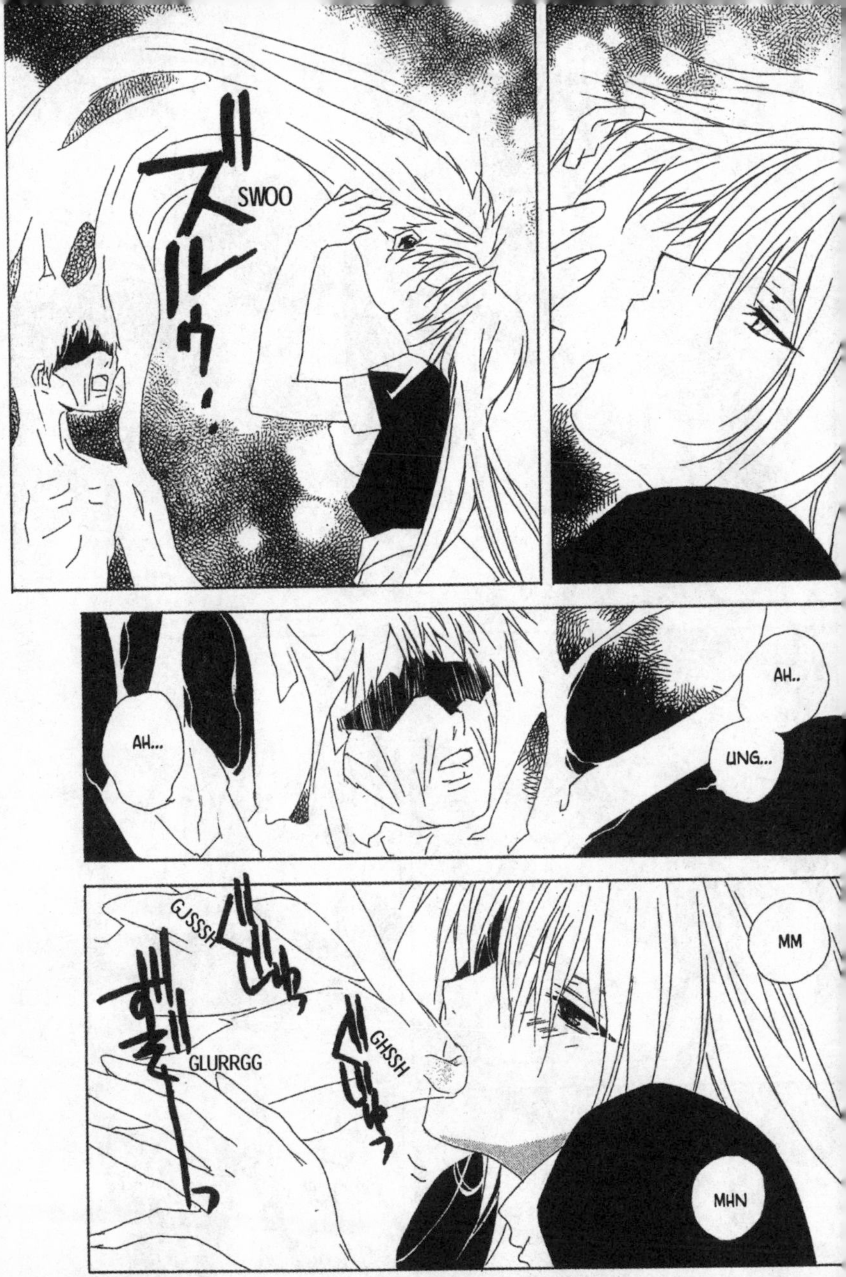
SWOO
AH..
UNG...
AH...
MM
MHN
GHSSH
GLURRGG
GJSSSH

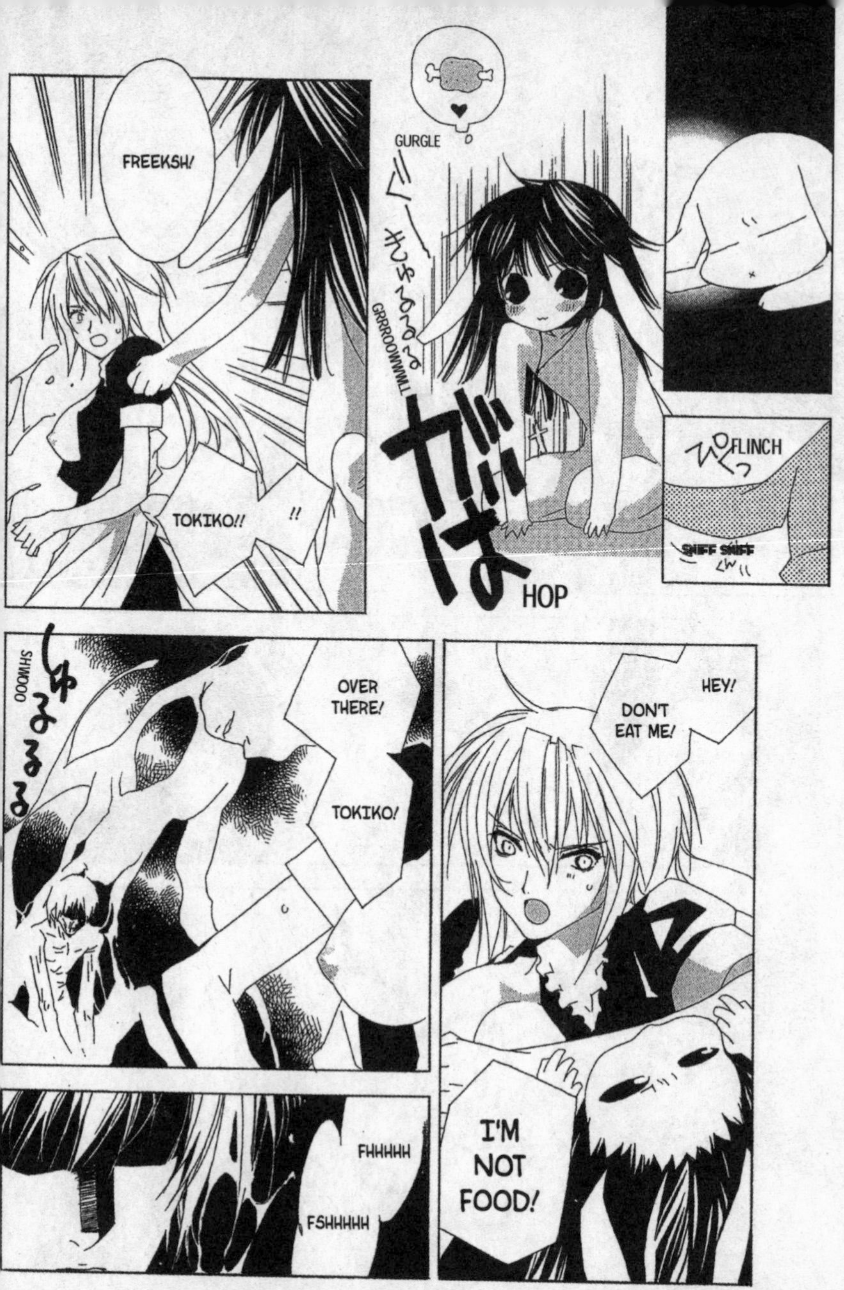
FLINCH
SNIFF SNIFF
GURGLE
GRRROOWWLL
がば
HOP
FREEKSH!
TOKIKO!!
!!
HEY!
DON'T EAT ME!
I'M NOT FOOD!
OVER THERE!
TOKIKO!
SHWOOO
FHHHHH
FSHHHHH

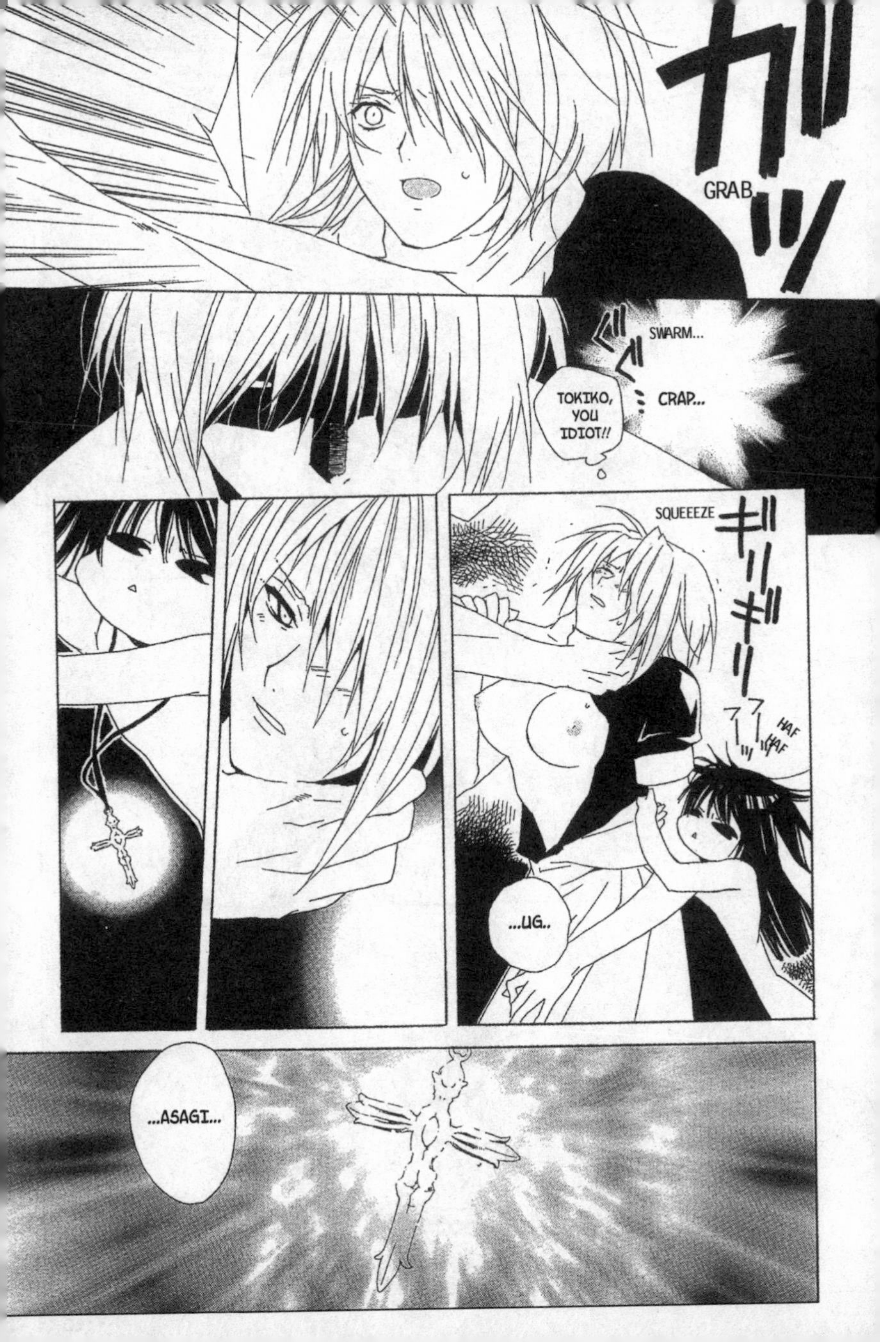
GRAB
SWARM...
CRAP...
TOKIKO, YOU IDIOT!!
SQUEEEZE
HAF HAF
...UG..
...ASAGI...

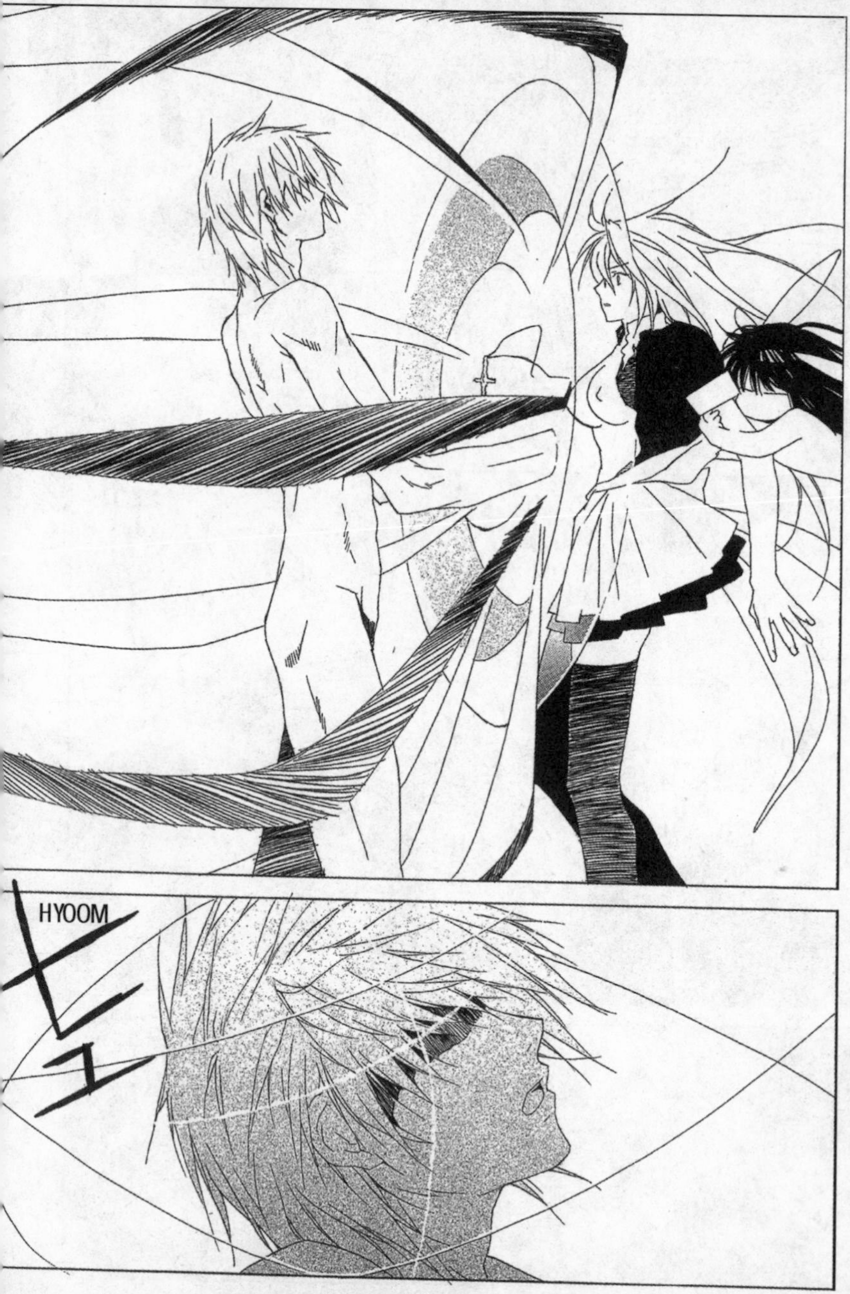
HYOOM

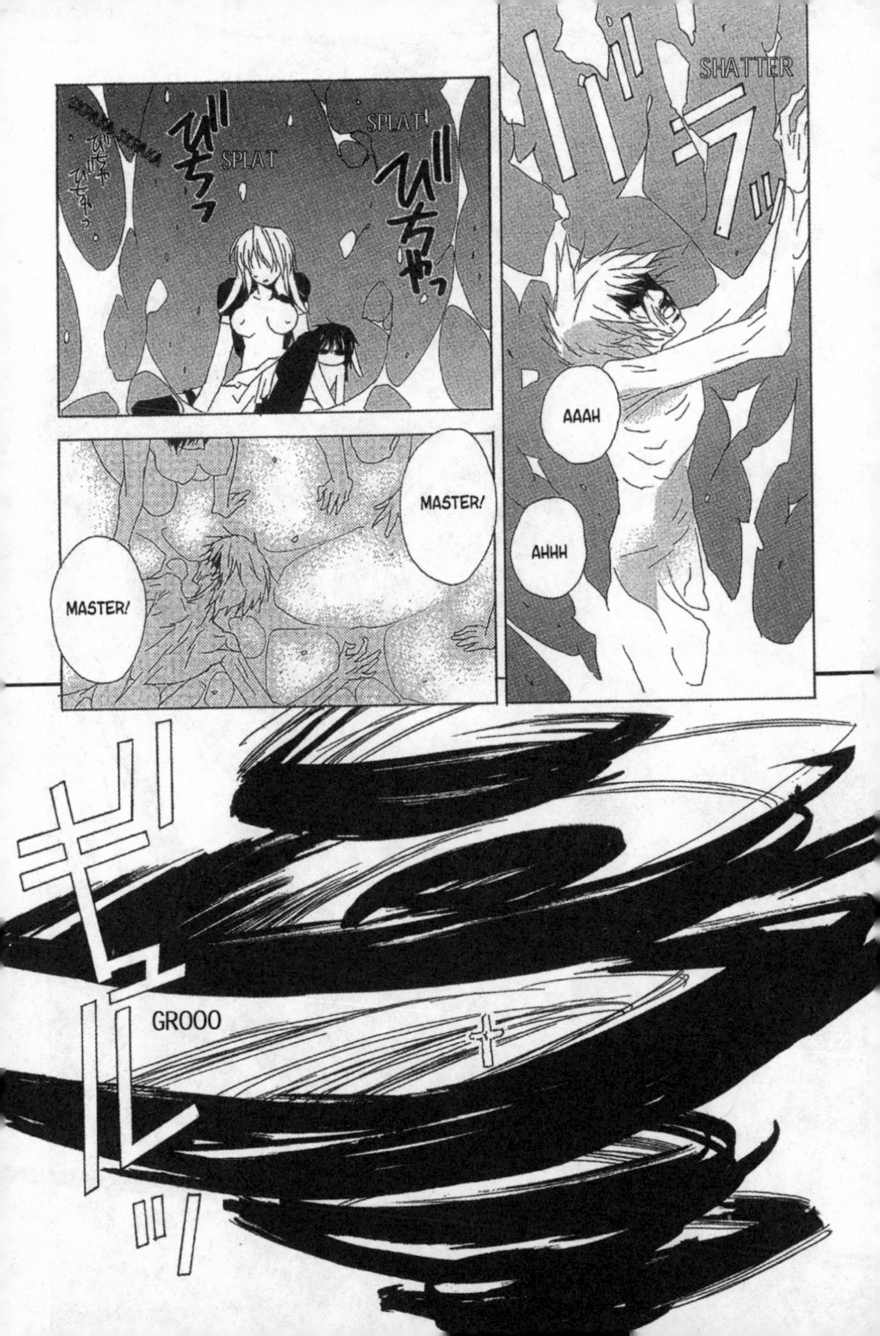
SHATTER
AAAH
AHHH
SPLAT
SPLAT
MASTER!
MASTER!
GROOO

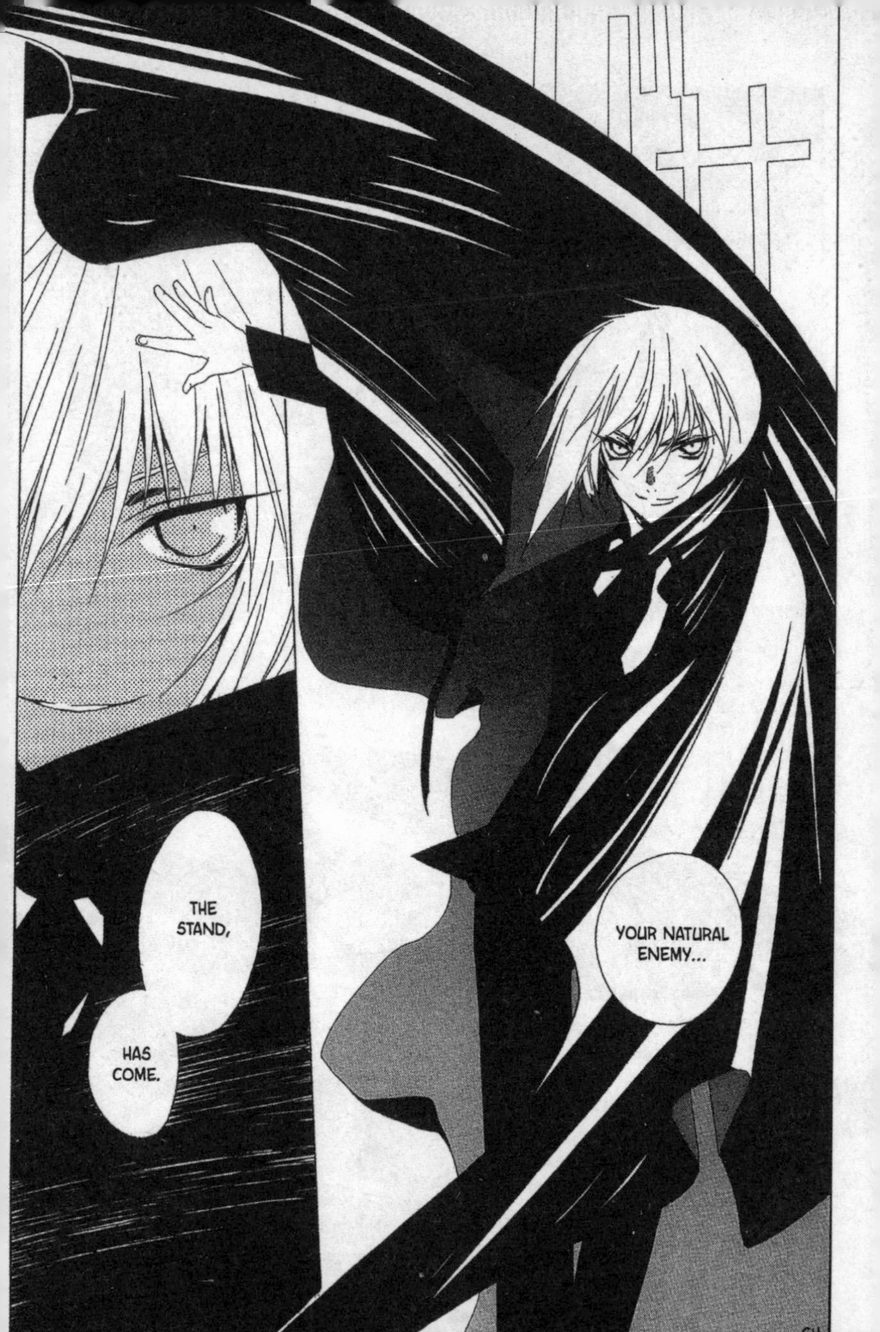
YOUR NATURAL ENEMY...
THE STAND,
HAS COME.

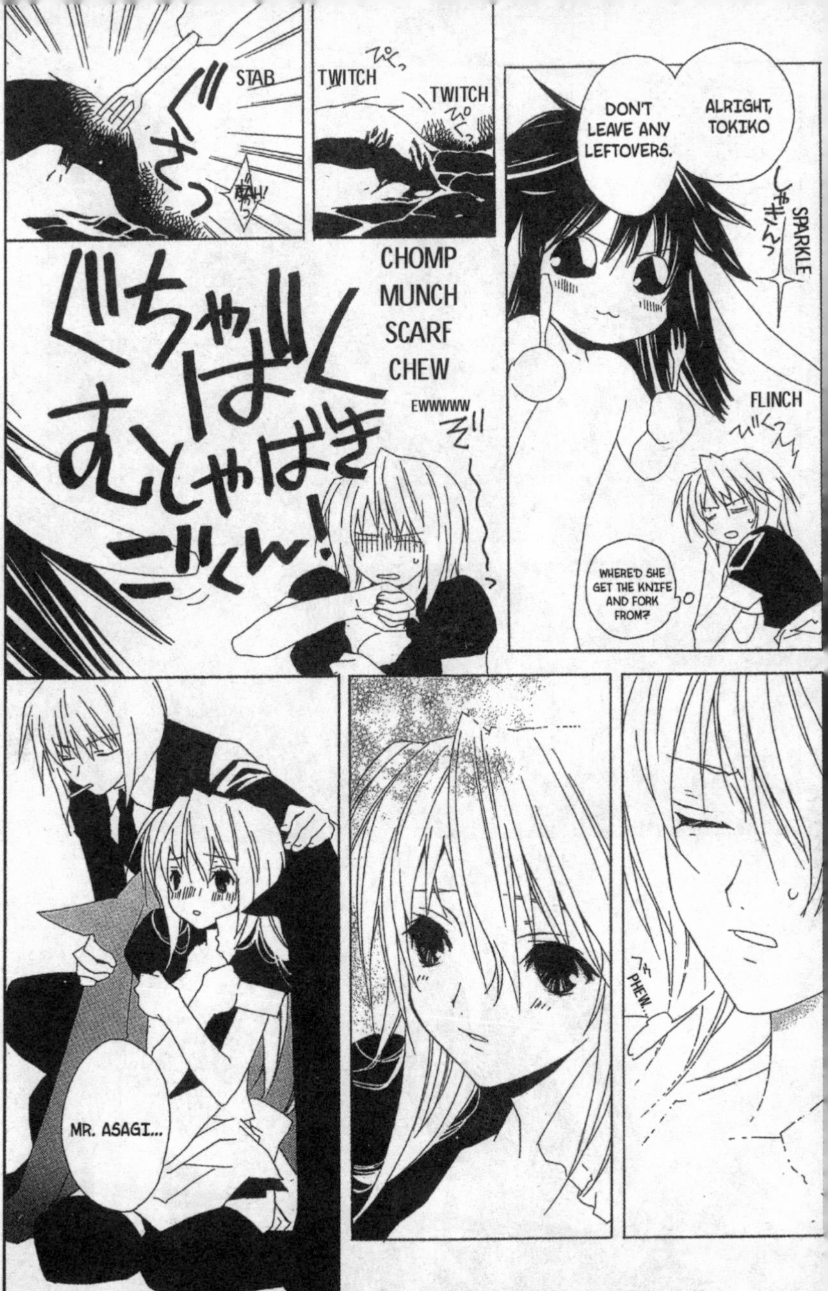
ALRIGHT, TOKIKO
DON'T LEAVE ANY LEFTOVERS.
SPARKLE
FLINCH
WHERE'D SHE GET THE KNIFE AND FORK FROM?
TWITCH
TWITCH
STAB
CHOMP
MUNCH
SCARF
CHEW
EWWWWW
PHEW...
MR. ASAGI...

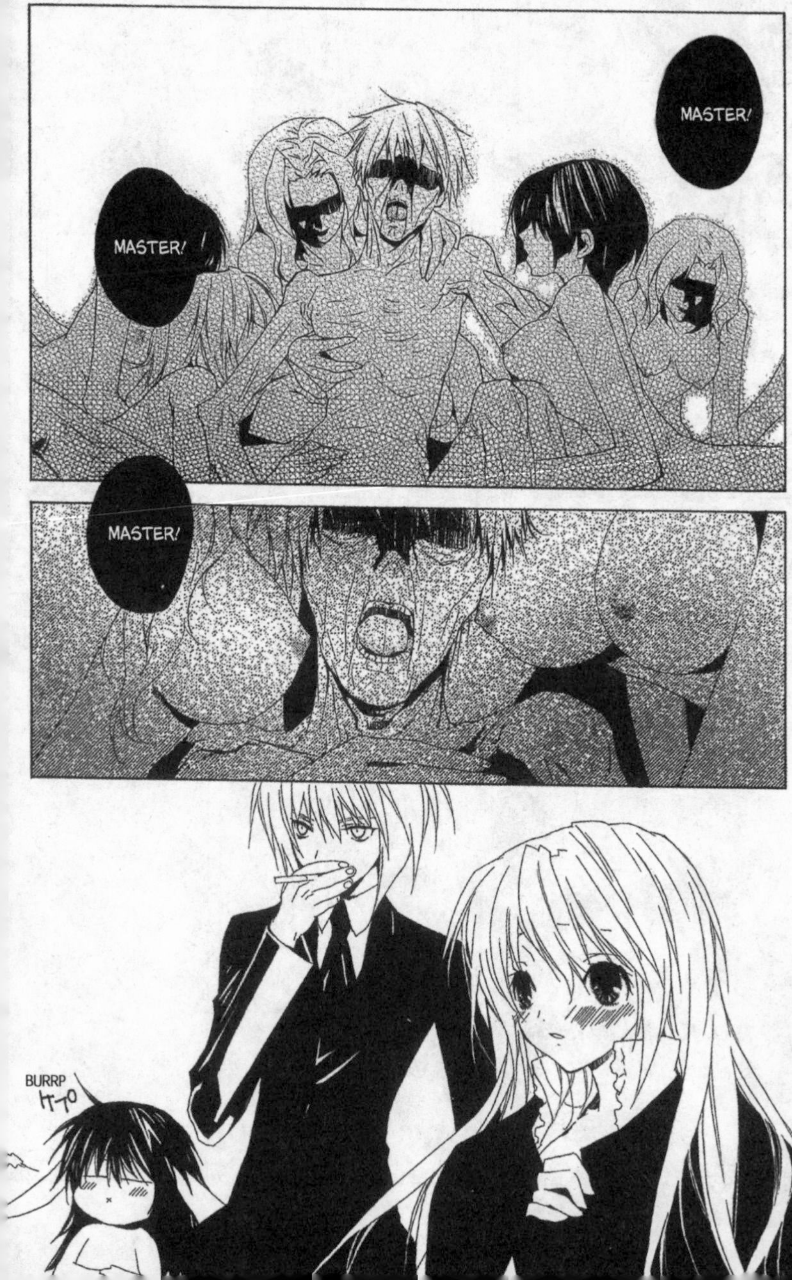
MASTER!
MASTER!
MASTER!
BURRP

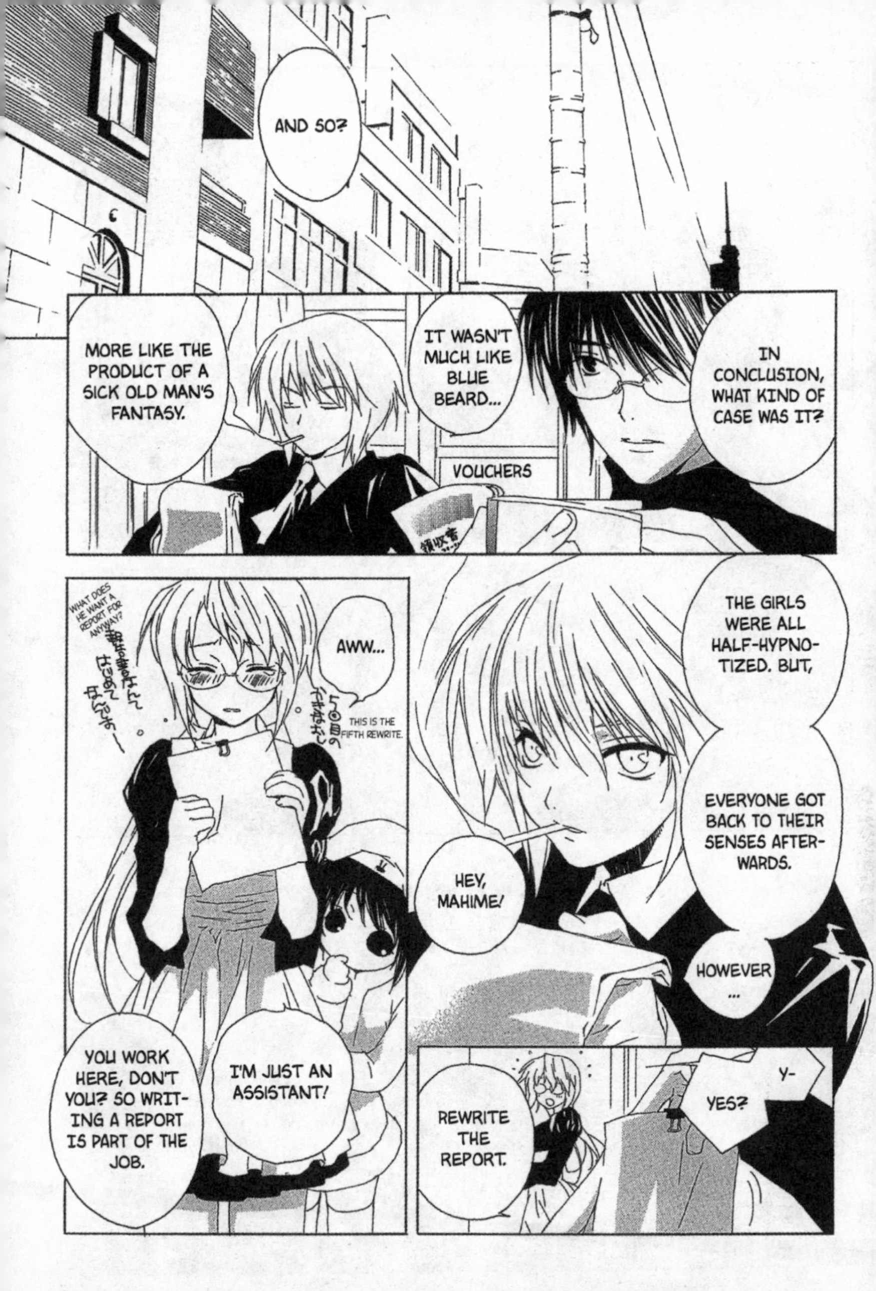
AND SO?
IN CONCLUSION, WHAT KIND OF CASE WAS IT?
IT WASN'T MUCH LIKE BLUE BEARD...
MORE LIKE THE PRODUCT OF A SICK OLD MAN'S FANTASY.
VOUCHERS
THE GIRLS WERE ALL HALF-HYPNO-TIZED. BUT,
EVERYONE GOT BACK TO THEIR SENSES AFTER-WARDS.
HOWEVER ...
HEY, MAHIME!
Y- YES?
REWRITE THE REPORT.
AWW...
THIS IS THE FIFTH REWRITE.
WHAT DOES HE WANT A REPORT FOR ANYWAY?
I'M JUST AN ASSISTANT!
YOU WORK HERE, DON'T YOU? SO WRITING A REPORT IS PART OF THE JOB.

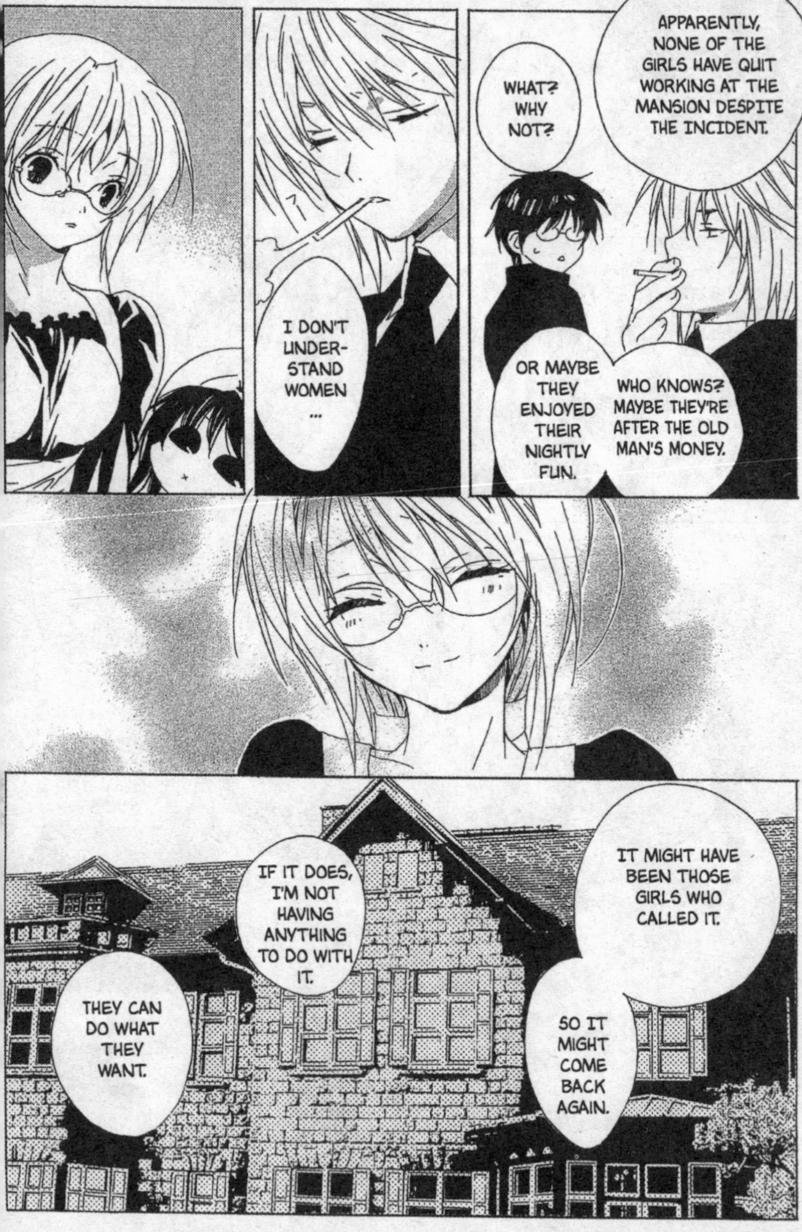
APPARENTLY, NONE OF THE GIRLS HAVE QUIT WORKING AT THE MANSION DESPITE THE INCIDENT.
WHAT? WHY NOT?
WHO KNOWS? MAYBE THEY'RE AFTER THE OLD MAN'S MONEY.
OR MAYBE THEY ENJOYED THEIR NIGHTLY FUN.
I DON'T UNDER-STAND WOMEN ...
IT MIGHT HAVE BEEN THOSE GIRLS WHO CALLED IT.
SO IT MIGHT COME BACK AGAIN.
IF IT DOES, I'M NOT HAVING ANYTHING TO DO WITH IT.
THEY CAN DO WHAT THEY WANT.

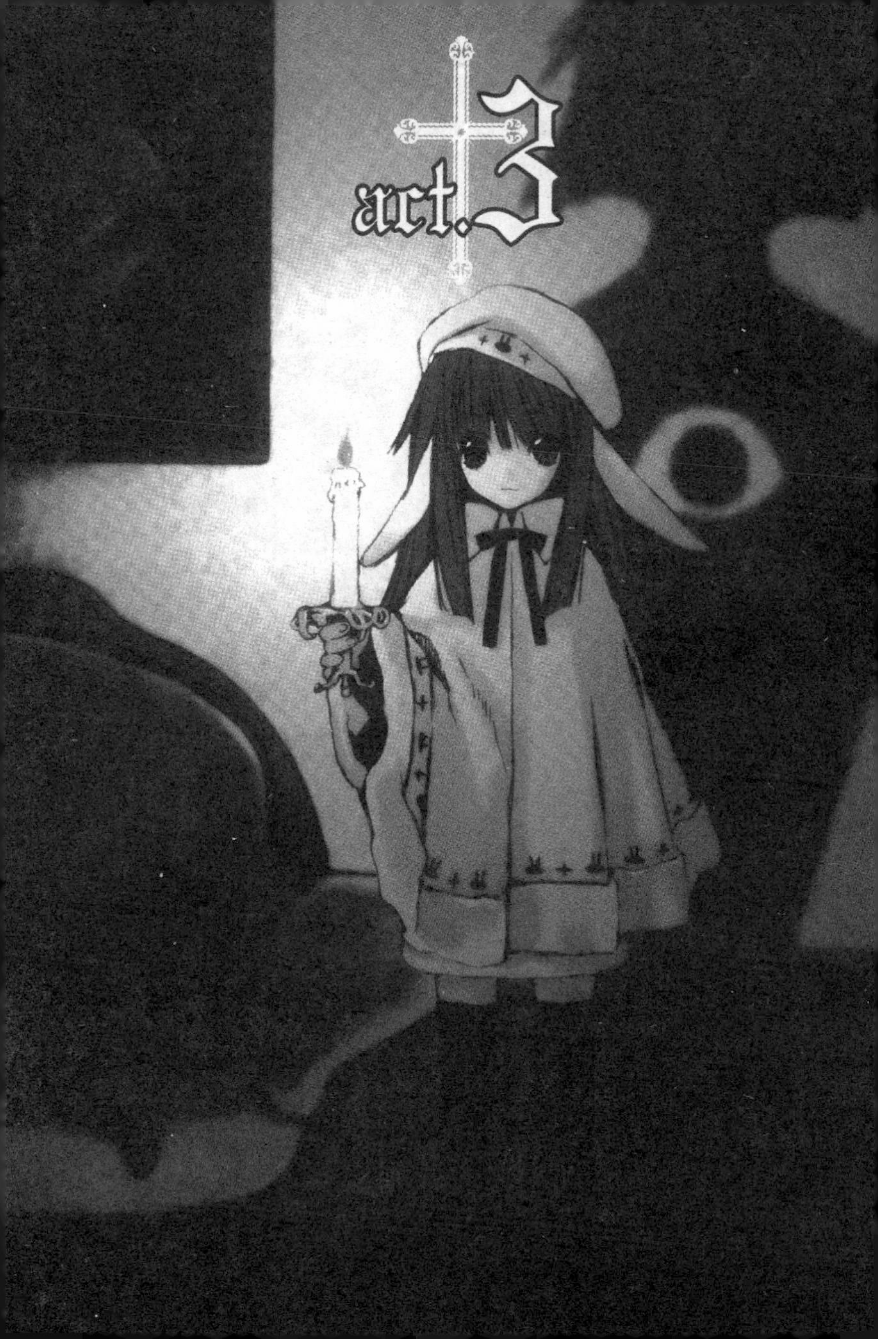
act.3

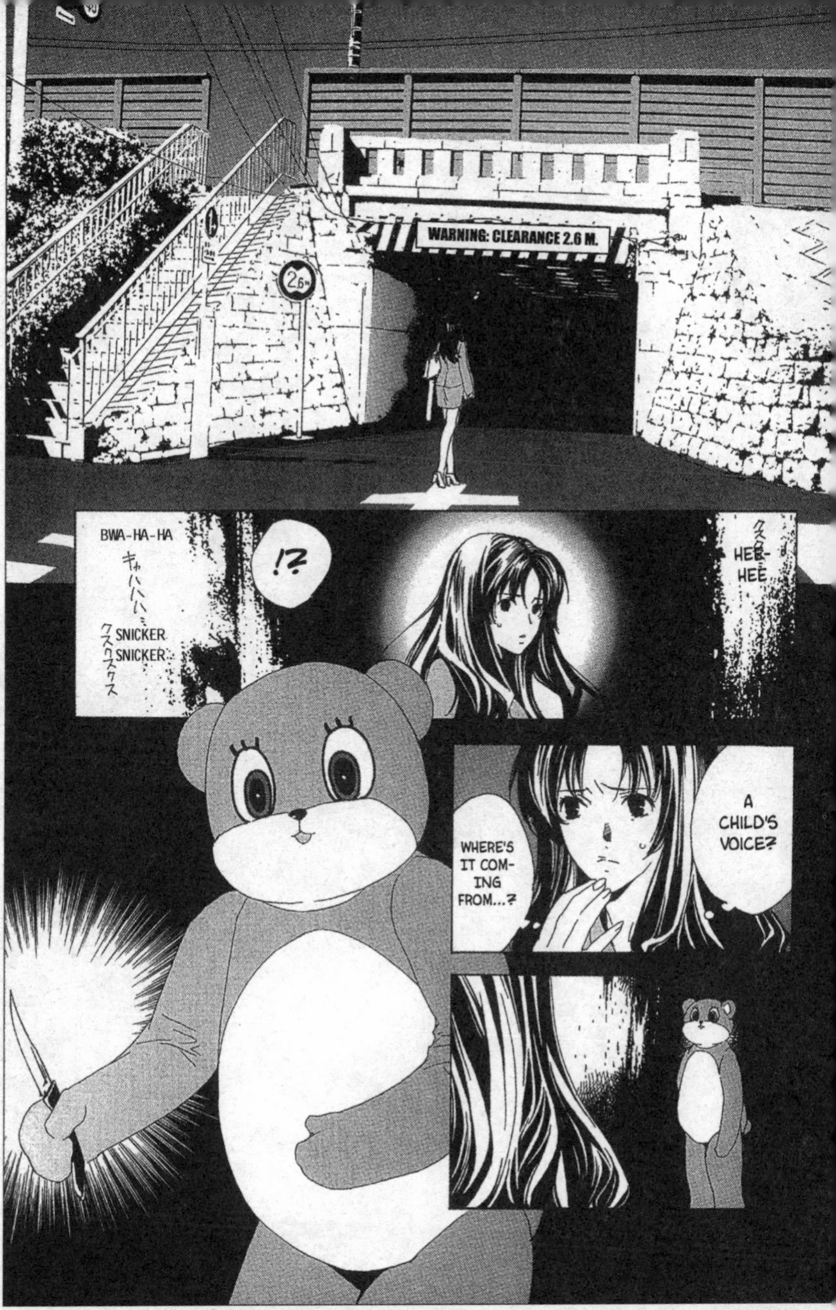
WARNING: CLEARANCE 2.6 M.
HEE-HEE
!?
BWA-HA-HA
キャハハハ
SNICKER SNICKER
クスクスクス
A CHILD'S VOICE?
WHERE'S IT COMING FROM...?

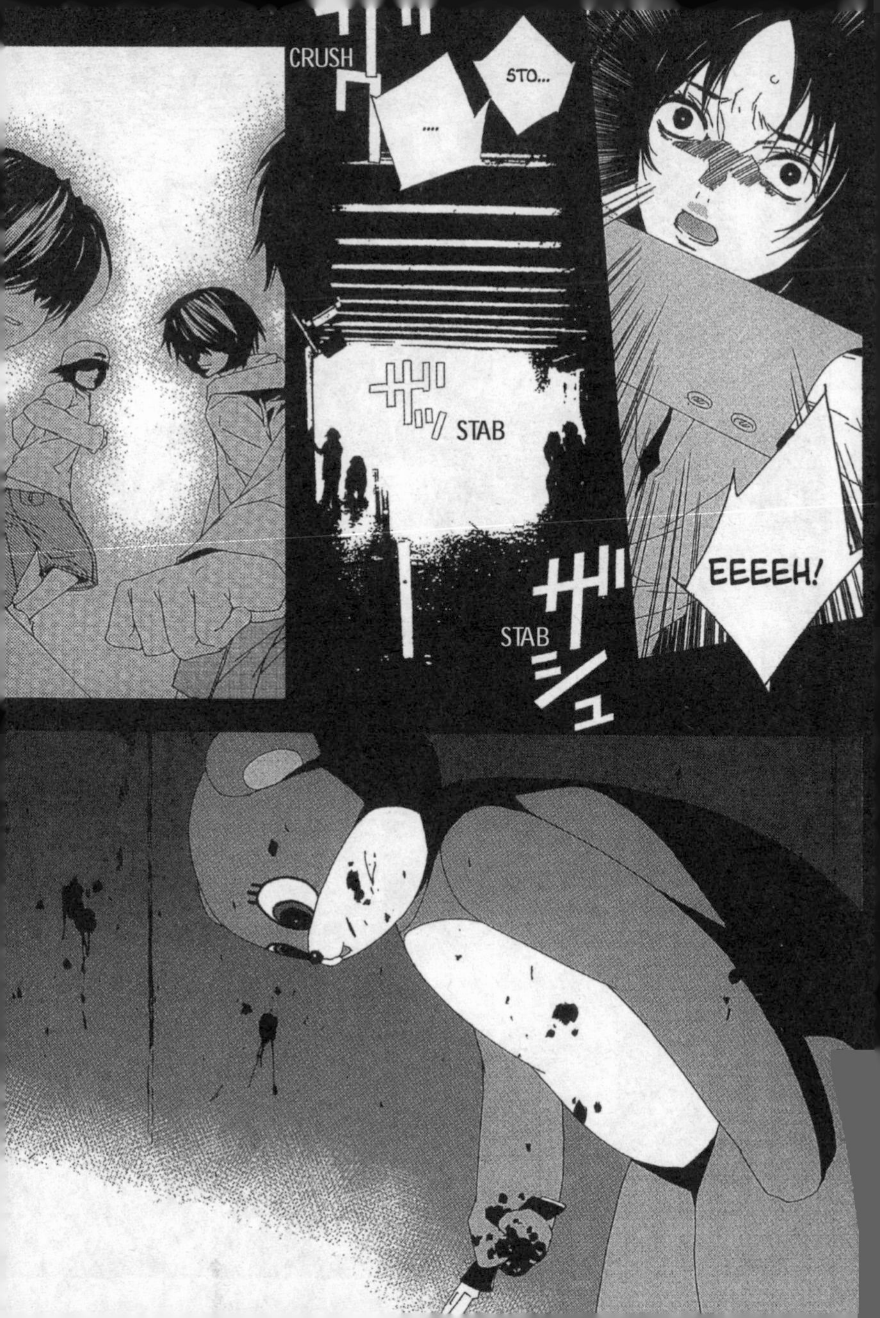

EEEEH!
STO...
....
CRUSH
ザッ
STAB
ザシュ
STAB

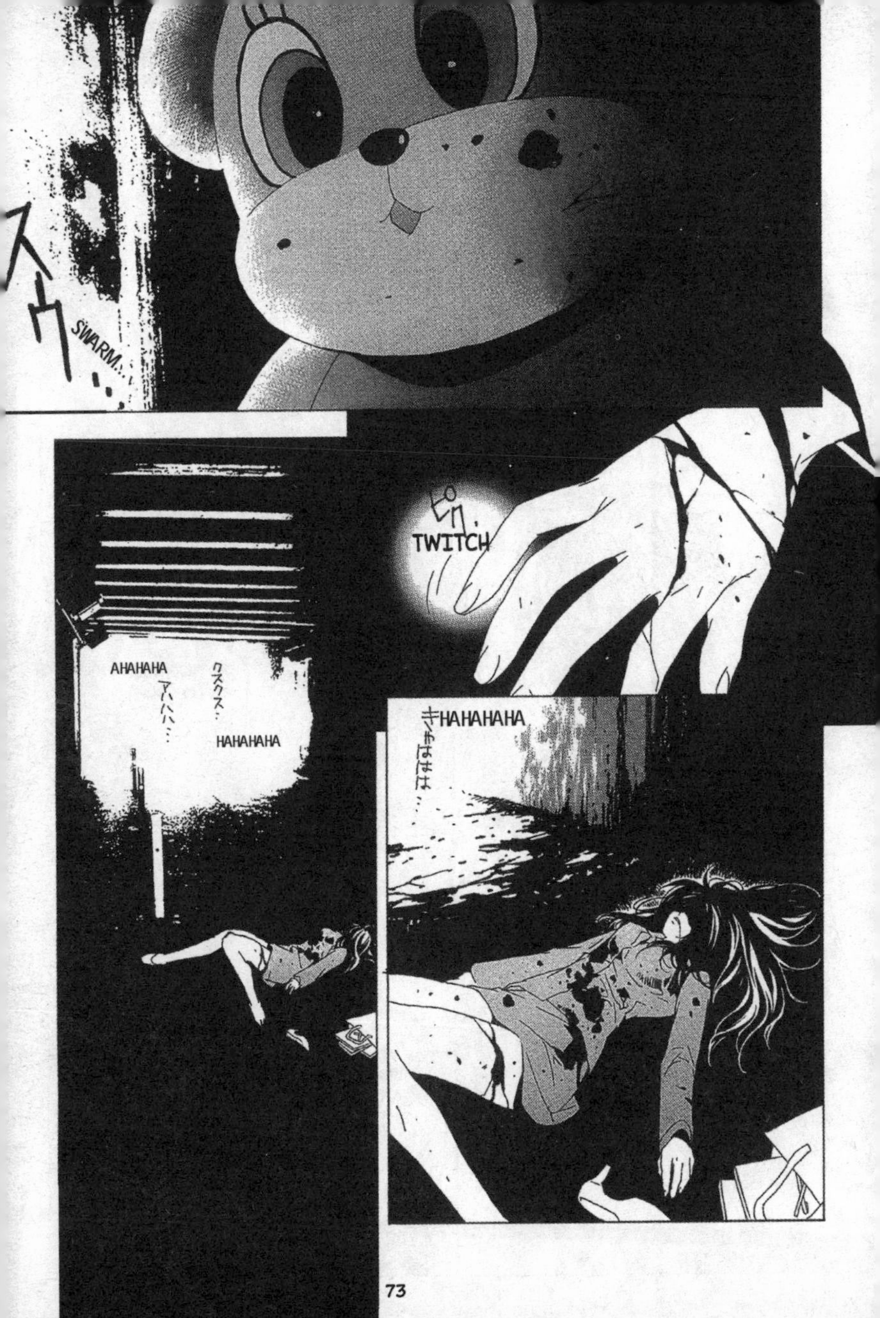

スゥ
SWARM...
ピクッ
TWITCH
クスクス…
アハハハ…
AHAHAHA
HAHAHAHA
きゃははは…
HAHAHAHA

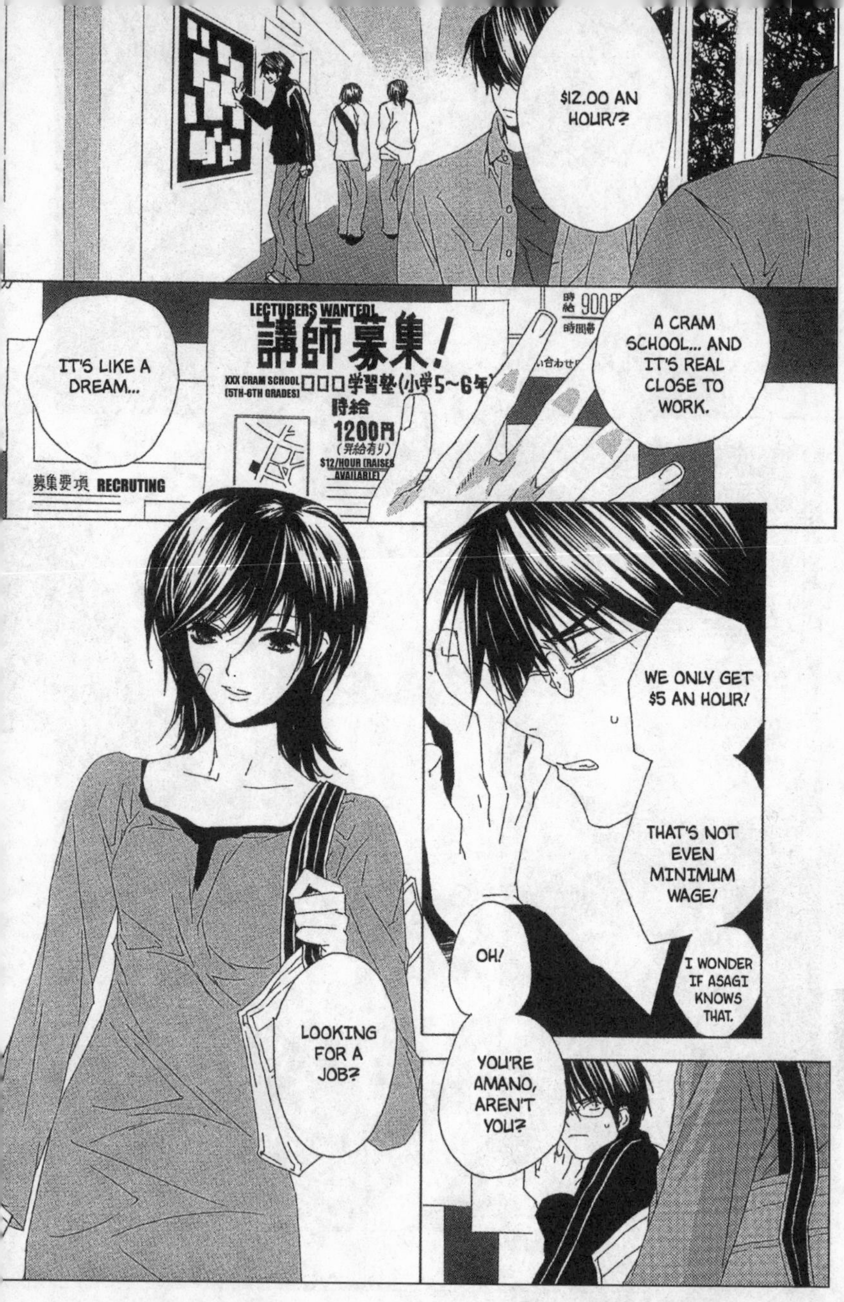
$12.00 AN HOUR!?
A CRAM SCHOOL... AND IT'S REAL CLOSE TO WORK.
IT'S LIKE A DREAM...
LECTURERS WANTED!
講師 募集！
XXX CRAM SCHOOL (5TH-6TH GRADES)
□□□学習塾(小学5～6年)
時給
1200円
(昇給有り)
$12/HOUR (RAISES AVAILABLE)
募集要項 RECRUTING
WE ONLY GET $5 AN HOUR!
THAT'S NOT EVEN MINIMUM WAGE!
I WONDER IF ASAGI KNOWS THAT.
OH!
YOU'RE AMANO, AREN'T YOU?
LOOKING FOR A JOB?

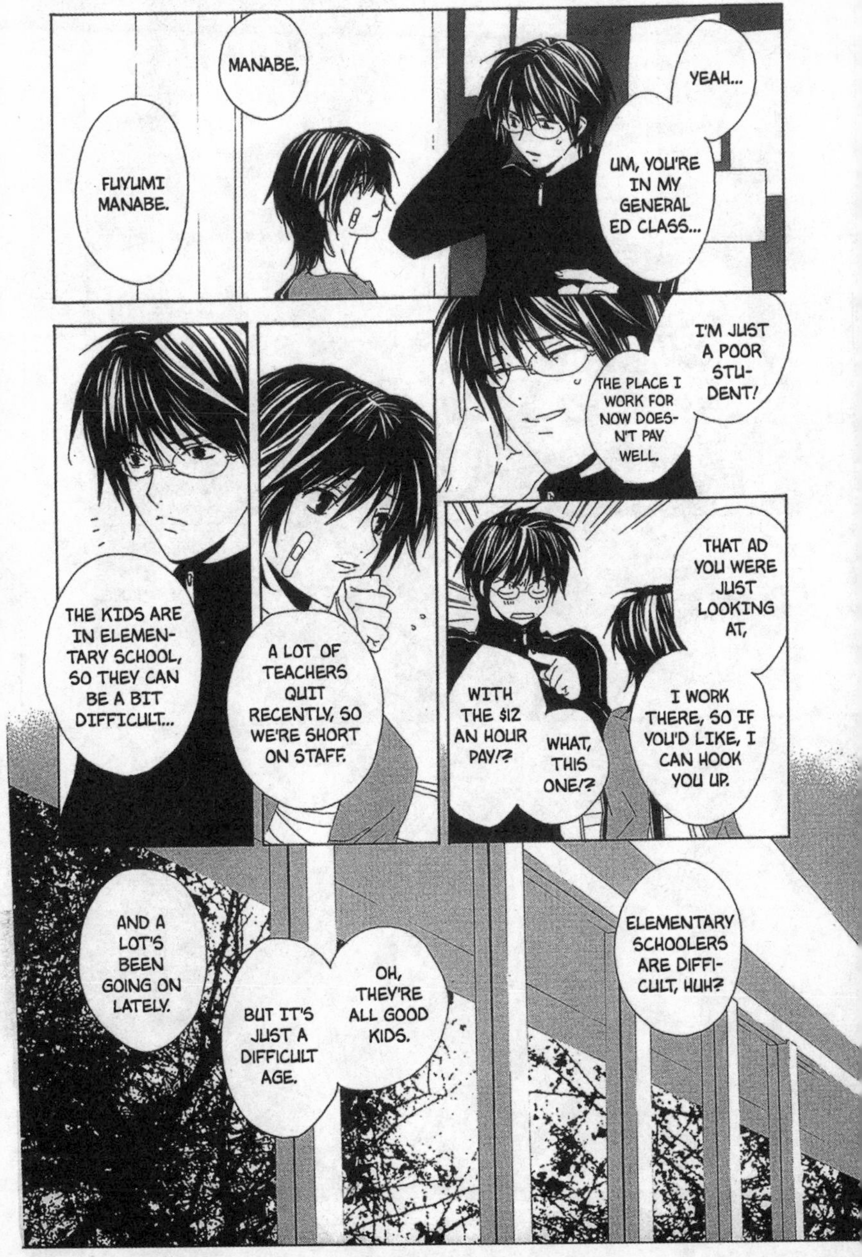
YEAH...
UM, YOU'RE IN MY GENERAL ED CLASS...
MANABE.
FUYUMI MANABE.
I'M JUST A POOR STU-DENT!
THE PLACE I WORK FOR NOW DOES-N'T PAY WELL.
THAT AD YOU WERE JUST LOOKING AT,
I WORK THERE, SO IF YOU'D LIKE, I CAN HOOK YOU UP.
WHAT, THIS ONE!?
WITH THE $12 AN HOUR PAY!?
A LOT OF TEACHERS QUIT RECENTLY, SO WE'RE SHORT ON STAFF.
THE KIDS ARE IN ELEMENTARY SCHOOL, SO THEY CAN BE A BIT DIFFICULT...
ELEMENTARY SCHOOLERS ARE DIFFI-CULT, HUH?
OH, THEY'RE ALL GOOD KIDS.
BUT IT'S JUST A DIFFICULT AGE.
AND A LOT'S BEEN GOING ON LATELY.

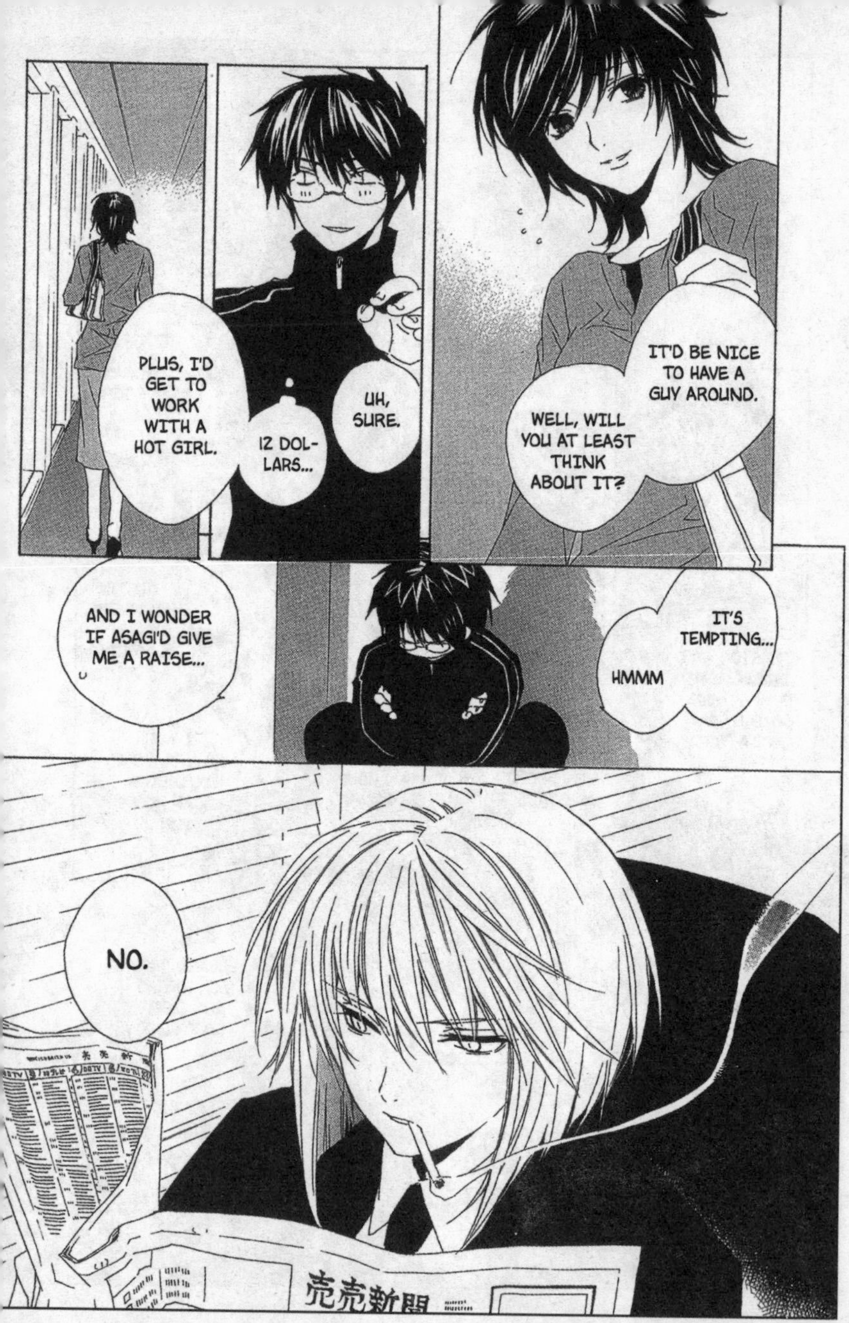
IT'D BE NICE TO HAVE A GUY AROUND.
WELL, WILL YOU AT LEAST THINK ABOUT IT?
UH, SURE.
12 DOL-LARS...
PLUS, I'D GET TO WORK WITH A HOT GIRL.
IT'S TEMPTING...
HMMM
AND I WONDER IF ASAGI'D GIVE ME A RAISE...
NO.
売売新聞

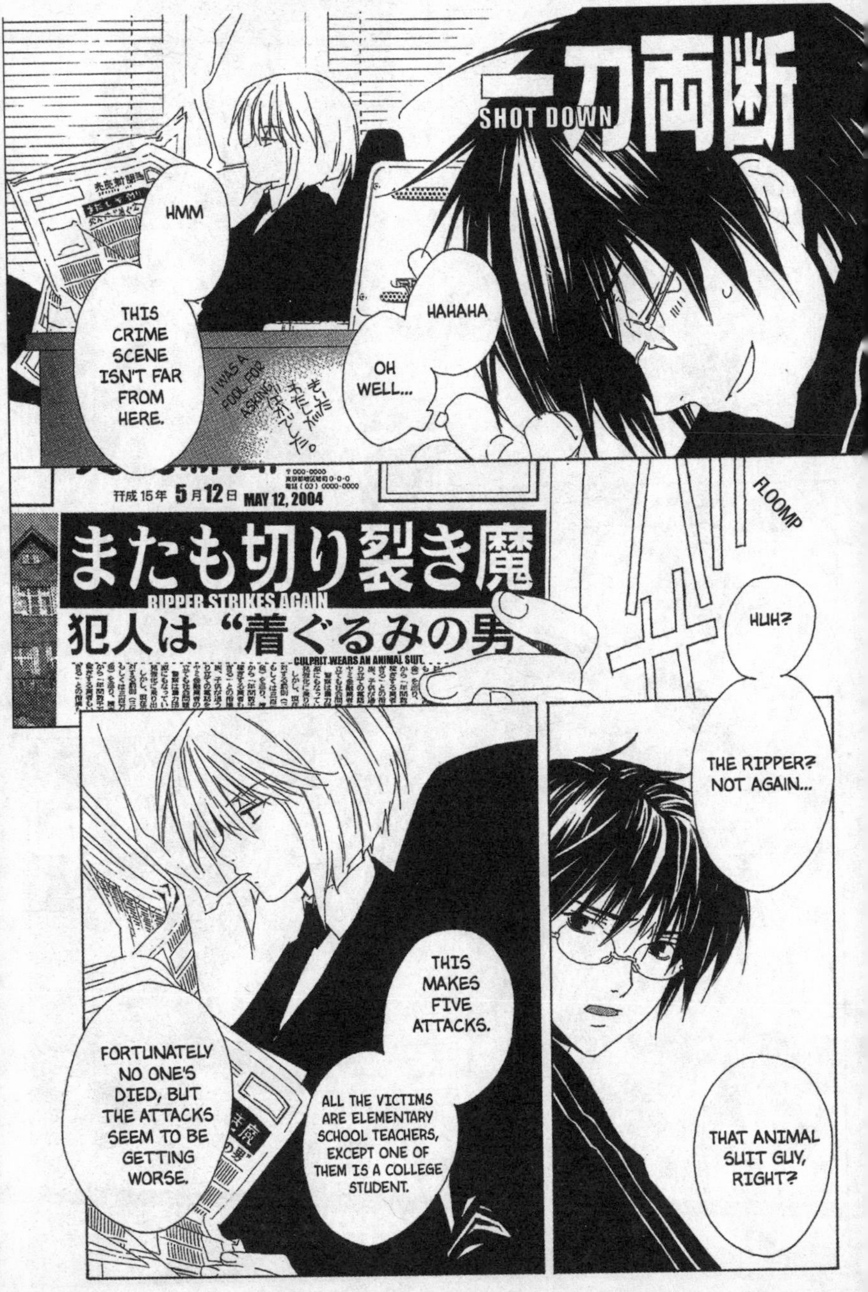
一刀両断
SHOT DOWN
HAHAHA
OH WELL...
I WAS A FOOL FOR ASKING.
HMM
THIS CRIME SCENE ISN'T FAR FROM HERE.
FLOOMP
平成15年 5月12日 MAY 12, 2004
またも切り裂き魔
RIPPER STRIKES AGAIN
犯人は"着ぐるみの男
CULPRIT WEARS AN ANIMAL SUIT
HUH?
THE RIPPER? NOT AGAIN...
THAT ANIMAL SUIT GUY, RIGHT?
THIS MAKES FIVE ATTACKS.
ALL THE VICTIMS ARE ELEMENTARY SCHOOL TEACHERS, EXCEPT ONE OF THEM IS A COLLEGE STUDENT.
FORTUNATELY NO ONE'S DIED, BUT THE ATTACKS SEEM TO BE GETTING WORSE.

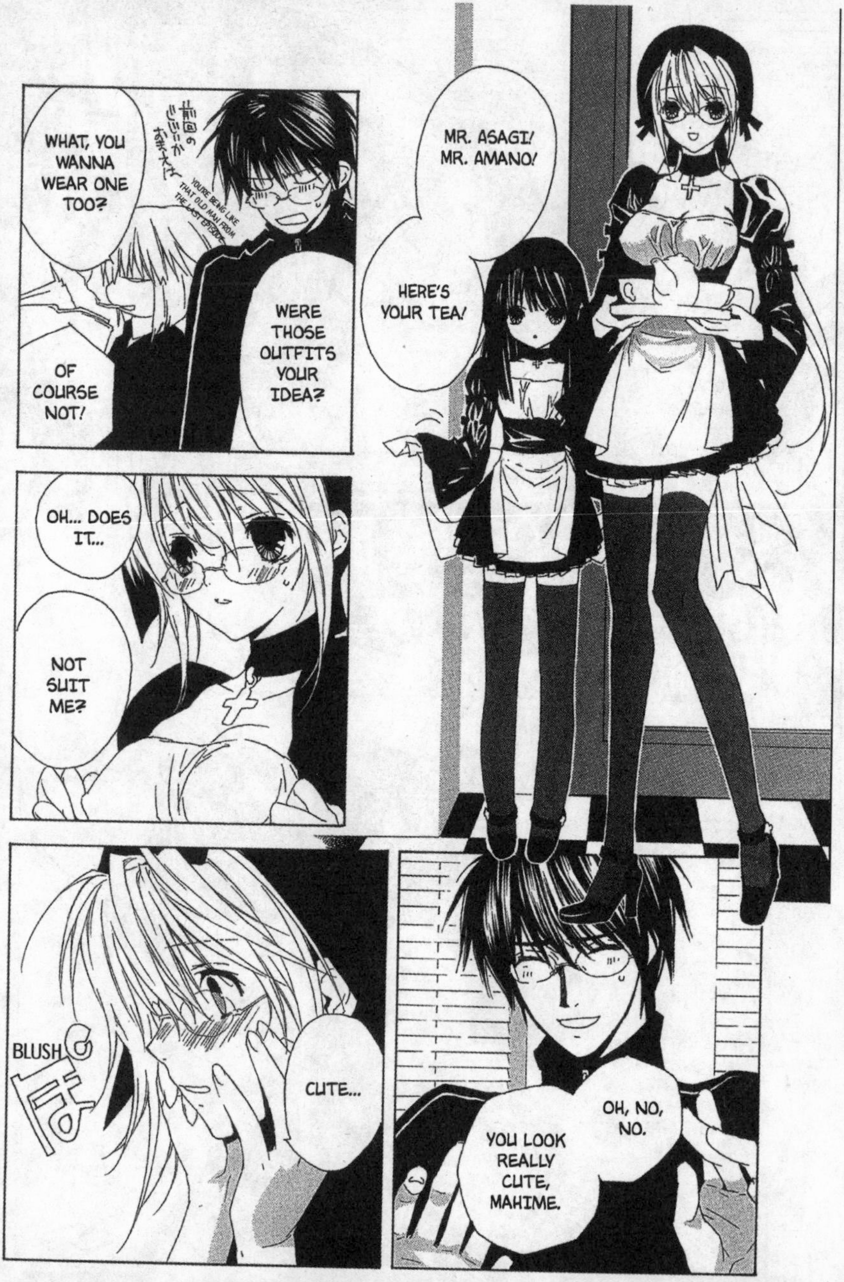
MR. ASAGI! MR. AMANO!
HERE'S YOUR TEA!
WERE THOSE OUTFITS YOUR IDEA?
OF COURSE NOT!
WHAT, YOU WANNA WEAR ONE TOO?
YOU'RE BEING LIKE THAT OLD MAN FROM THE LAST EPISODE
OH... DOES IT...
NOT SUIT ME?
OH, NO, NO.
YOU LOOK REALLY CUTE, MAHIME.
CUTE...
BLUSH
ぽ

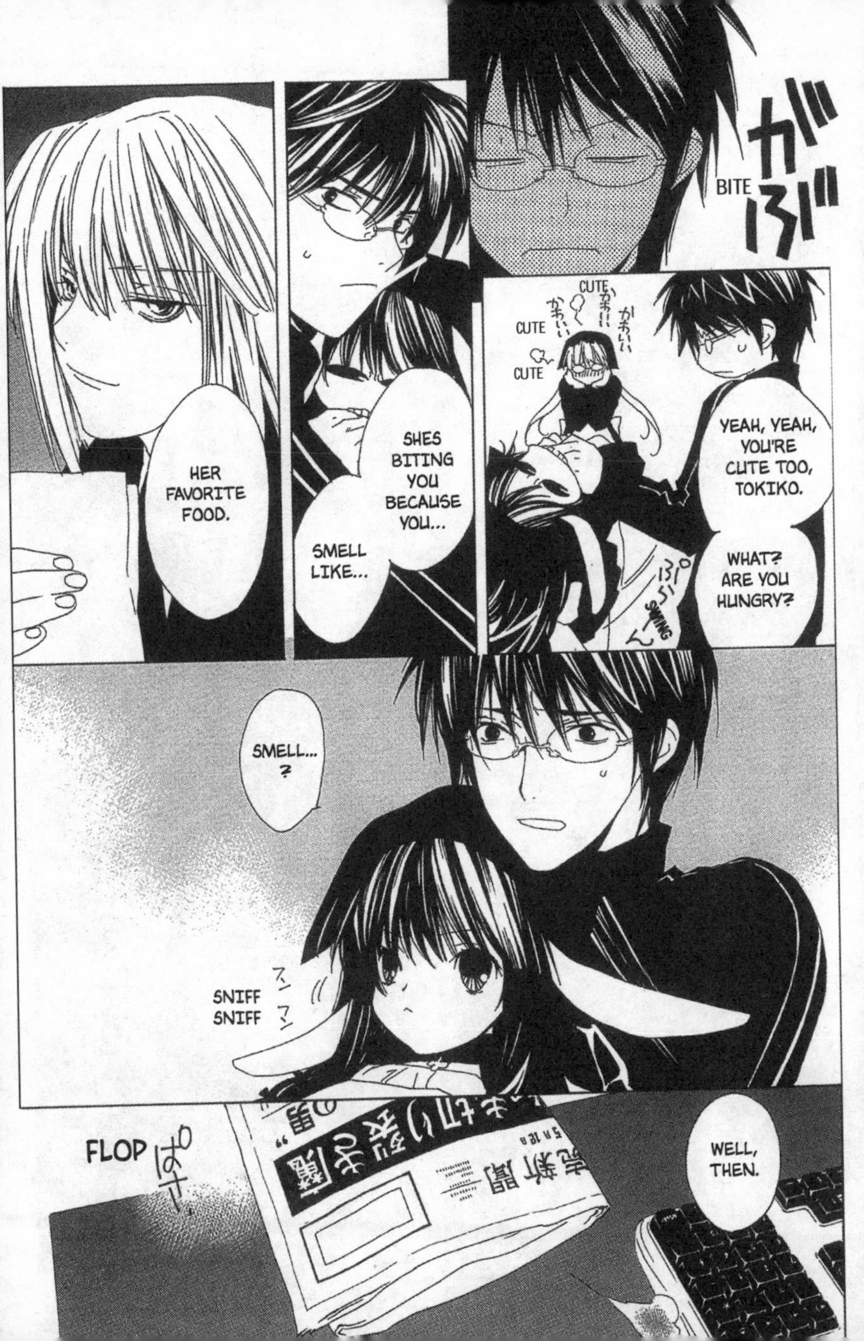
BITE
CUTE
CUTE
CUTE
YEAH, YEAH, YOU'RE CUTE TOO, TOKIKO.
WHAT? ARE YOU HUNGRY?
SWING
SHES BITING YOU BECAUSE YOU...
SMELL LIKE...
HER FAVORITE FOOD.
SMELL... ?
SNIFF SNIFF
WELL, THEN.
FLOP

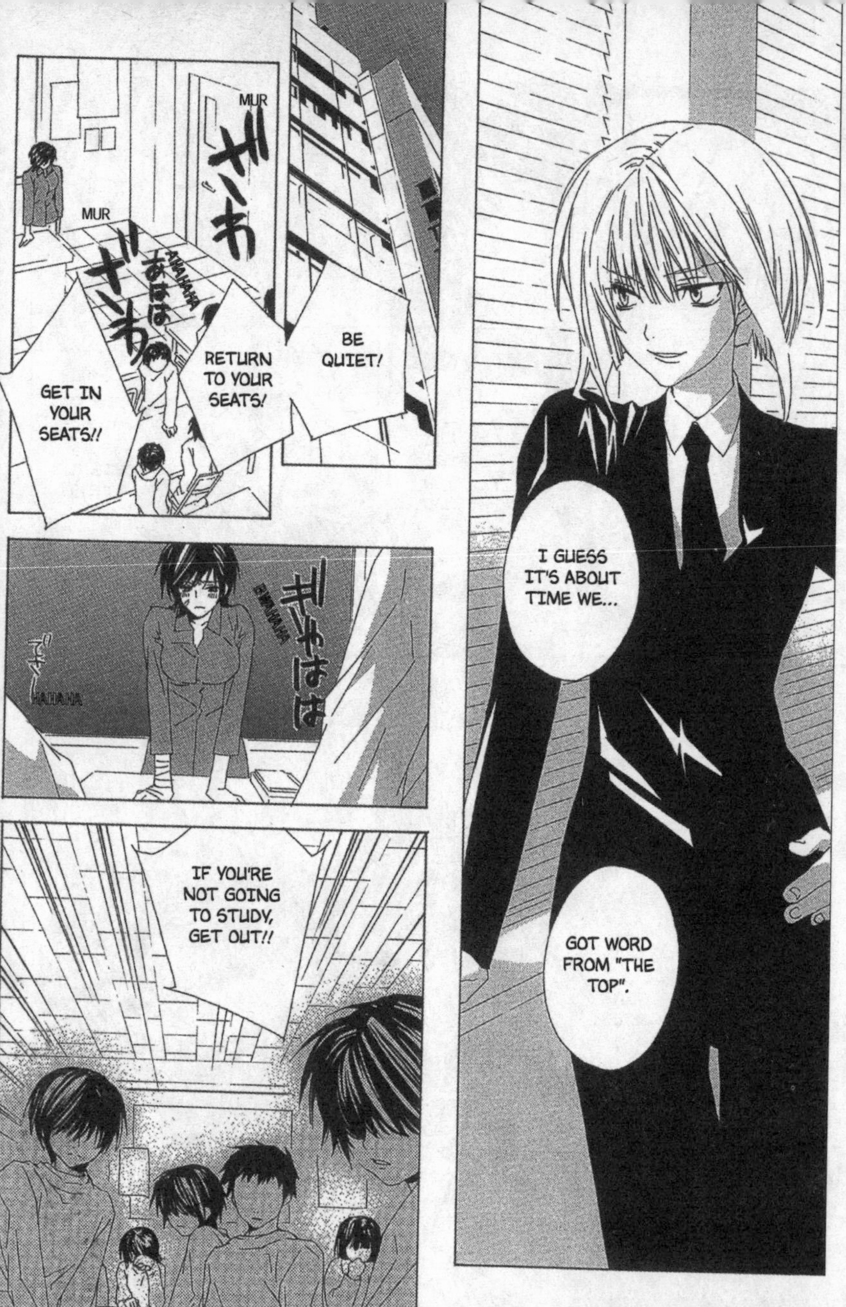
I GUESS IT'S ABOUT TIME WE...
GOT WORD FROM "THE TOP".
MUR
MUR
AHAHAHA
BE QUIET!
RETURN TO YOUR SEATS!
GET IN YOUR SEATS!!
IF YOU'RE NOT GOING TO STUDY, GET OUT!!

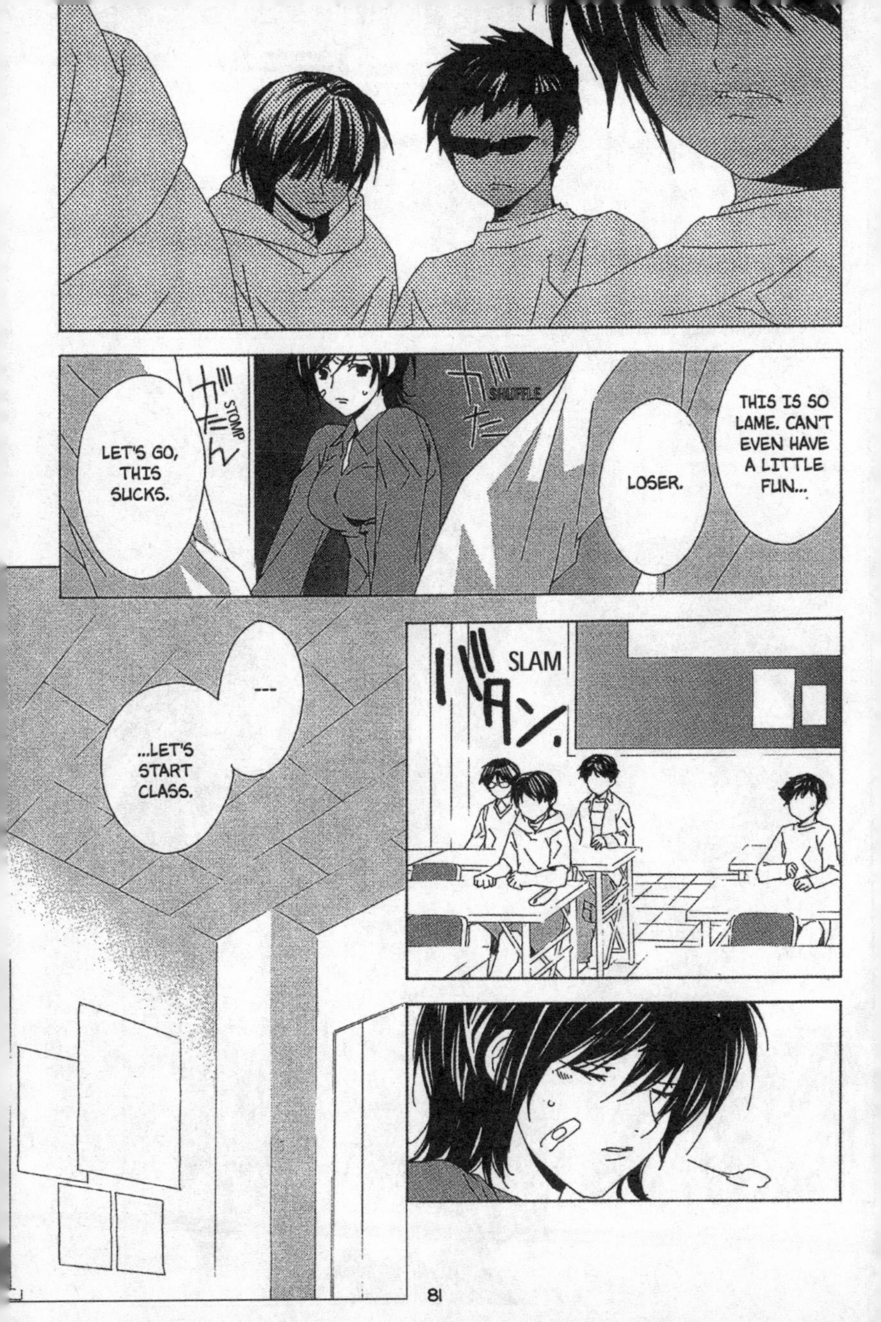
THIS IS SO LAME. CAN'T EVEN HAVE A LITTLE FUN...
LOSER.
SHUFFLE
STOMP
LET'S GO, THIS SUCKS.
SLAM

...LET'S START CLASS.

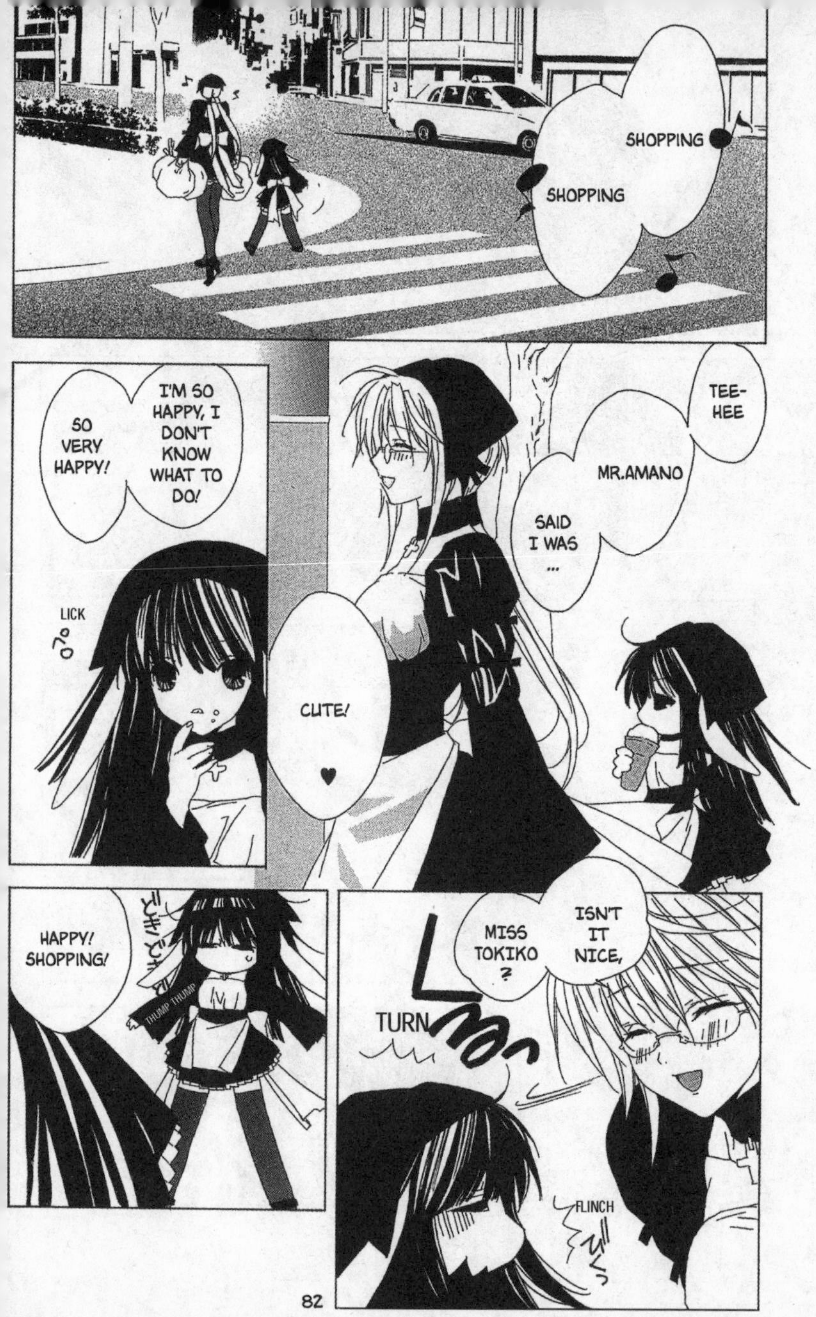
SHOPPING
SHOPPING
TEE-HEE
MR.AMANO SAID I WAS ...
CUTE! ♥
I'M SO HAPPY, I DON'T KNOW WHAT TO DO!
SO VERY HAPPY!
LICK
ISN'T IT NICE,
MISS TOKIKO?
TURN
FLINCH
HAPPY! SHOPPING!
THUMP THUMP

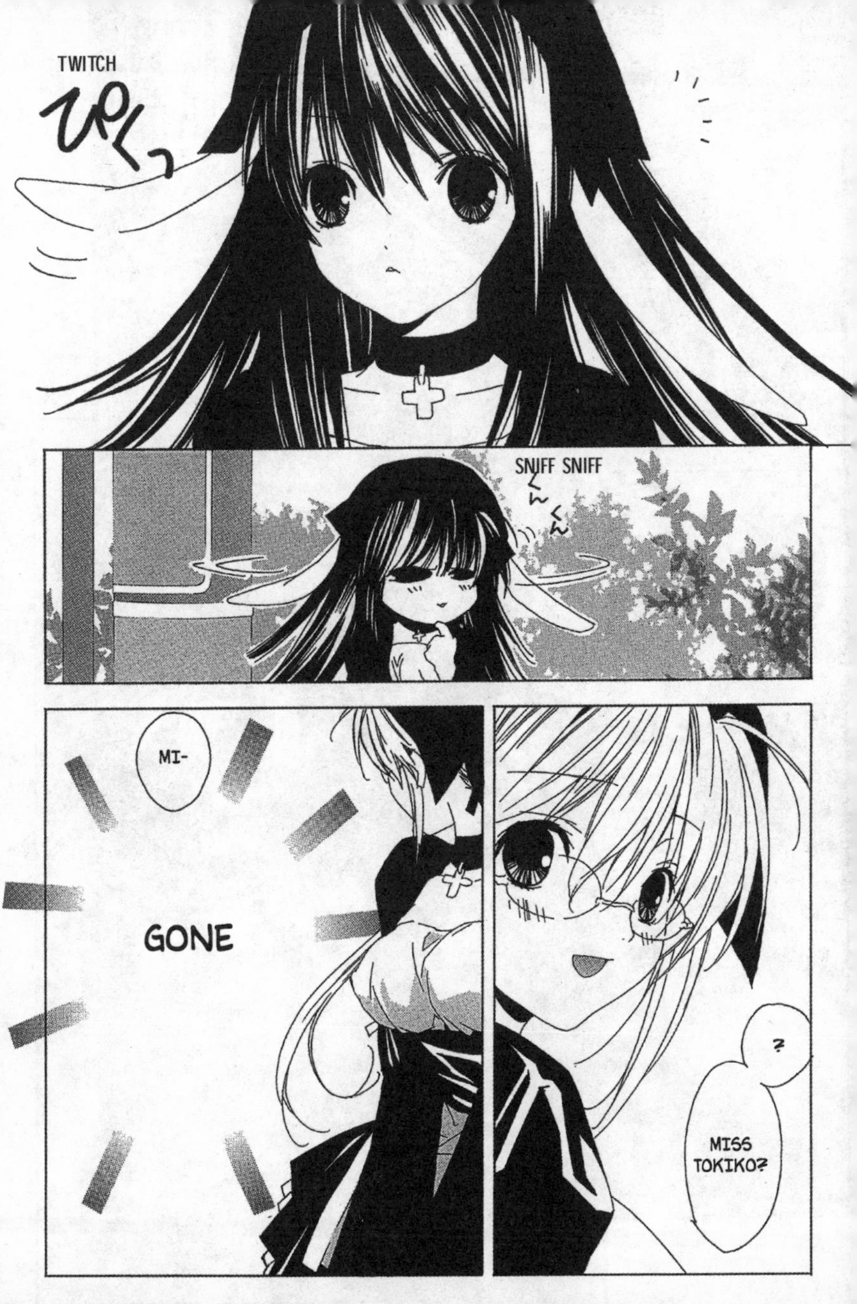

TWITCH
ぴくっ
SNIFF SNIFF
くんくん
MI-
GONE
?
MISS TOKIKO?

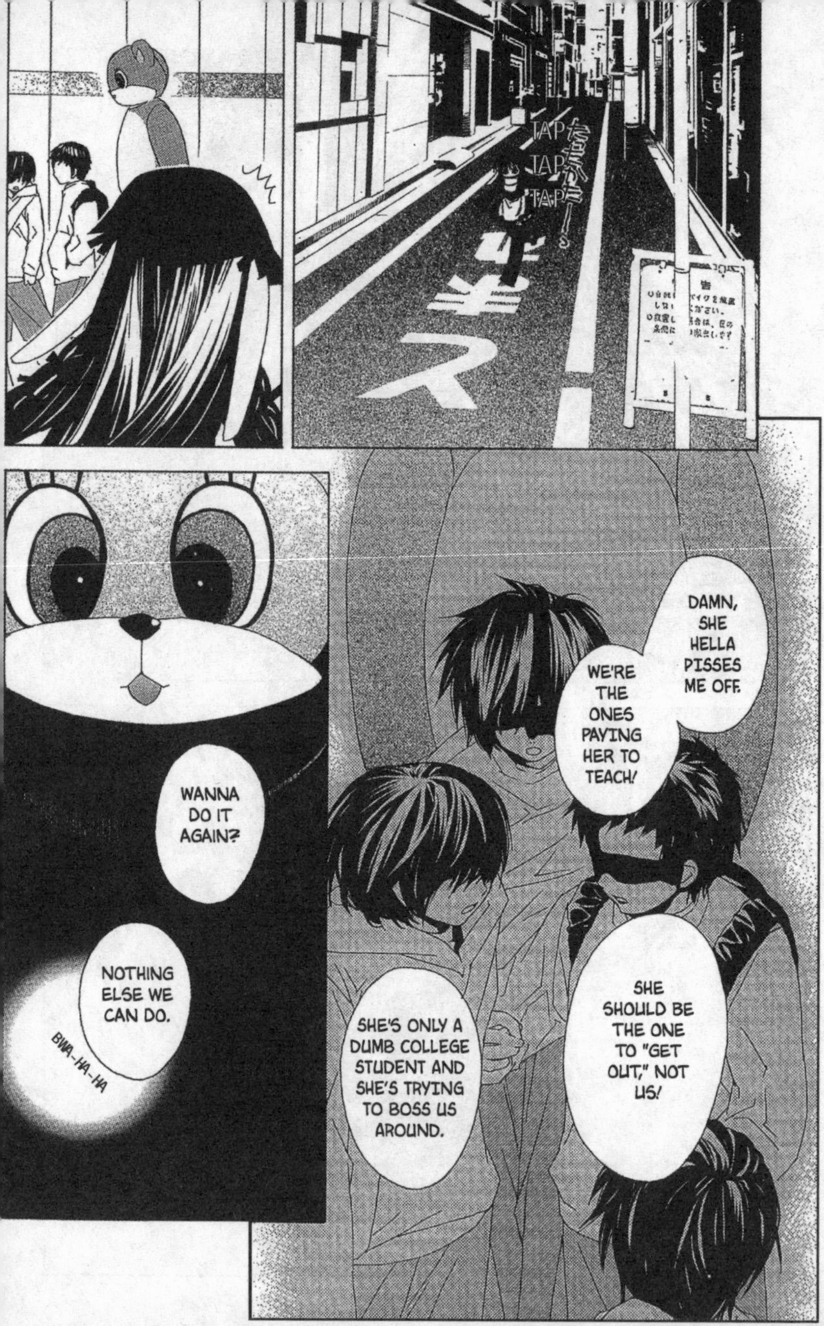
TAP
TAP
TAP
DAMN, SHE HELLA PISSES ME OFF.
WE'RE THE ONES PAYING HER TO TEACH!
SHE SHOULD BE THE ONE TO "GET OUT," NOT US!
SHE'S ONLY A DUMB COLLEGE STUDENT AND SHE'S TRYING TO BOSS US AROUND.
WANNA DO IT AGAIN?
NOTHING ELSE WE CAN DO.
BWA-HA-HA

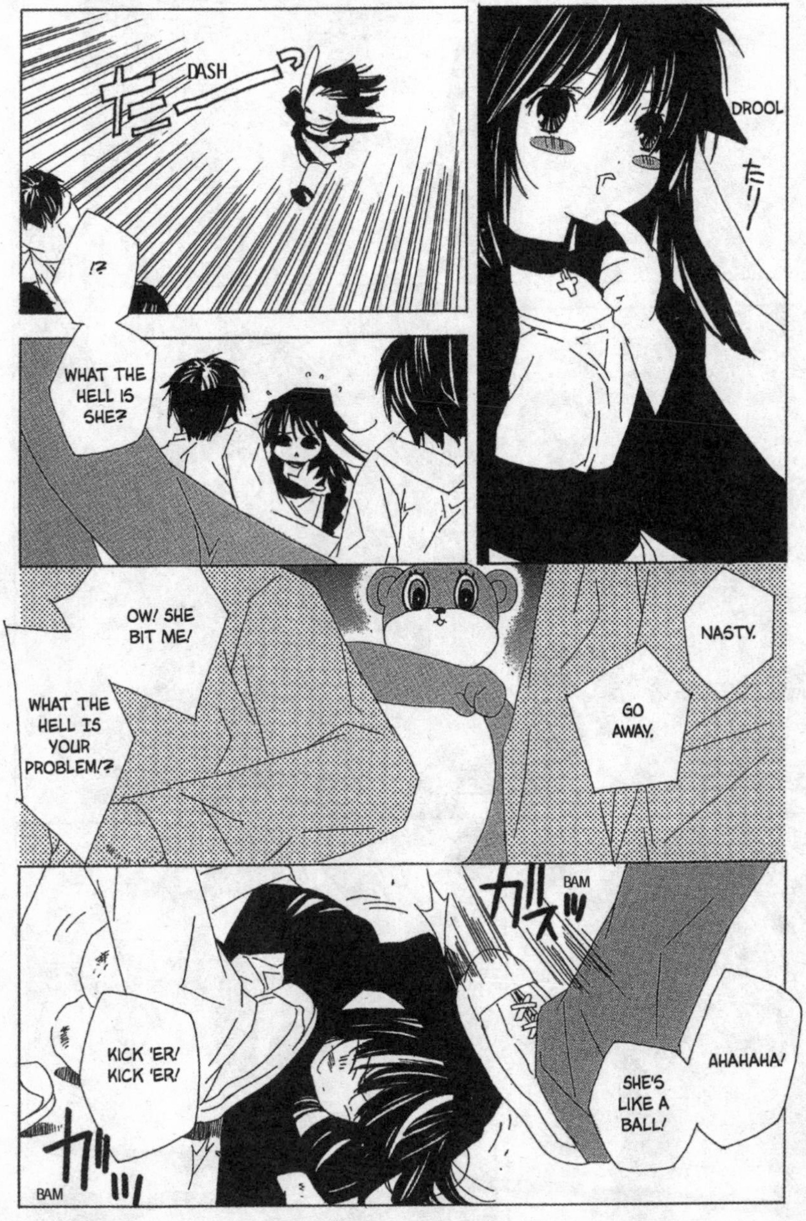
DROOL
DASH
!?
WHAT THE HELL IS SHE?
NASTY.
GO AWAY.
OW! SHE BIT ME!
WHAT THE HELL IS YOUR PROBLEM!?
BAM
AHAHAHA!
SHE'S LIKE A BALL!
KICK 'ER! KICK 'ER!
BAM

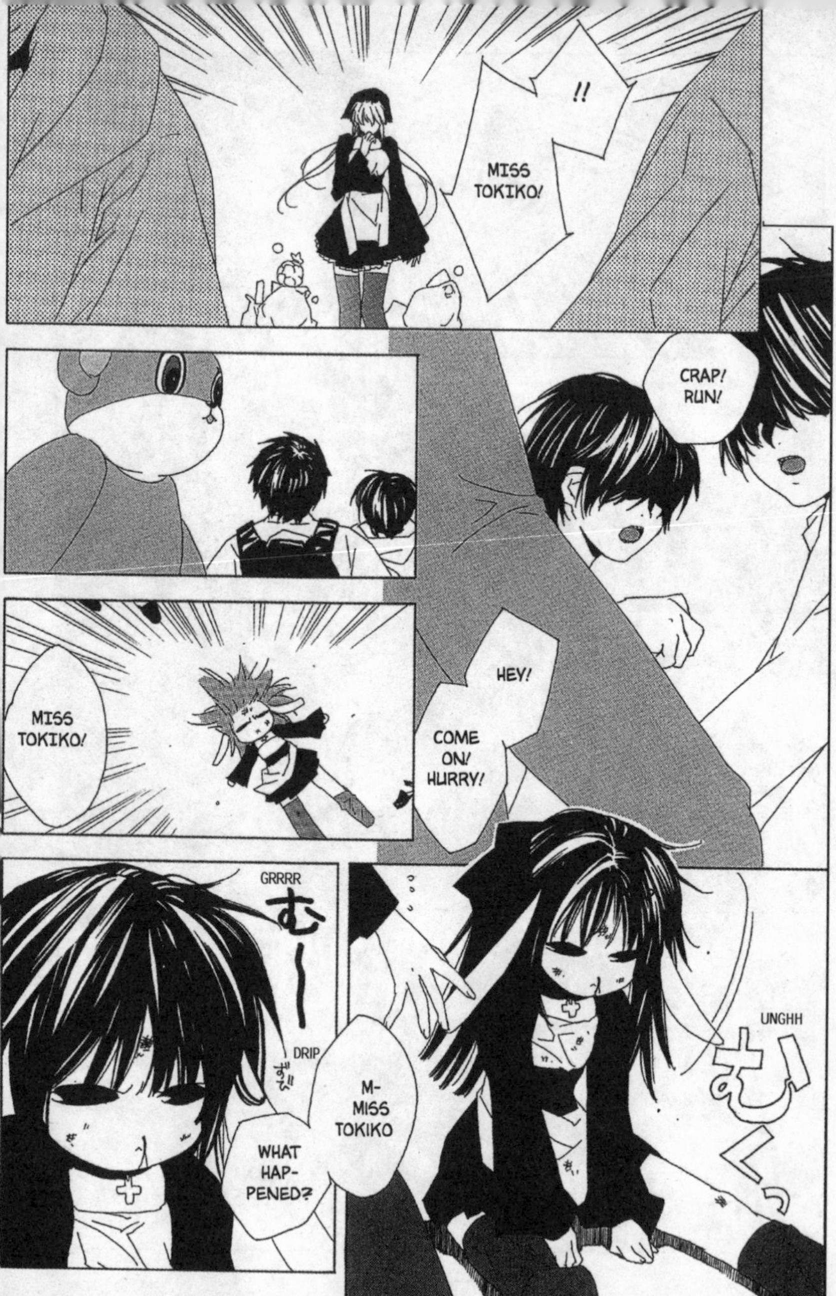

!!
MISS TOKIKO!
CRAP! RUN!
HEY!
COME ON! HURRY!
MISS TOKIKO!
UNGHH
M- MISS TOKIKO
WHAT HAP-PENED?
GRRRR
むー
DRIP

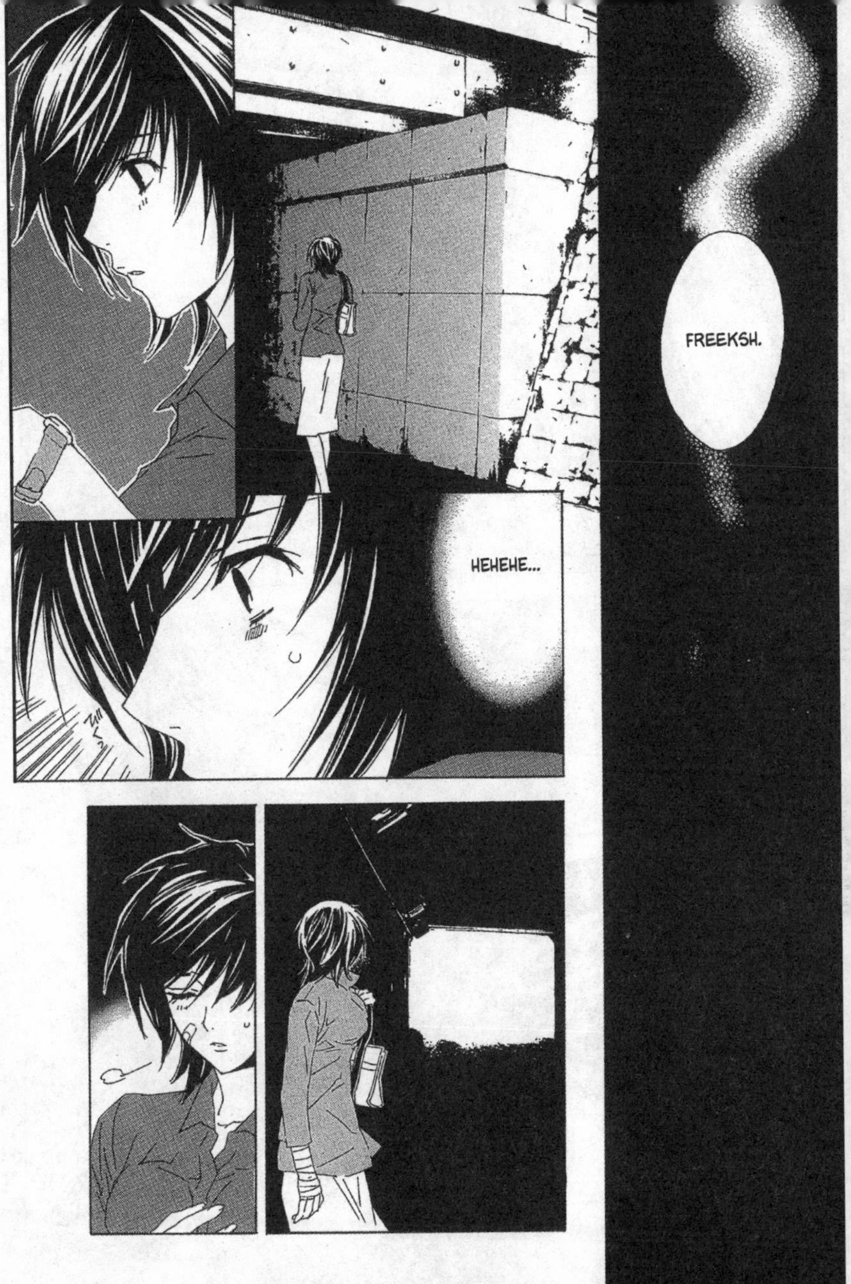
FREEKSH.
HEHEHE...

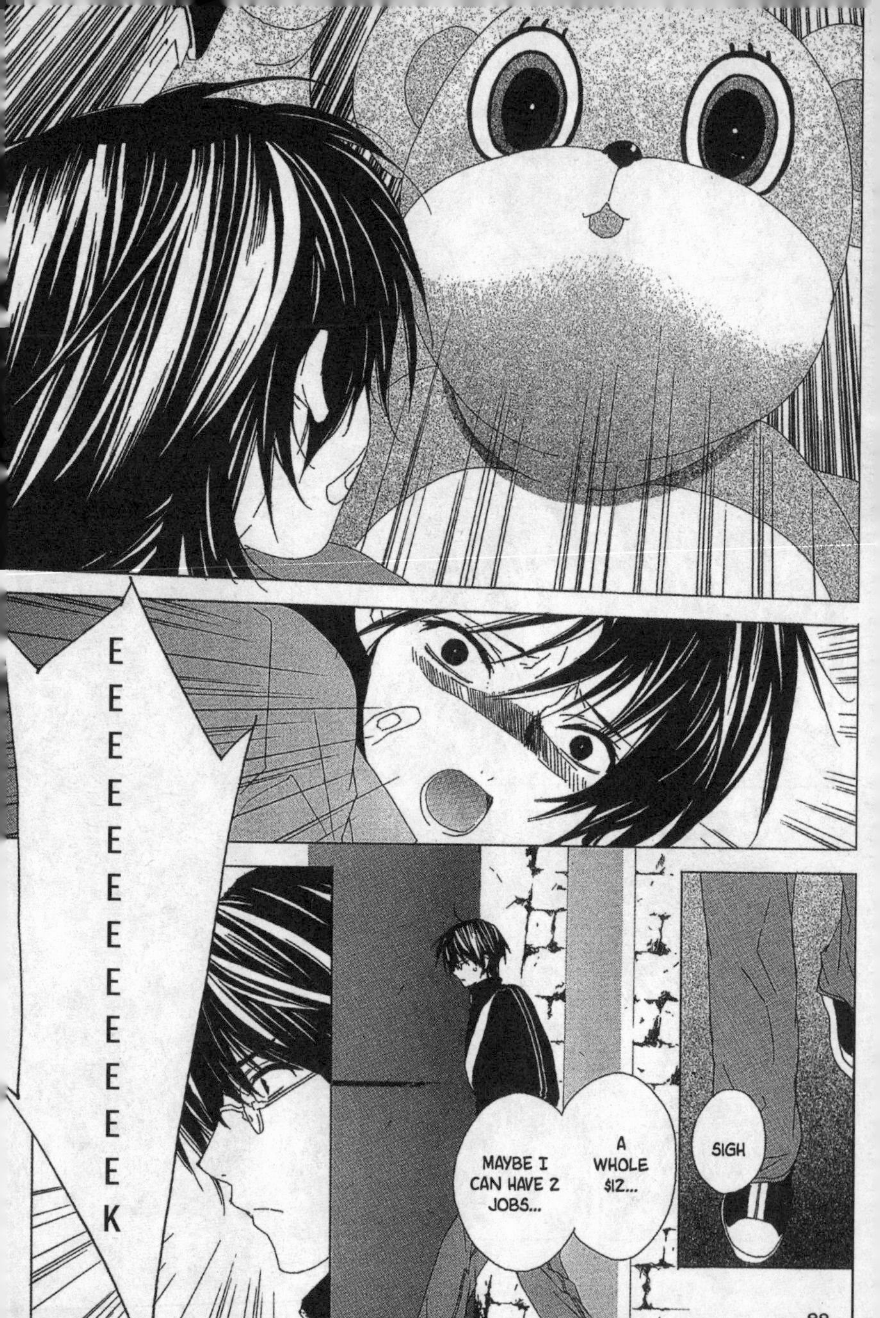
EEEEEEEEEEEEK
SIGH
A WHOLE $12...
MAYBE I CAN HAVE 2 JOBS...

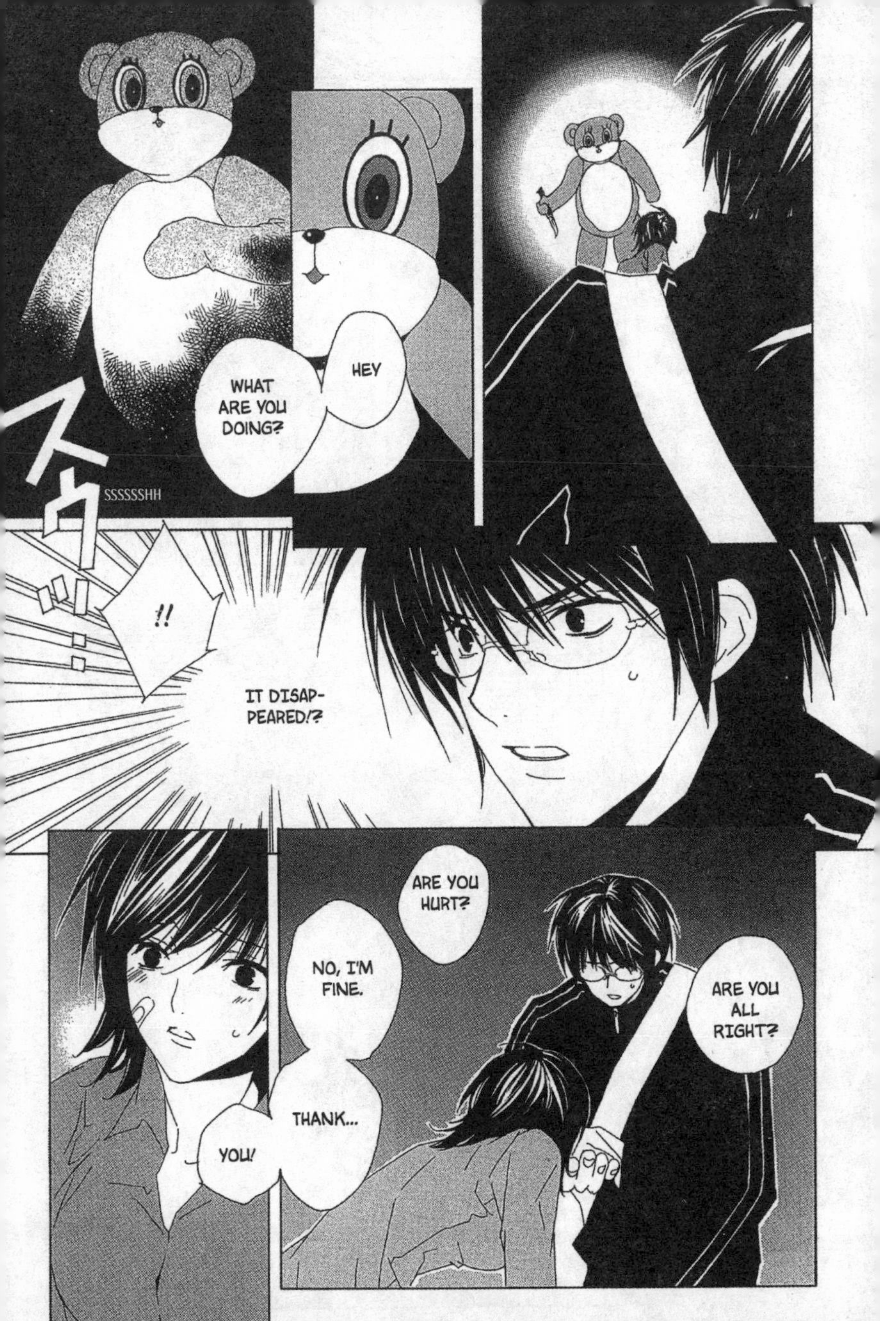
HEY
WHAT ARE YOU DOING?
SSSSSSHH
!!
IT DISAPPEARED!?
ARE YOU ALL RIGHT?
ARE YOU HURT?
NO, I'M FINE.
THANK...
YOU!

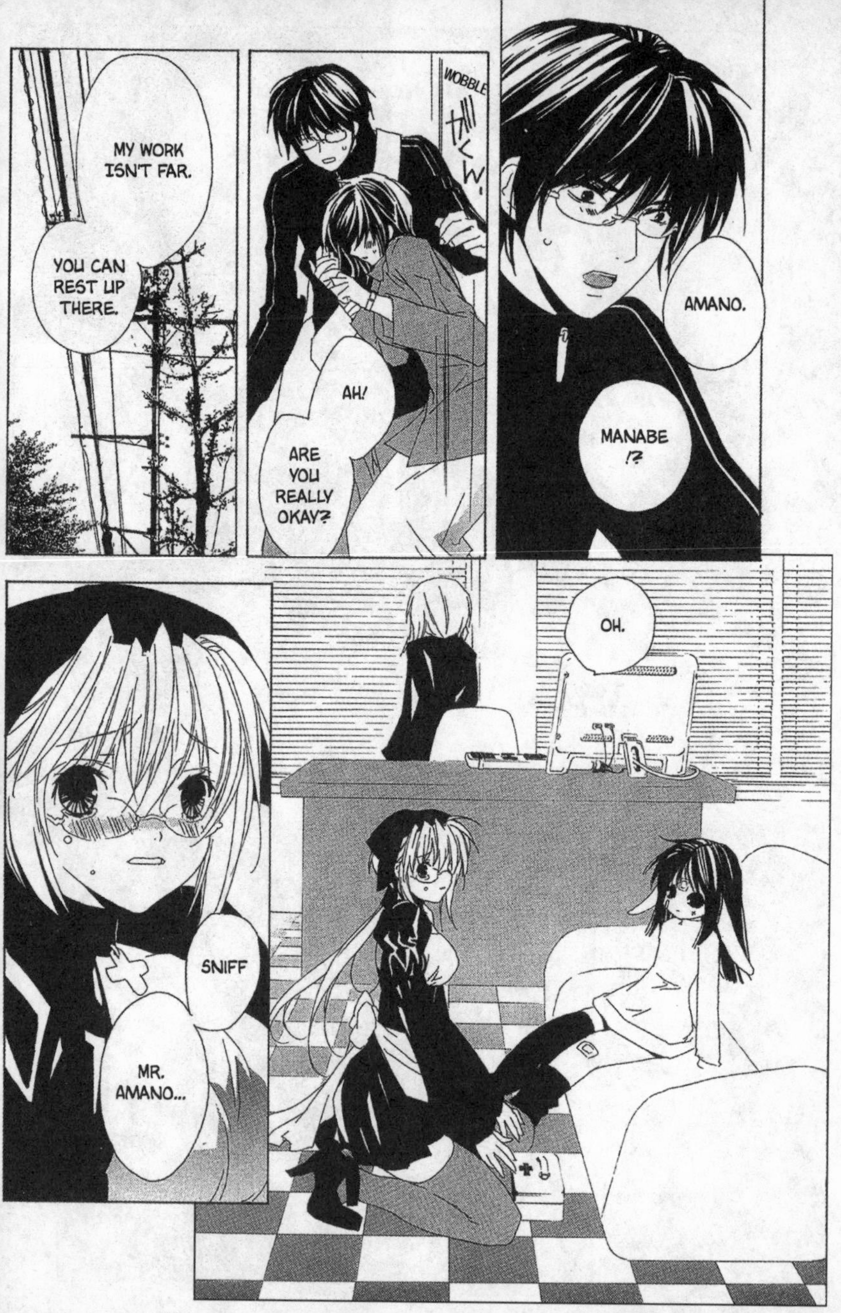
AMANO.
MANABE !?
WOBBLE
AH!
ARE YOU REALLY OKAY?
MY WORK ISN'T FAR.
YOU CAN REST UP THERE.
OH.
SNIFF
MR. AMANO...

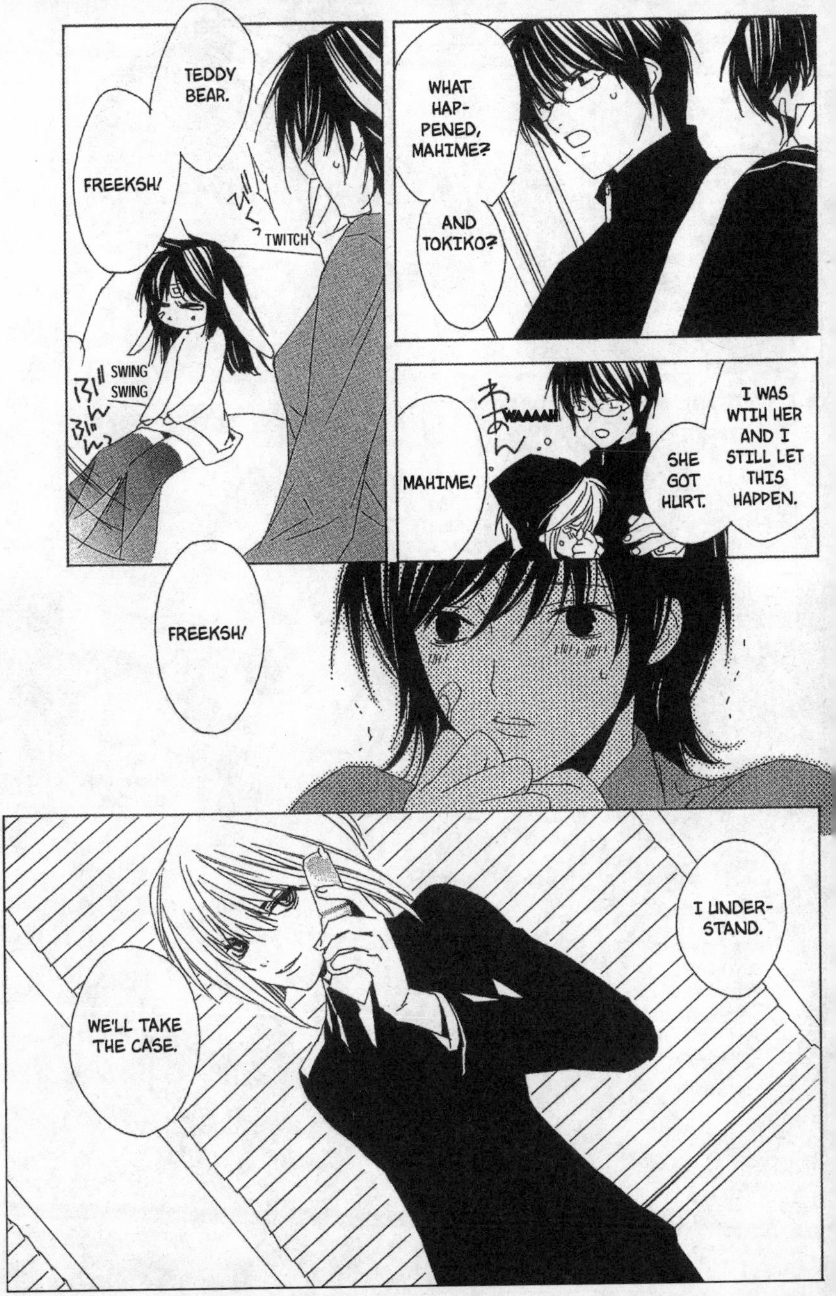
WHAT HAP-PENED, MAHIME?
AND TOKIKO?
TEDDY BEAR.
FREEKSH!
TWITCH
SWING SWING
I WAS WTIH HER AND I STILL LET THIS HAPPEN.
SHE GOT HURT.
WAAAAH
MAHIME!
FREEKSH!
I UNDER-STAND.
WE'LL TAKE THE CASE.

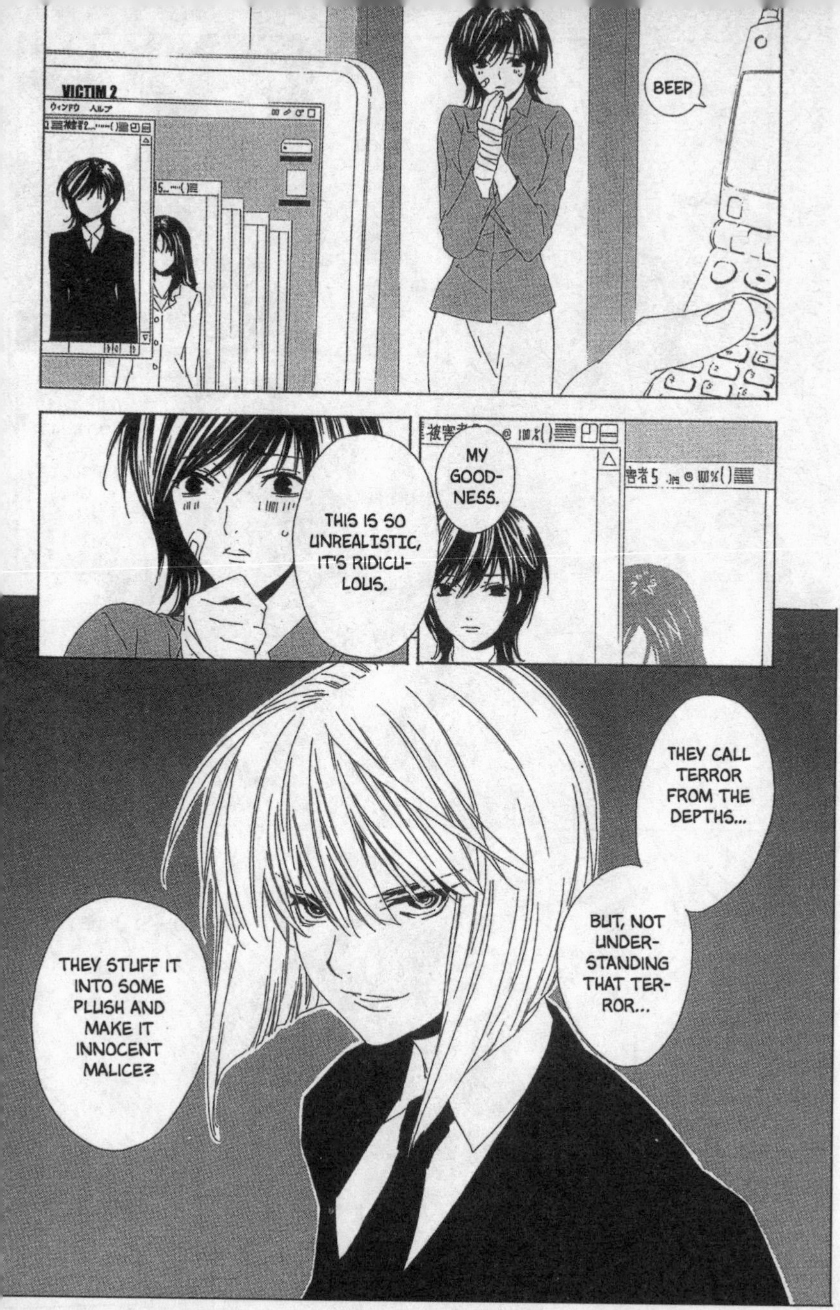
BEEP
VICTIM 2
MY GOOD-NESS.
THIS IS SO UNREALISTIC, IT'S RIDICULOUS.
THEY CALL TERROR FROM THE DEPTHS...
BUT, NOT UNDER-STANDING THAT TER-ROR...
THEY STUFF IT INTO SOME PLUSH AND MAKE IT INNOCENT MALICE?

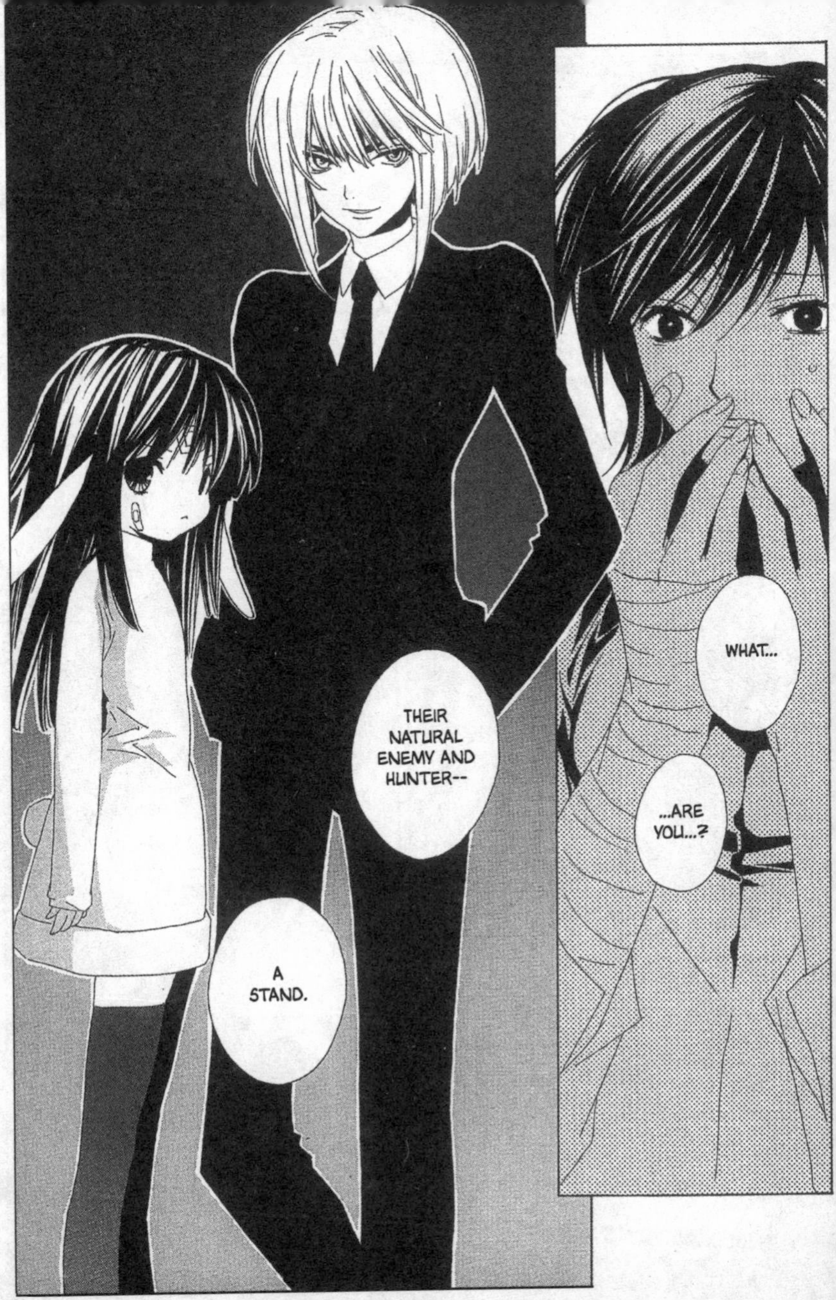
WHAT...
...ARE YOU...?
THEIR NATURAL ENEMY AND HUNTER--
A STAND.

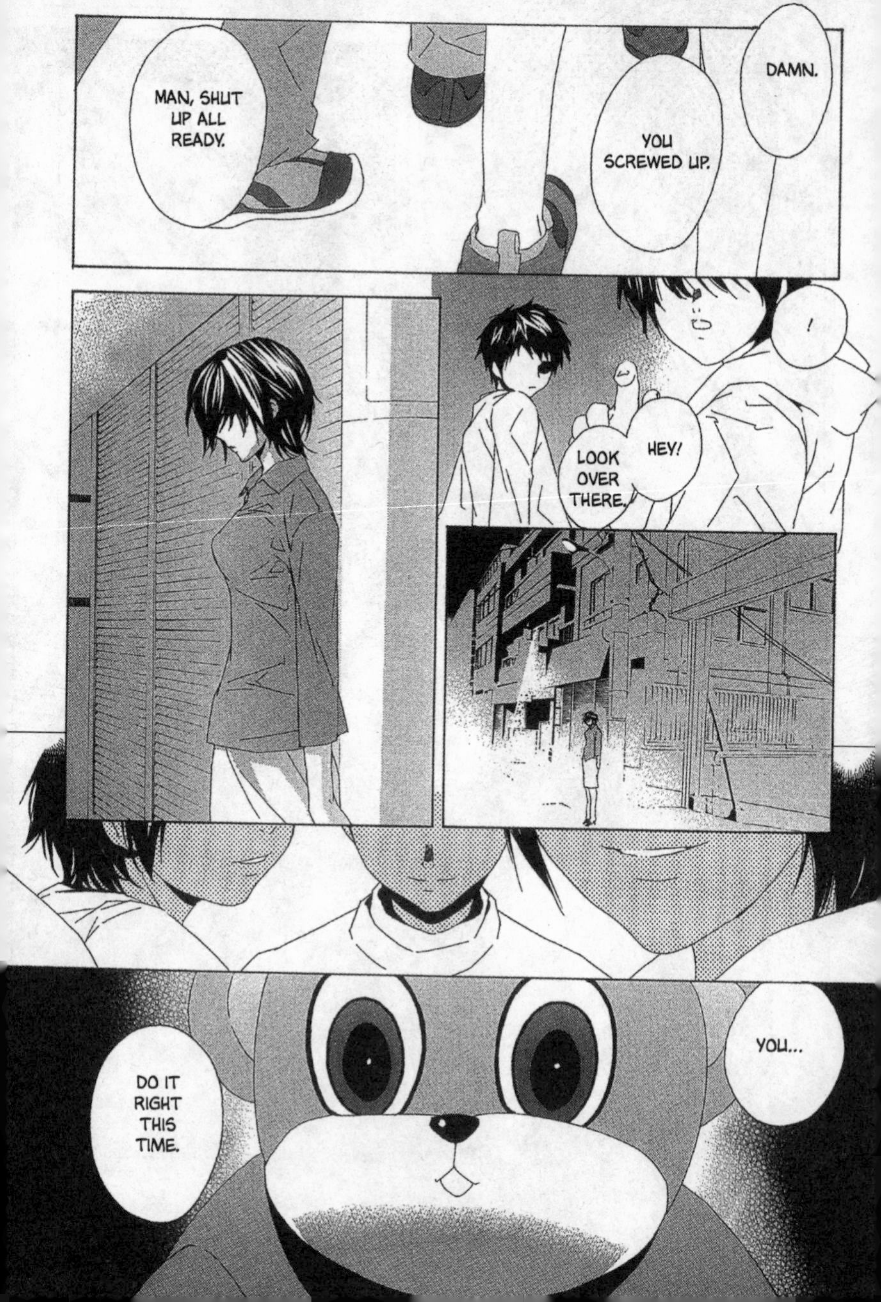
DAMN.
YOU SCREWED UP.
MAN, SHUT UP ALL READY.
!
HEY!
LOOK OVER THERE.
YOU...
DO IT RIGHT THIS TIME.

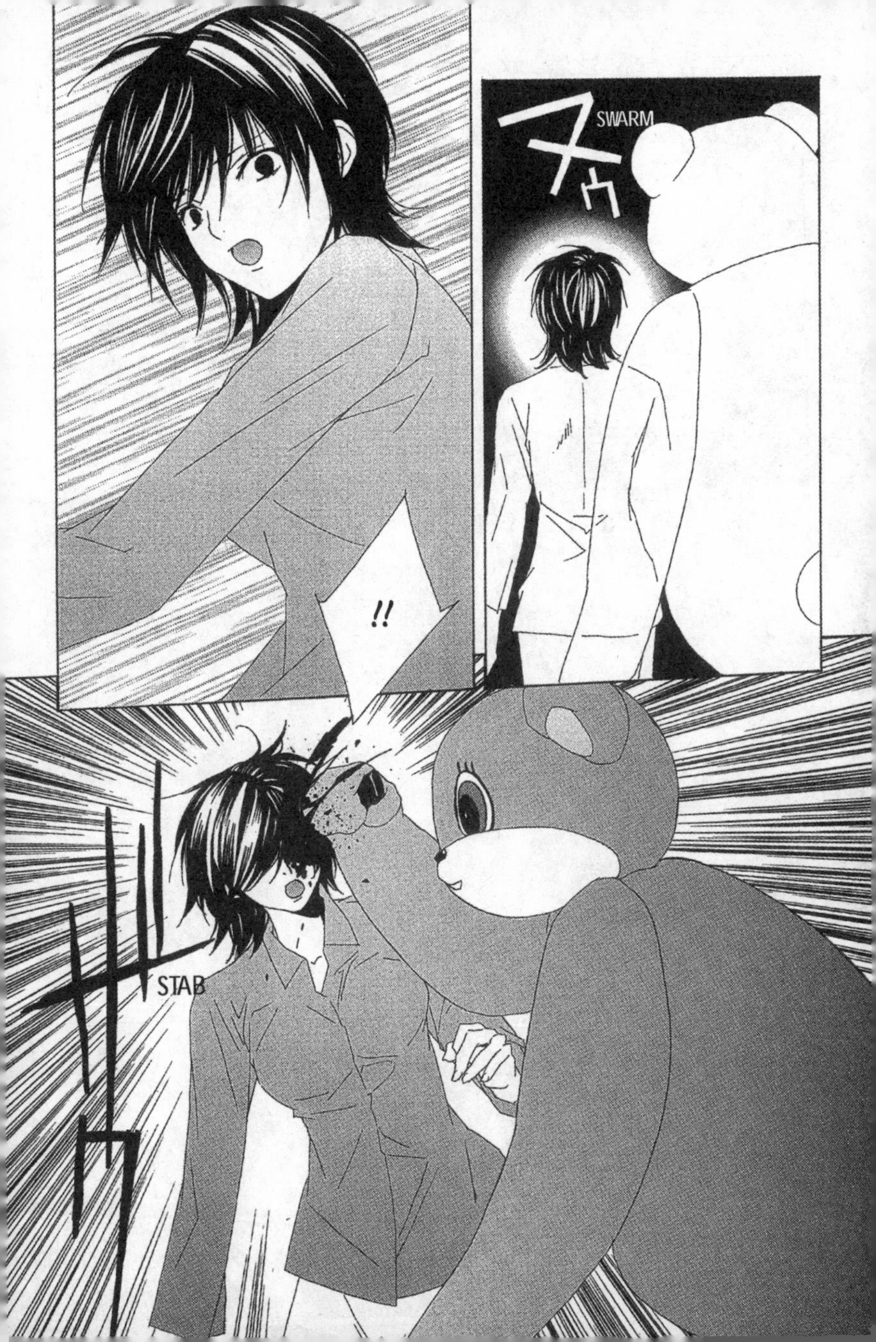

SWARM
!!
STAB

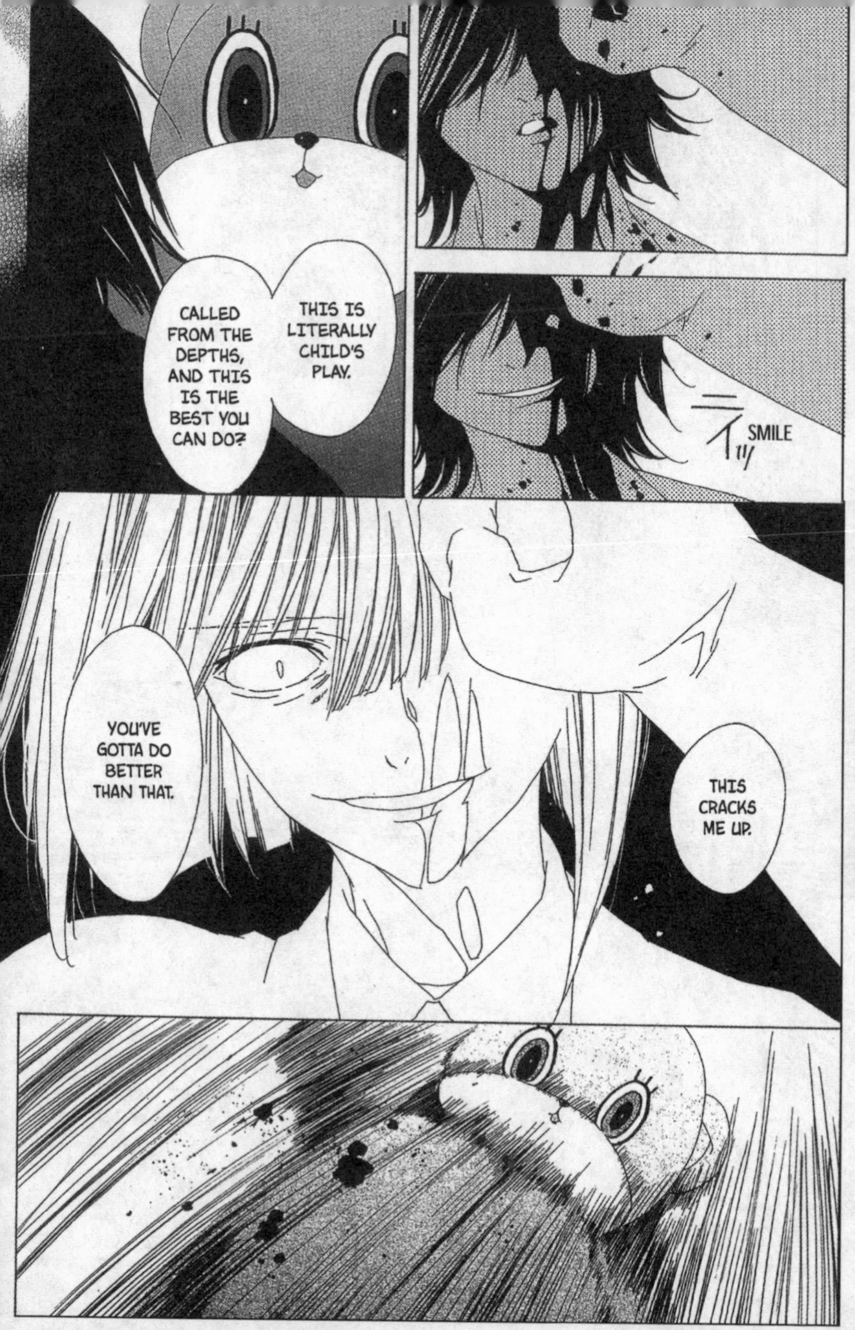
THIS IS LITERALLY CHILD'S PLAY.
CALLED FROM THE DEPTHS, AND THIS IS THE BEST YOU CAN DO?
SMILE
THIS CRACKS ME UP.
YOU'VE GOTTA DO BETTER THAN THAT.

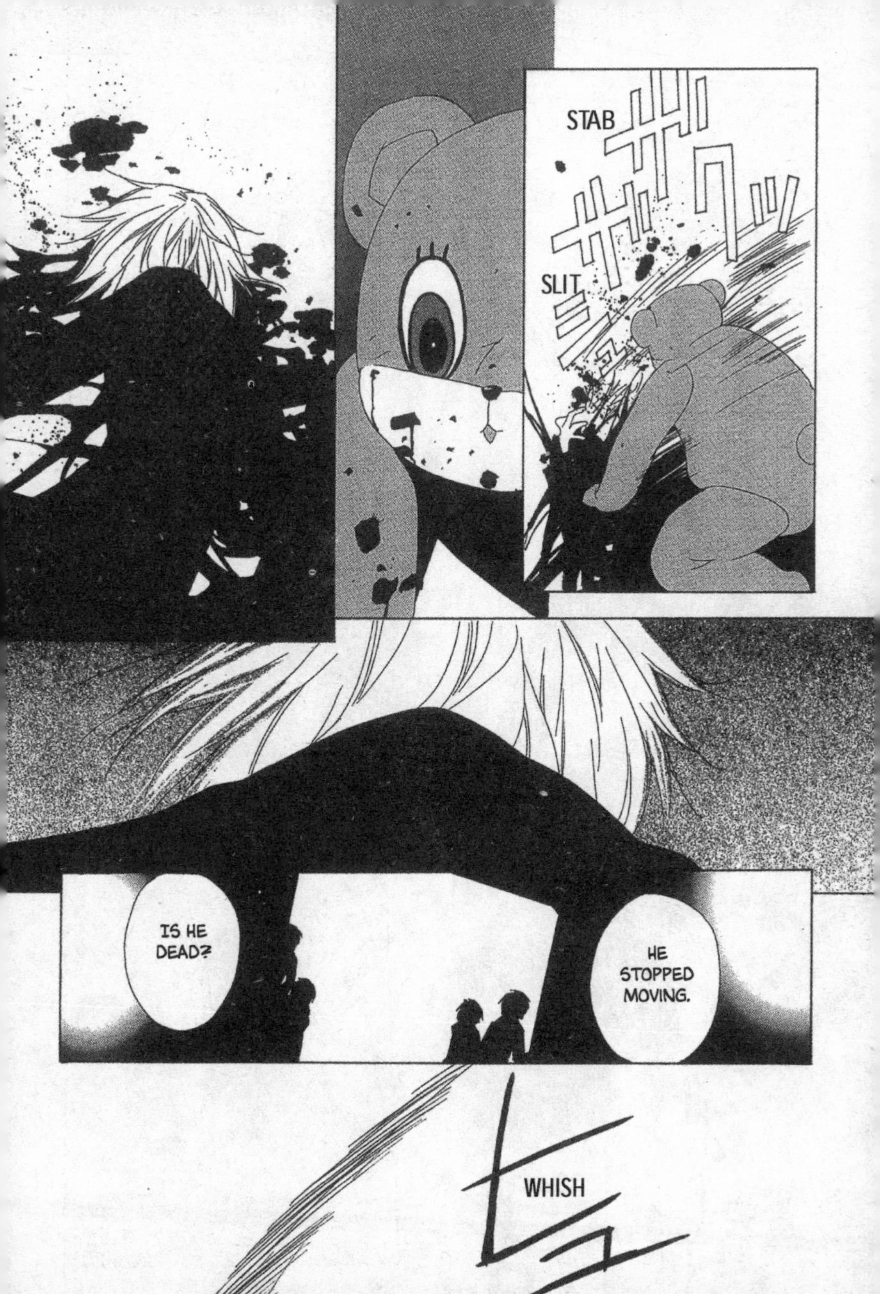
STAB
SLIT
IS HE DEAD?
HE STOPPED MOVING.
WHISH

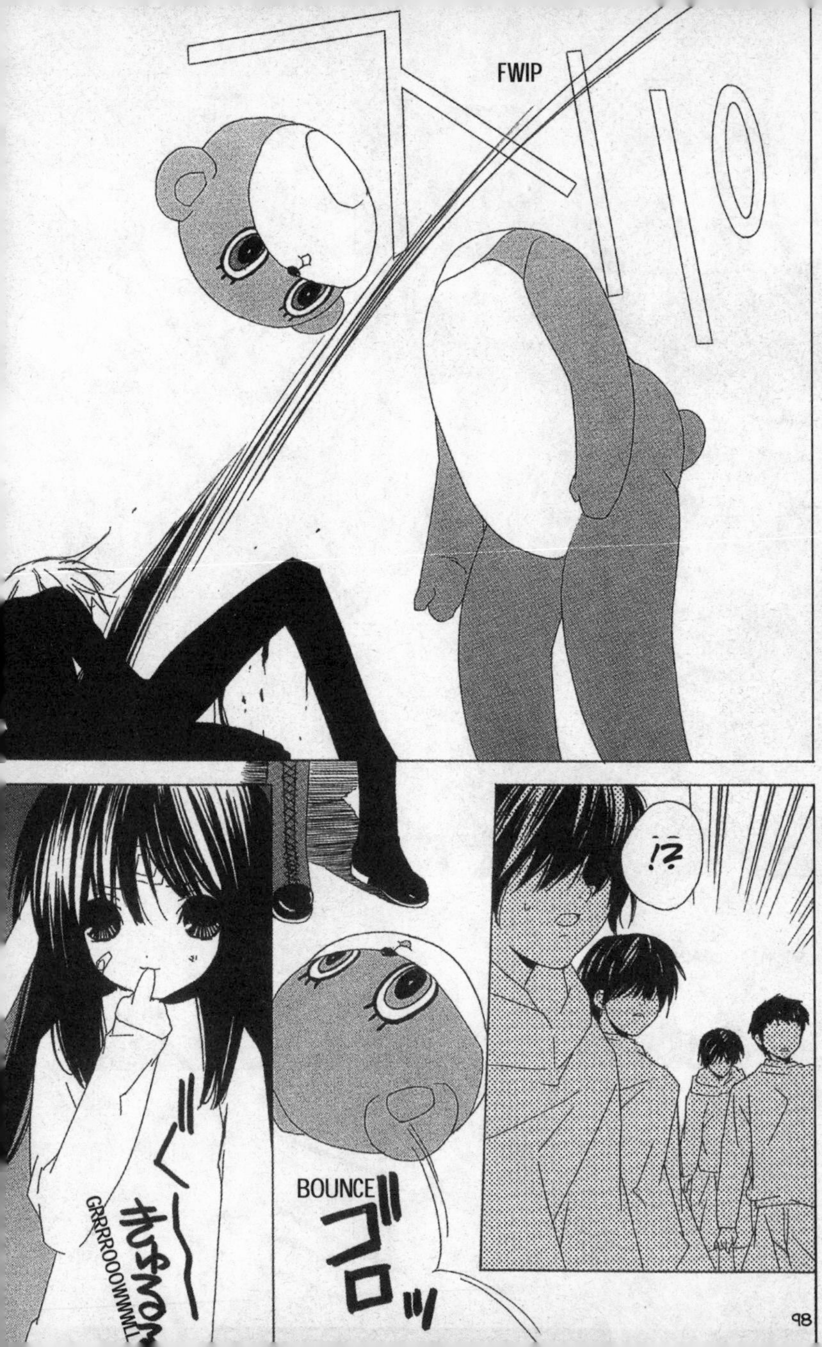
FWIP
!?
BOUNCE
ゴロッ
ぐ〜
GRRROOOWWLL

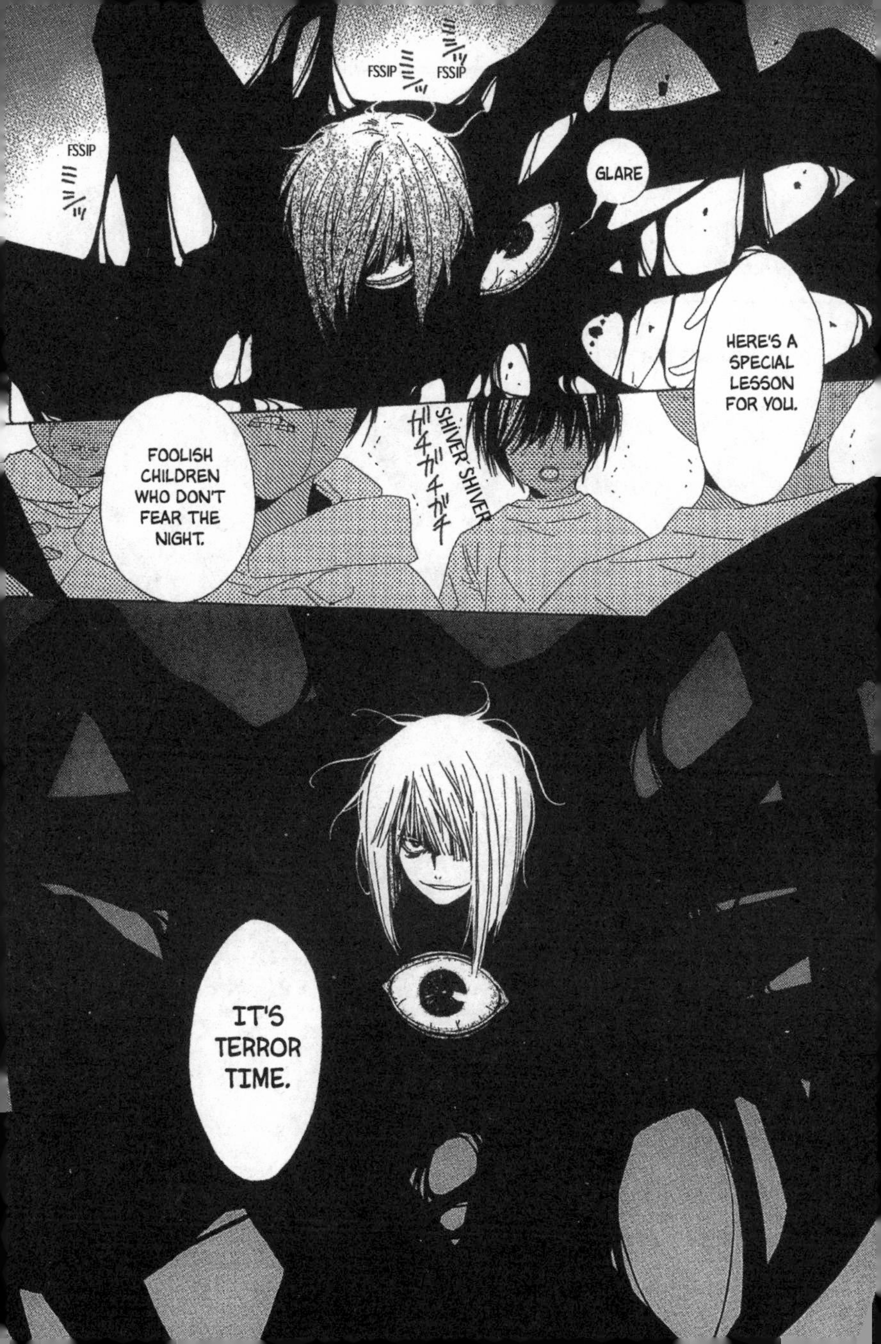
FSSIP
FSSIP
FSSIP
GLARE
HERE'S A SPECIAL LESSON FOR YOU.
SHIVER SHIVER
ガチガチ
FOOLISH CHILDREN WHO DON'T FEAR THE NIGHT.
IT'S TERROR TIME.

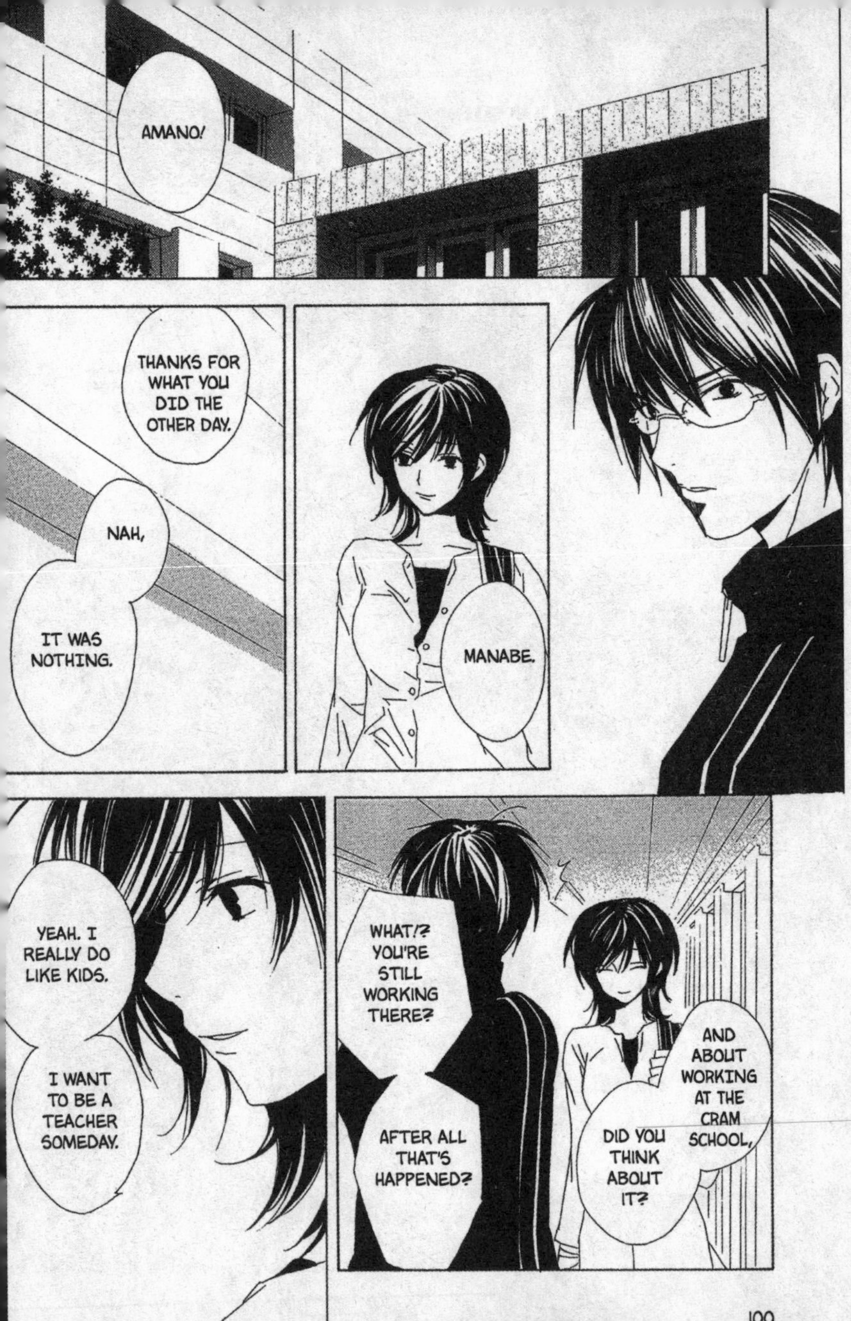
AMANO!
MANABE.
THANKS FOR WHAT YOU DID THE OTHER DAY.
NAH,
IT WAS NOTHING.
AND ABOUT WORKING AT THE CRAM SCHOOL,
DID YOU THINK ABOUT IT?
WHAT!? YOU'RE STILL WORKING THERE?
AFTER ALL THAT'S HAPPENED?
YEAH. I REALLY DO LIKE KIDS.
I WANT TO BE A TEACHER SOMEDAY.

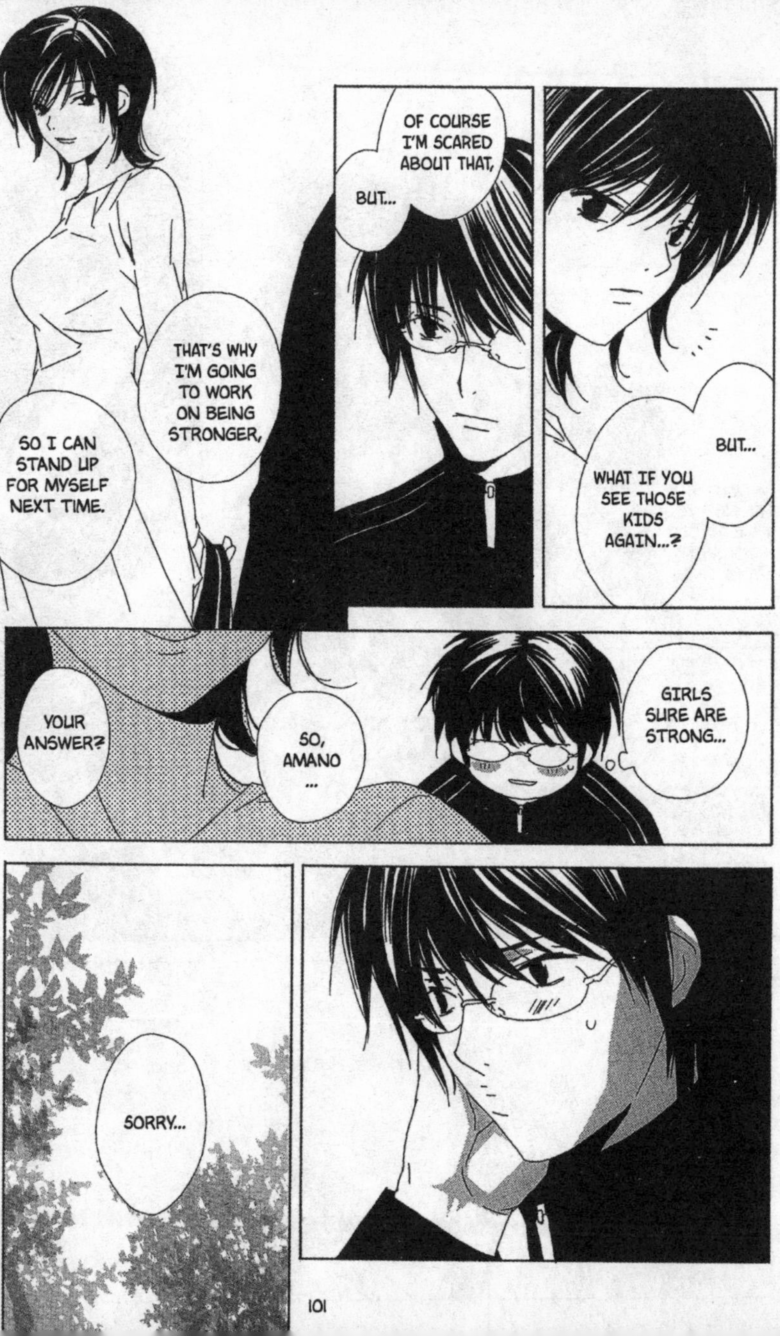
BUT...
WHAT IF YOU SEE THOSE KIDS AGAIN...?
OF COURSE I'M SCARED ABOUT THAT,
BUT...
THAT'S WHY I'M GOING TO WORK ON BEING STRONGER,
SO I CAN STAND UP FOR MYSELF NEXT TIME.
GIRLS SURE ARE STRONG...
SO, AMANO ...
YOUR ANSWER?
SORRY...

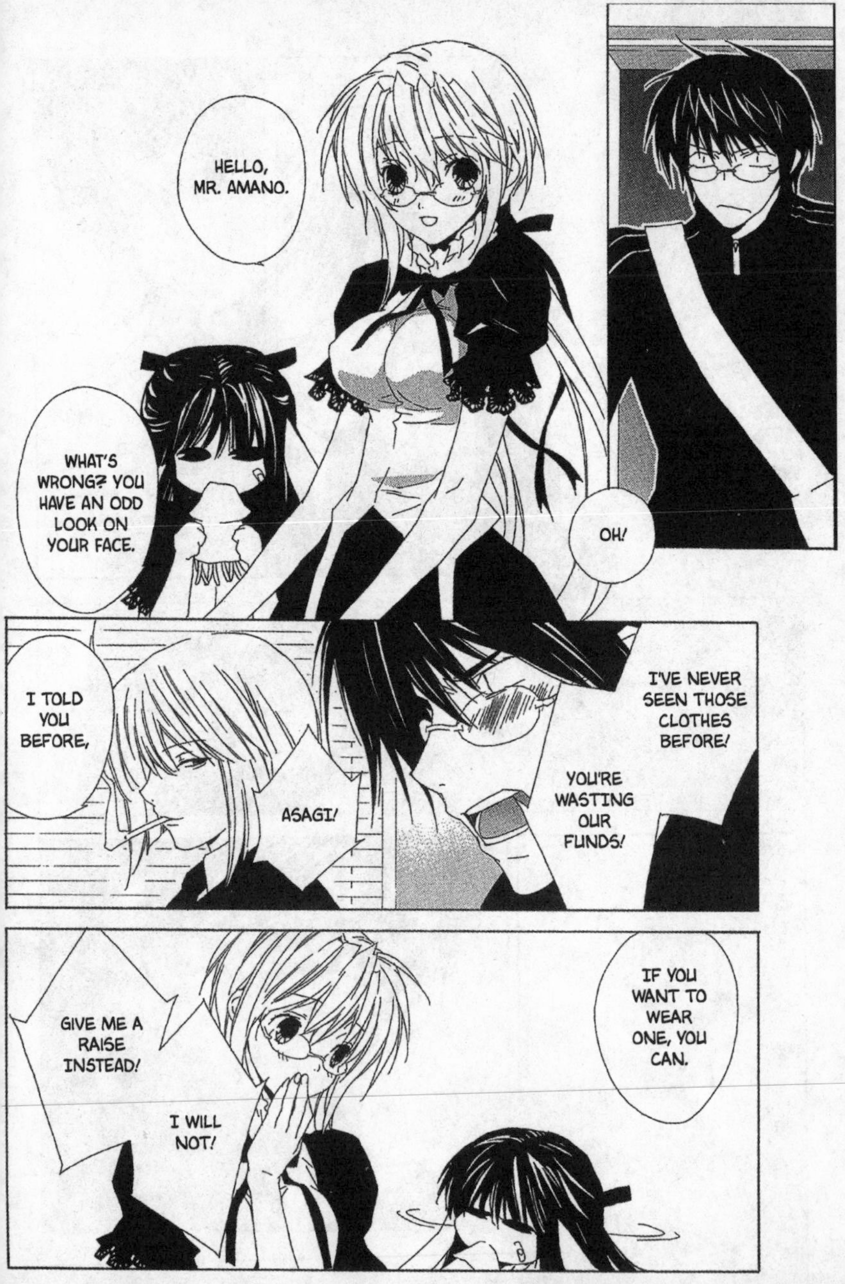
HELLO, MR. AMANO.
OH!
WHAT'S WRONG? YOU HAVE AN ODD LOOK ON YOUR FACE.
I'VE NEVER SEEN THOSE CLOTHES BEFORE!
YOU'RE WASTING OUR FUNDS!
ASAGI!
I TOLD YOU BEFORE,
IF YOU WANT TO WEAR ONE, YOU CAN.
GIVE ME A RAISE INSTEAD!
I WILL NOT!

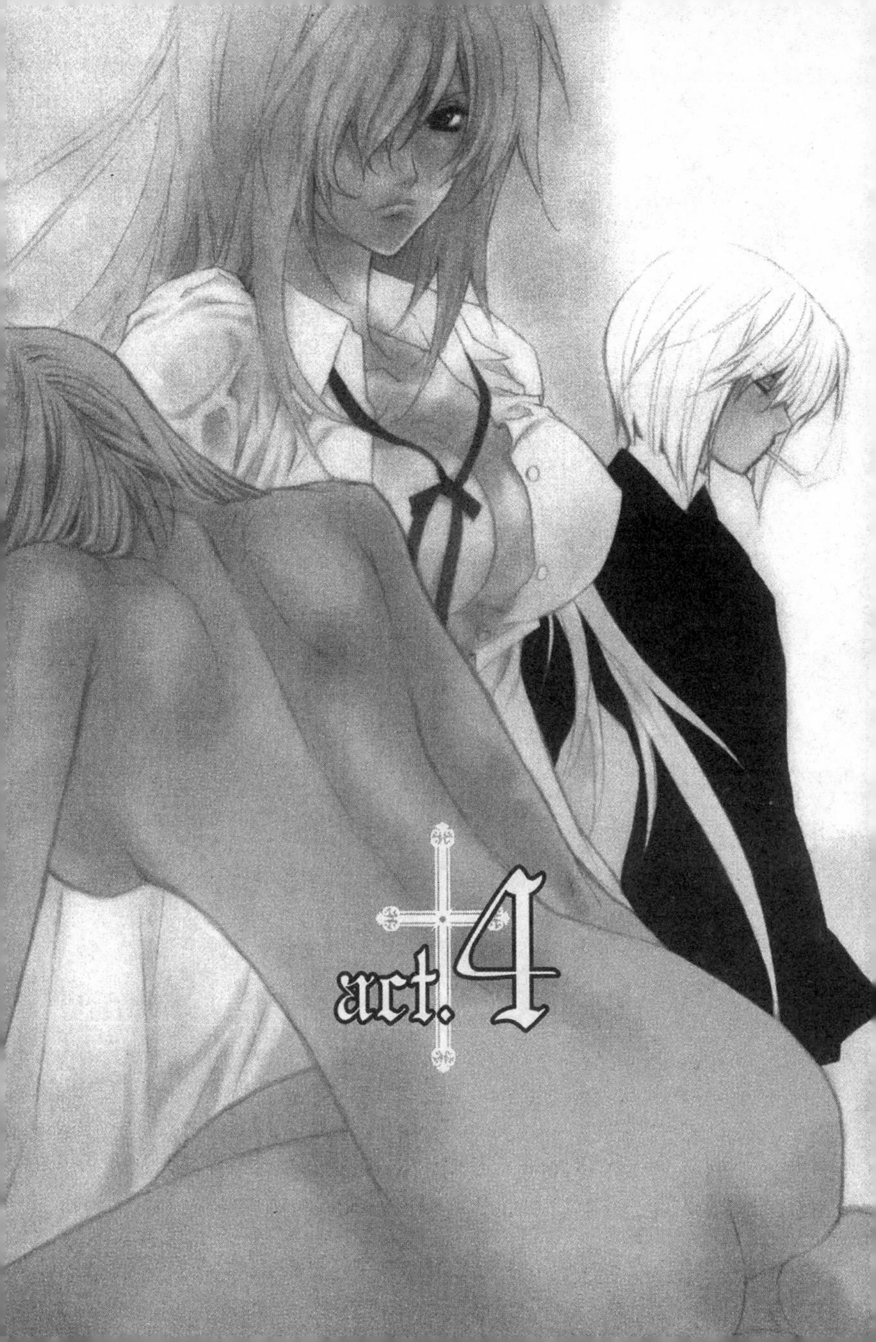
act. 4

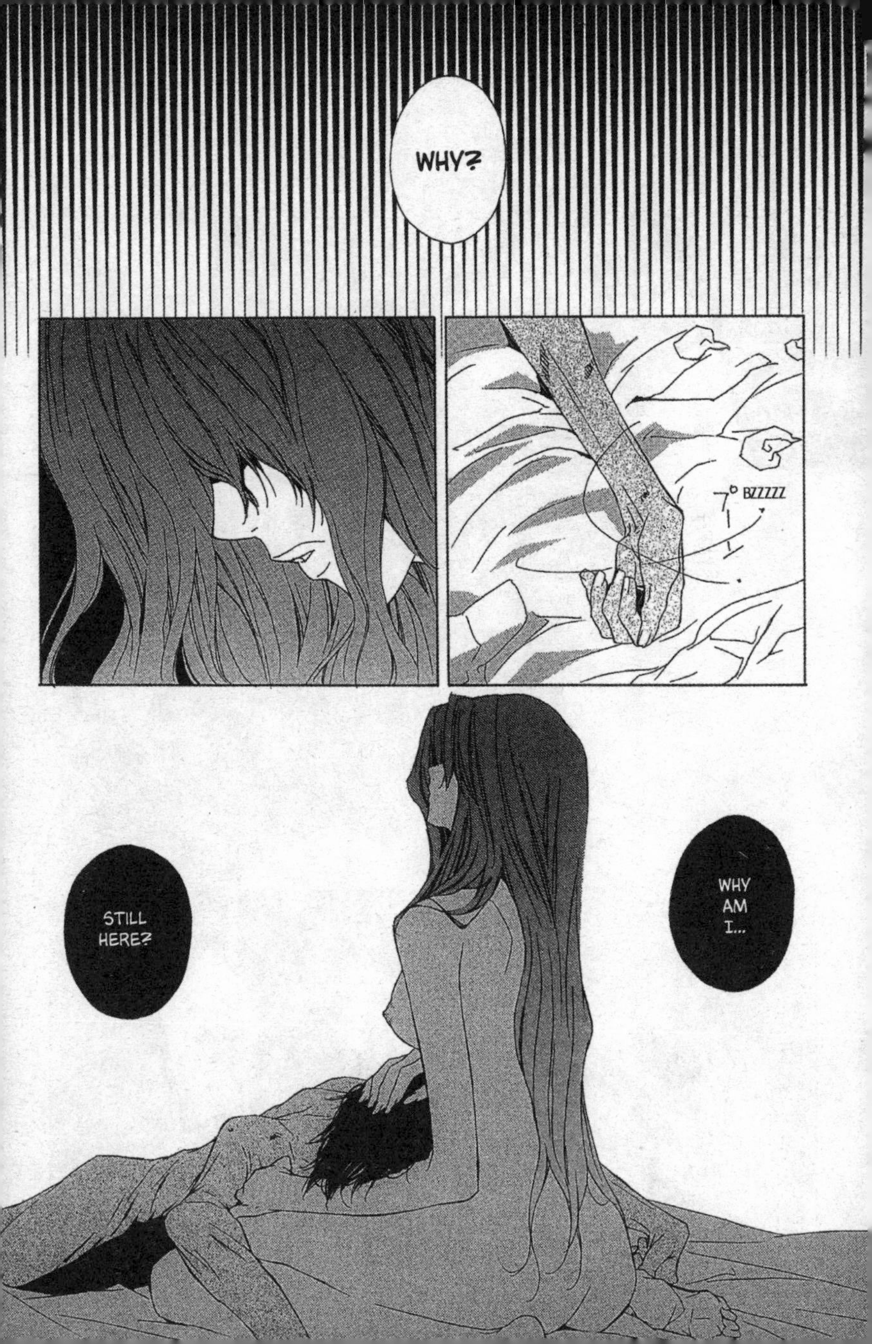
WHY?
BZZZZZ
WHY AM I...
STILL HERE?

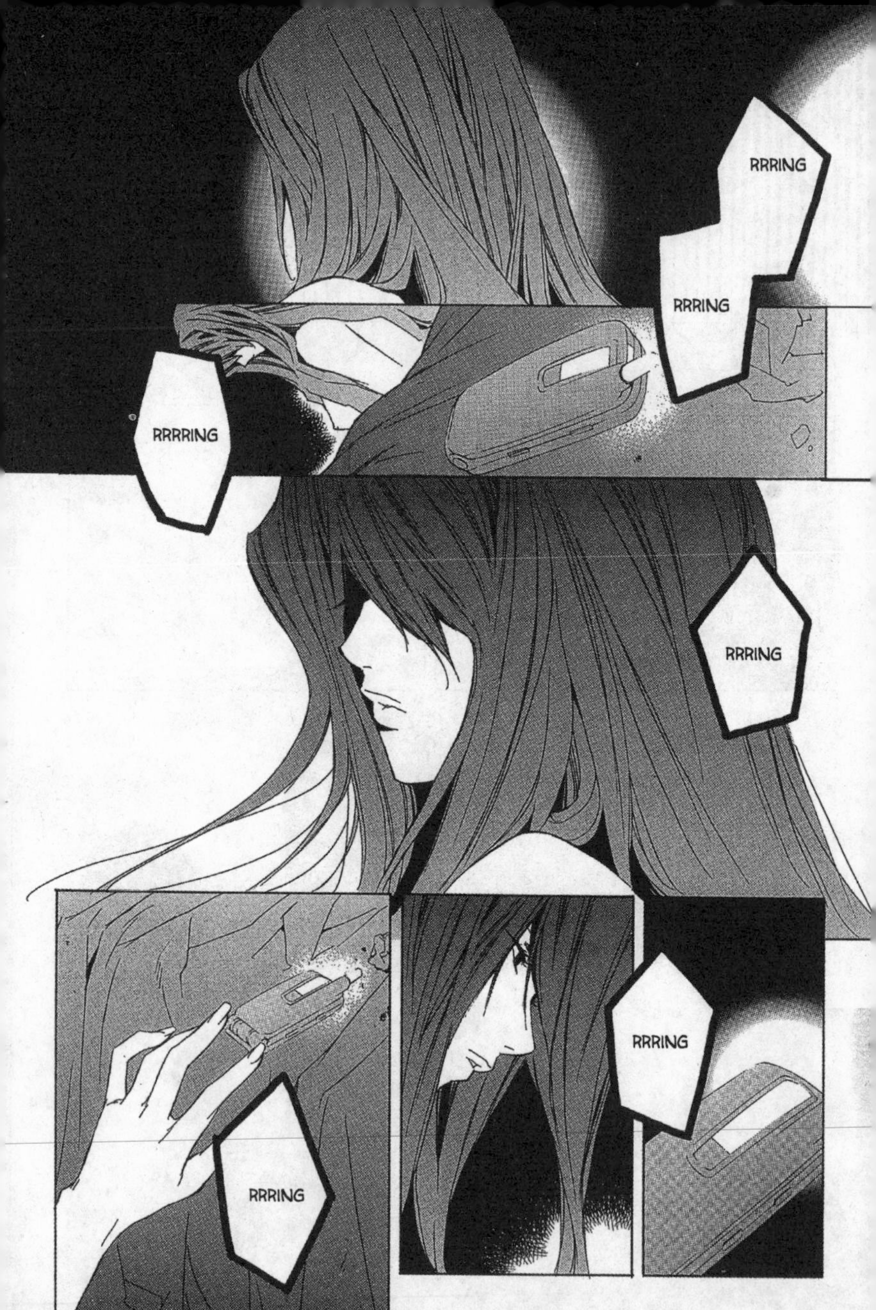
RRRING
RRRING
RRRRING
RRRING
RRRING
RRRING

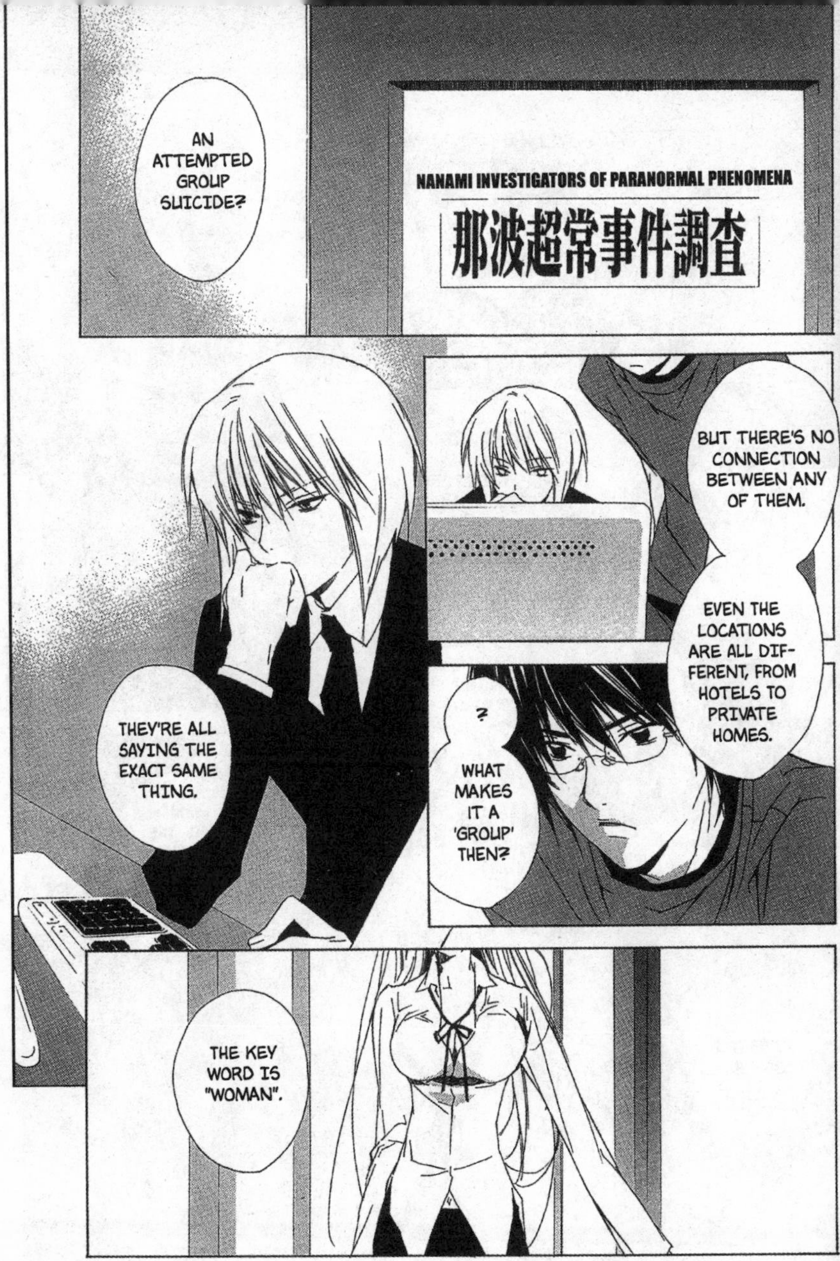
NANAMI INVESTIGATORS OF PARANORMAL PHENOMENA
那波超常事件調査
AN ATTEMPTED GROUP SUICIDE?
BUT THERE'S NO CONNECTION BETWEEN ANY OF THEM.
EVEN THE LOCATIONS ARE ALL DIF-FERENT, FROM HOTELS TO PRIVATE HOMES.
?
WHAT MAKES IT A 'GROUP' THEN?
THEY'RE ALL SAYING THE EXACT SAME THING.
THE KEY WORD IS "WOMAN".

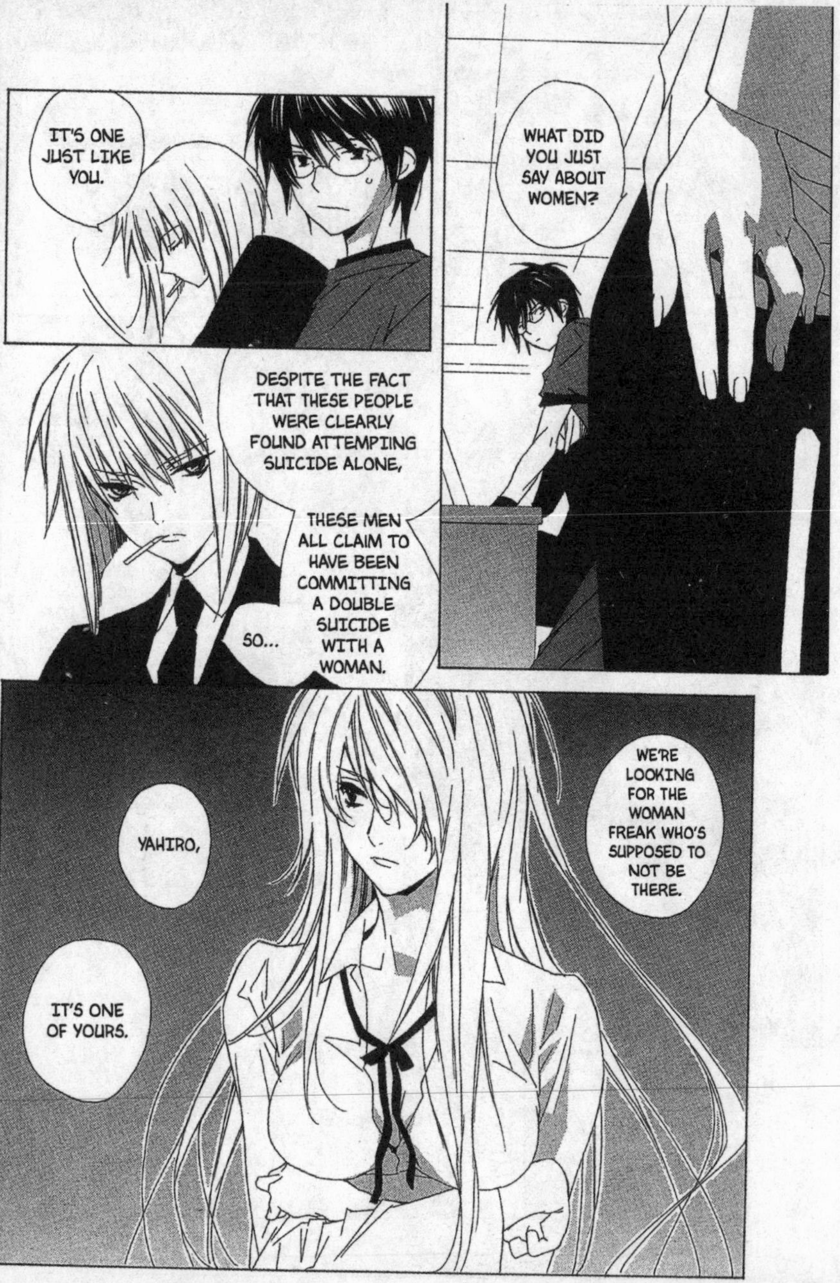
WHAT DID YOU JUST SAY ABOUT WOMEN?
IT'S ONE JUST LIKE YOU.
DESPITE THE FACT THAT THESE PEOPLE WERE CLEARLY FOUND ATTEMPTING SUICIDE ALONE,
THESE MEN ALL CLAIM TO HAVE BEEN COMMITTING A DOUBLE SUICIDE WITH A WOMAN.
SO...
WE'RE LOOKING FOR THE WOMAN FREAK WHO'S SUPPOSED TO NOT BE THERE.
YAHIRO,
IT'S ONE OF YOURS.

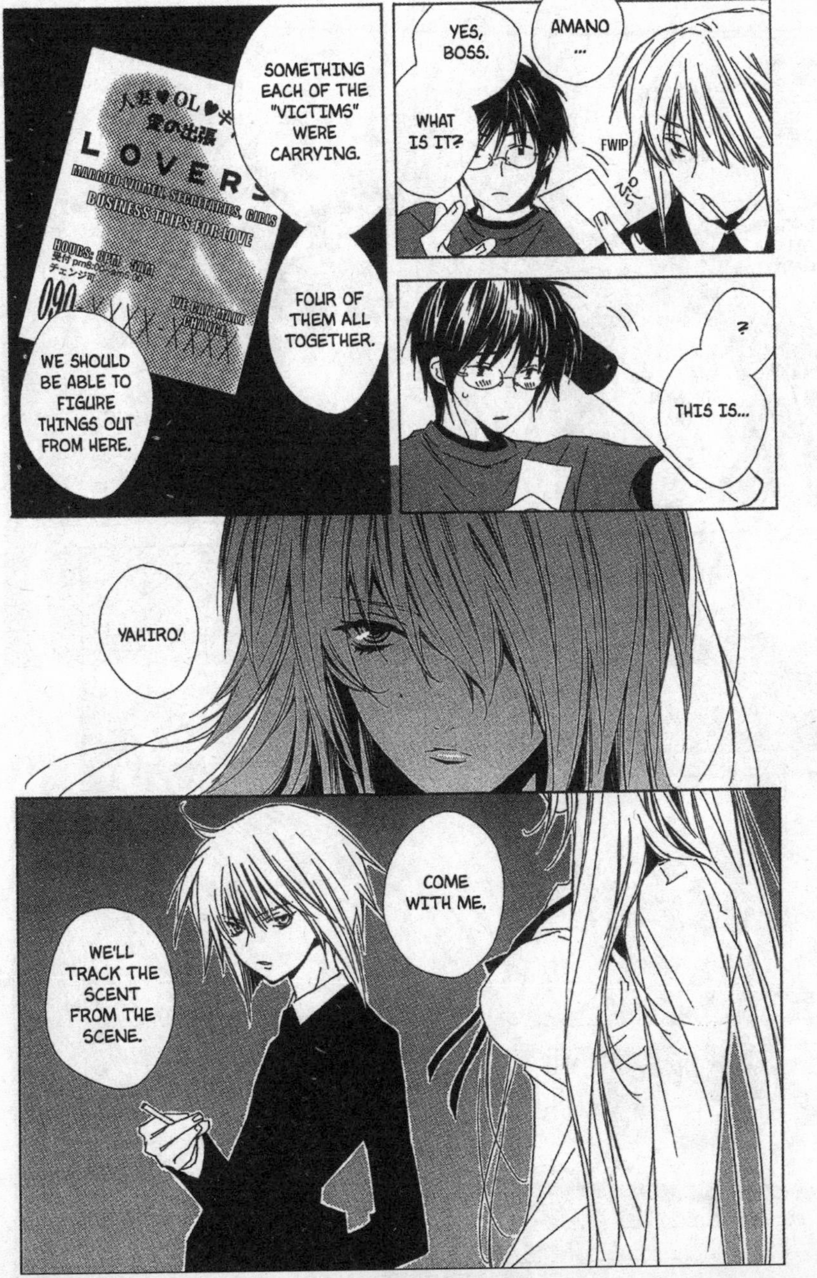
AMANO ...
YES, BOSS.
WHAT IS IT?
FWIP
?
THIS IS...
LOVERS
MARRIED WOMEN, SECRETARIES, GIRLS
BUSINESS TRIPS FOR LOVE
SOMETHING EACH OF THE "VICTIMS" WERE CARRYING.
FOUR OF THEM ALL TOGETHER.
WE SHOULD BE ABLE TO FIGURE THINGS OUT FROM HERE.
YAHIRO!
COME WITH ME.
WE'LL TRACK THE SCENT FROM THE SCENE.

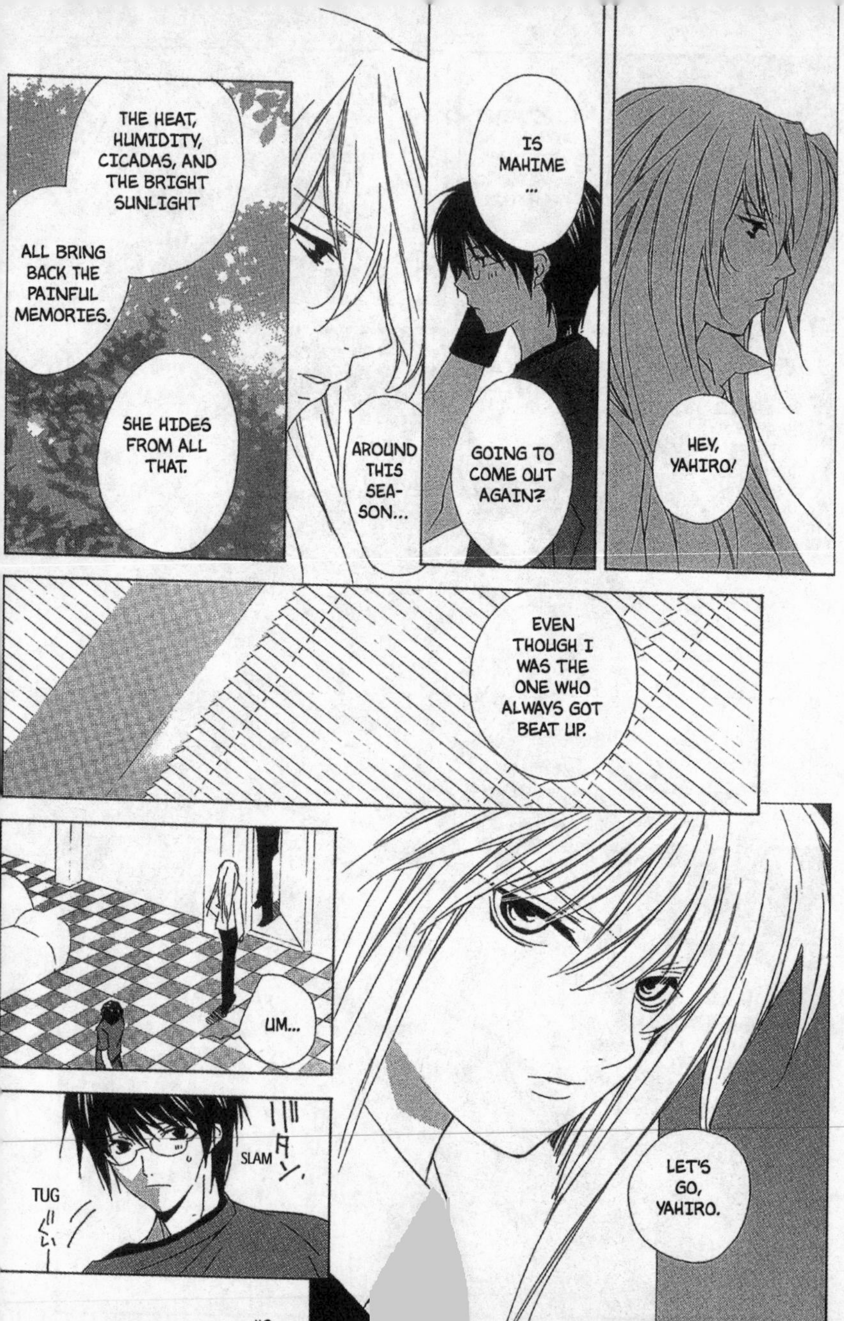
HEY, YAHIRO!
IS MAHIME ...
GOING TO COME OUT AGAIN?
AROUND THIS SEA-SON...
THE HEAT, HUMIDITY, CICADAS, AND THE BRIGHT SUNLIGHT
ALL BRING BACK THE PAINFUL MEMORIES.
SHE HIDES FROM ALL THAT.
EVEN THOUGH I WAS THE ONE WHO ALWAYS GOT BEAT UP.
LET'S GO, YAHIRO.
UM...
SLAM
TUG

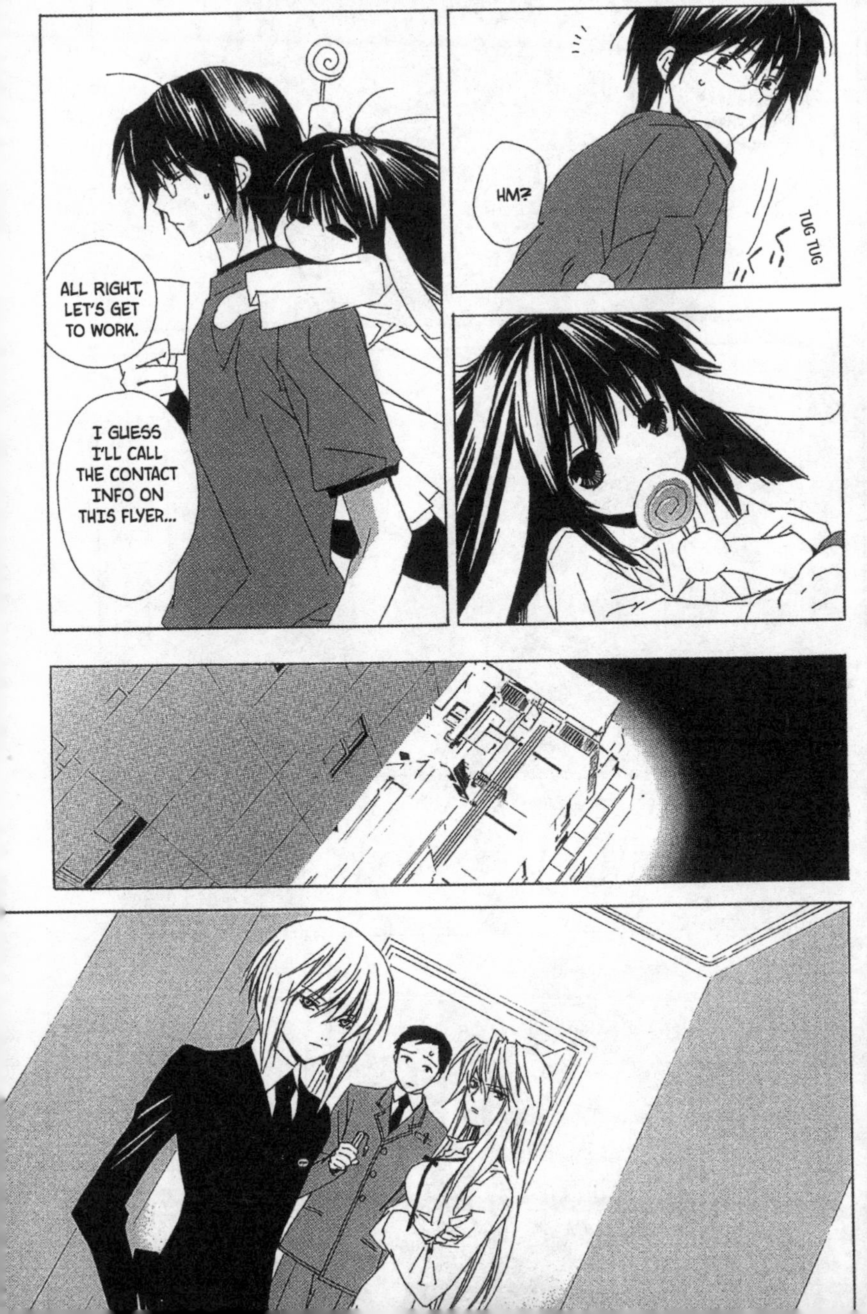
TUG TUG
HM?
ALL RIGHT, LET'S GET TO WORK.
I GUESS I'LL CALL THE CONTACT INFO ON THIS FLYER...

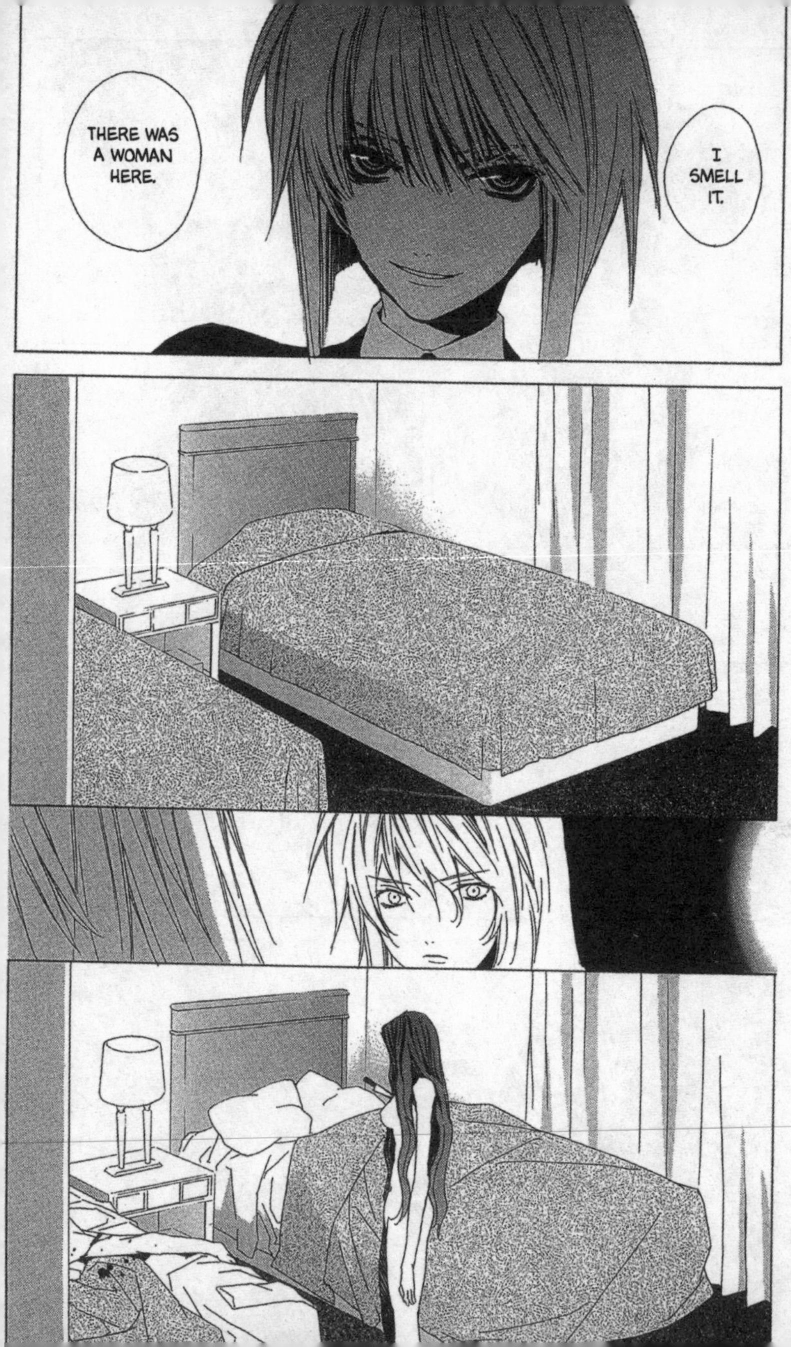
I SMELL IT.
THERE WAS A WOMAN HERE.

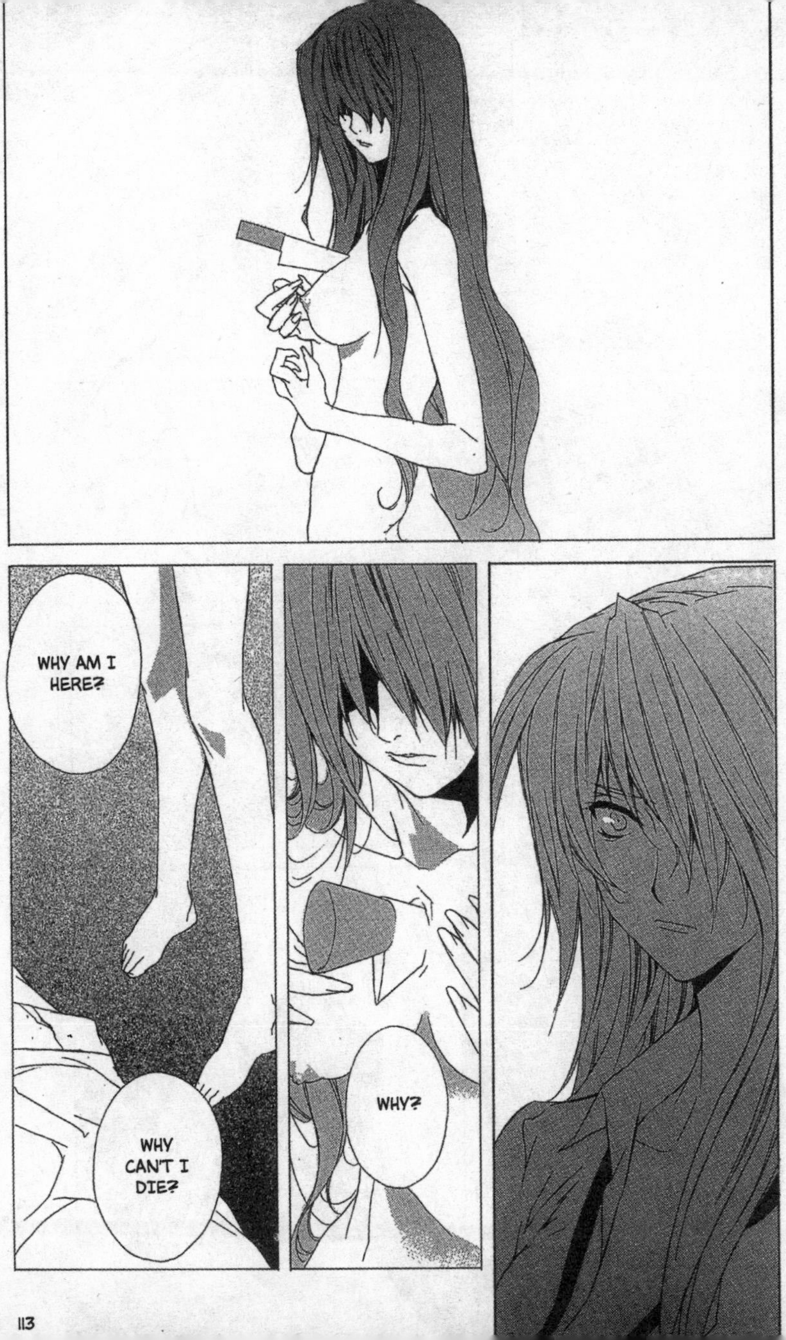
WHY?
WHY AM I HERE?
WHY CAN'T I DIE?

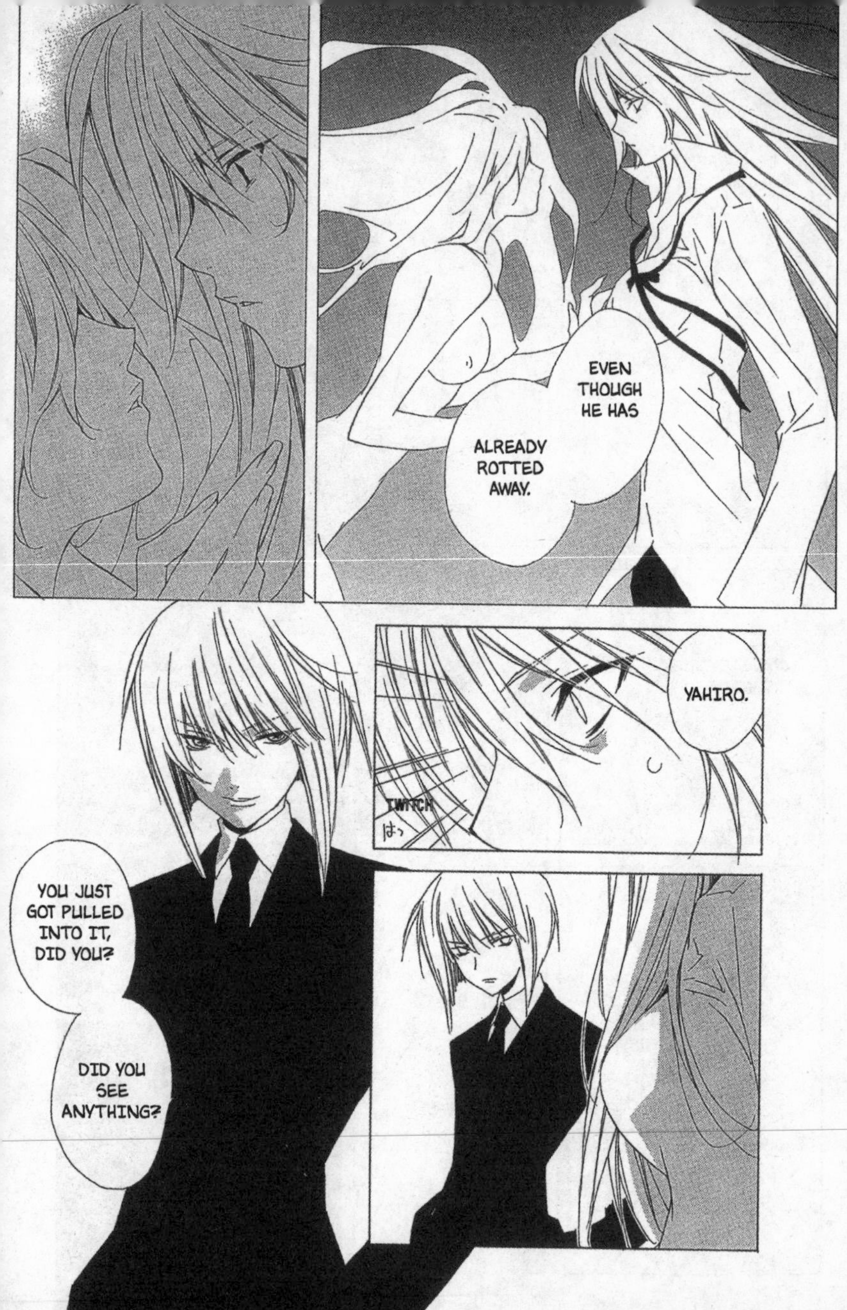
EVEN THOUGH HE HAS
ALREADY ROTTED AWAY.
YAHIRO.
TWITCH
はっ
YOU JUST GOT PULLED INTO IT, DID YOU?
DID YOU SEE ANYTHING?

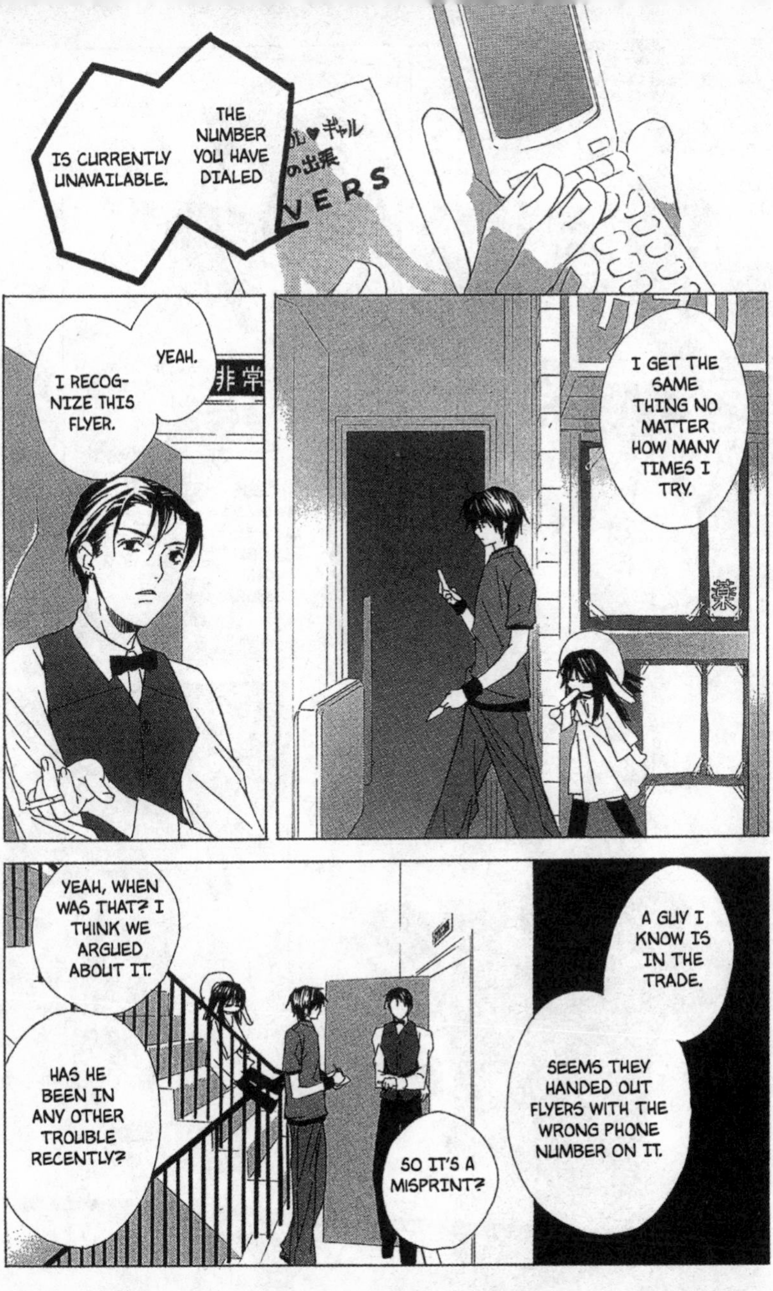
THE NUMBER YOU HAVE DIALED
IS CURRENTLY UNAVAILABLE.
I GET THE SAME THING NO MATTER HOW MANY TIMES I TRY.
YEAH.
I RECOGNIZE THIS FLYER.
非常
A GUY I KNOW IS IN THE TRADE.
SEEMS THEY HANDED OUT FLYERS WITH THE WRONG PHONE NUMBER ON IT.
SO IT'S A MISPRINT?
YEAH, WHEN WAS THAT? I THINK WE ARGUED ABOUT IT.
HAS HE BEEN IN ANY OTHER TROUBLE RECENTLY?

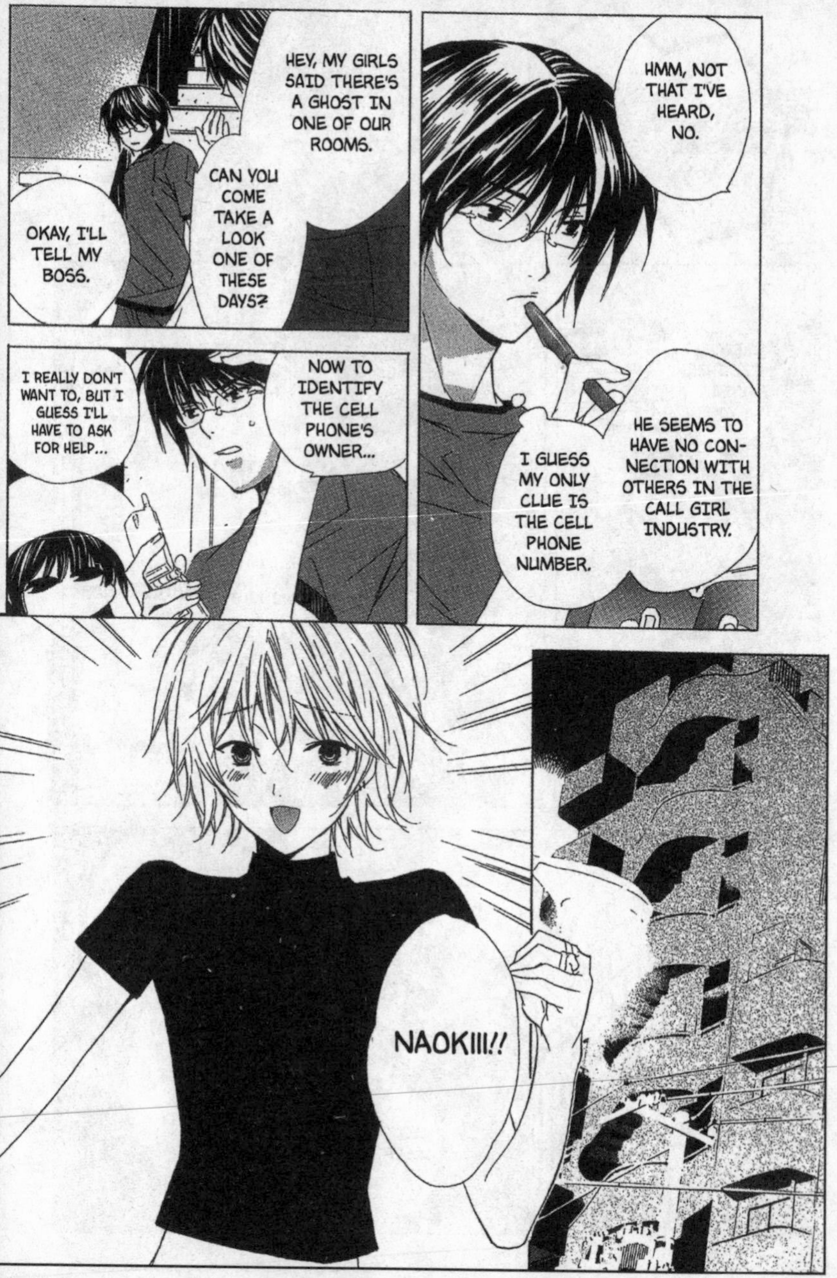
HMM, NOT THAT I'VE HEARD, NO.
HE SEEMS TO HAVE NO CON-NECTION WITH OTHERS IN THE CALL GIRL INDUSTRY.
I GUESS MY ONLY CLUE IS THE CELL PHONE NUMBER.
HEY, MY GIRLS SAID THERE'S A GHOST IN ONE OF OUR ROOMS.
CAN YOU COME TAKE A LOOK ONE OF THESE DAYS?
OKAY, I'LL TELL MY BOSS.
NOW TO IDENTIFY THE CELL PHONE'S OWNER...
I REALLY DON'T WANT TO, BUT I GUESS I'LL HAVE TO ASK FOR HELP...
NAOKIII!!

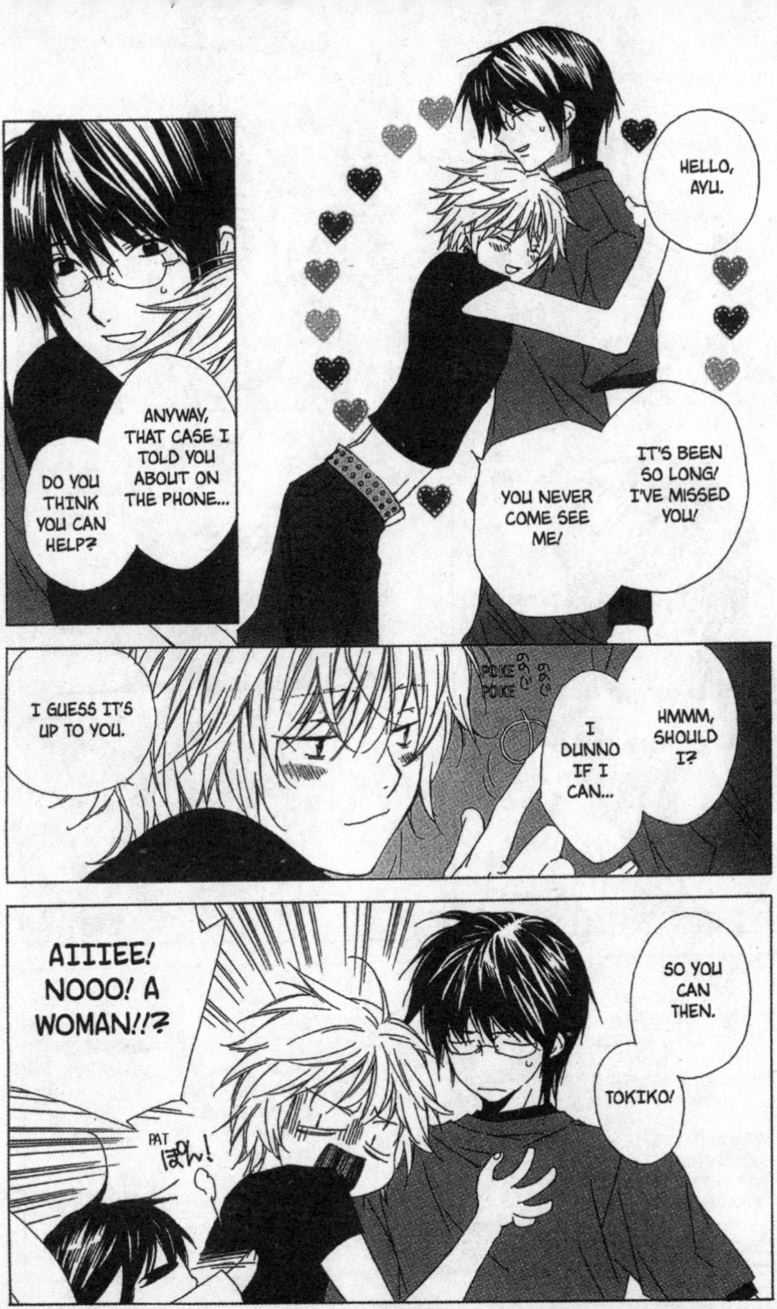
HELLO, AYU.
IT'S BEEN SO LONG! I'VE MISSED YOU!
YOU NEVER COME SEE ME!
ANYWAY, THAT CASE I TOLD YOU ABOUT ON THE PHONE...
DO YOU THINK YOU CAN HELP?
POKE POKE
HMMM, SHOULD I?
I DUNNO IF I CAN...
I GUESS IT'S UP TO YOU.
SO YOU CAN THEN.
TOKIKO!
AIIIEE! NOOO! A WOMAN!!?
PAT
ぽんっ!

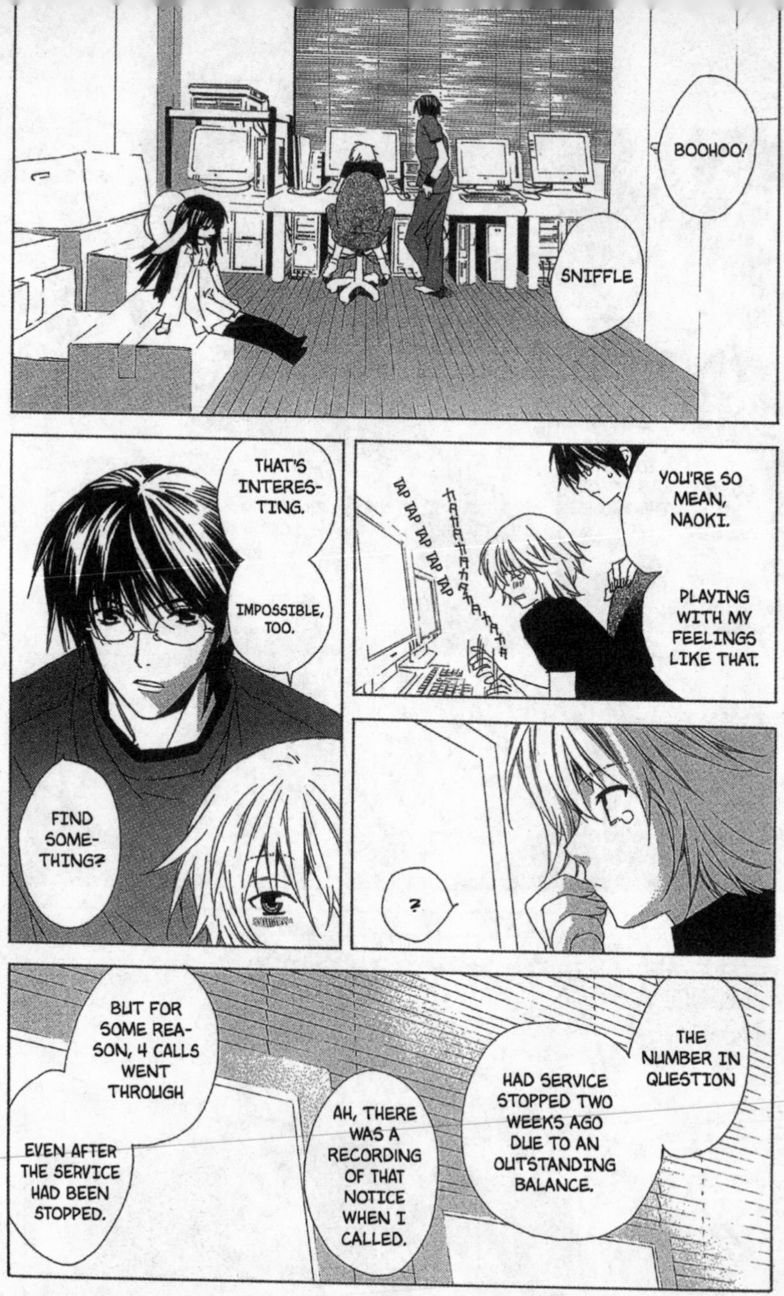

BOOHOO!
SNIFFLE
YOU'RE SO MEAN, NAOKI.
TAP TAP TAP TAP TAP
PLAYING WITH MY FEELINGS LIKE THAT.
?
THAT'S INTERES-TING.
IMPOSSIBLE, TOO.
FIND SOME-THING?
THE NUMBER IN QUESTION
HAD SERVICE STOPPED TWO WEEKS AGO DUE TO AN OUTSTANDING BALANCE.
AH, THERE WAS A RECORDING OF THAT NOTICE WHEN I CALLED.
BUT FOR SOME REA-SON, 4 CALLS WENT THROUGH
EVEN AFTER THE SERVICE HAD BEEN STOPPED.

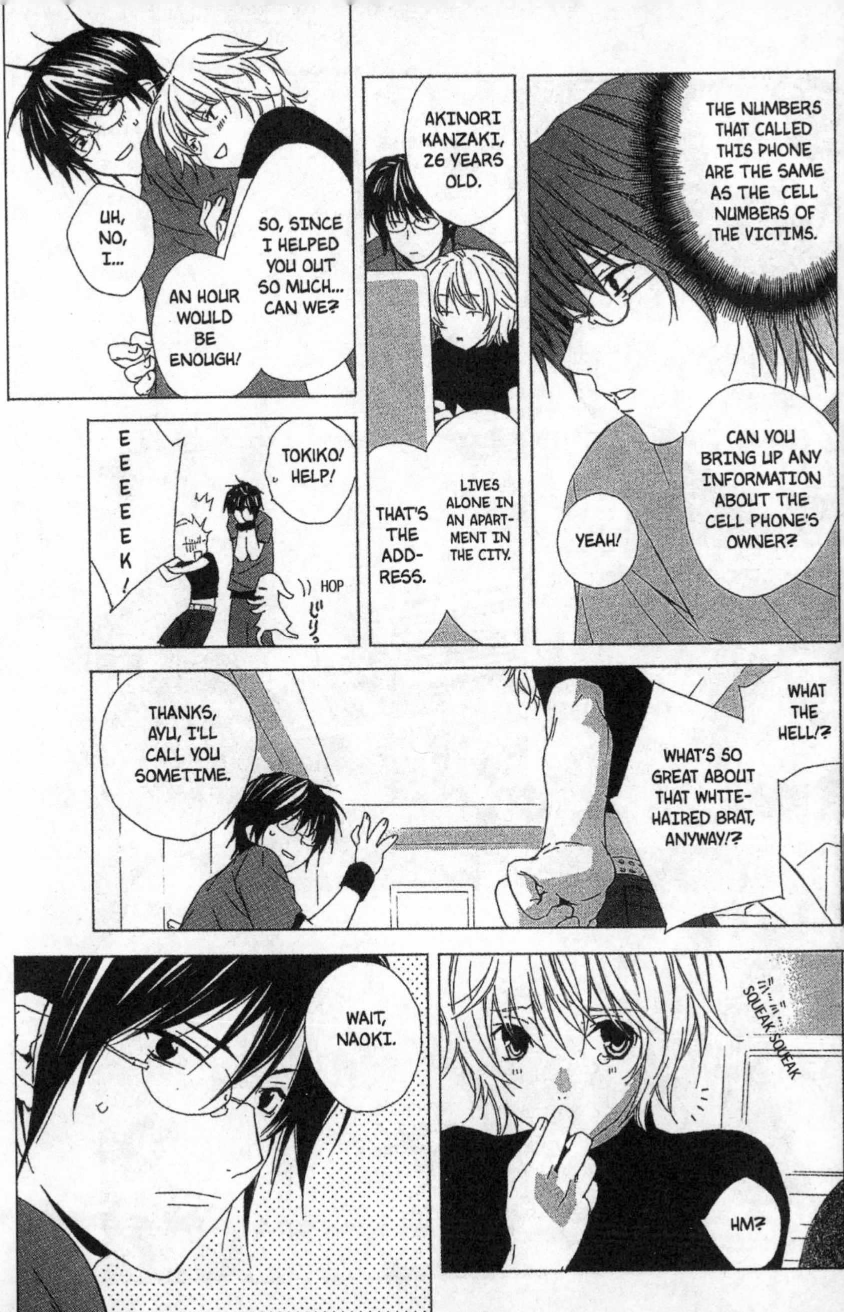
THE NUMBERS THAT CALLED THIS PHONE ARE THE SAME AS THE CELL NUMBERS OF THE VICTIMS.
CAN YOU BRING UP ANY INFORMATION ABOUT THE CELL PHONE'S OWNER?
YEAH!
AKINORI KANZAKI, 26 YEARS OLD.
LIVES ALONE IN AN APARTMENT IN THE CITY.
THAT'S THE ADDRESS.
SO, SINCE I HELPED YOU OUT SO MUCH... CAN WE?
AN HOUR WOULD BE ENOUGH!
UH, NO, I...
TOKIKO! HELP!
EEEEEEK!
HOP
WHAT THE HELL!?
WHAT'S SO GREAT ABOUT THAT WHTTE-HAIRED BRAT, ANYWAY!?
THANKS, AYU, I'LL CALL YOU SOMETIME.
SQUEAK SQUEAK
HM?
WAIT, NAOKI.

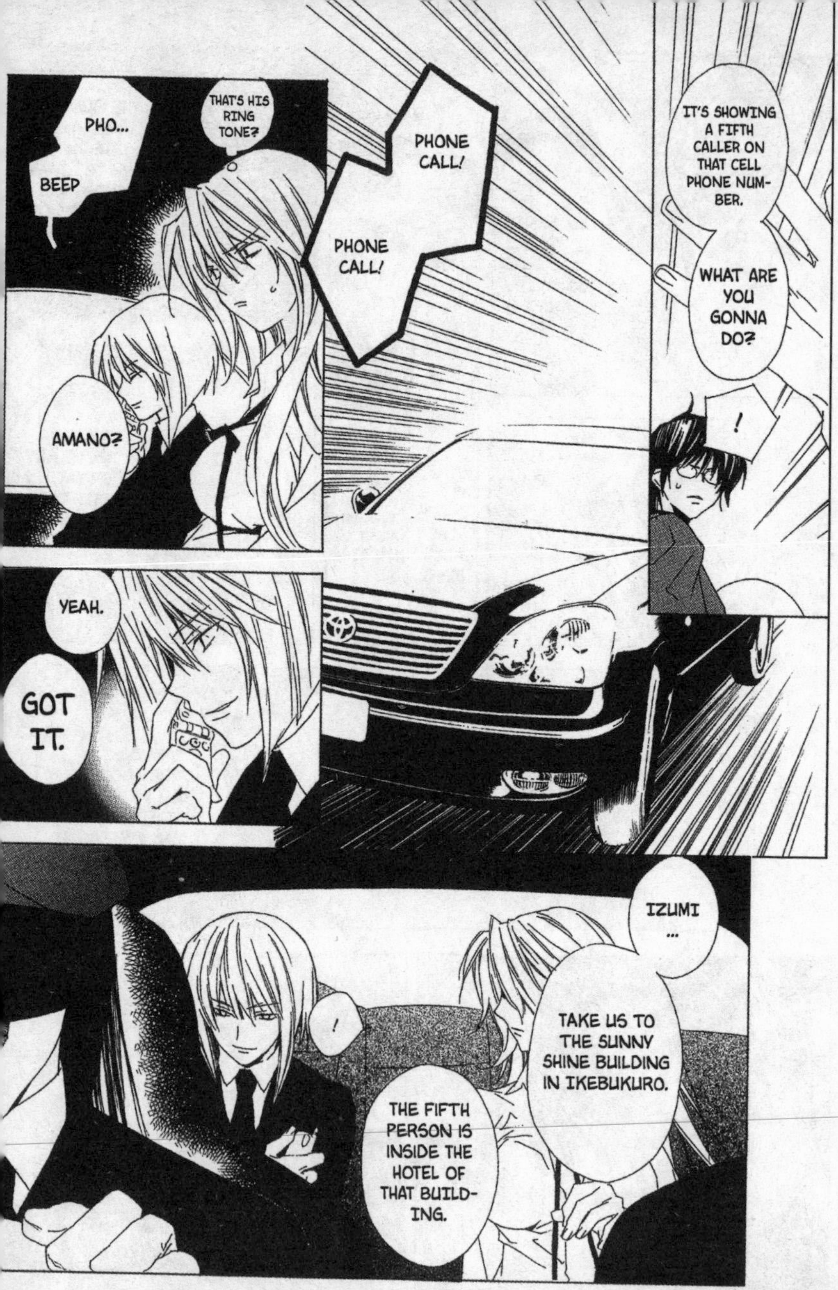

IT'S SHOWING A FIFTH CALLER ON THAT CELL PHONE NUMBER.
WHAT ARE YOU GONNA DO?
!
PHONE CALL!
PHONE CALL!
THAT'S HIS RING TONE?
PHO...
BEEP
AMANO?
YEAH.
GOT IT.
IZUMI ...
TAKE US TO THE SUNNY SHINE BUILDING IN IKEBUKURO.
THE FIFTH PERSON IS INSIDE THE HOTEL OF THAT BUILDING.
!

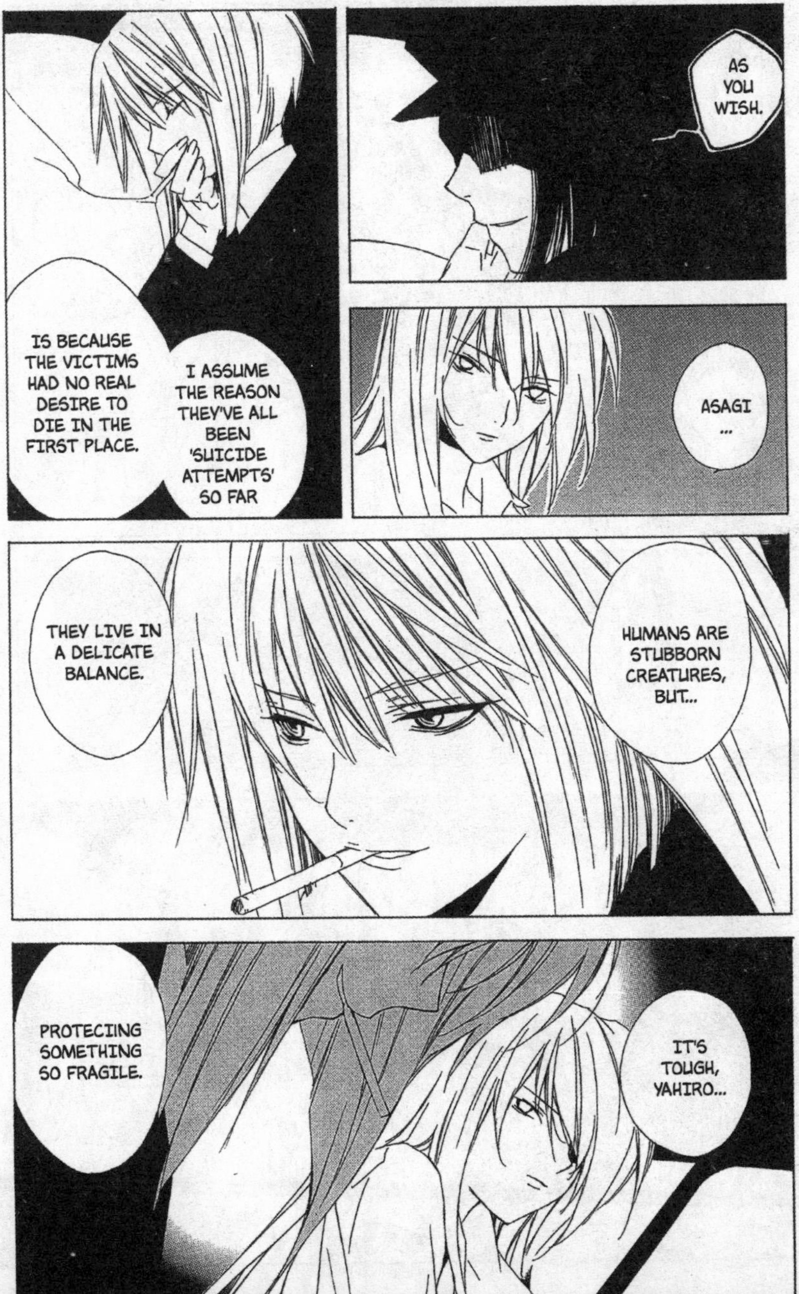
AS YOU WISH.
ASAGI ...
I ASSUME THE REASON THEY'VE ALL BEEN 'SUICIDE ATTEMPTS' SO FAR
IS BECAUSE THE VICTIMS HAD NO REAL DESIRE TO DIE IN THE FIRST PLACE.
HUMANS ARE STUBBORN CREATURES, BUT...
THEY LIVE IN A DELICATE BALANCE.
IT'S TOUGH, YAHIRO...
PROTECTING SOMETHING SO FRAGILE.

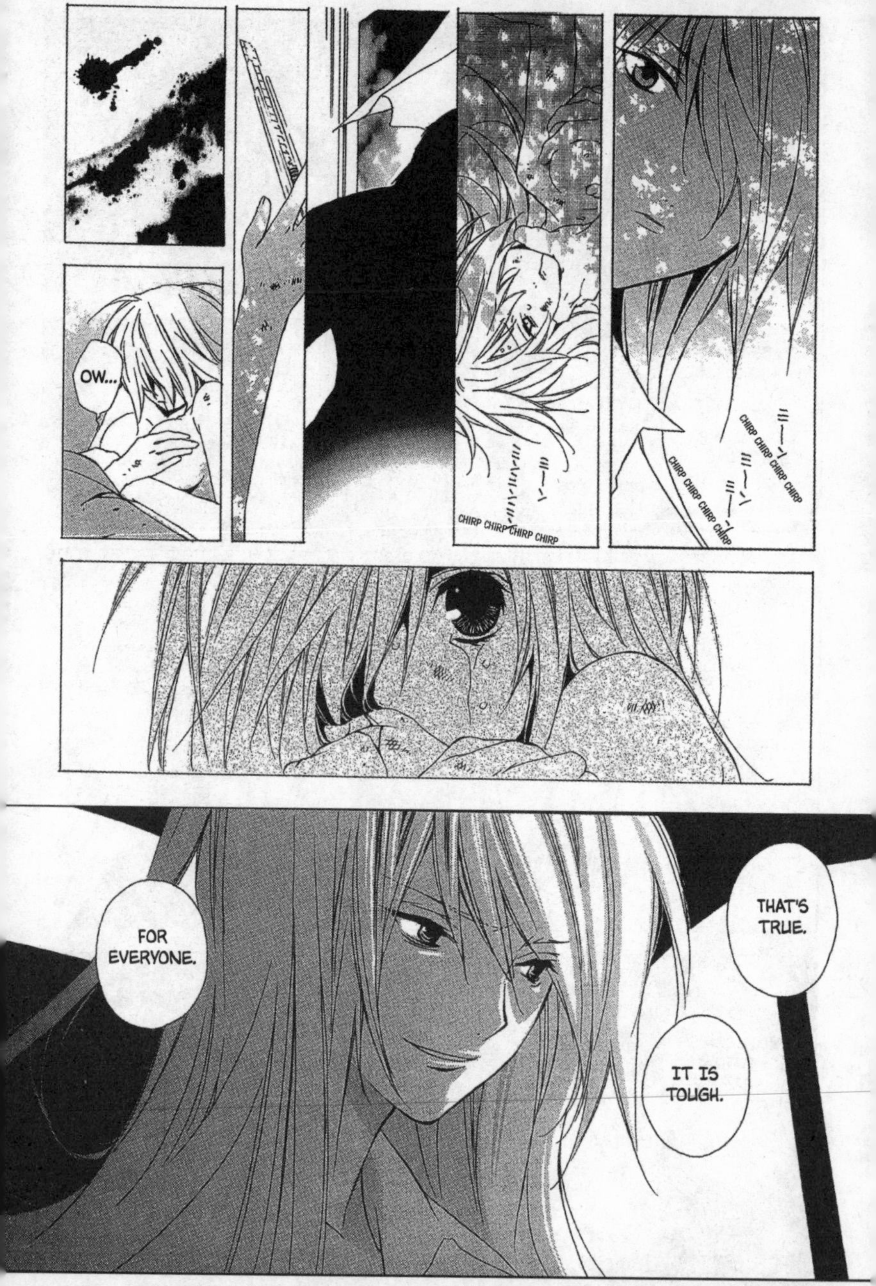
CHIRP CHIRP CHIRP CHIRP
CHIRP CHIRP CHIRP CHIRP
CHIRP CHIRP CHIRP CHIRP
OW...
THAT'S TRUE.
IT IS TOUGH.
FOR EVERYONE.

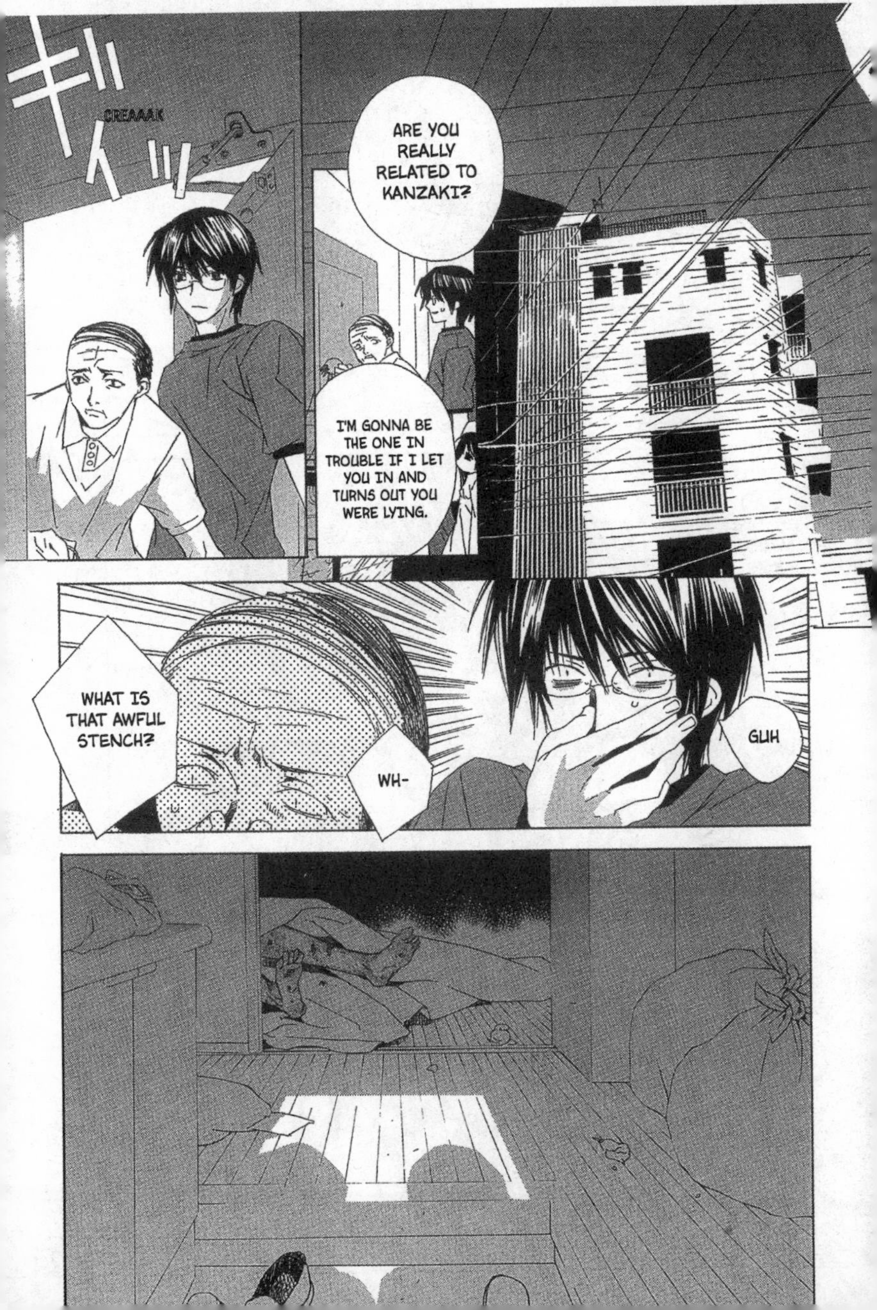
ARE YOU REALLY RELATED TO KANZAKI?
I'M GONNA BE THE ONE IN TROUBLE IF I LET YOU IN AND TURNS OUT YOU WERE LYING.
キィ
CREAAAK
GUH
WH-
WHAT IS THAT AWFUL STENCH?

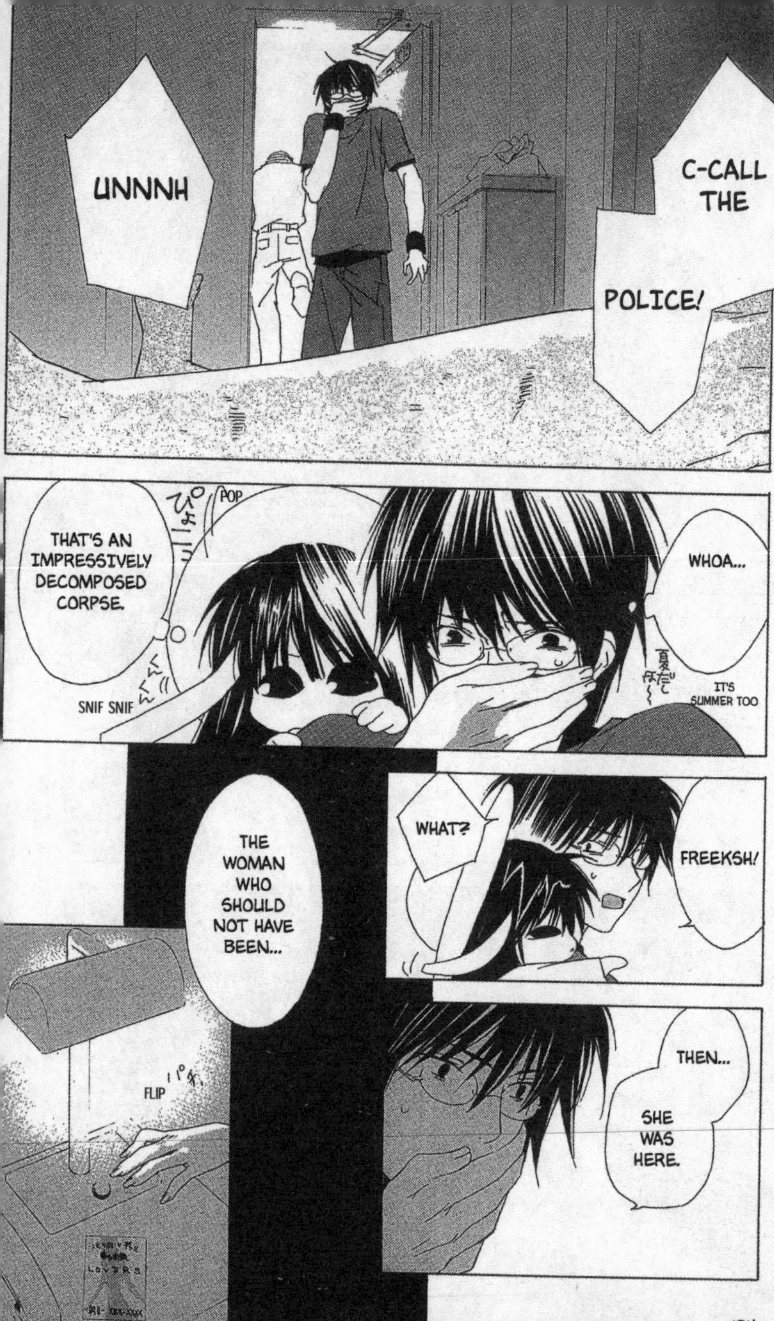
C-CALL THE POLICE!
UNNNH
WHOA...
IT'S SUMMER TOO
POP
THAT'S AN IMPRESSIVELY DECOMPOSED CORPSE.
SNIF SNIF
FREEKSH!
WHAT?
THE WOMAN WHO SHOULD NOT HAVE BEEN...
THEN...
SHE WAS HERE.
FLIP

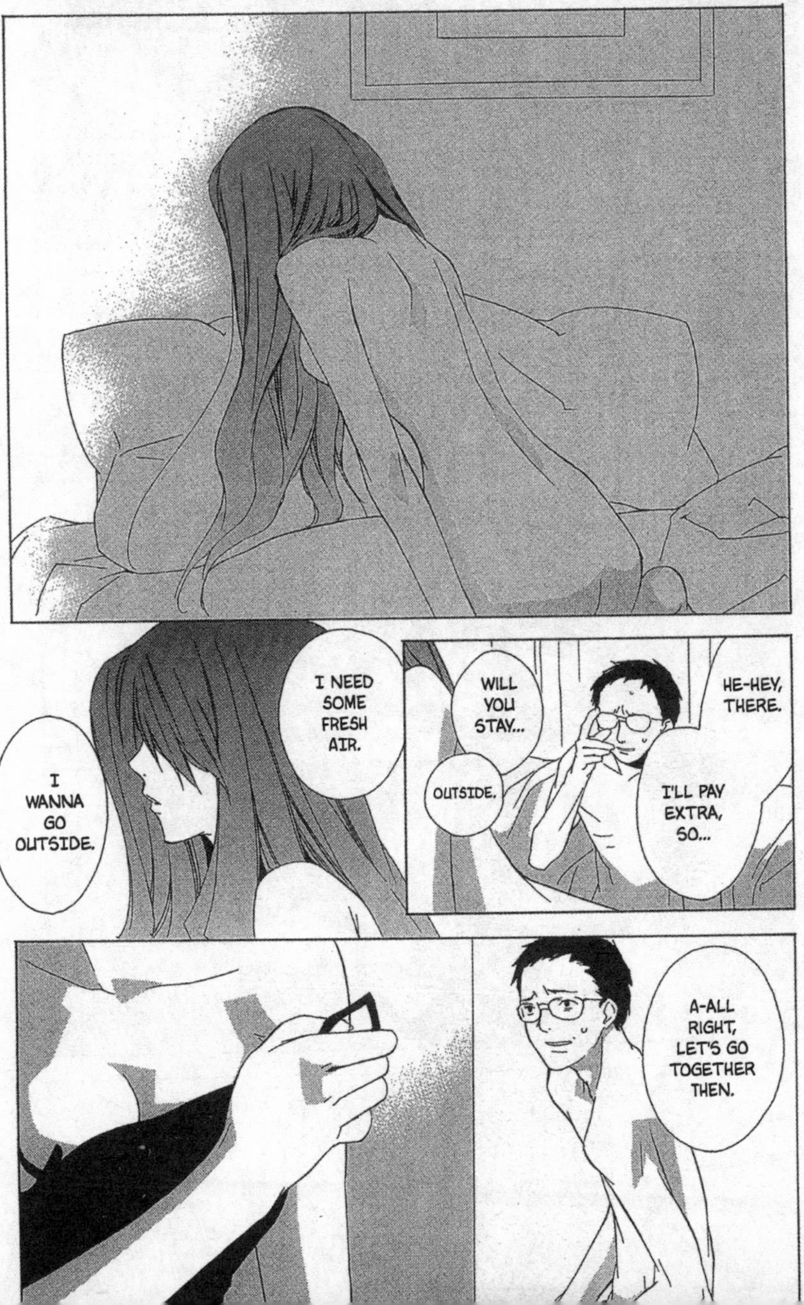
HE-HEY, THERE.
WILL YOU STAY...
I'LL PAY EXTRA, SO...
OUTSIDE.
I NEED SOME FRESH AIR.
I WANNA GO OUTSIDE.
A-ALL RIGHT, LET'S GO TOGETHER THEN.

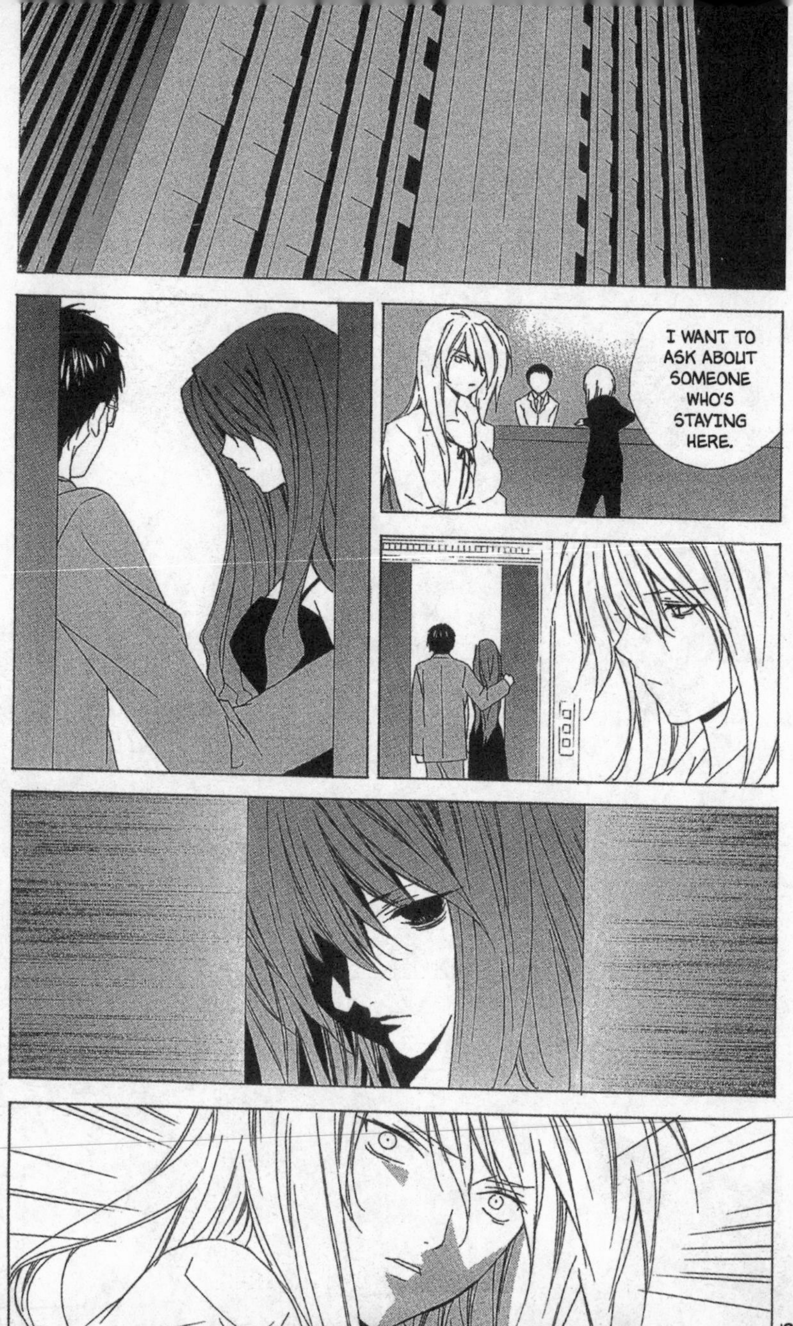
I WANT TO ASK ABOUT SOMEONE WHO'S STAYING HERE.

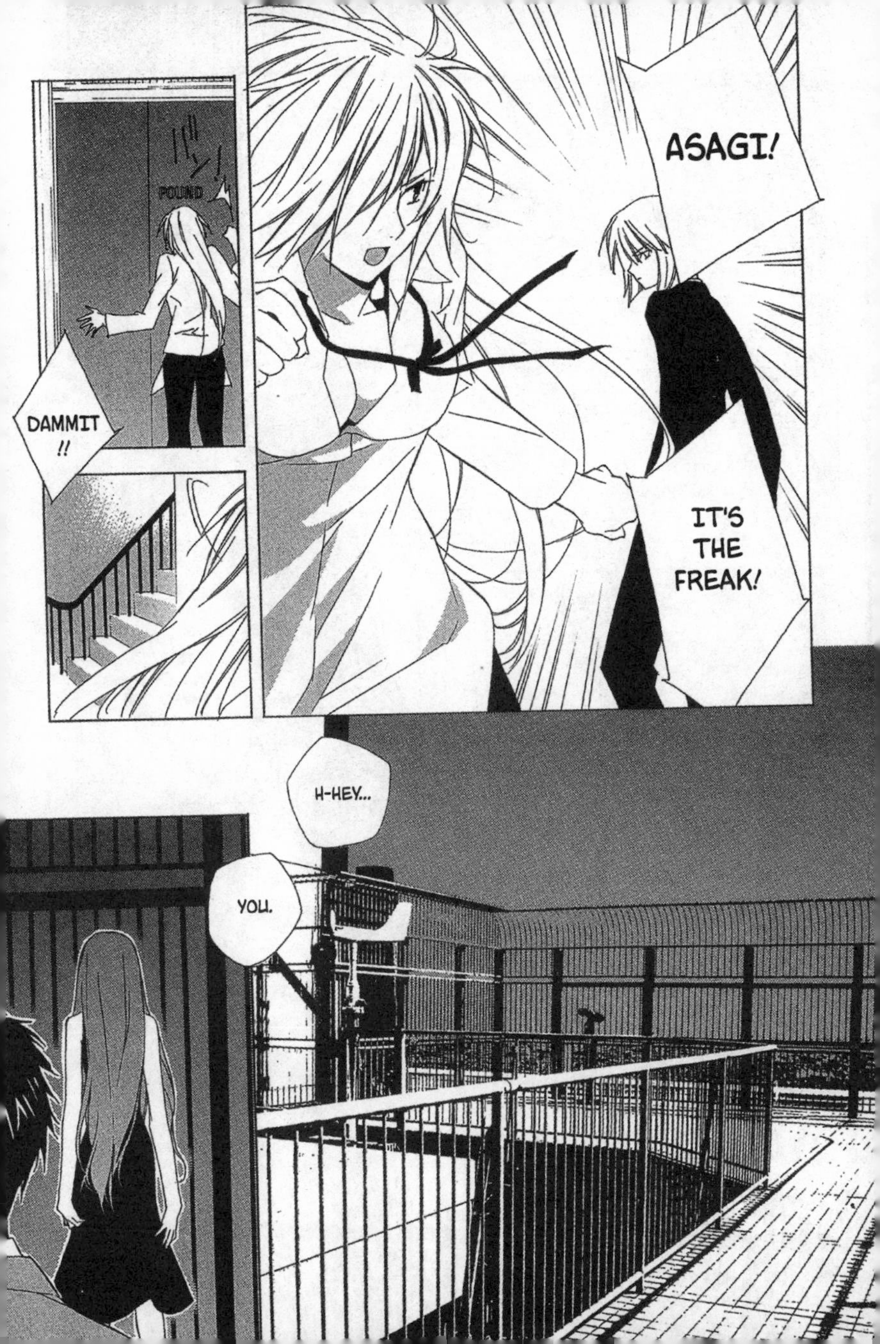
ASAGI!
IT'S THE FREAK!
バン!
POUND
DAMMIT !!
H-HEY...
YOU.

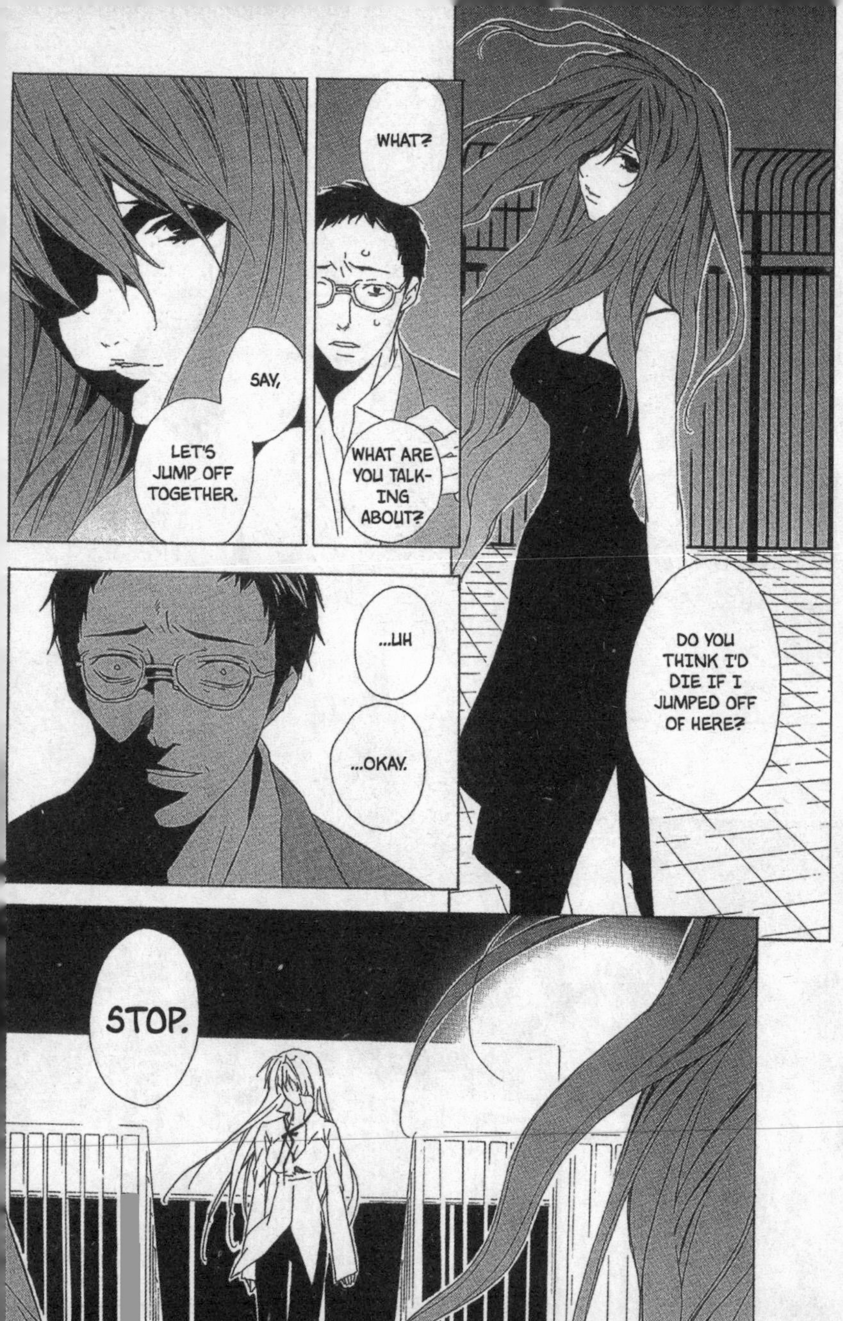
DO YOU THINK I'D DIE IF I JUMPED OFF OF HERE?
WHAT?
WHAT ARE YOU TALK-ING ABOUT?
SAY,
LET'S JUMP OFF TOGETHER.
...UH
...OKAY.
STOP.

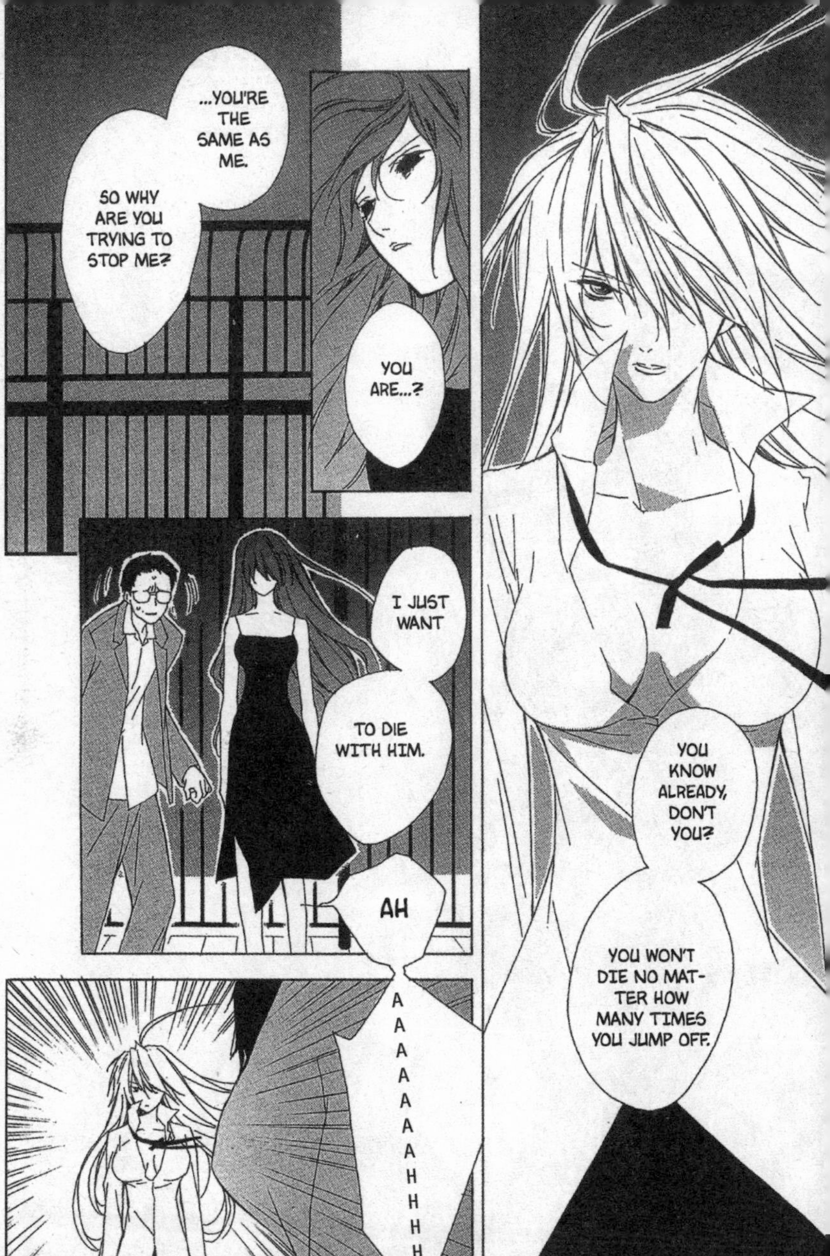
YOU ARE...?
...YOU'RE THE SAME AS ME.
SO WHY ARE YOU TRYING TO STOP ME?
YOU KNOW ALREADY, DON'T YOU?
YOU WON'T DIE NO MAT-TER HOW MANY TIMES YOU JUMP OFF.
I JUST WANT
TO DIE WITH HIM.
AH
AAAAAAAAHHHHHH

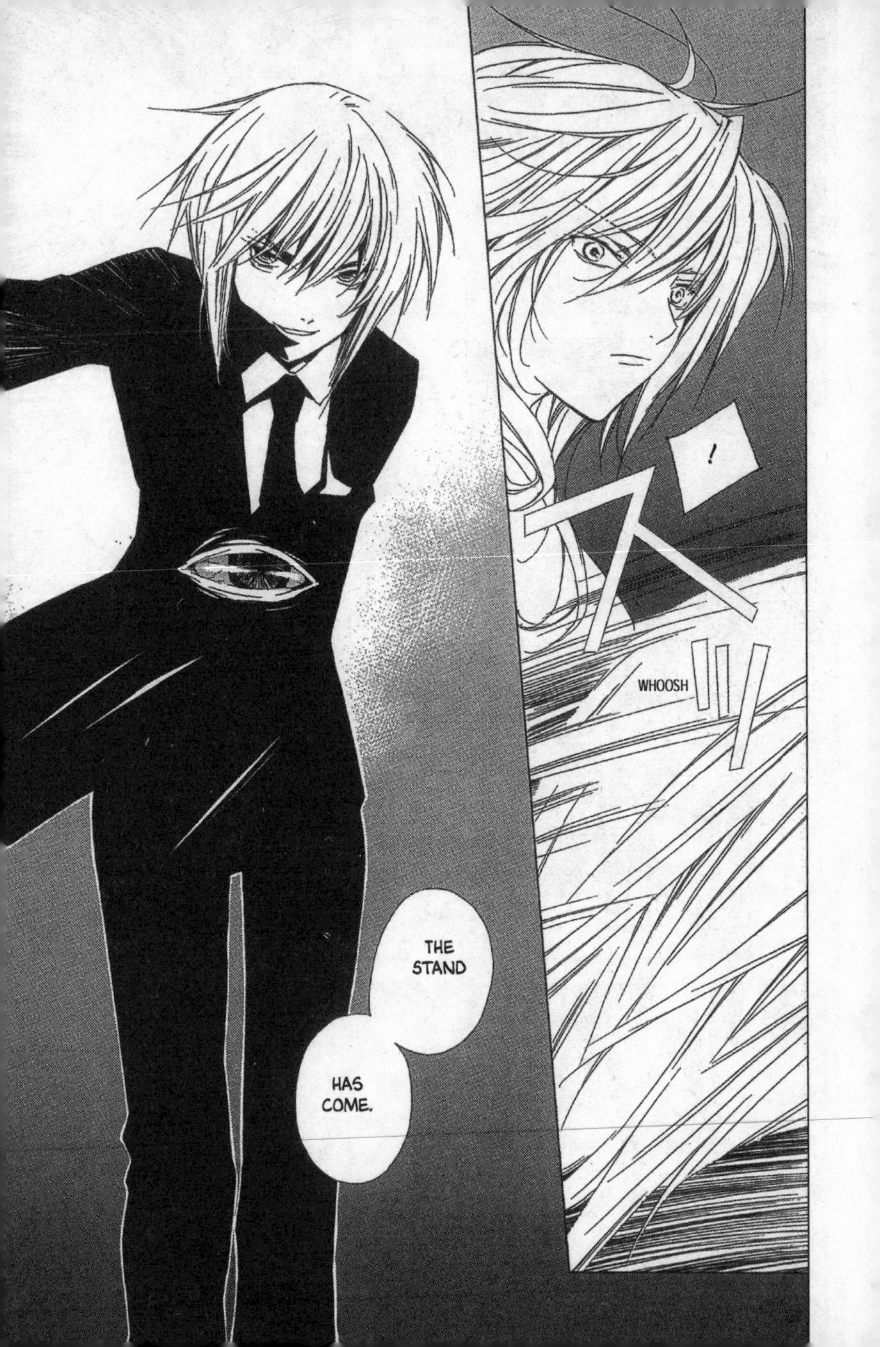
!
WHOOSH
THE STAND
HAS COME.

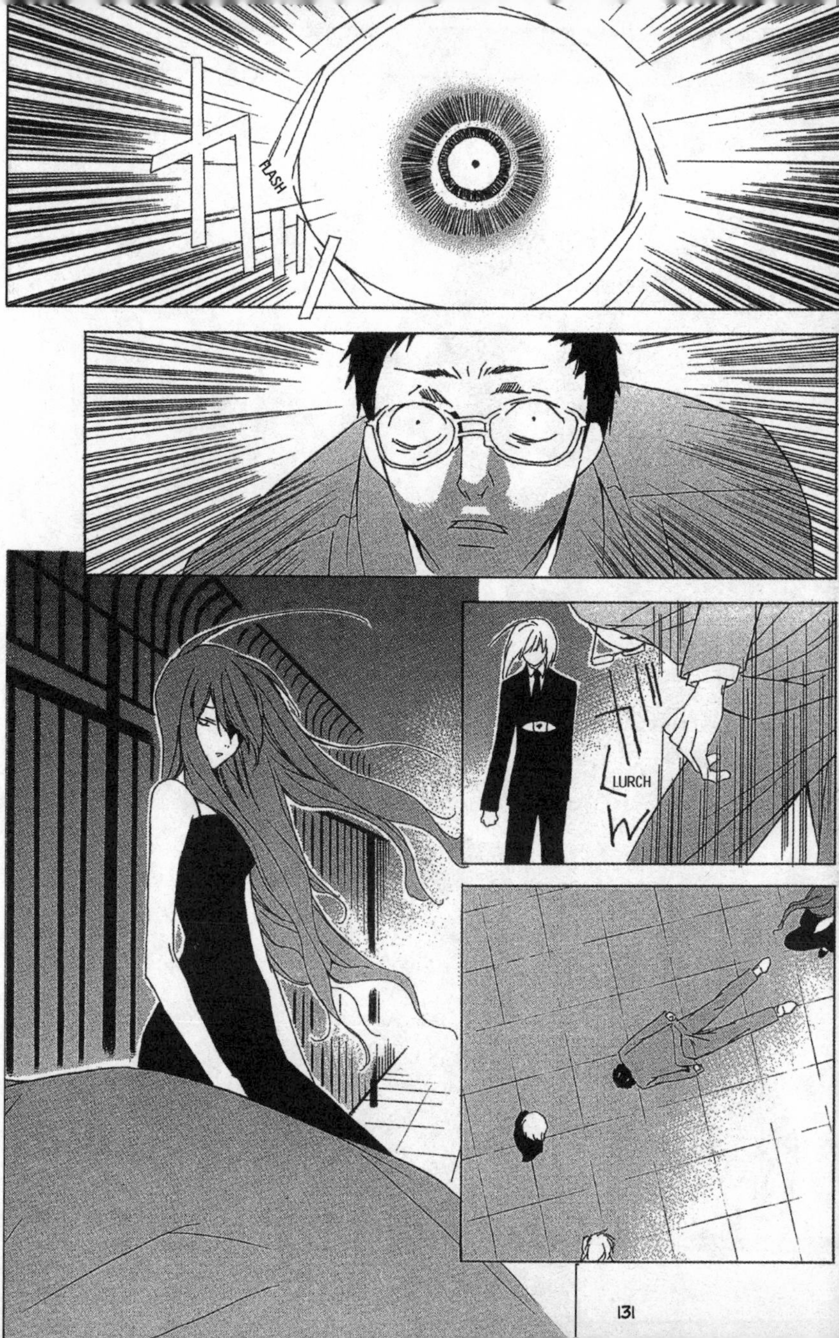

FLASH
LURCH

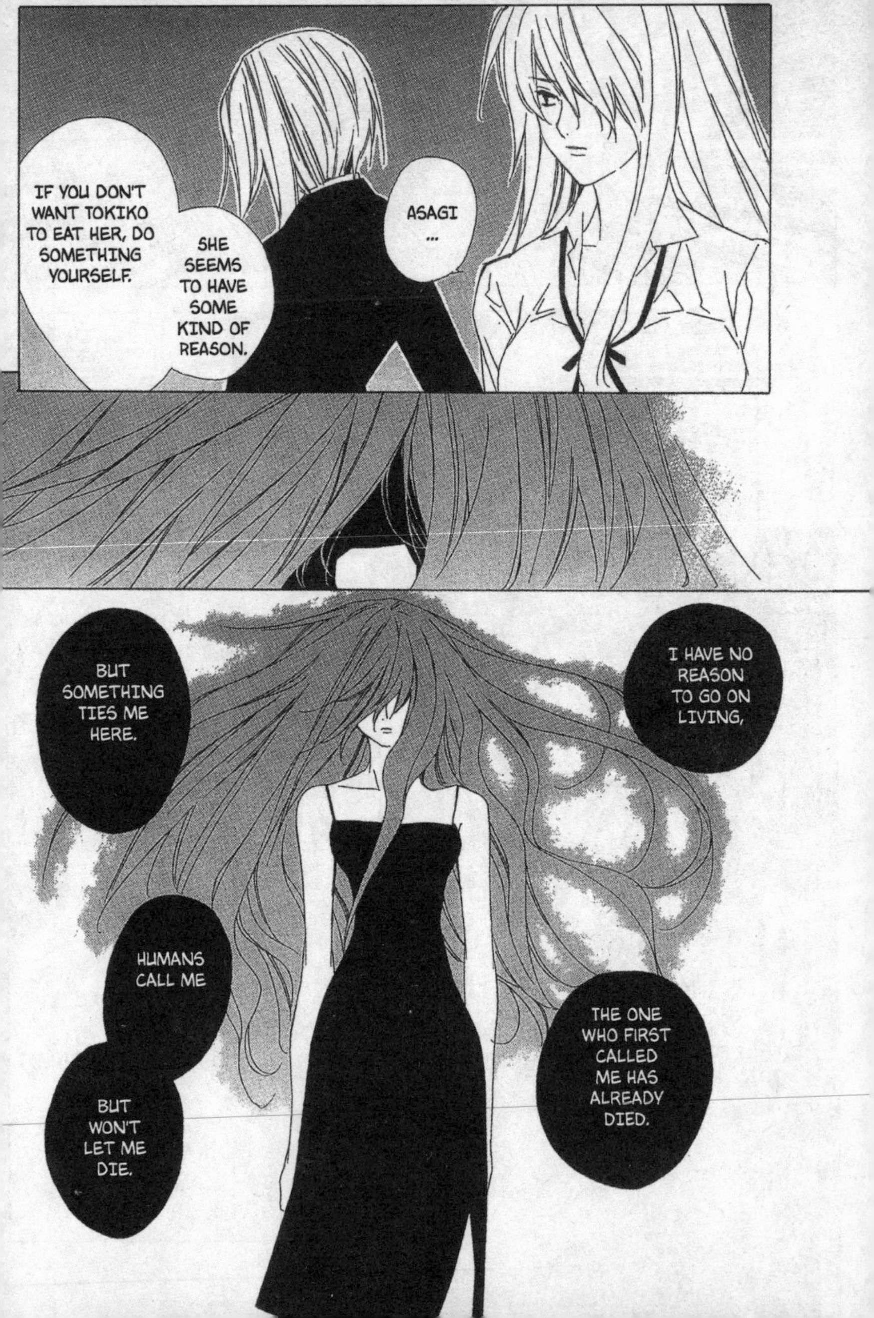
ASAGI ...
SHE SEEMS TO HAVE SOME KIND OF REASON.
IF YOU DON'T WANT TOKIKO TO EAT HER, DO SOMETHING YOURSELF.
I HAVE NO REASON TO GO ON LIVING,
BUT SOMETHING TIES ME HERE.
THE ONE WHO FIRST CALLED ME HAS ALREADY DIED.
HUMANS CALL ME
BUT WON'T LET ME DIE.

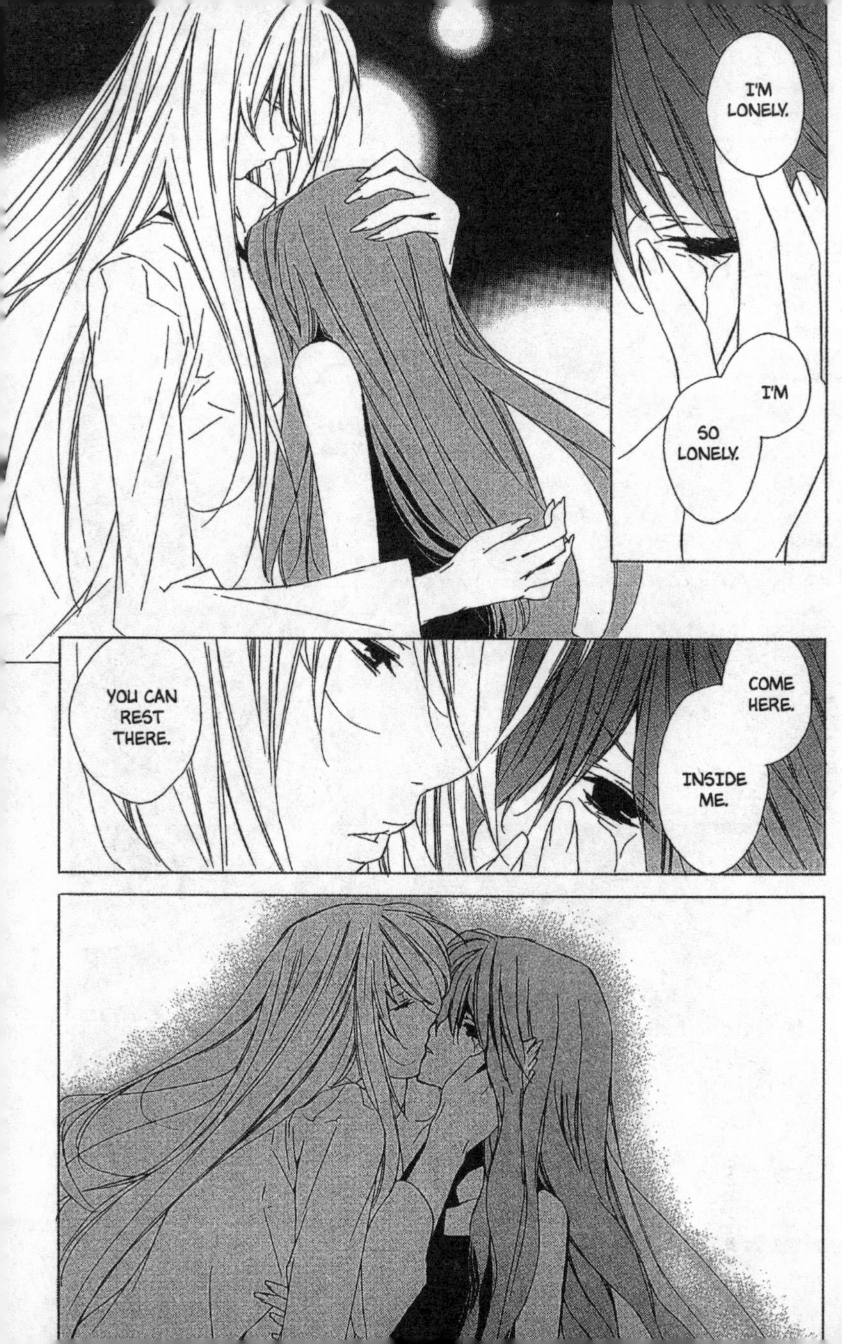
I'M LONELY.
I'M SO LONELY.
COME HERE. INSIDE ME.
YOU CAN REST THERE.

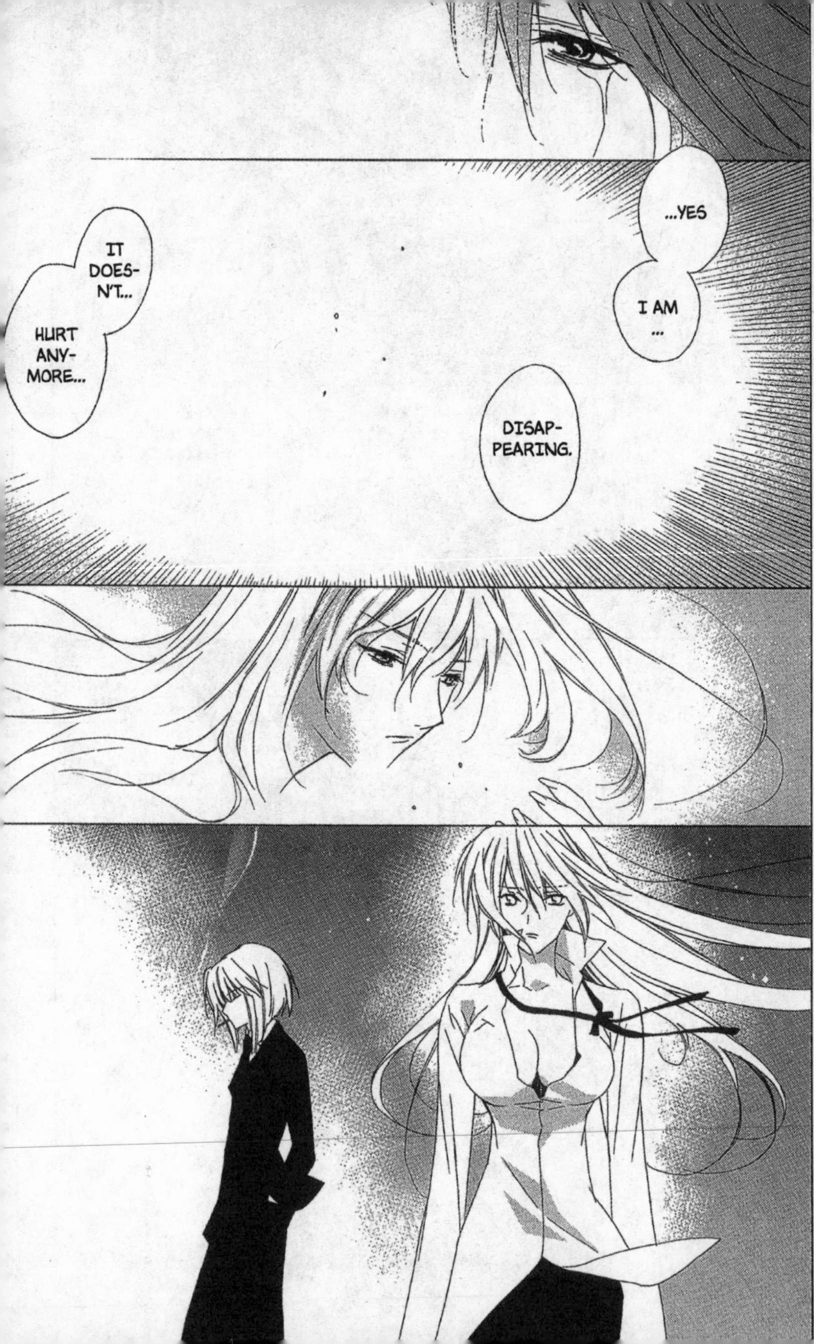
...YES
I AM ...
DISAP-PEARING.
IT DOES-N'T...
HURT ANY-MORE...

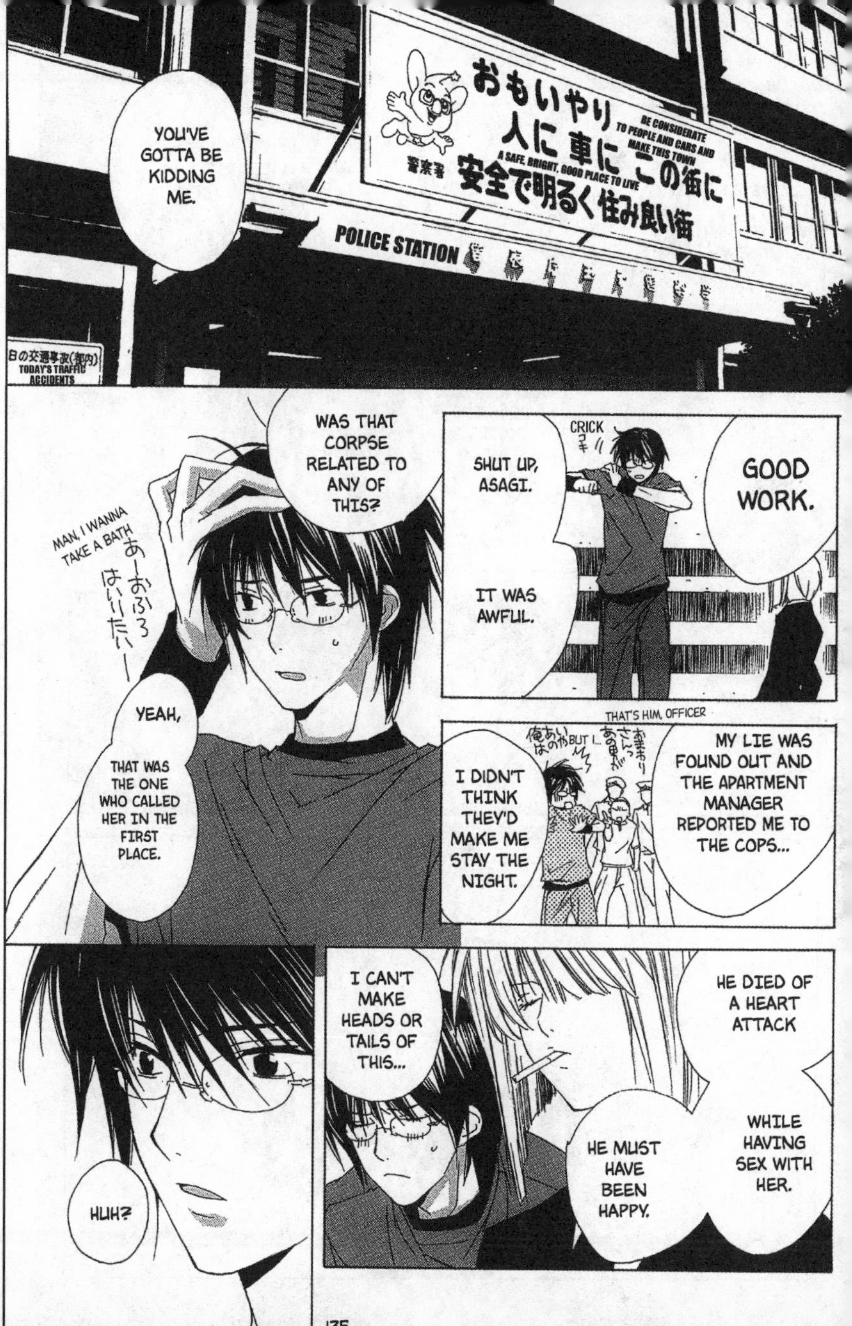
おもいやり
人に車に この街に
BE CONSIDERATE TO PEOPLE AND CARS AND MAKE THIS TOWN
A SAFE, BRIGHT, GOOD PLACE TO LIVE
安全で明るく住み良い街
POLICE STATION
TODAY'S TRAFFIC ACCIDENTS
YOU'VE GOTTA BE KIDDING ME.
GOOD WORK.
CRICK
SHUT UP, ASAGI.
IT WAS AWFUL.
MY LIE WAS FOUND OUT AND THE APARTMENT MANAGER REPORTED ME TO THE COPS...
THAT'S HIM, OFFICER
BUT I...
I DIDN'T THINK THEY'D MAKE ME STAY THE NIGHT.
WAS THAT CORPSE RELATED TO ANY OF THIS?
MAN, I WANNA TAKE A BATH
あーおふろはいりたいー
YEAH,
THAT WAS THE ONE WHO CALLED HER IN THE FIRST PLACE.
HE DIED OF A HEART ATTACK
WHILE HAVING SEX WITH HER.
HE MUST HAVE BEEN HAPPY.
I CAN'T MAKE HEADS OR TAILS OF THIS...
HUH?

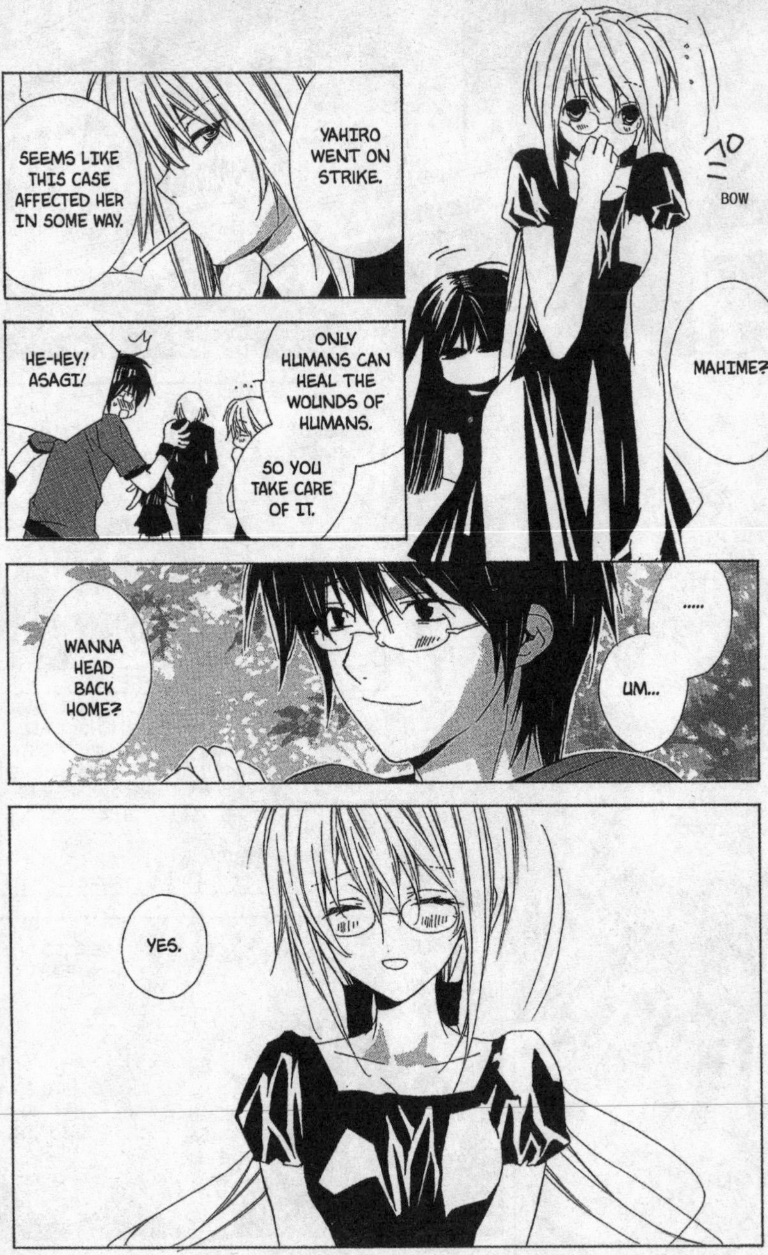
YAHIRO WENT ON STRIKE.
SEEMS LIKE THIS CASE AFFECTED HER IN SOME WAY.
ONLY HUMANS CAN HEAL THE WOUNDS OF HUMANS.
SO YOU TAKE CARE OF IT.
...
HE-HEY! ASAGI!
BOW
MAHIME?
.....
UM...
WANNA HEAD BACK HOME?
YES.

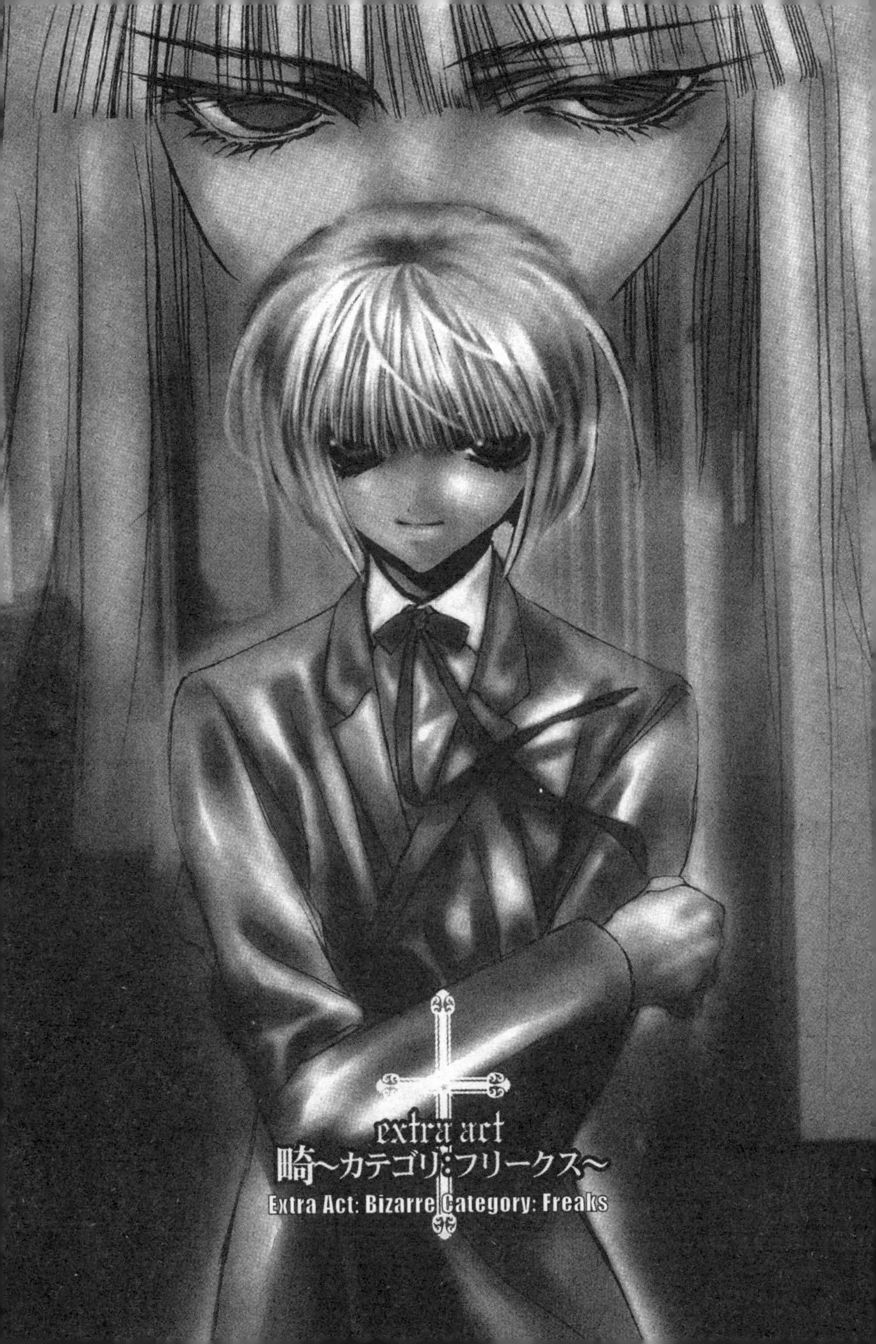
extra act
畸～カテゴリ：フリークス～
Extra Act: Bizarre Category: Freaks

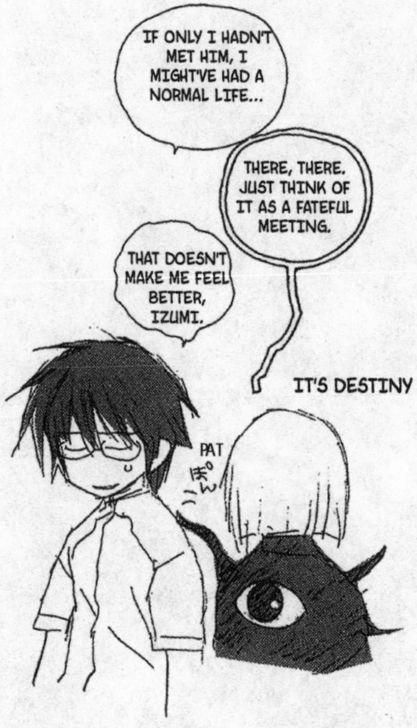
IF ONLY I HADN'T MET HIM, I MIGHT'VE HAD A NORMAL LIFE...
THERE, THERE. JUST THINK OF IT AS A FATEFUL MEETING.
THAT DOESN'T MAKE ME FEEL BETTER, IZUMI.
IT'S DESTINY
PAT
ぽん

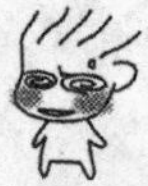

I WROTE THIS CHAPTER AS A STAND ALONE FOR A GIRLS' MYSTERY MAGAZINE BEFORE SIGNING ON WITH COMIC BIRZ. IT SEEMS LIKE AGES AGO. I COULD NOT EVEN REMEMBER WHEN I WROTE IT UNTIL I SAW IT AGAIN. FOUR YEARS AGO. THE DRAWINGS LOOK COMPLETELY DIFFERENT; IT'S A LITTLE EMBARRASSING! ASAGI IS LOOKING PRETTY SPIFFY IN THAT STRING TIE AND AMANO IS IN MIDDLE SCHOOL. I BELIEVE I HAD DESIGNED TOKIKO AT THIS POINT, BUT I GUESS I NEVER GOT PAST JUST NAMING HER. THERE IS NO SIGN OF EITHER MAHIME OR YAHIRO IN THIS VERSION. MY CONCEPT FOR THE PLOT WHEN I WAS PLANNING THIS WAS "AN OCCULT HORROR STORY IN WHICH FEW DIE." THAT IS STILL THE BASIC CONCEPT OF THE SERIES.

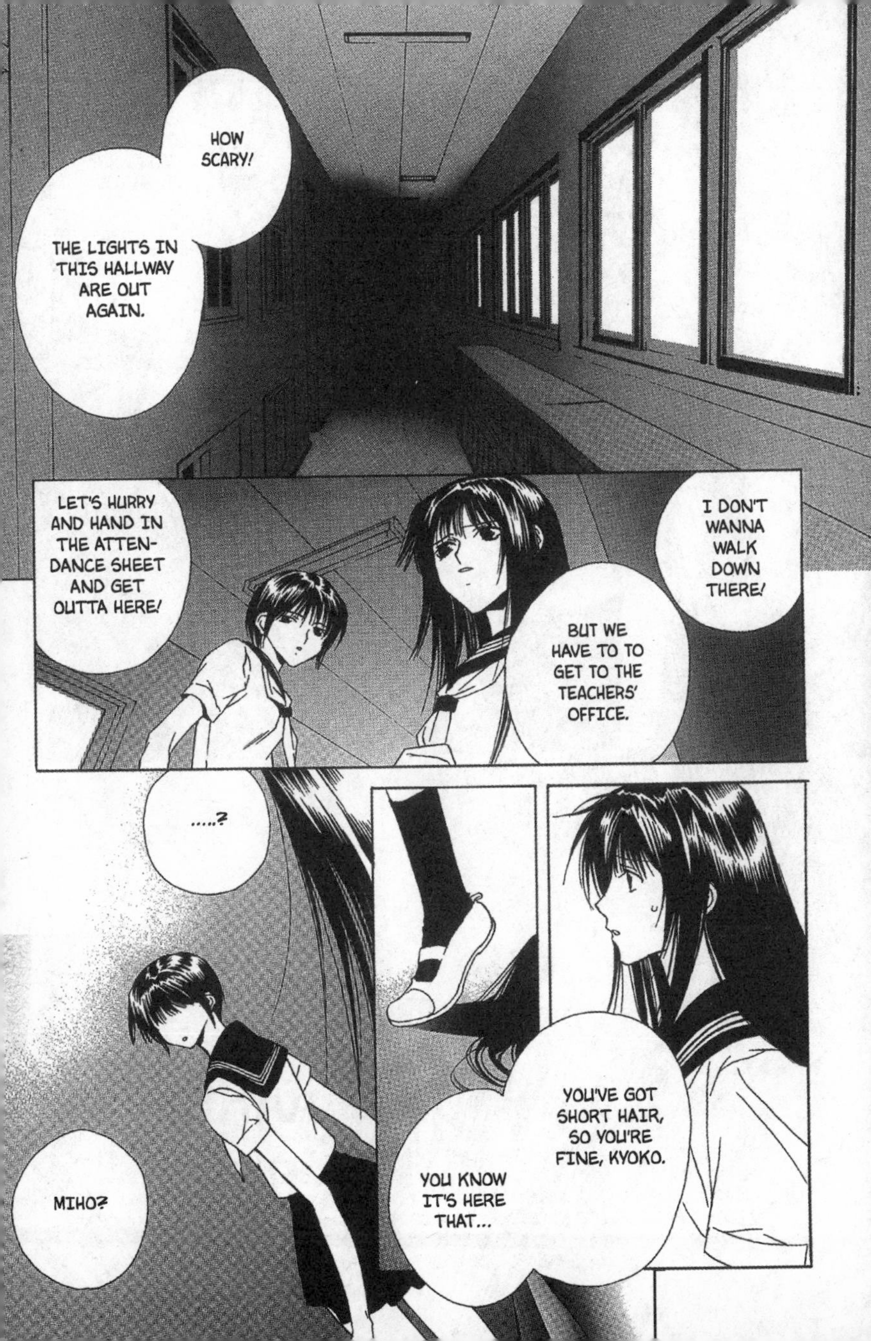
HOW SCARY!
THE LIGHTS IN THIS HALLWAY ARE OUT AGAIN.
I DON'T WANNA WALK DOWN THERE!
BUT WE HAVE TO TO GET TO THE TEACHERS' OFFICE.
LET'S HURRY AND HAND IN THE ATTEN-DANCE SHEET AND GET OUTTA HERE!
YOU'VE GOT SHORT HAIR, SO YOU'RE FINE, KYOKO.
YOU KNOW IT'S HERE THAT...
.....?
MIHO?

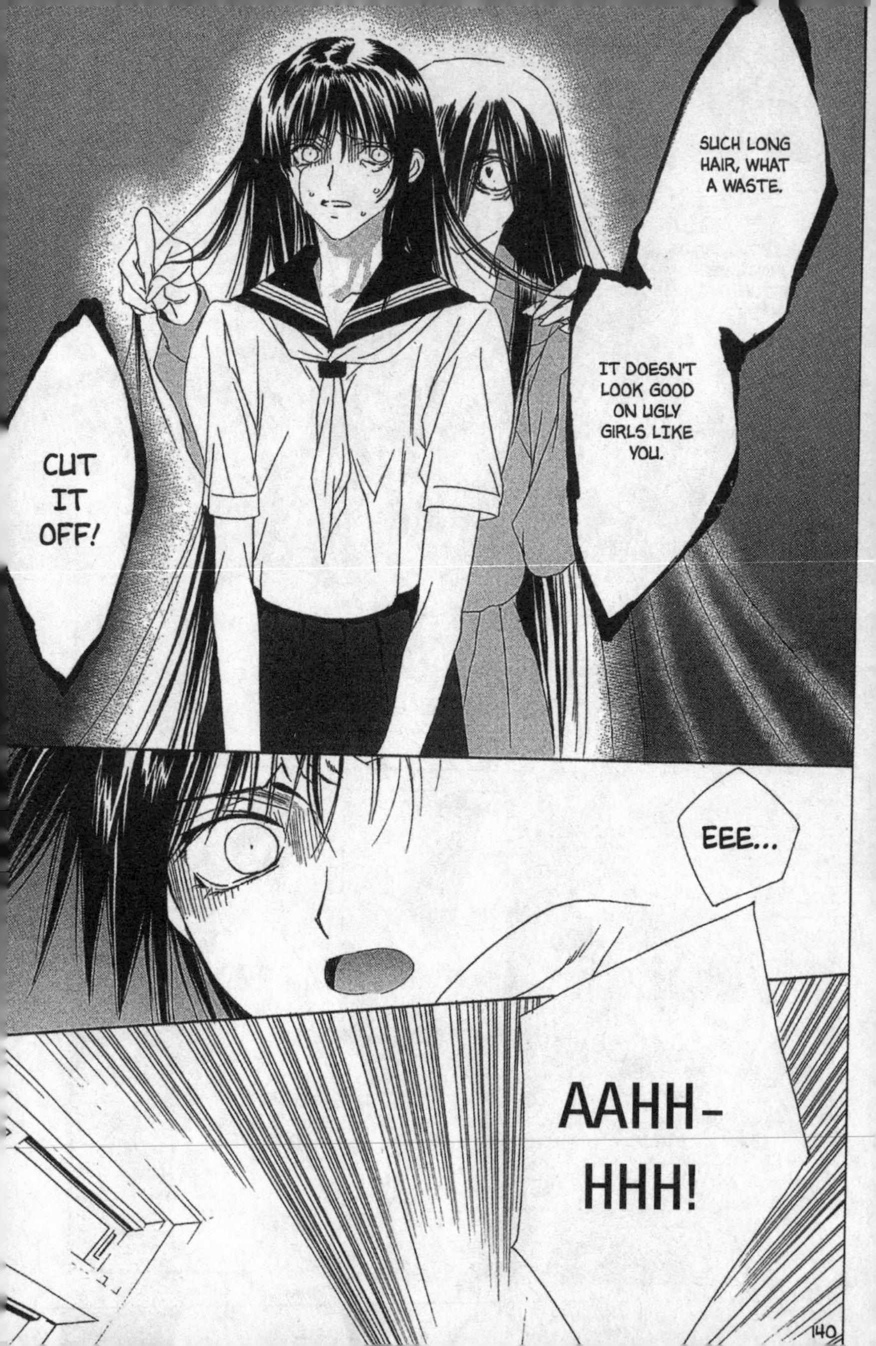
SUCH LONG HAIR, WHAT A WASTE.
IT DOESN'T LOOK GOOD ON UGLY GIRLS LIKE YOU.
CUT IT OFF!
EEE...
AAHH-HHH!

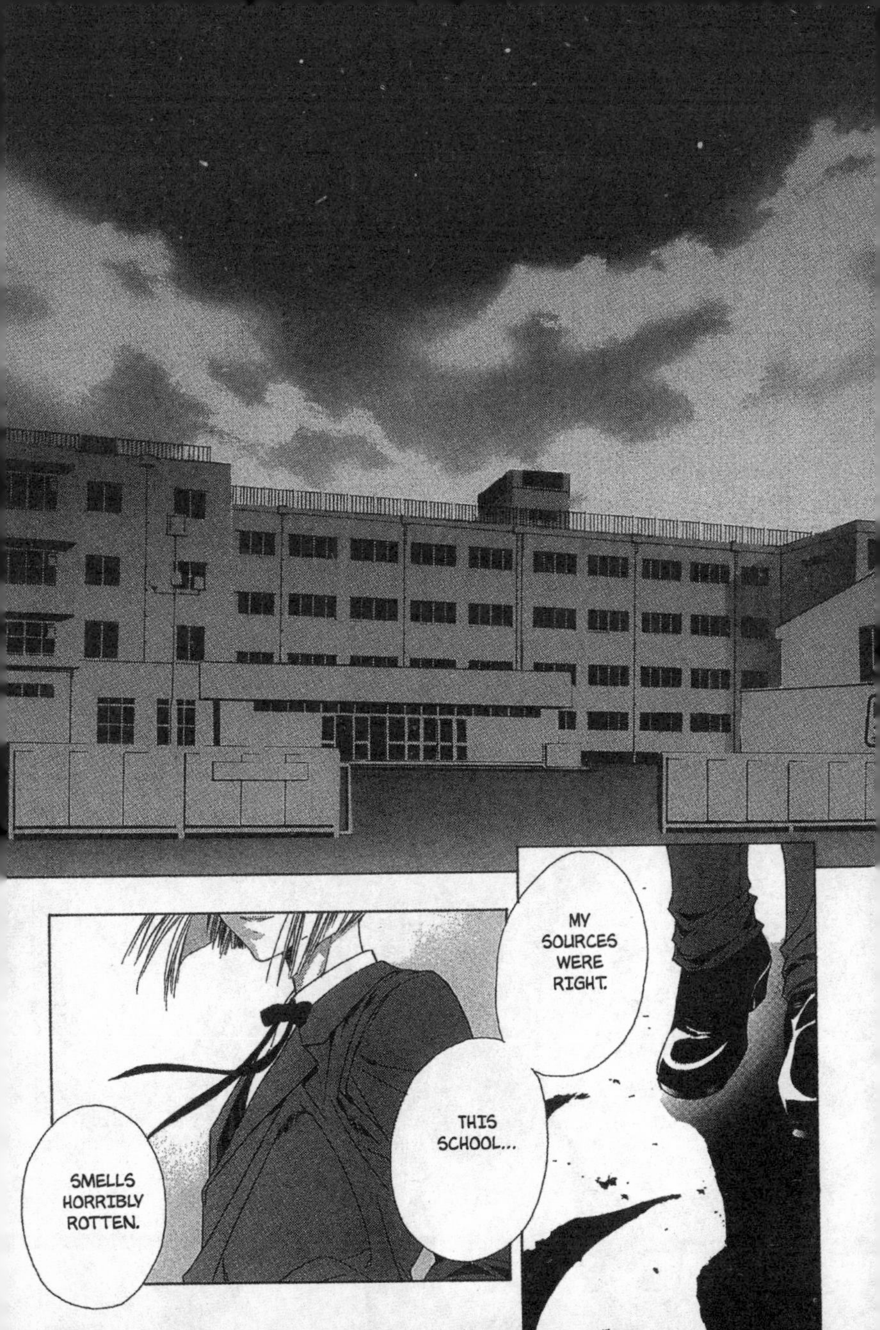
MY SOURCES WERE RIGHT.
THIS SCHOOL...
SMELLS HORRIBLY ROTTEN.

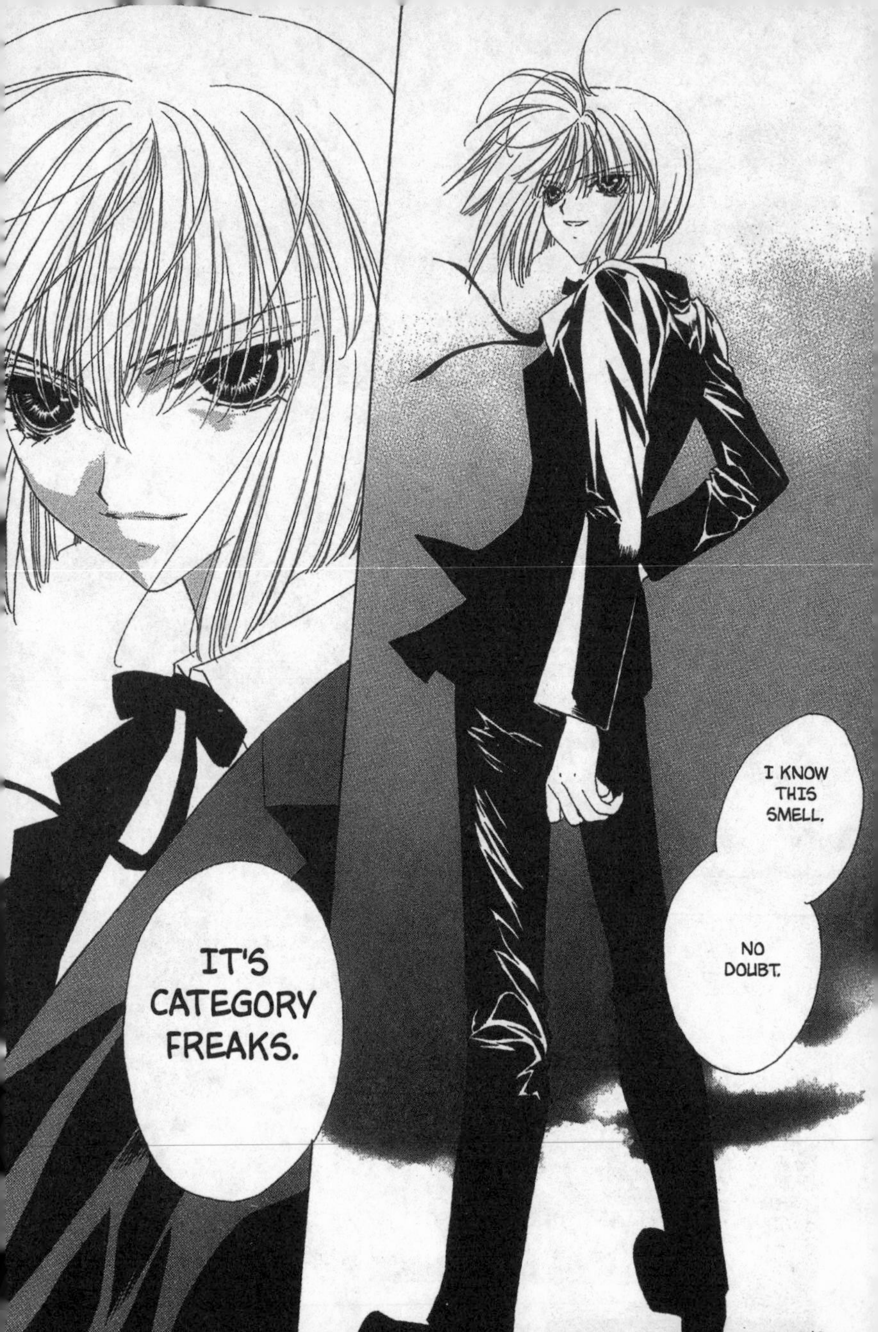
I KNOW THIS SMELL.
NO DOUBT.
IT'S CATEGORY FREAKS.

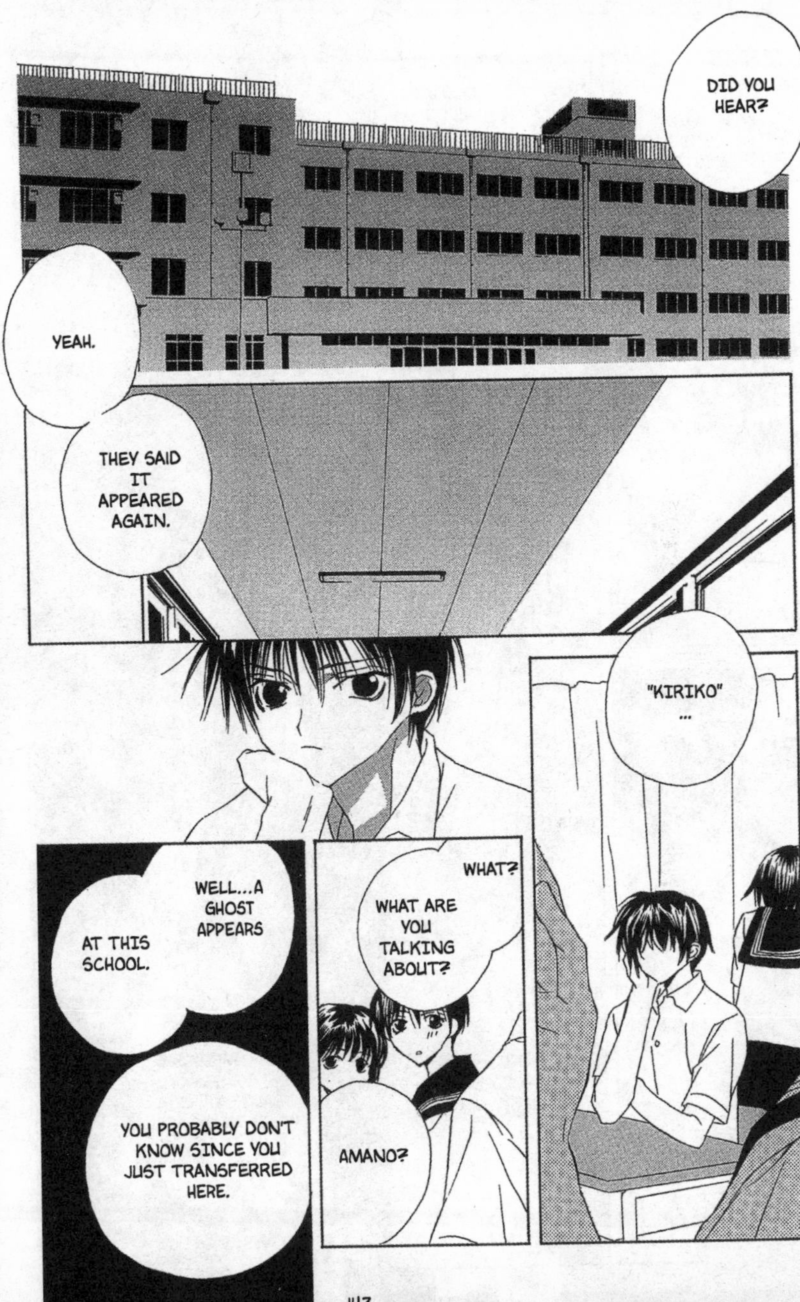
DID YOU HEAR?
YEAH.
THEY SAID IT APPEARED AGAIN.
"KIRIKO"...
WHAT?
WHAT ARE YOU TALKING ABOUT?
AMANO?
WELL...A GHOST APPEARS
AT THIS SCHOOL.
YOU PROBABLY DON'T KNOW SINCE YOU JUST TRANSFERRED HERE.

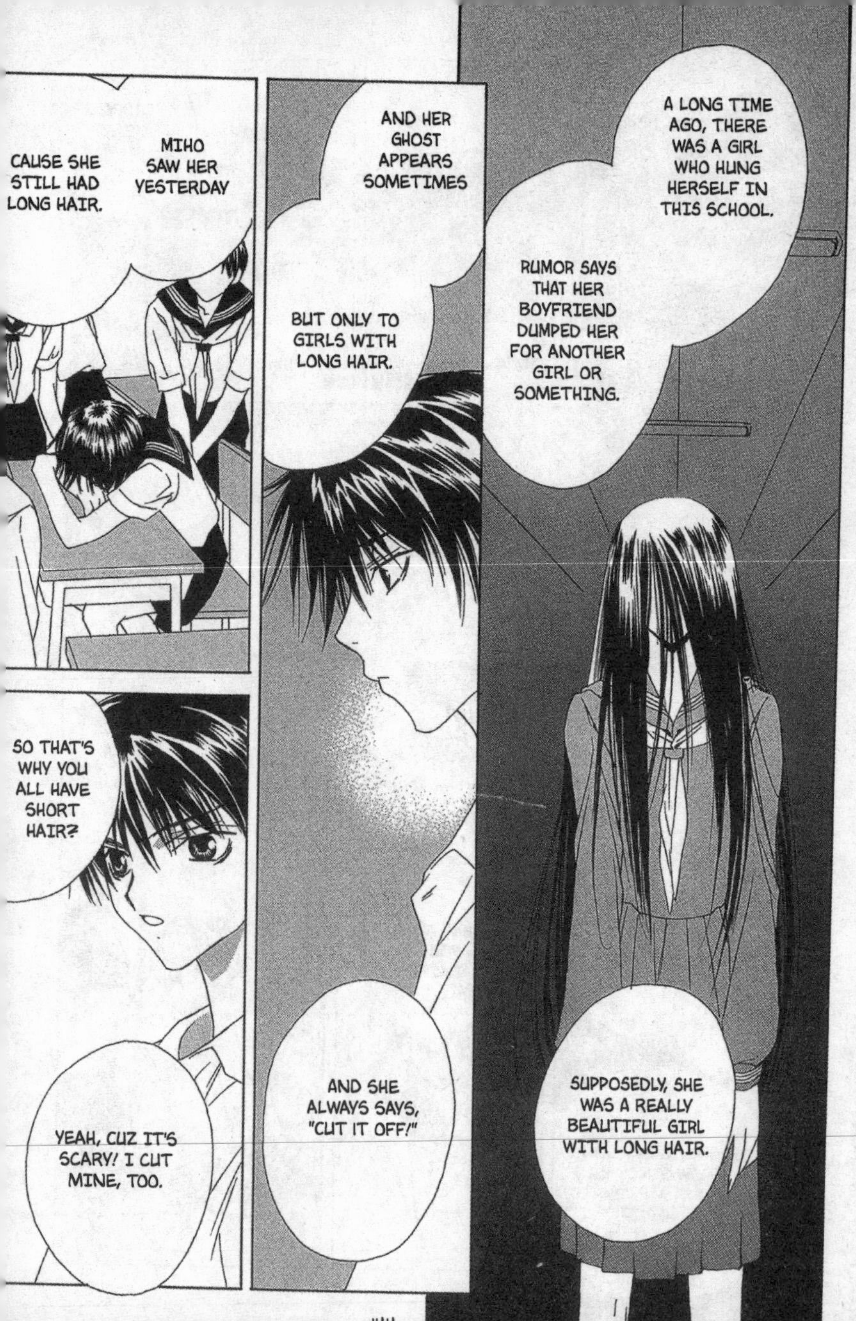
A LONG TIME AGO, THERE WAS A GIRL WHO HUNG HERSELF IN THIS SCHOOL.
RUMOR SAYS THAT HER BOYFRIEND DUMPED HER FOR ANOTHER GIRL OR SOMETHING.
SUPPOSEDLY, SHE WAS A REALLY BEAUTIFUL GIRL WITH LONG HAIR.
AND HER GHOST APPEARS SOMETIMES
BUT ONLY TO GIRLS WITH LONG HAIR.
AND SHE ALWAYS SAYS, "CUT IT OFF!"
MIHO SAW HER YESTERDAY
CAUSE SHE STILL HAD LONG HAIR.
SO THAT'S WHY YOU ALL HAVE SHORT HAIR?
YEAH, CUZ IT'S SCARY! I CUT MINE, TOO.

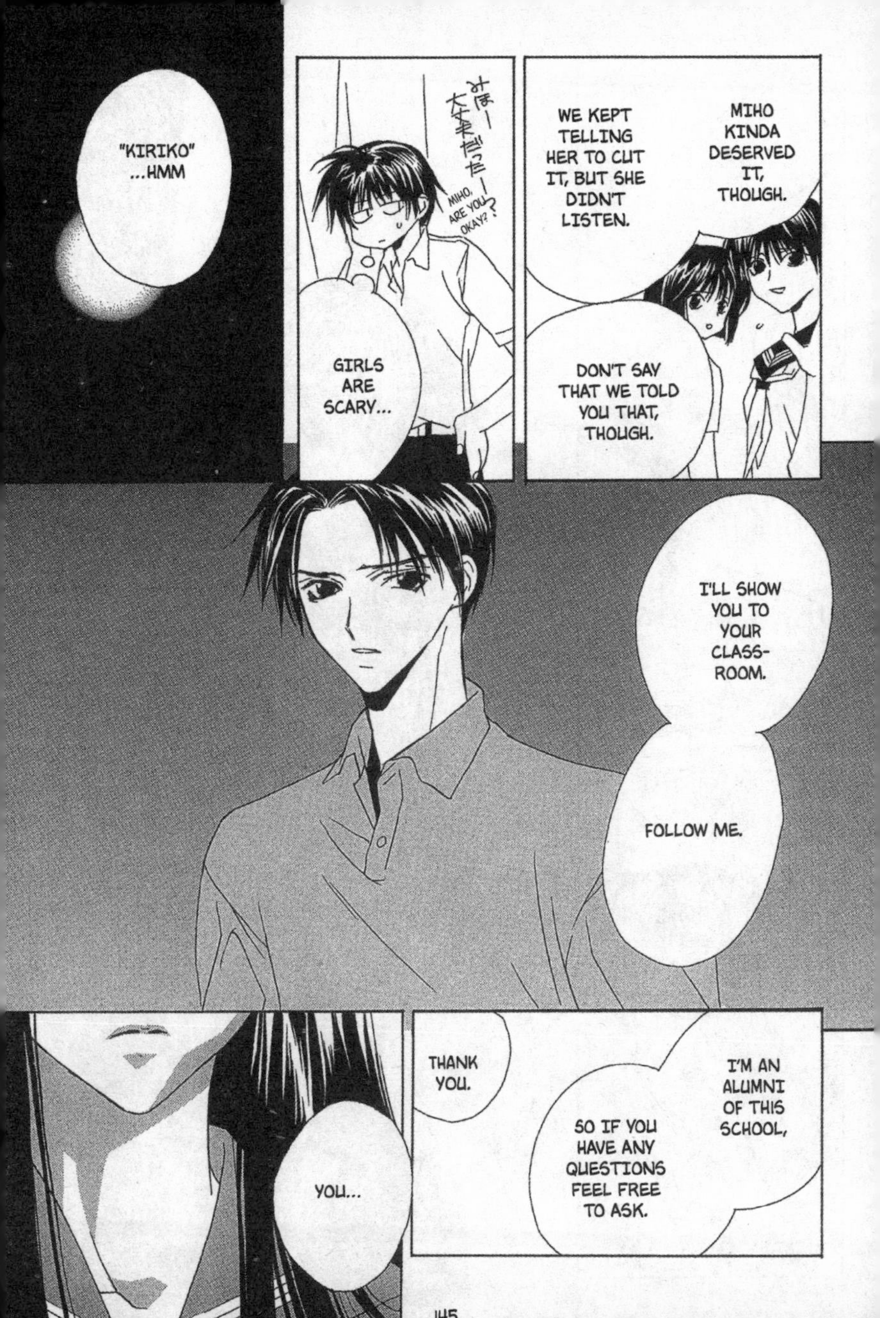
MIHO KINDA DESERVED IT, THOUGH.
WE KEPT TELLING HER TO CUT IT, BUT SHE DIDN'T LISTEN.
DON'T SAY THAT WE TOLD YOU THAT, THOUGH.
みほー大丈夫だったー!?
MIHO, ARE YOU OKAY?
GIRLS ARE SCARY...
"KIRIKO" ...HMM
I'LL SHOW YOU TO YOUR CLASS-ROOM.
FOLLOW ME.
I'M AN ALUMNI OF THIS SCHOOL,
SO IF YOU HAVE ANY QUESTIONS FEEL FREE TO ASK.
THANK YOU.
YOU...

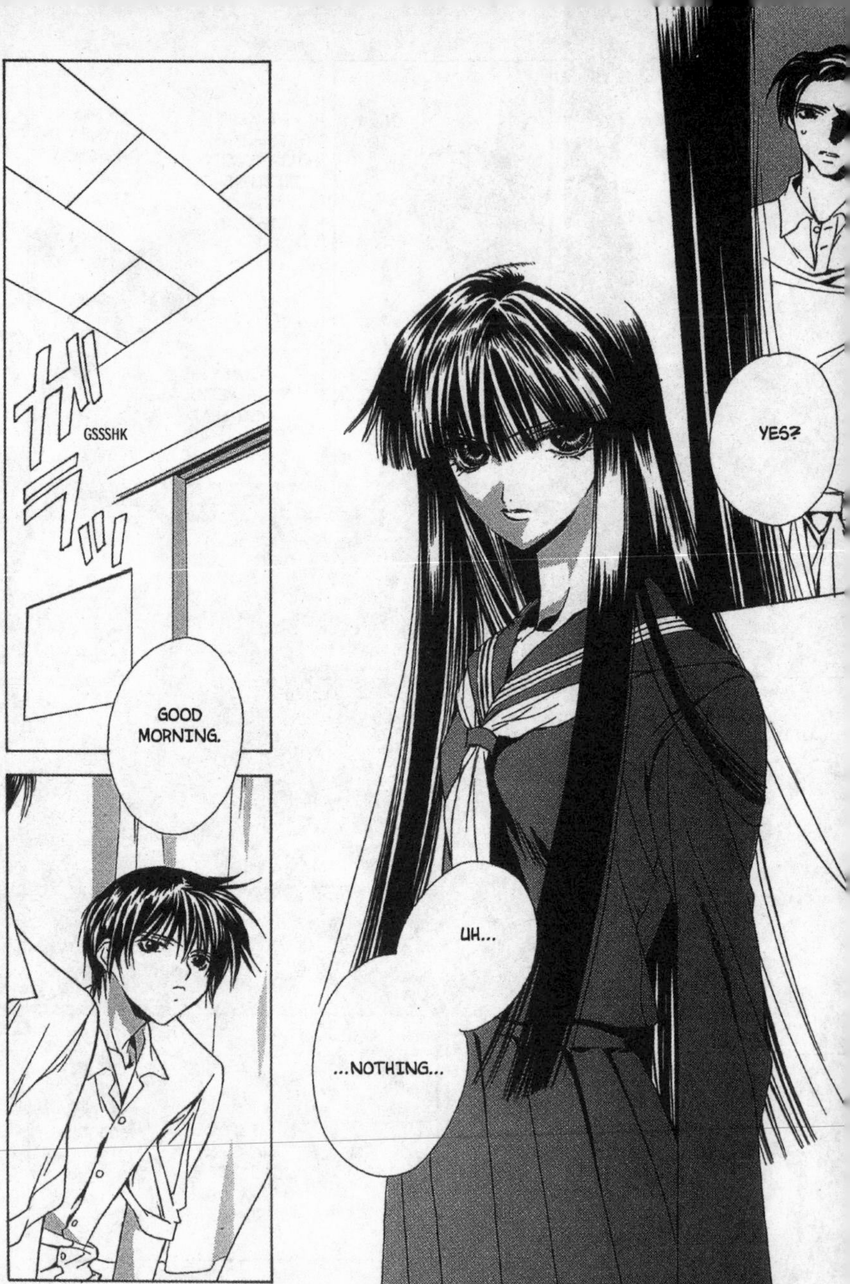
YES?
UH...
...NOTHING...
GSSSHK
GOOD MORNING.

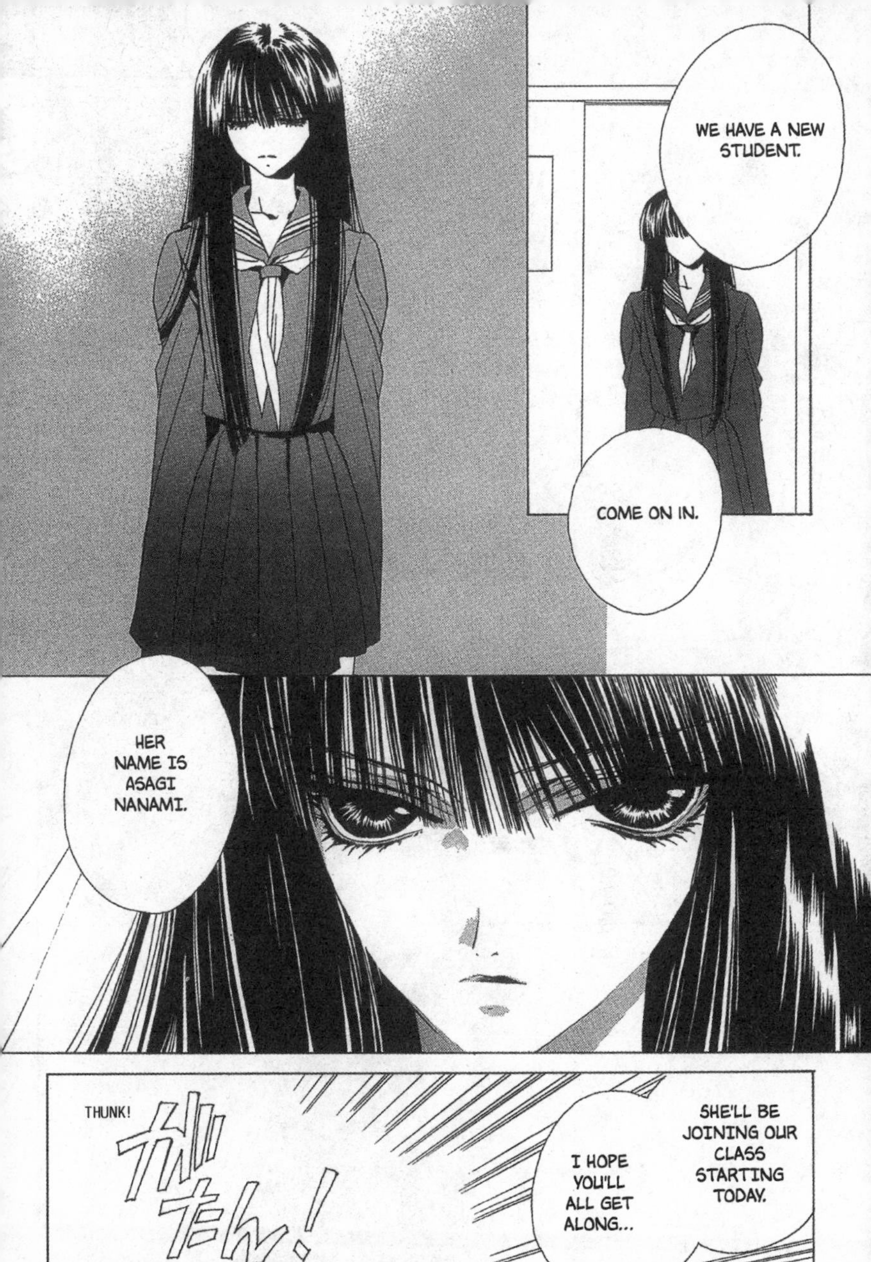
WE HAVE A NEW STUDENT.
COME ON IN.
HER NAME IS ASAGI NANAMI.
SHE'LL BE JOINING OUR CLASS STARTING TODAY.
I HOPE YOU'LL ALL GET ALONG...
THUNK!
がたん!

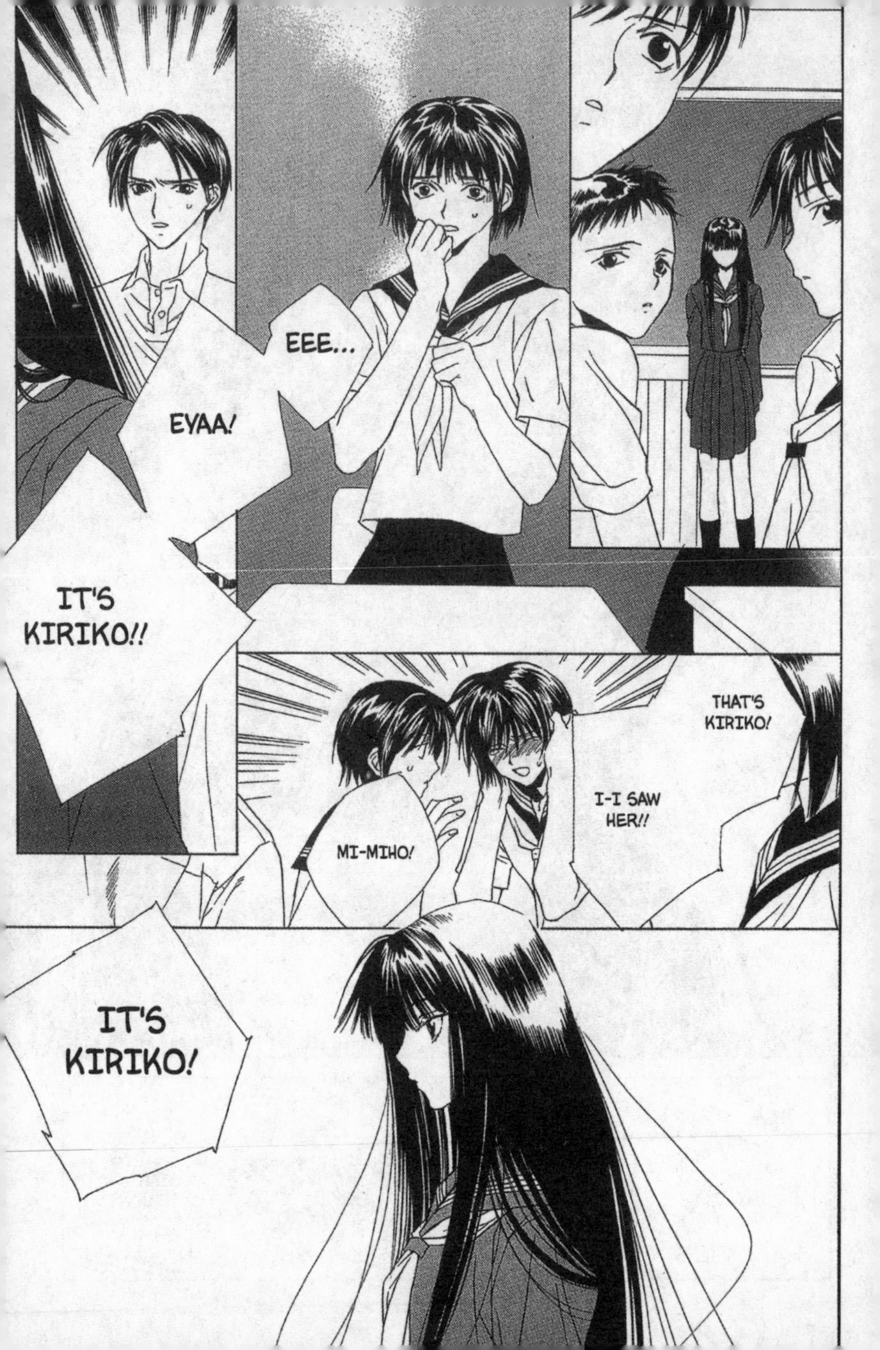
EEE...
EYAA!
IT'S KIRIKO!!
THAT'S KIRIKO!
I-I SAW HER!!
MI-MIHO!
IT'S KIRIKO!

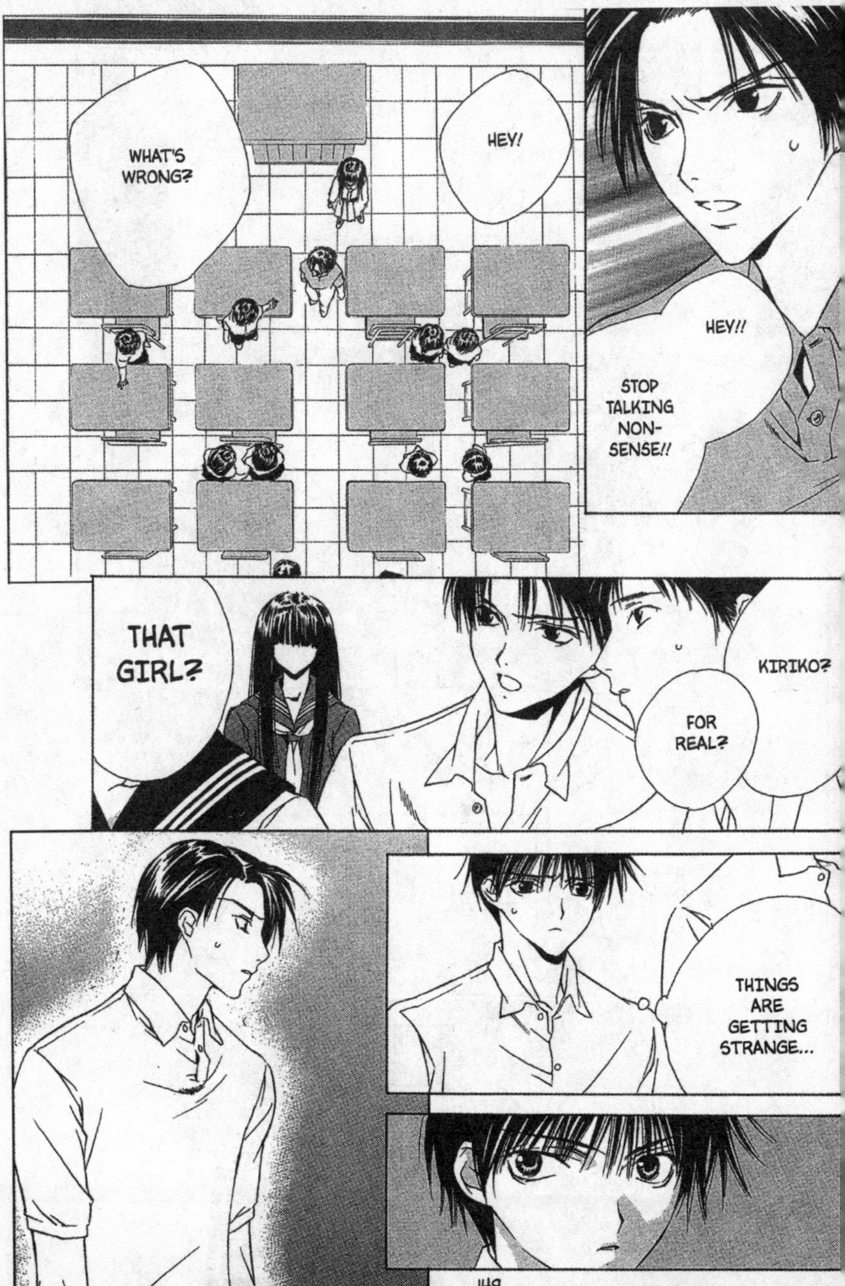
HEY!!
STOP TALKING NON-SENSE!!
HEY!
WHAT'S WRONG?
KIRIKO?
FOR REAL?
THAT GIRL?
THINGS ARE GETTING STRANGE...

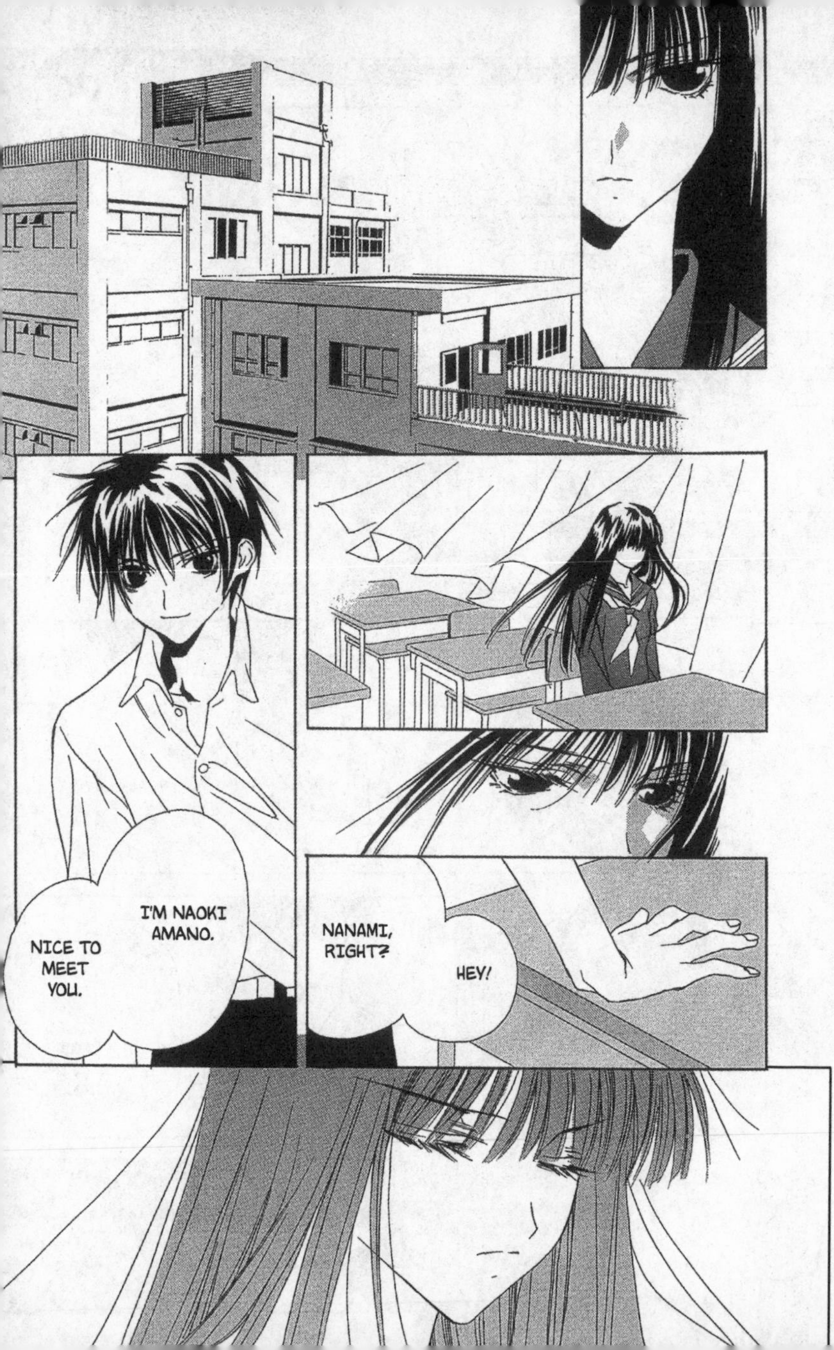
HEY!
NANAMI, RIGHT?
I'M NAOKI AMANO.
NICE TO MEET YOU.

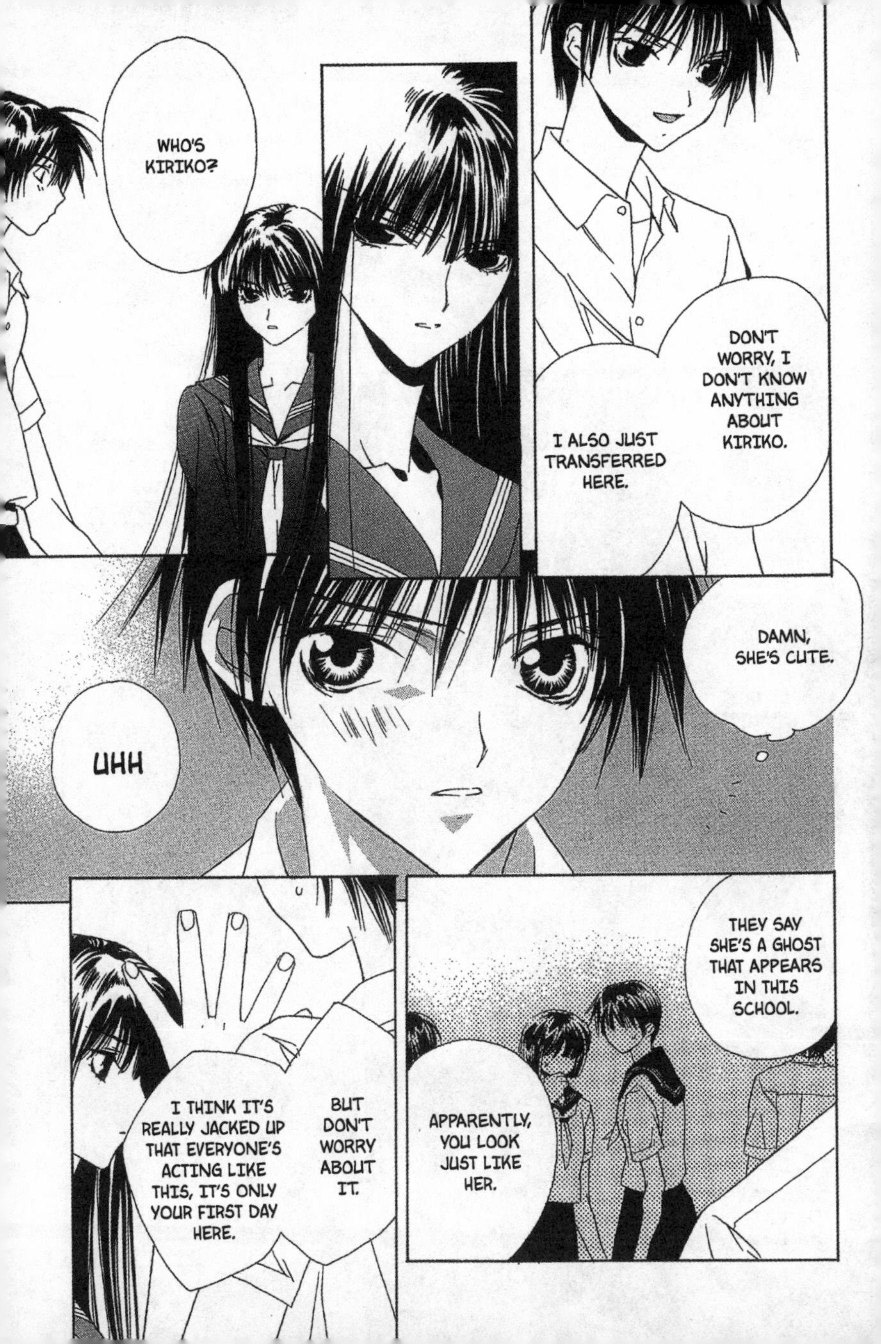
WHO'S KIRIKO?
DON'T WORRY, I DON'T KNOW ANYTHING ABOUT KIRIKO.
I ALSO JUST TRANSFERRED HERE.
DAMN, SHE'S CUTE.
UHH
THEY SAY SHE'S A GHOST THAT APPEARS IN THIS SCHOOL.
APPARENTLY, YOU LOOK JUST LIKE HER.
BUT DON'T WORRY ABOUT IT.
I THINK IT'S REALLY JACKED UP THAT EVERYONE'S ACTING LIKE THIS, IT'S ONLY YOUR FIRST DAY HERE.

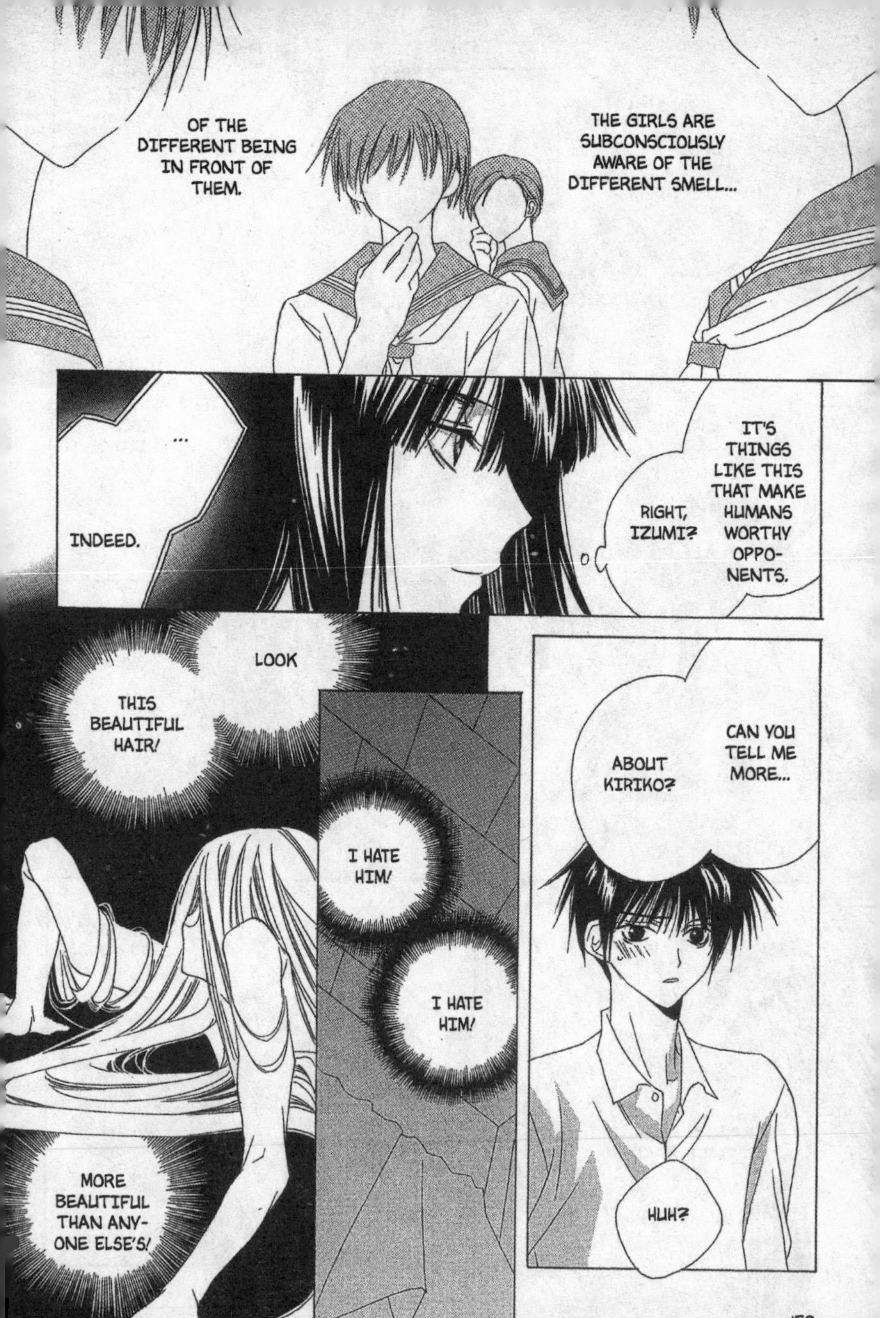
THE GIRLS ARE SUBCONSCIOUSLY AWARE OF THE DIFFERENT SMELL...
OF THE DIFFERENT BEING IN FRONT OF THEM.
IT'S THINGS LIKE THIS THAT MAKE HUMANS WORTHY OPPO-NENTS.
RIGHT, IZUMI?
...
INDEED.
CAN YOU TELL ME MORE...
ABOUT KIRIKO?
HUH?
LOOK
THIS BEAUTIFUL HAIR!
I HATE HIM!
I HATE HIM!
MORE BEAUTIFUL THAN ANY-ONE ELSE'S!

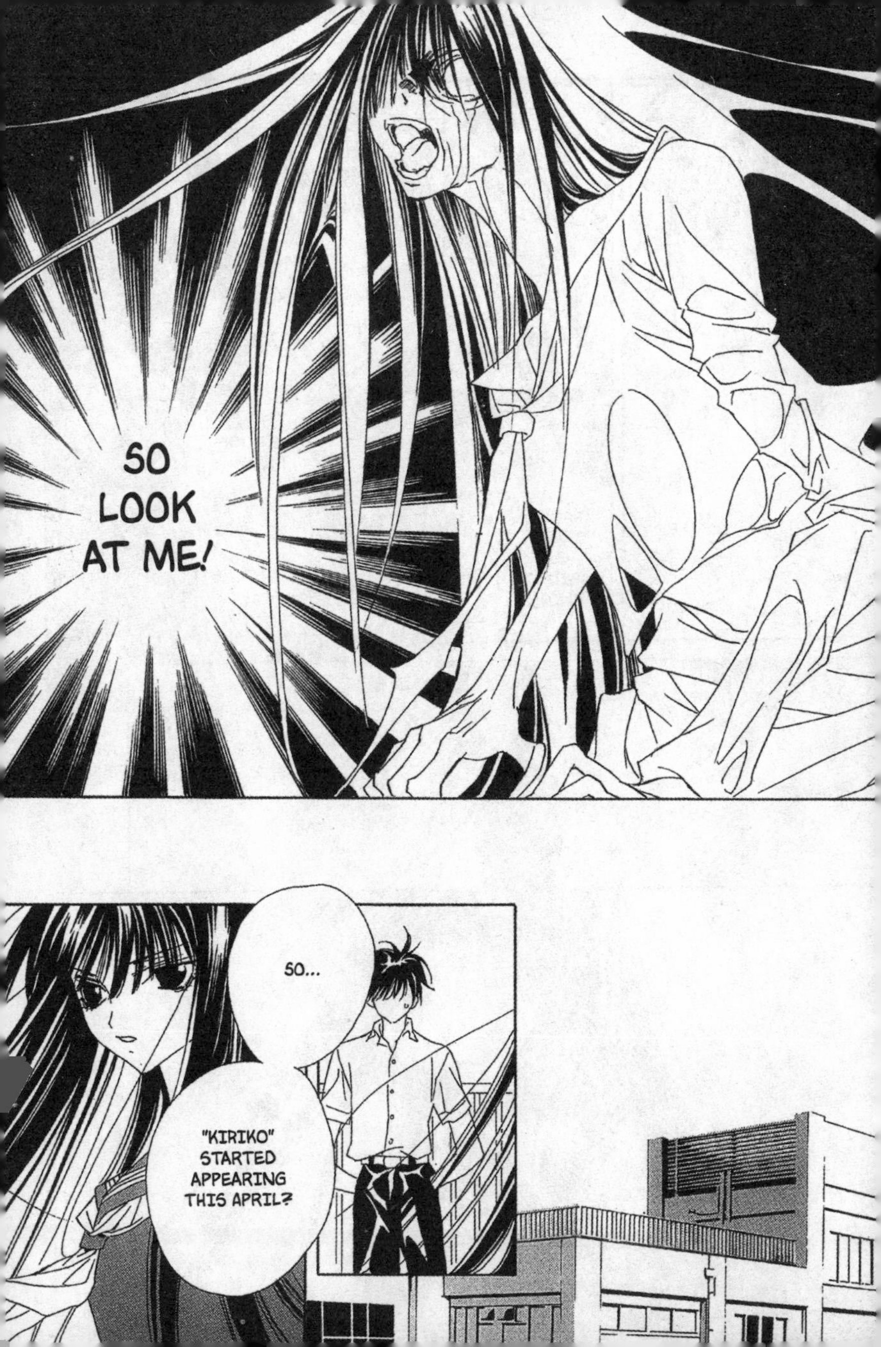
SO LOOK AT ME!
SO...
"KIRIKO" STARTED APPEARING THIS APRIL?

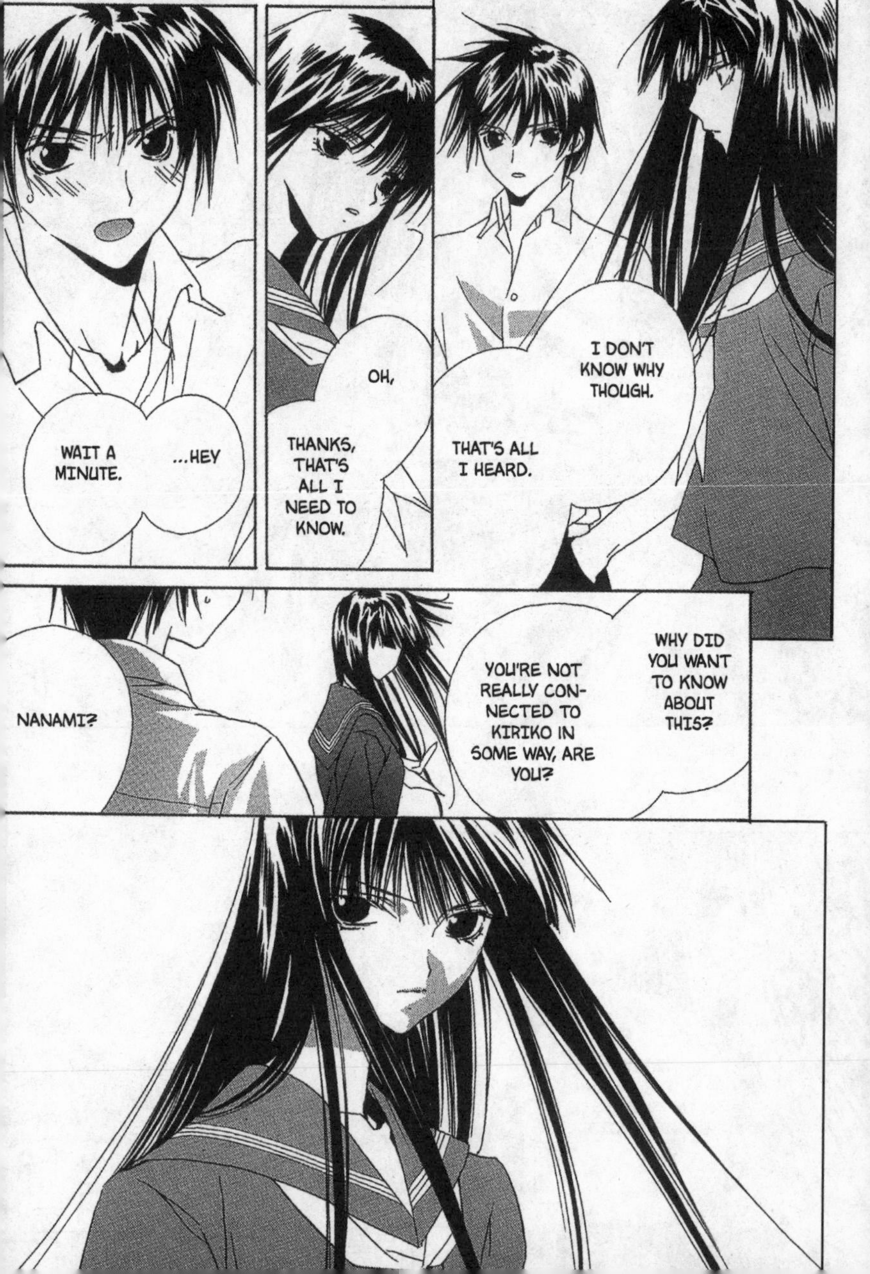
I DON'T KNOW WHY THOUGH.
THAT'S ALL I HEARD.
OH,
THANKS, THAT'S ALL I NEED TO KNOW.
...HEY
WAIT A MINUTE.
WHY DID YOU WANT TO KNOW ABOUT THIS?
YOU'RE NOT REALLY CON-NECTED TO KIRIKO IN SOME WAY, ARE YOU?
NANAMI?

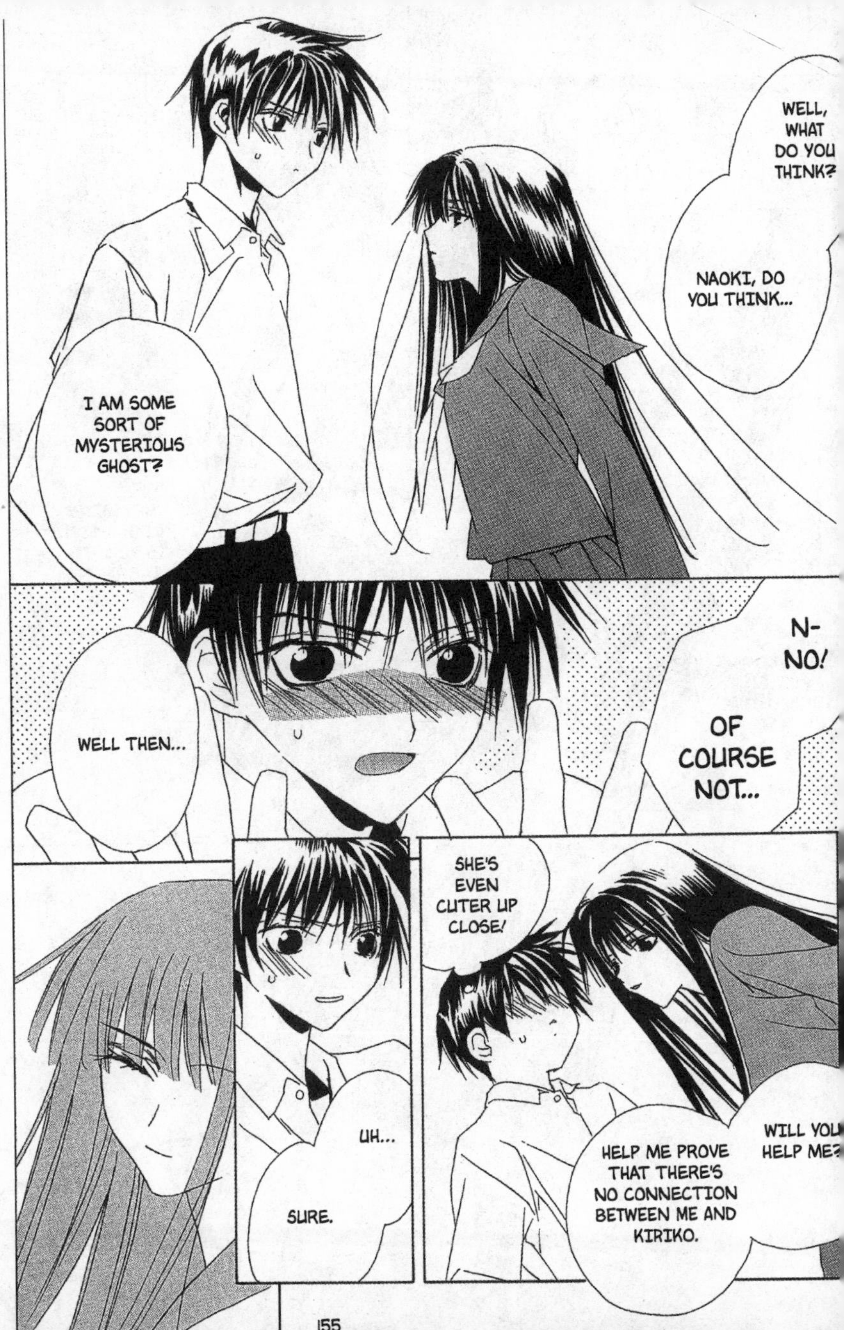
WELL, WHAT DO YOU THINK?
NAOKI, DO YOU THINK...
I AM SOME SORT OF MYSTERIOUS GHOST?
N- NO!
OF COURSE NOT...
WELL THEN...
WILL YOU HELP ME?
HELP ME PROVE THAT THERE'S NO CONNECTION BETWEEN ME AND KIRIKO.
SHE'S EVEN CUTER UP CLOSE!
UH...
SURE.

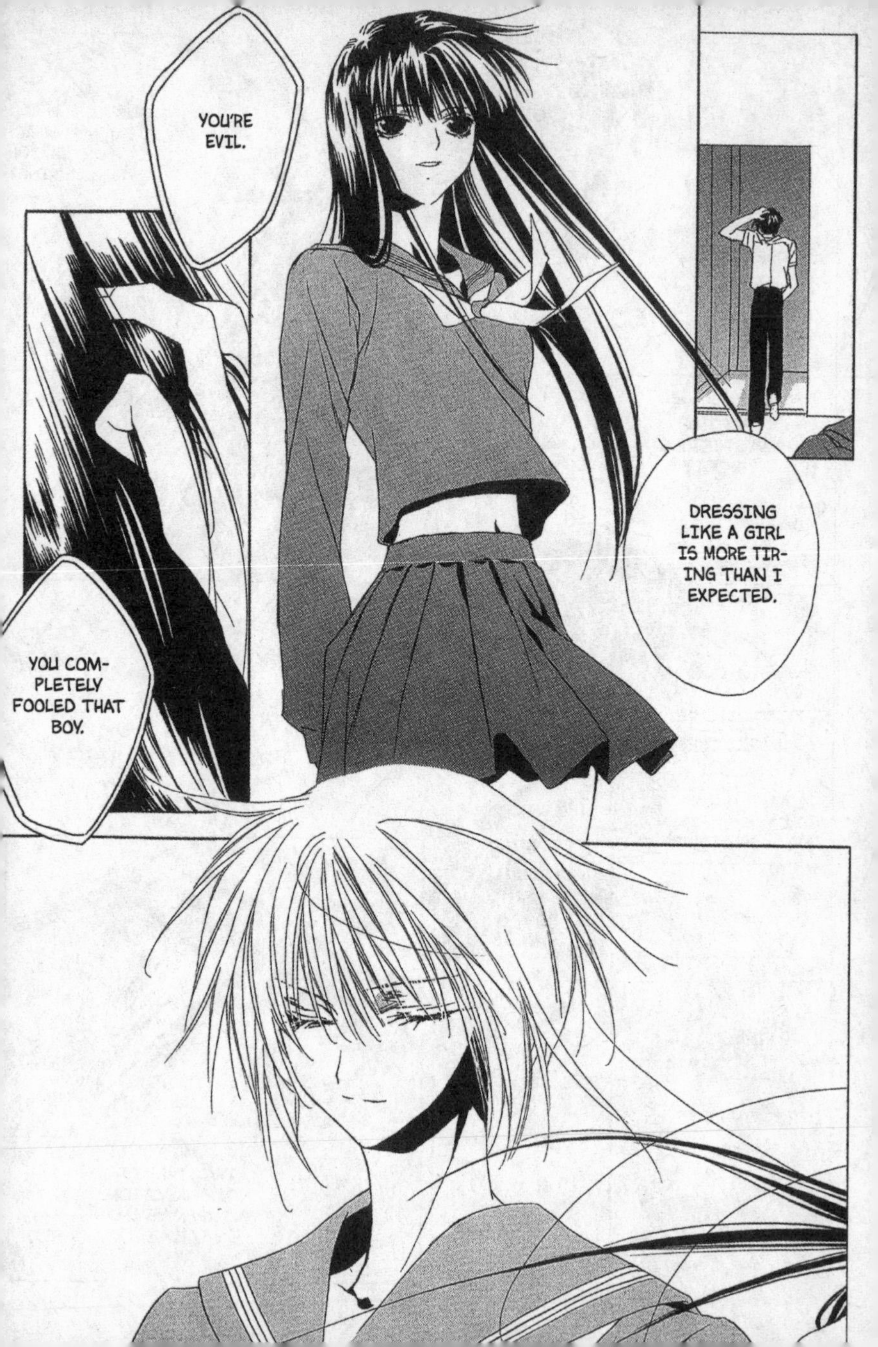
DRESSING LIKE A GIRL IS MORE TIR-ING THAN I EXPECTED.
YOU'RE EVIL.
YOU COM-PLETELY FOOLED THAT BOY.

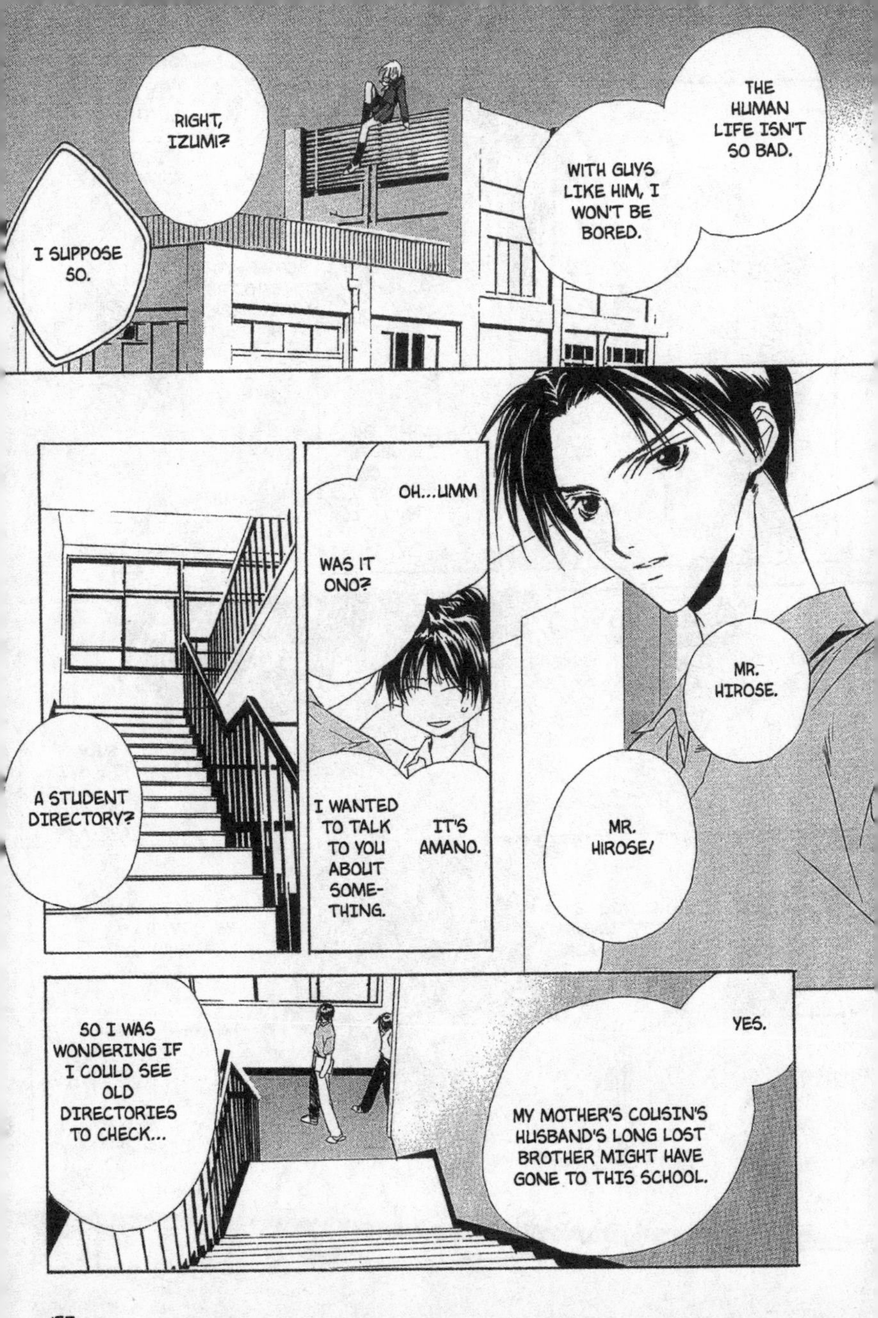
THE HUMAN LIFE ISN'T SO BAD.
WITH GUYS LIKE HIM, I WON'T BE BORED.
RIGHT, IZUMI?
I SUPPOSE SO.
MR. HIROSE.
MR. HIROSE!
OH...UMM
WAS IT ONO?
IT'S AMANO.
I WANTED TO TALK TO YOU ABOUT SOME-THING.
A STUDENT DIRECTORY?
YES.
MY MOTHER'S COUSIN'S HUSBAND'S LONG LOST BROTHER MIGHT HAVE GONE TO THIS SCHOOL.
SO I WAS WONDERING IF I COULD SEE OLD DIRECTORIES TO CHECK...

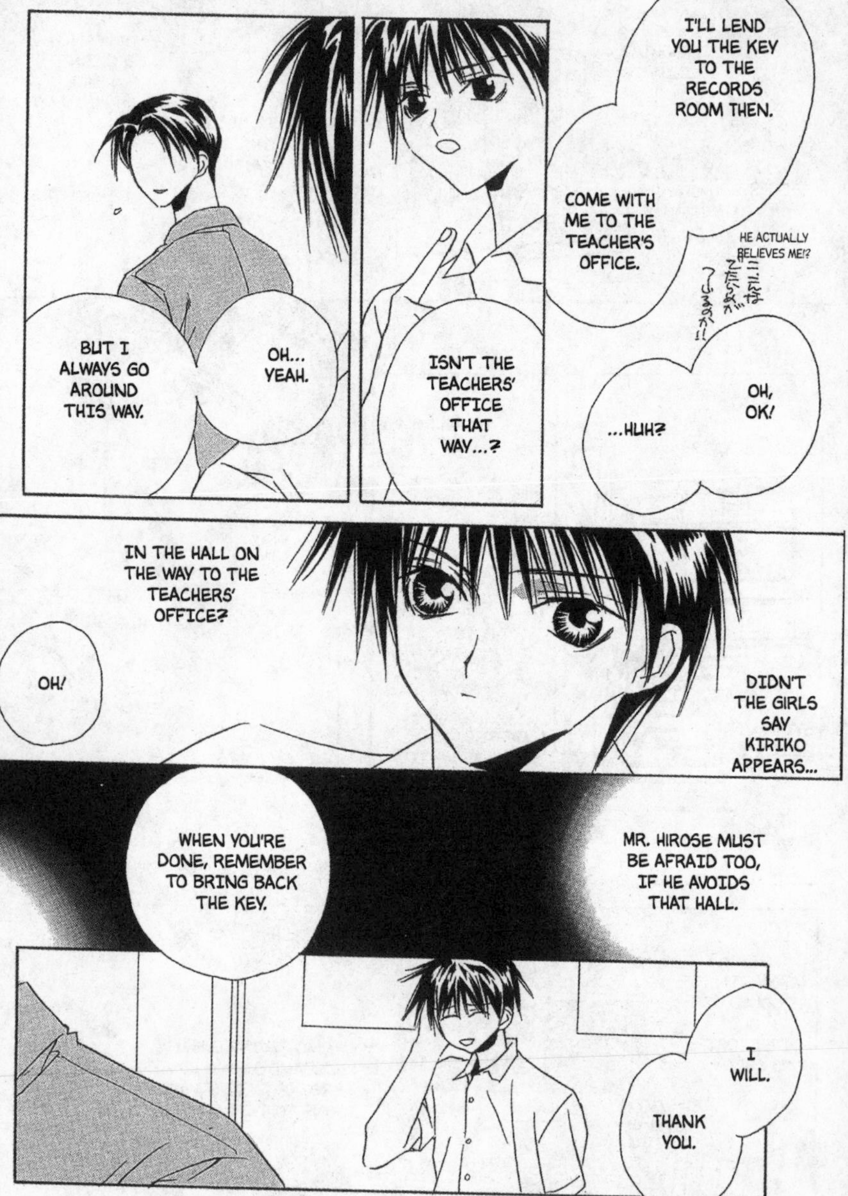
I'LL LEND YOU THE KEY TO THE RECORDS ROOM THEN.
COME WITH ME TO THE TEACHER'S OFFICE.
HE ACTUALLY BELIEVES ME!?
OH, OK!
...HUH?
ISN'T THE TEACHERS' OFFICE THAT WAY...?
OH... YEAH.
BUT I ALWAYS GO AROUND THIS WAY.
DIDN'T THE GIRLS SAY KIRIKO APPEARS...
IN THE HALL ON THE WAY TO THE TEACHERS' OFFICE?
OH!
MR. HIROSE MUST BE AFRAID TOO, IF HE AVOIDS THAT HALL.
WHEN YOU'RE DONE, REMEMBER TO BRING BACK THE KEY.
I WILL.
THANK YOU.

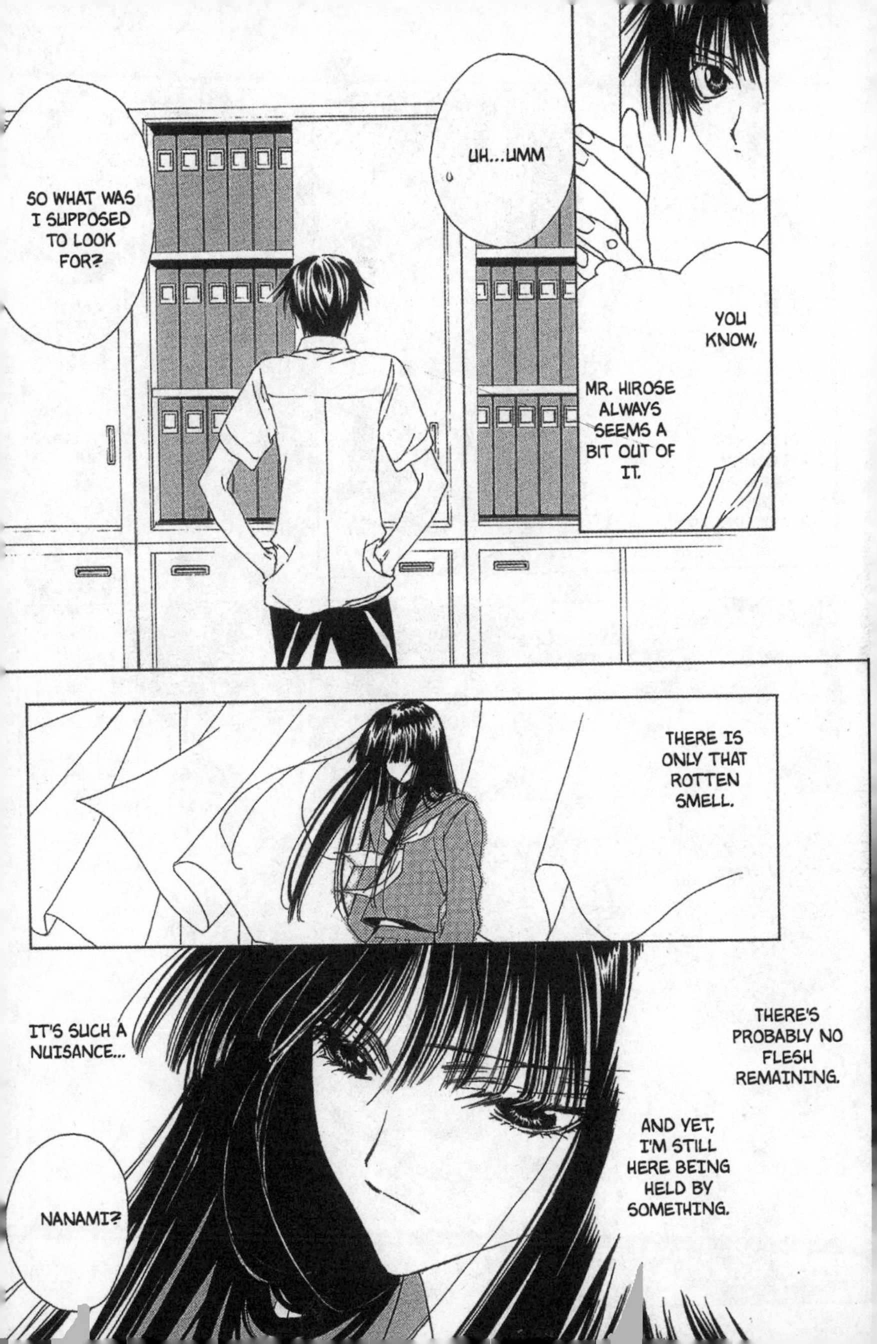
YOU KNOW,
MR. HIROSE ALWAYS SEEMS A BIT OUT OF IT.
UH...UMM
SO WHAT WAS I SUPPOSED TO LOOK FOR?
THERE IS ONLY THAT ROTTEN SMELL.
THERE'S PROBABLY NO FLESH REMAINING.
AND YET, I'M STILL HERE BEING HELD BY SOMETHING.
IT'S SUCH A NUISANCE...
NANAMI?

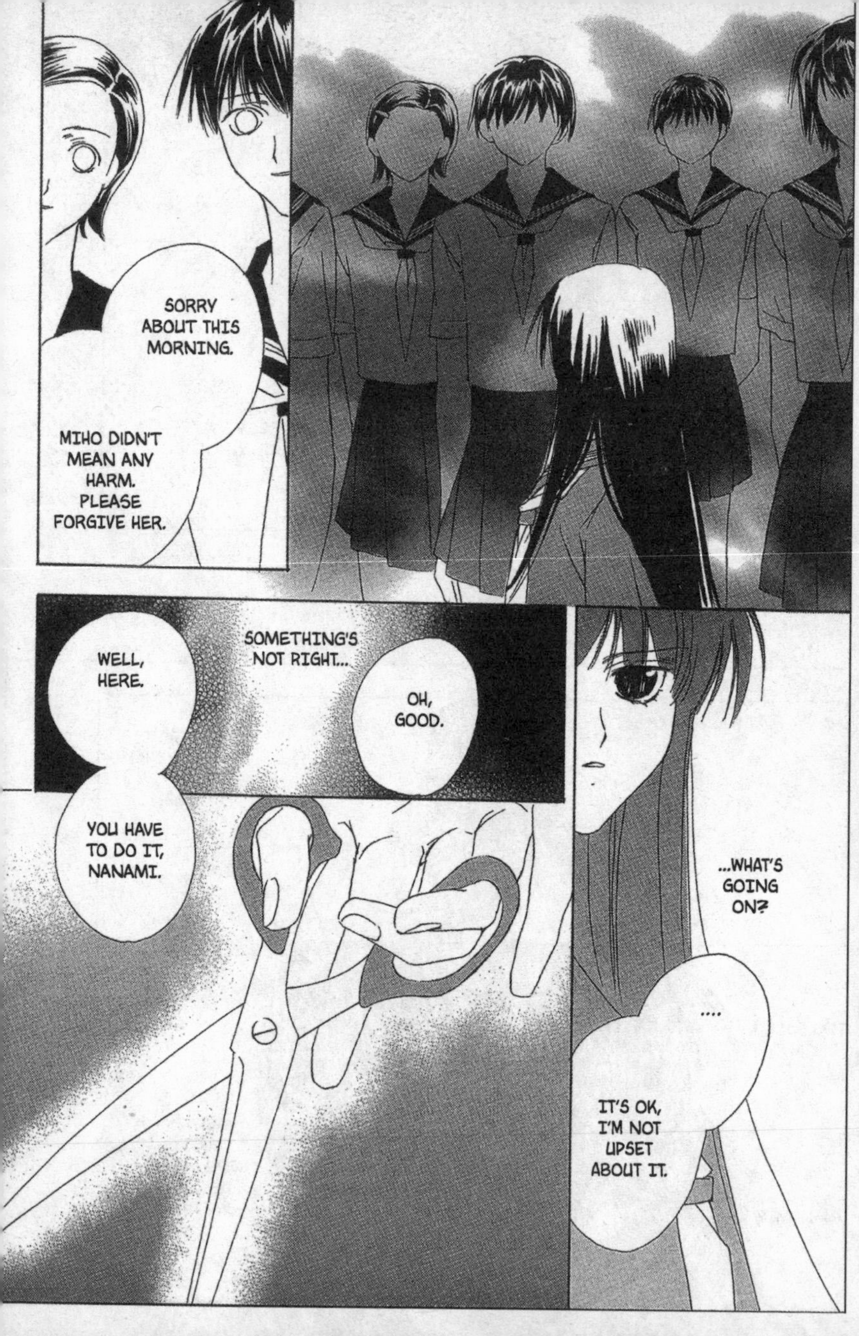
SORRY ABOUT THIS MORNING.
MIHO DIDN'T MEAN ANY HARM. PLEASE FORGIVE HER.
....
IT'S OK, I'M NOT UPSET ABOUT IT.
OH, GOOD.
SOMETHING'S NOT RIGHT...
...WHAT'S GOING ON?
WELL, HERE.
YOU HAVE TO DO IT, NANAMI.

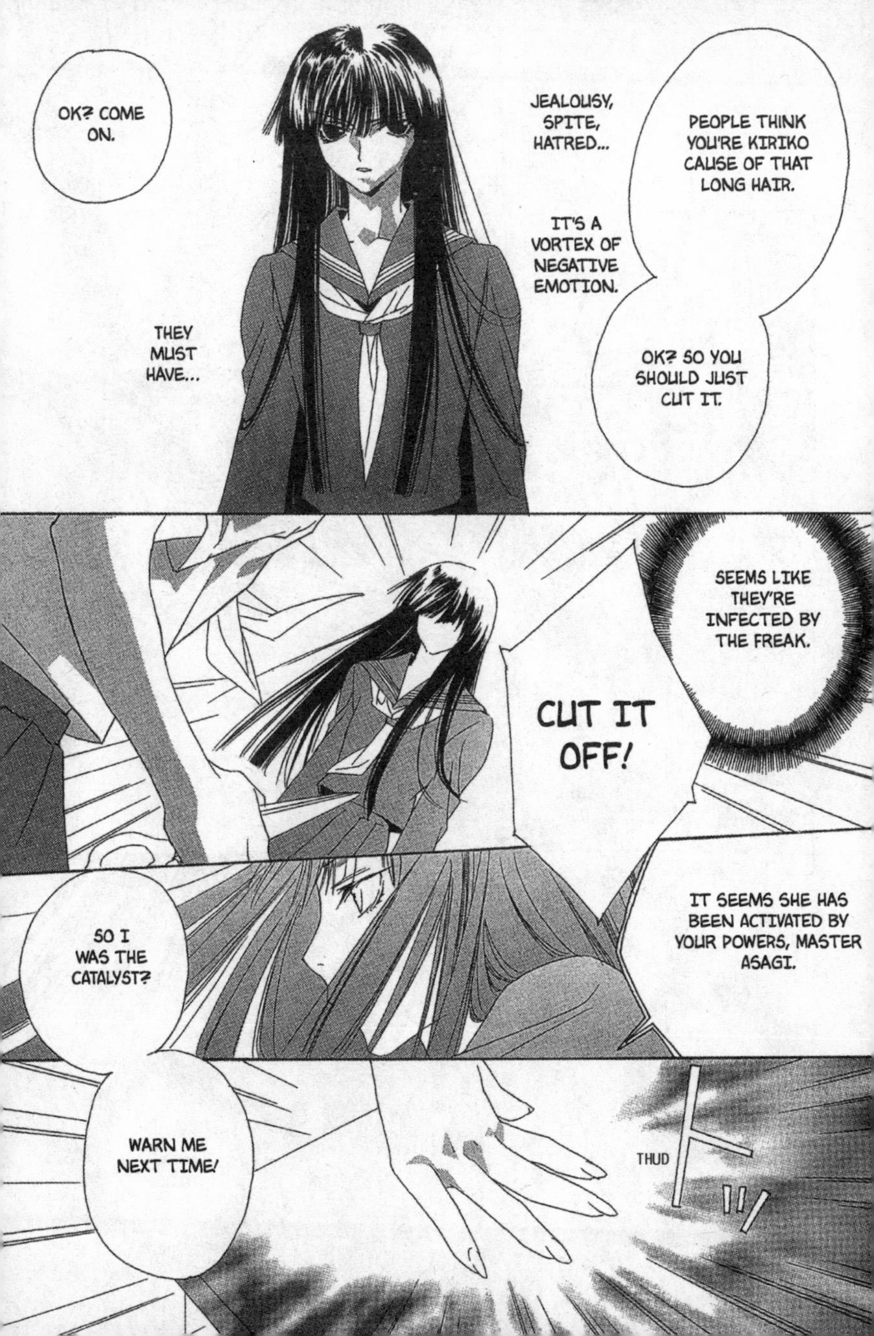
PEOPLE THINK YOU'RE KIRIKO CAUSE OF THAT LONG HAIR.
OK? SO YOU SHOULD JUST CUT IT.
JEALOUSY, SPITE, HATRED...
IT'S A VORTEX OF NEGATIVE EMOTION.
THEY MUST HAVE...
OK? COME ON.
SEEMS LIKE THEY'RE INFECTED BY THE FREAK.
CUT IT OFF!
IT SEEMS SHE HAS BEEN ACTIVATED BY YOUR POWERS, MASTER ASAGI.
SO I WAS THE CATALYST?
THUD
WARN ME NEXT TIME!

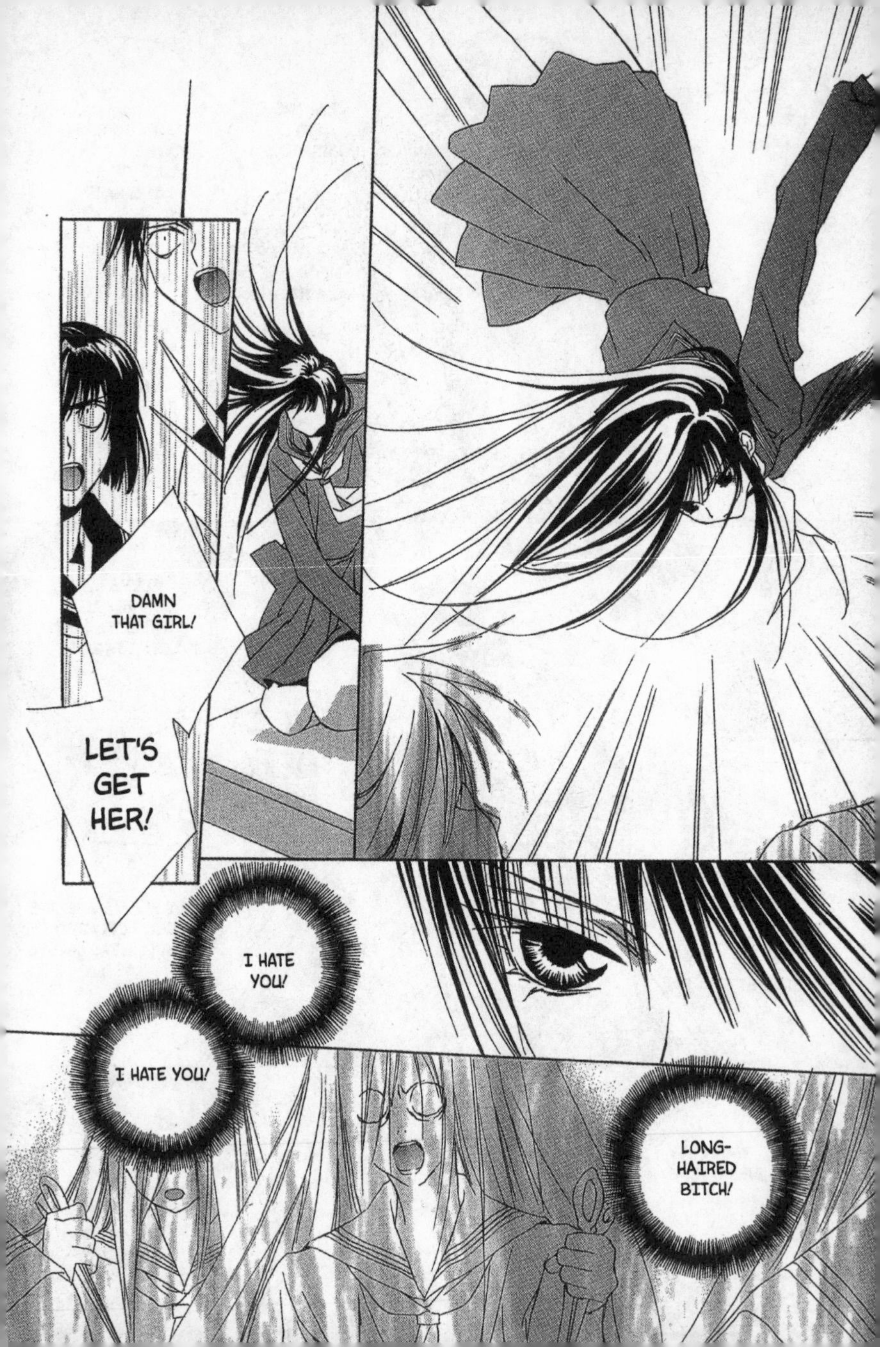
DAMN THAT GIRL!
LET'S GET HER!
I HATE YOU!
LONG-HAIRED BITCH!
I HATE YOU!

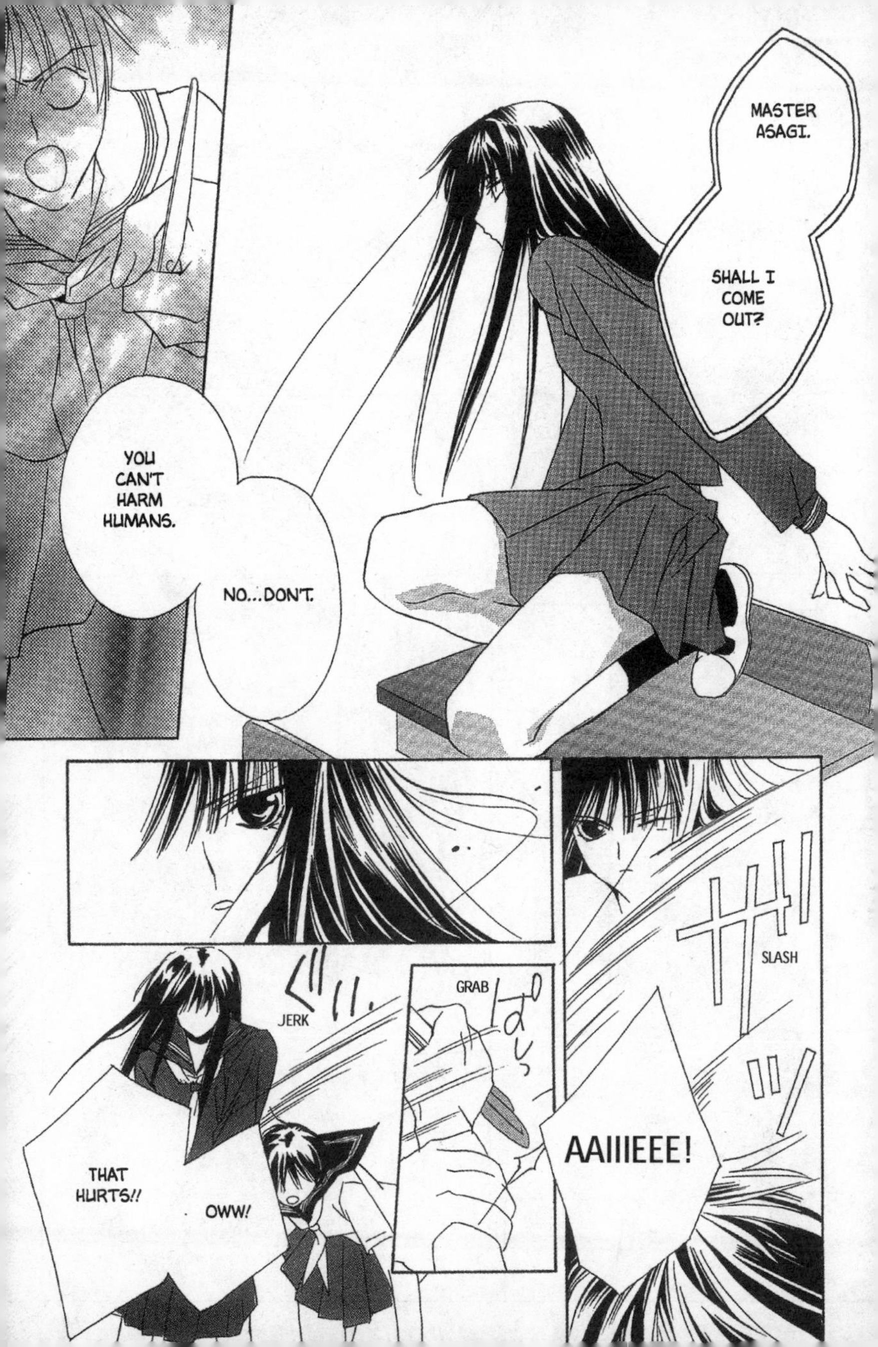
MASTER ASAGI.
SHALL I COME OUT?
NO...DON'T.
YOU CAN'T HARM HUMANS.
SLASH
AAIIIEEE!
GRAB
JERK
OWW!
THAT HURTS!!

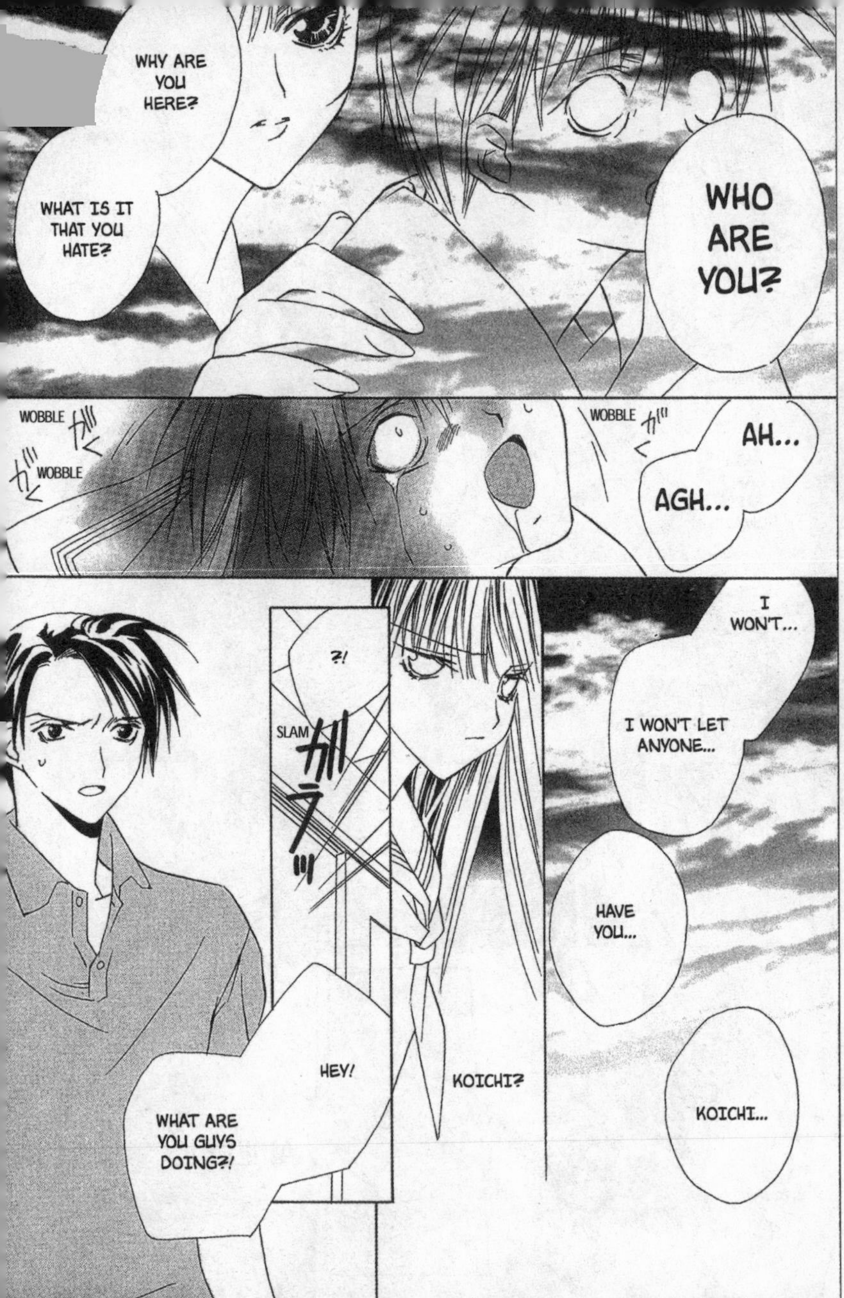
WHO ARE YOU?
WHY ARE YOU HERE?
WHAT IS IT THAT YOU HATE?
WOBBLE
AH...
AGH...
WOBBLE
WOBBLE
I WON'T...
I WON'T LET ANYONE...
HAVE YOU...
KOICHI...
SLAM
?!
KOICHI?
HEY!
WHAT ARE YOU GUYS DOING?!

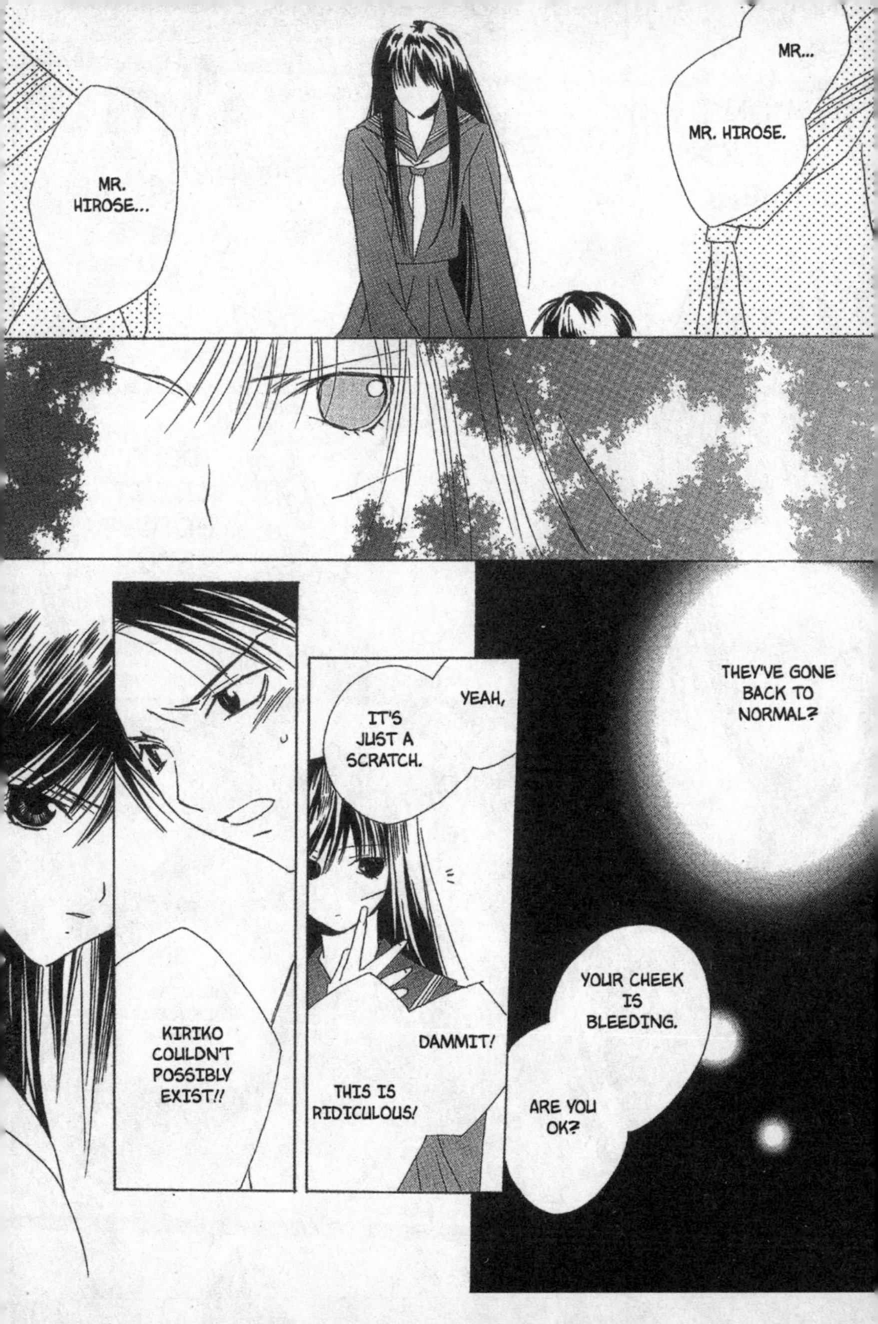
MR...
MR. HIROSE.
MR. HIROSE...
THEY'VE GONE BACK TO NORMAL?
YOUR CHEEK IS BLEEDING.
ARE YOU OK?
YEAH,
IT'S JUST A SCRATCH.
DAMMIT!
THIS IS RIDICULOUS!
KIRIKO COULDN'T POSSIBLY EXIST!!

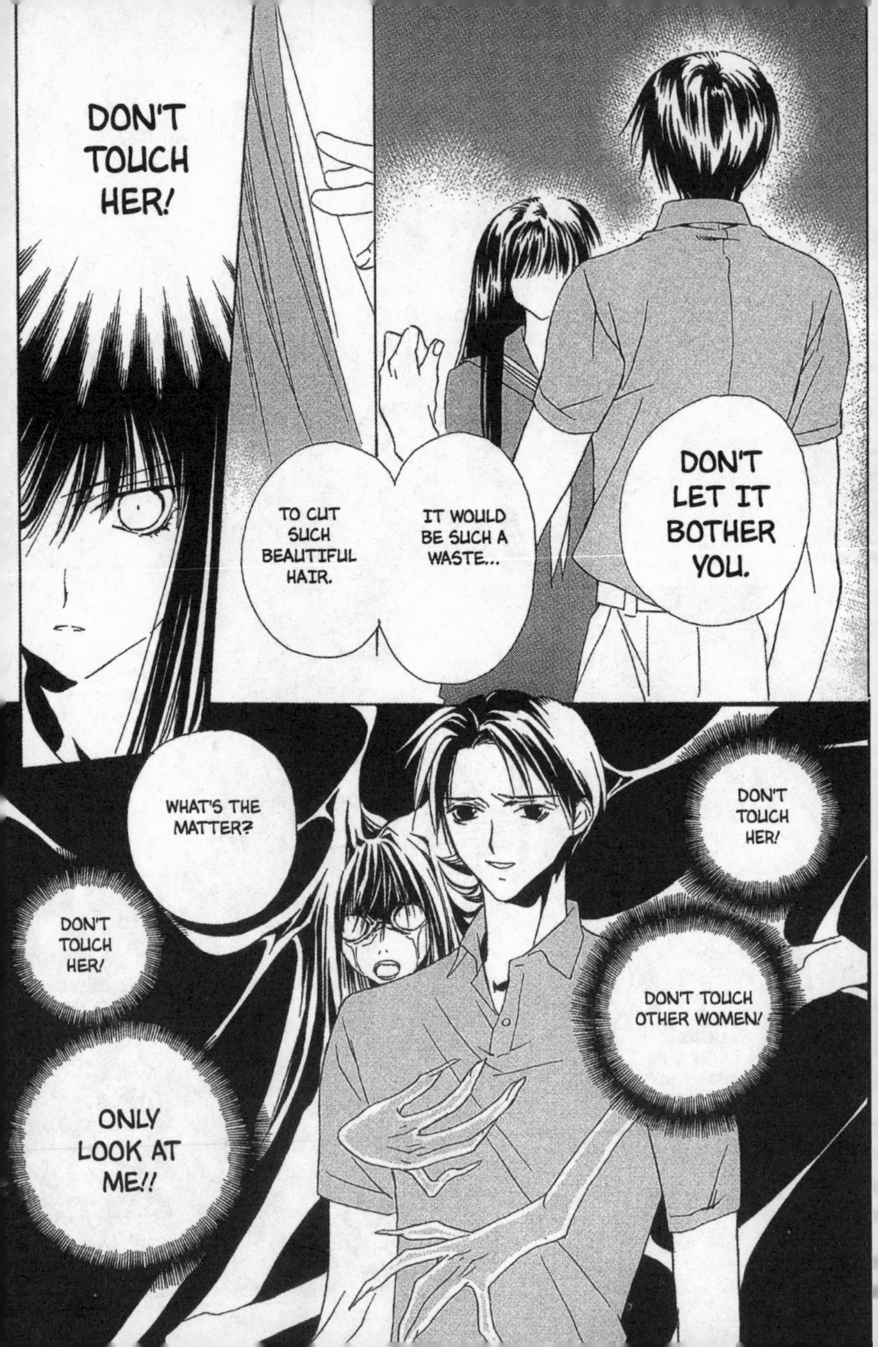
DON'T LET IT BOTHER YOU.
IT WOULD BE SUCH A WASTE...
TO CUT SUCH BEAUTIFUL HAIR.
DON'T TOUCH HER!
WHAT'S THE MATTER?
DON'T TOUCH HER!
DON'T TOUCH HER!
DON'T TOUCH OTHER WOMEN!
ONLY LOOK AT ME!!

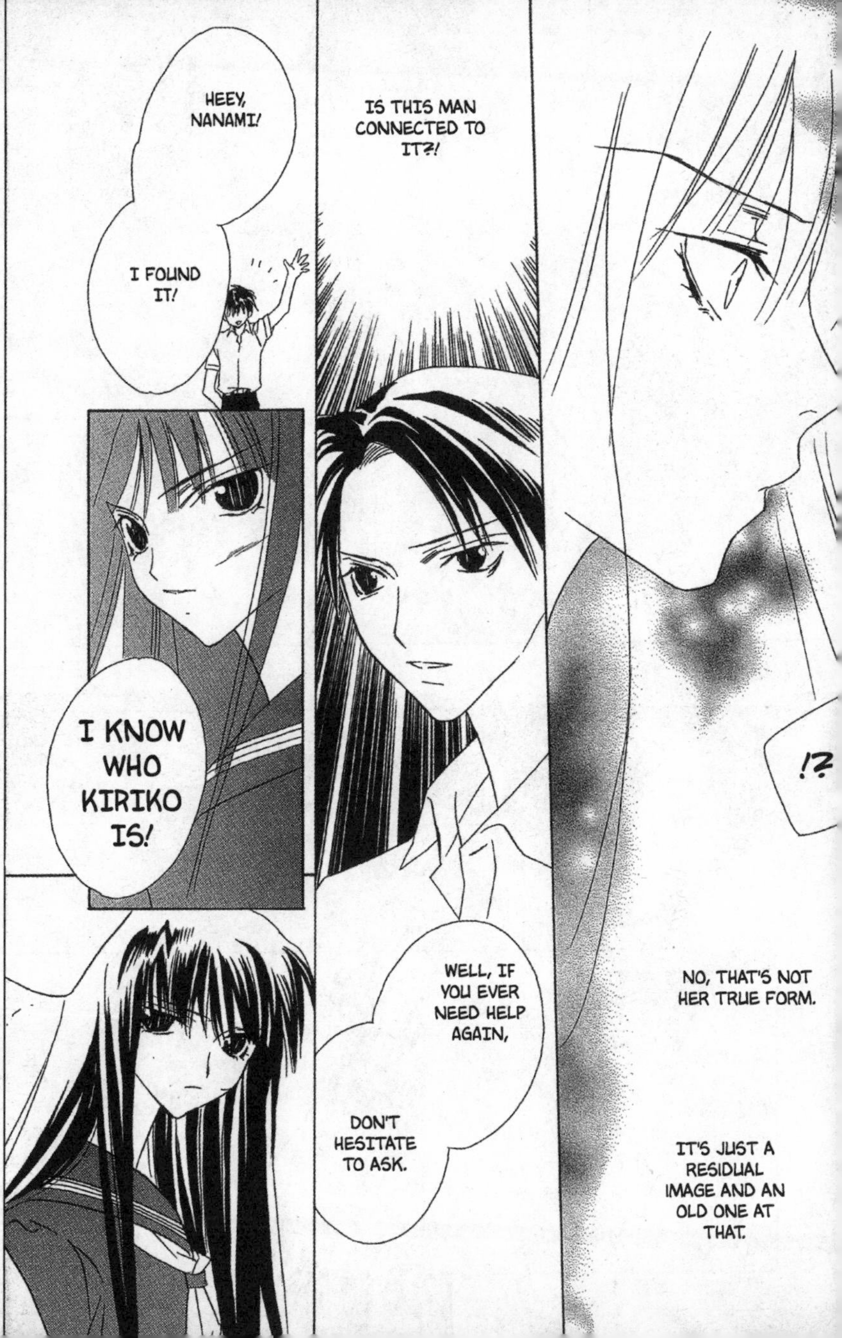
!?
NO, THAT'S NOT HER TRUE FORM.
IT'S JUST A RESIDUAL IMAGE AND AN OLD ONE AT THAT.
IS THIS MAN CONNECTED TO IT?!
WELL, IF YOU EVER NEED HELP AGAIN,
DON'T HESITATE TO ASK.
HEEY, NANAMI!
I FOUND IT!
I KNOW WHO KIRIKO IS!

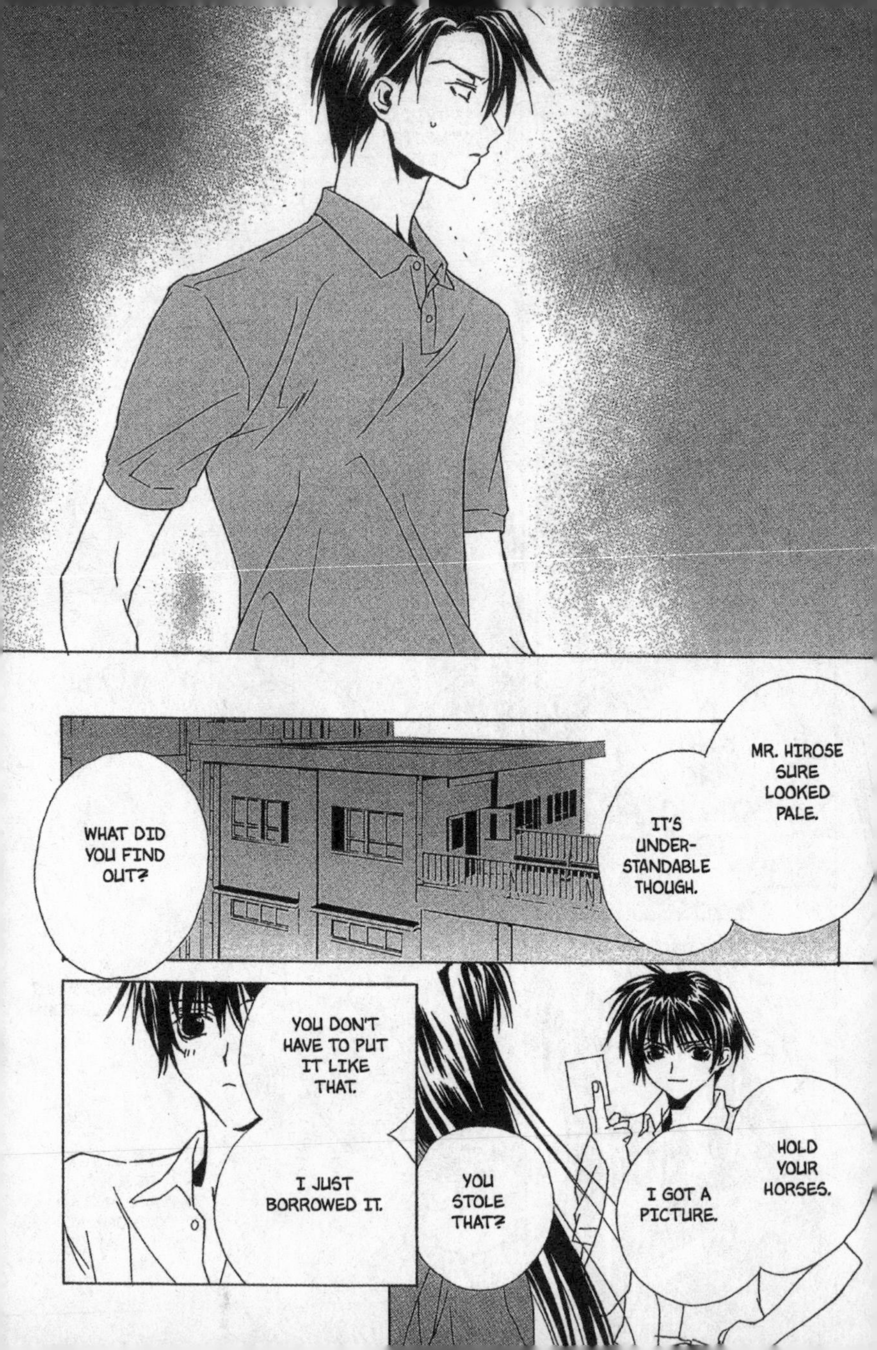
MR. HIROSE SURE LOOKED PALE.
IT'S UNDER-STANDABLE THOUGH.
WHAT DID YOU FIND OUT?
HOLD YOUR HORSES.
I GOT A PICTURE.
YOU STOLE THAT?
YOU DON'T HAVE TO PUT IT LIKE THAT.
I JUST BORROWED IT.

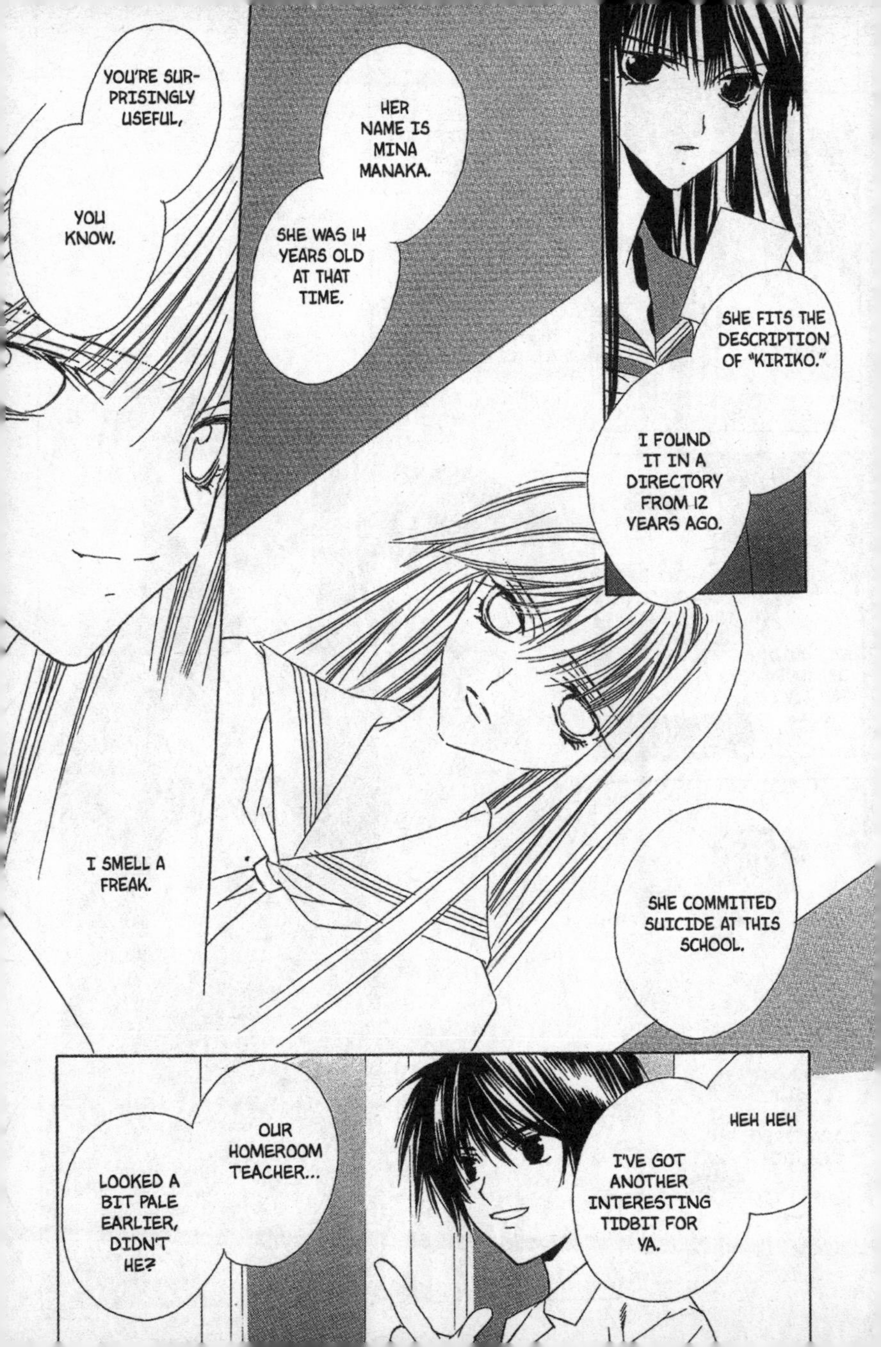
SHE FITS THE DESCRIPTION OF "KIRIKO."
I FOUND IT IN A DIRECTORY FROM 12 YEARS AGO.
HER NAME IS MINA MANAKA.
SHE WAS 14 YEARS OLD AT THAT TIME.
SHE COMMITTED SUICIDE AT THIS SCHOOL.
YOU'RE SURPRISINGLY USEFUL,
YOU KNOW.
I SMELL A FREAK.
HEH HEH
I'VE GOT ANOTHER INTERESTING TIDBIT FOR YA.
OUR HOMEROOM TEACHER...
LOOKED A BIT PALE EARLIER, DIDN'T HE?

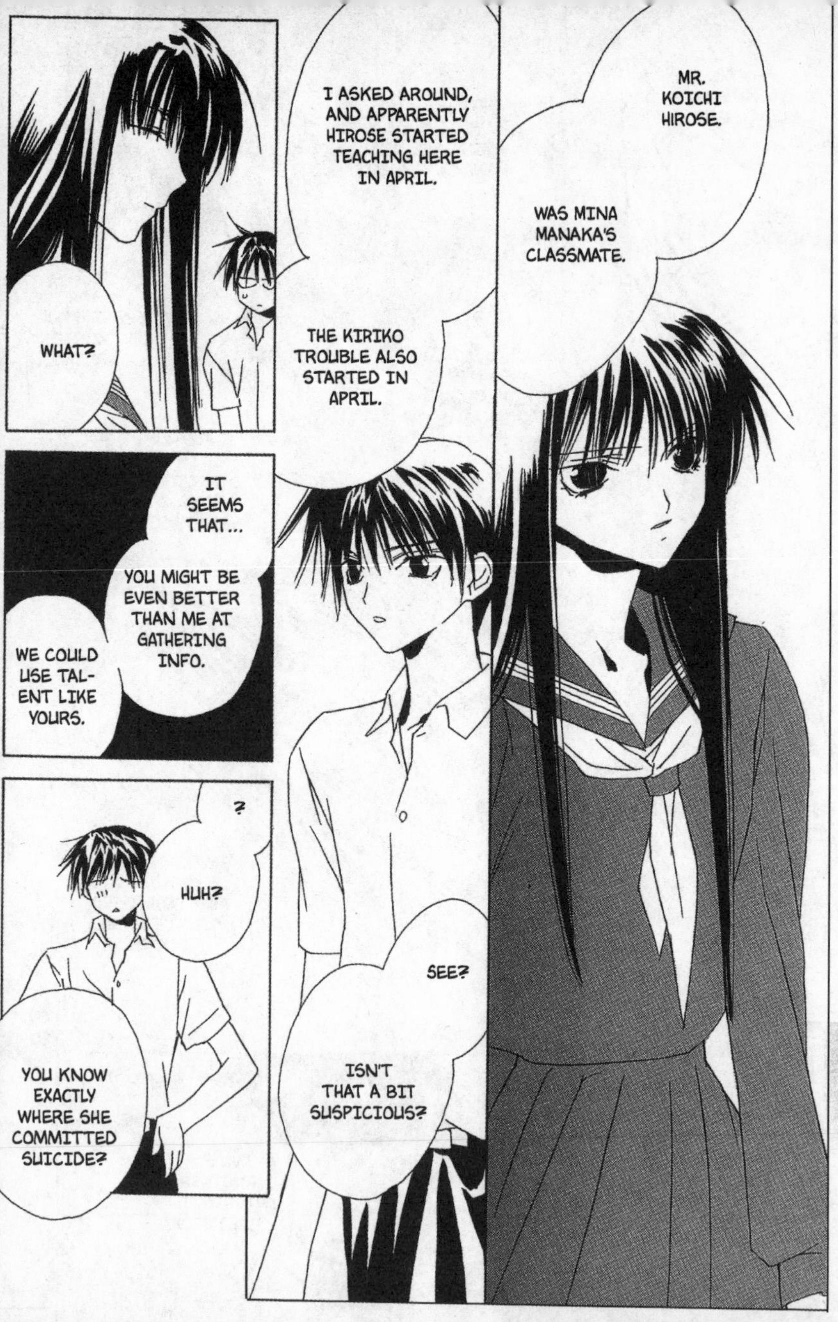
MR. KOICHI HIROSE.
WAS MINA MANAKA'S CLASSMATE.
I ASKED AROUND, AND APPARENTLY HIROSE STARTED TEACHING HERE IN APRIL.
THE KIRIKO TROUBLE ALSO STARTED IN APRIL.
SEE?
ISN'T THAT A BIT SUSPICIOUS?
WHAT?
IT SEEMS THAT...
YOU MIGHT BE EVEN BETTER THAN ME AT GATHERING INFO.
WE COULD USE TAL-ENT LIKE YOURS.
?
HUH?
YOU KNOW EXACTLY WHERE SHE COMMITTED SUICIDE?

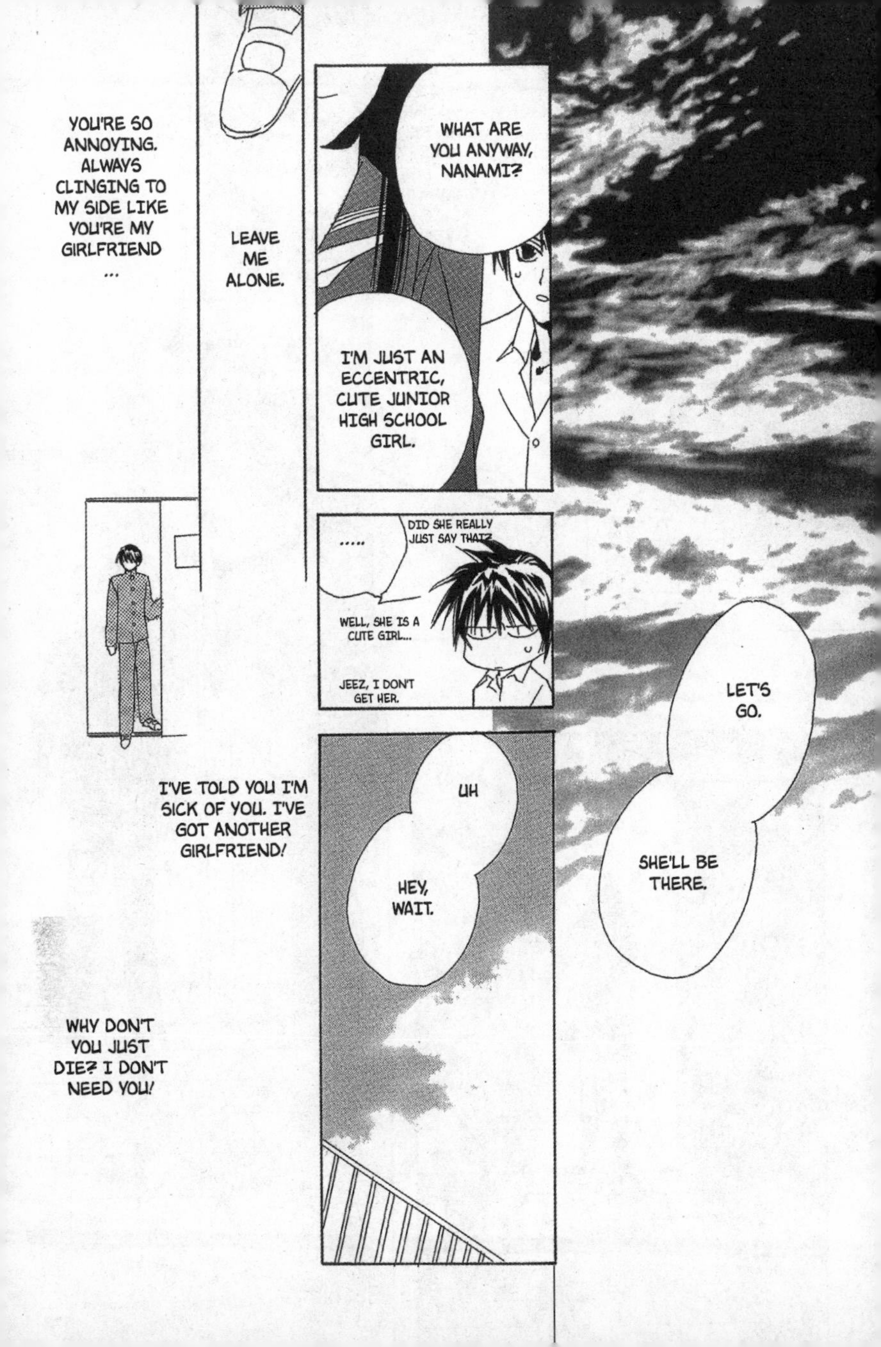

WHAT ARE YOU ANYWAY, NANAMI?
I'M JUST AN ECCENTRIC, CUTE JUNIOR HIGH SCHOOL GIRL.
.....
DID SHE REALLY JUST SAY THAT?
WELL, SHE IS A CUTE GIRL...
JEEZ, I DON'T GET HER.
LET'S GO.
SHE'LL BE THERE.
UH
HEY, WAIT.
YOU'RE SO ANNOYING. ALWAYS CLINGING TO MY SIDE LIKE YOU'RE MY GIRLFRIEND ...
LEAVE ME ALONE.
I'VE TOLD YOU I'M SICK OF YOU. I'VE GOT ANOTHER GIRLFRIEND!
WHY DON'T YOU JUST DIE? I DON'T NEED YOU!

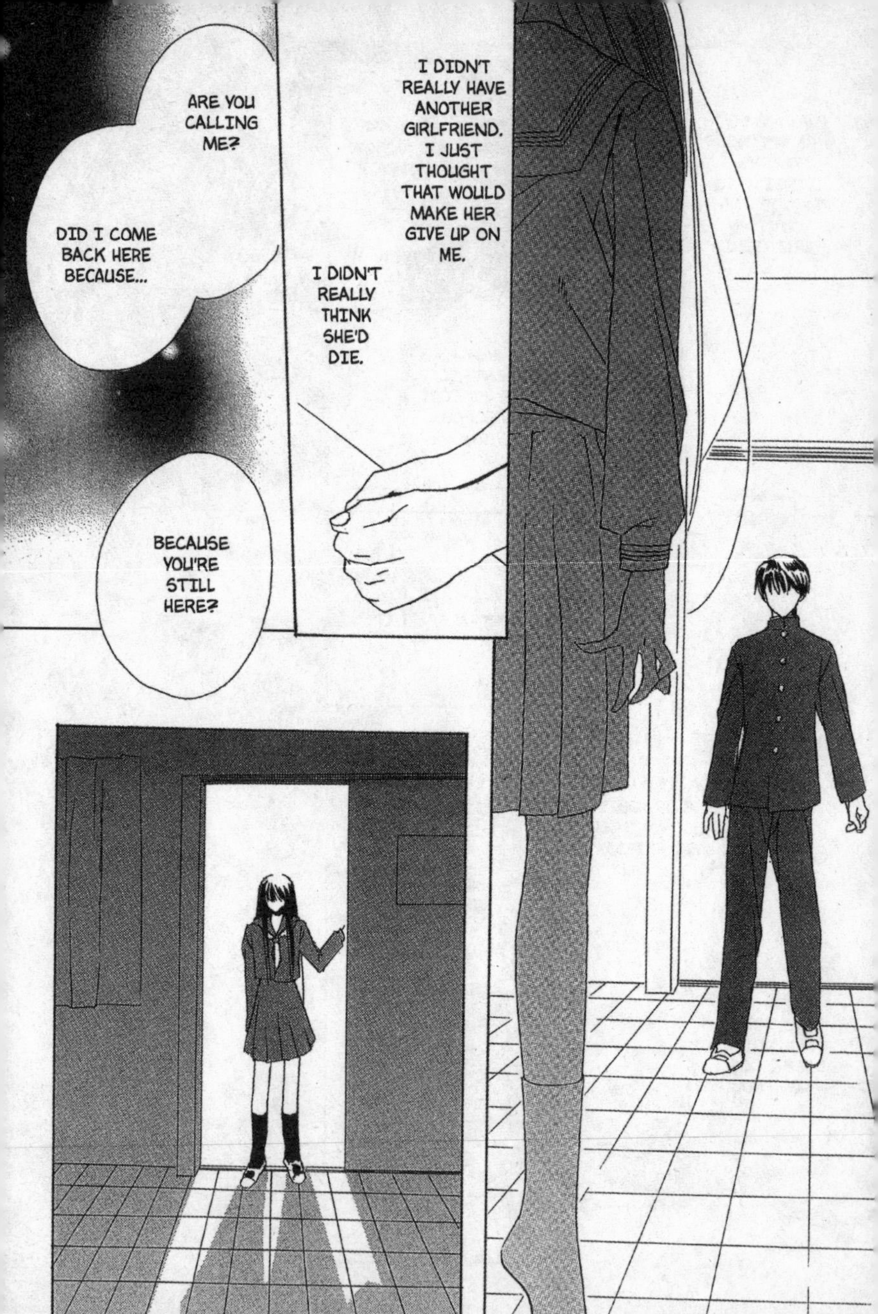
I DIDN'T REALLY HAVE ANOTHER GIRLFRIEND. I JUST THOUGHT THAT WOULD MAKE HER GIVE UP ON ME.
I DIDN'T REALLY THINK SHE'D DIE.
ARE YOU CALLING ME?
DID I COME BACK HERE BECAUSE...
BECAUSE YOU'RE STILL HERE?

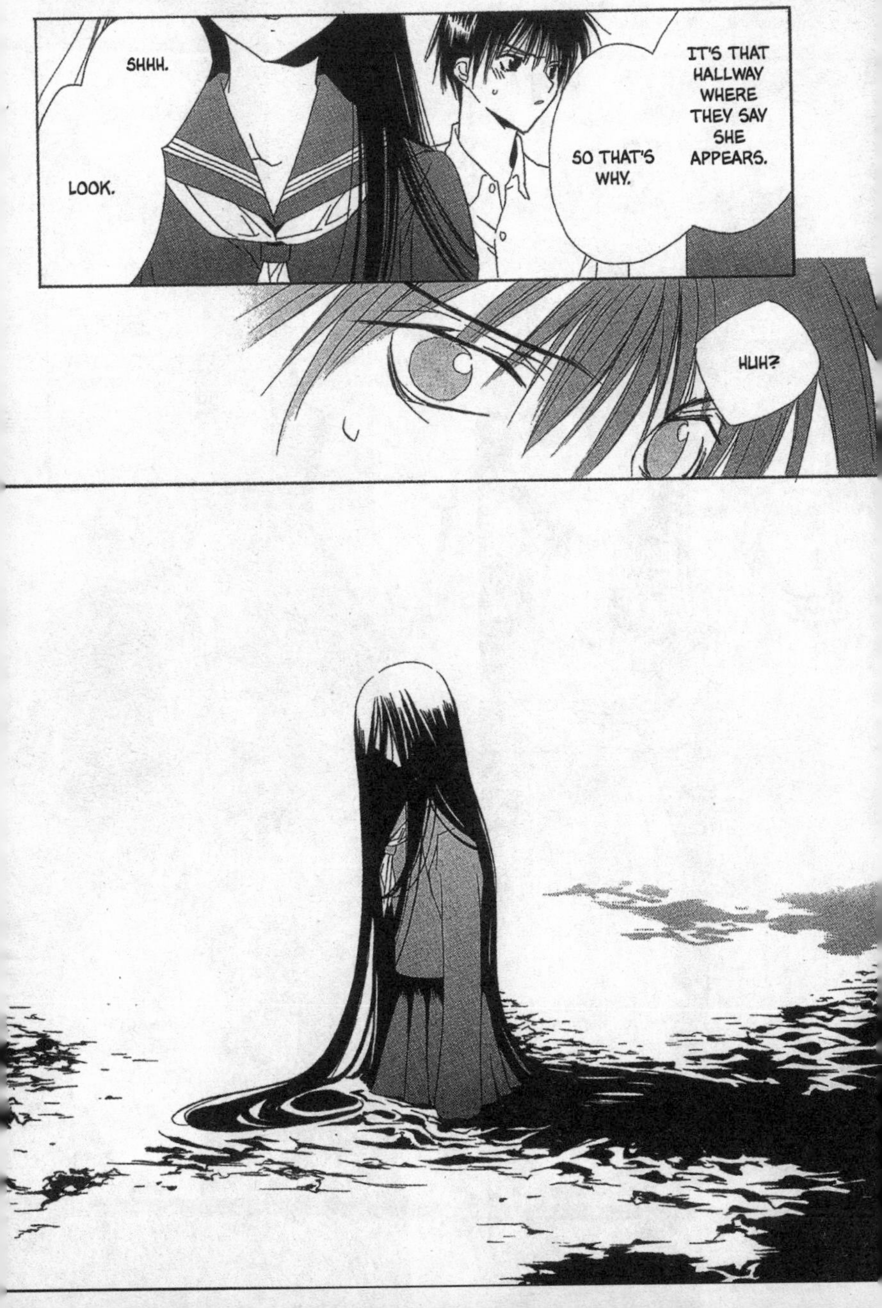
IT'S THAT HALLWAY WHERE THEY SAY SHE APPEARS.
SO THAT'S WHY.
SHHH.
LOOK.
HUH?

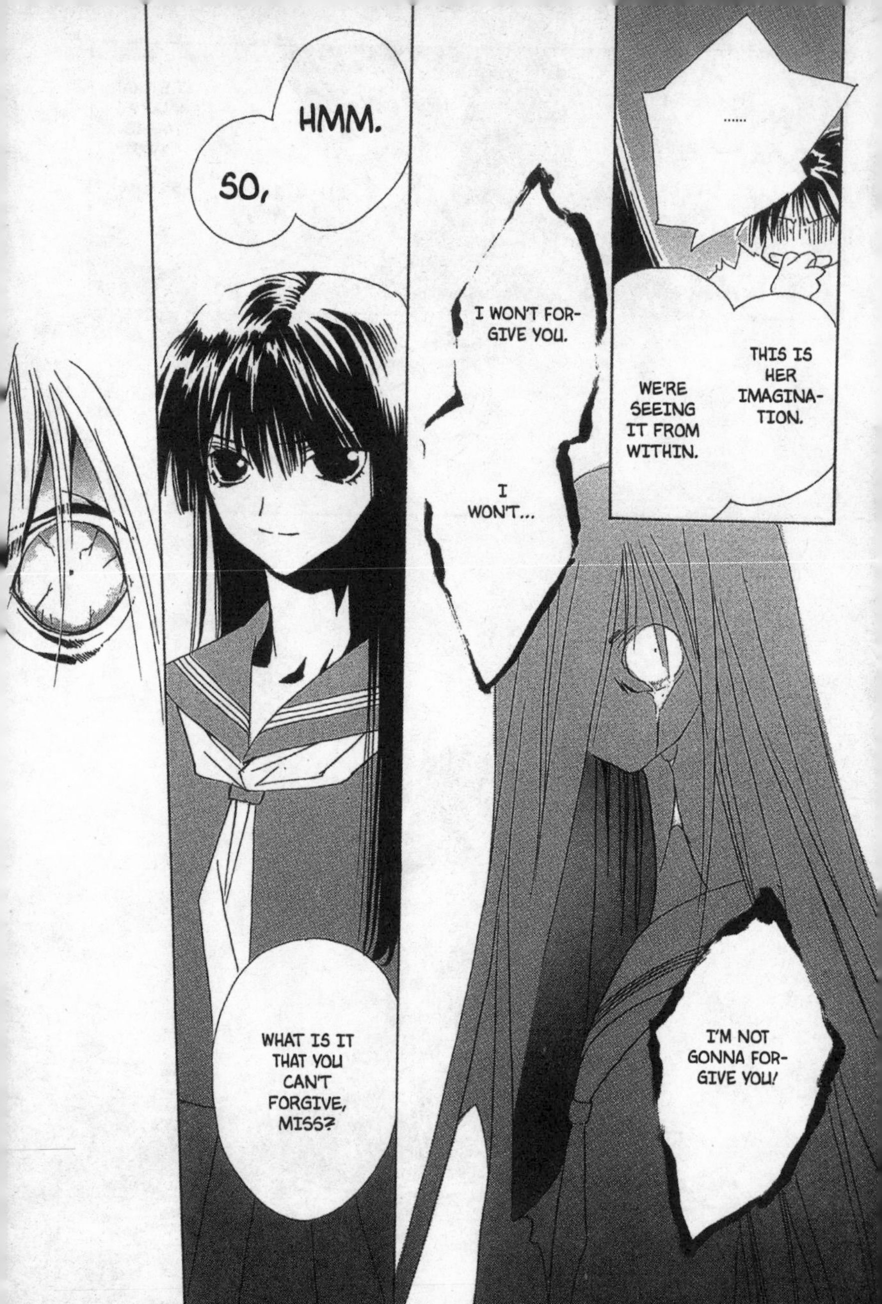
......
THIS IS HER IMAGINATION.
WE'RE SEEING IT FROM WITHIN.
I WON'T FOR-GIVE YOU.
I WON'T...
HMM.
SO,
I'M NOT GONNA FOR-GIVE YOU!
WHAT IS IT THAT YOU CAN'T FORGIVE, MISS?

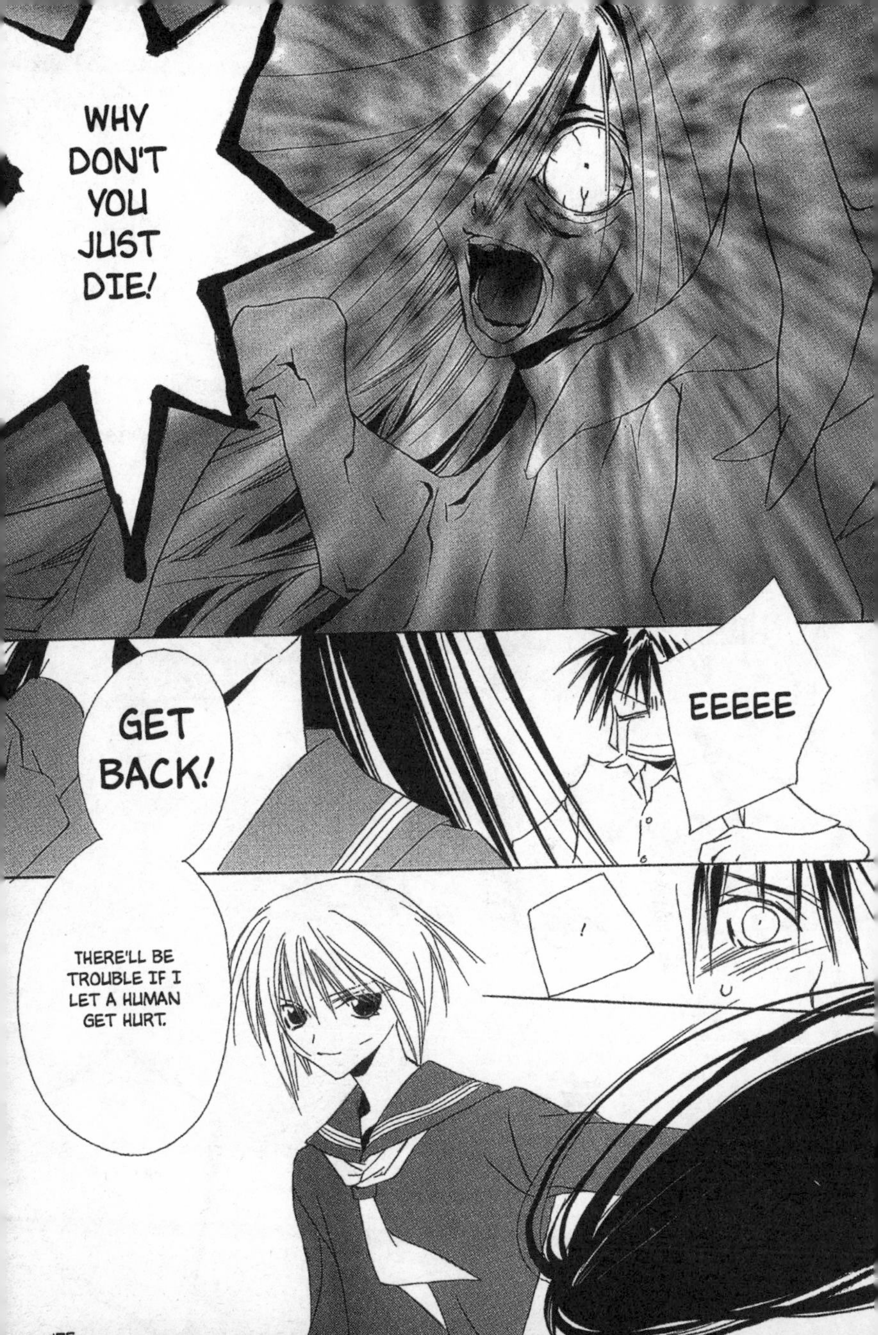
WHY DON'T YOU JUST DIE!
EEEEE
GET BACK!
!
THERE'LL BE TROUBLE IF I LET A HUMAN GET HURT.

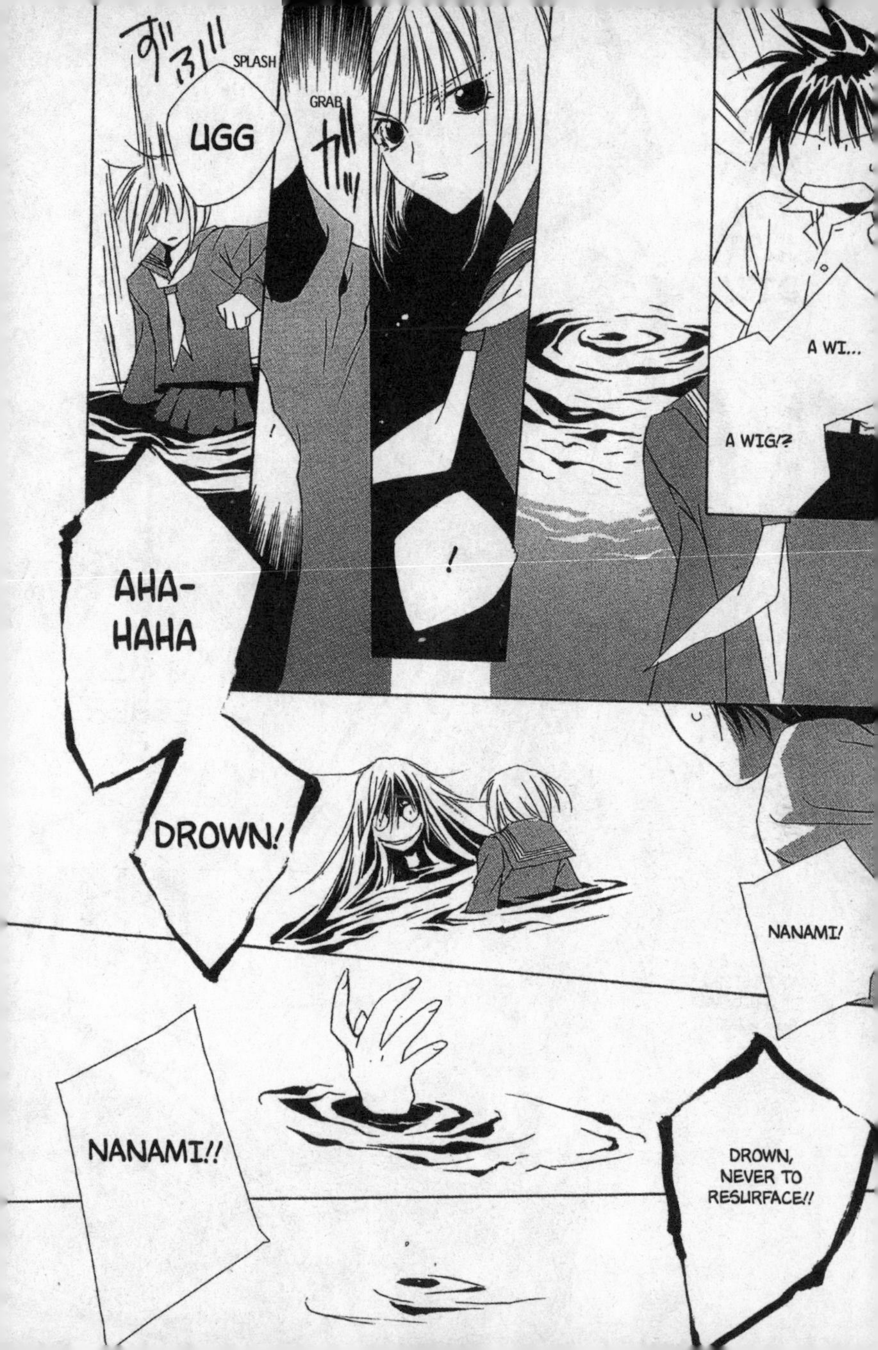
A WI...
A WIG!?
すぶ!!
SPLASH
UGG
GRAB
ガッ
!
!
AHA-
HAHA
DROWN!
NANAMI!
DROWN,
NEVER TO
RESURFACE!!
NANAMI!!

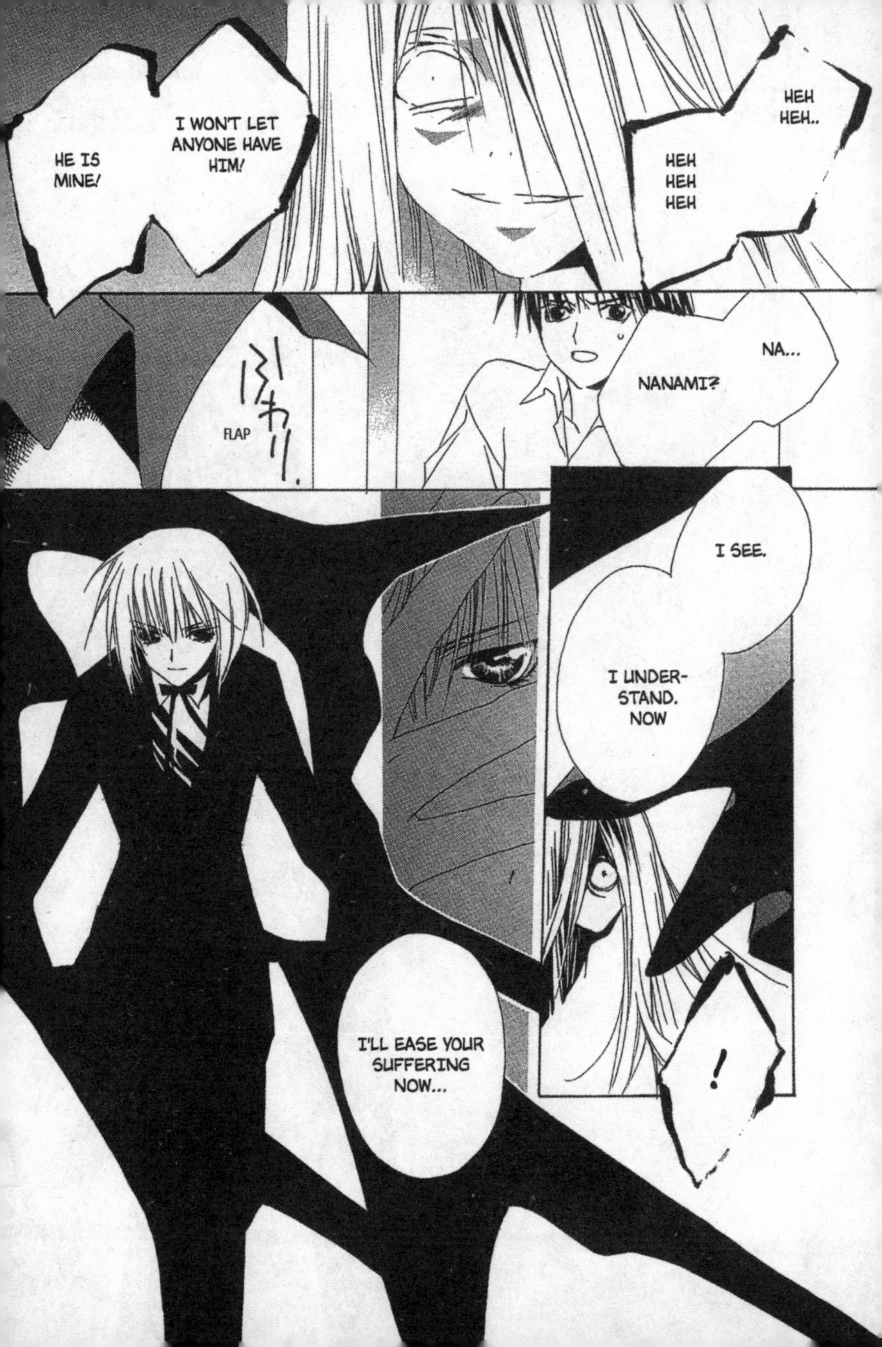
HEH HEH..
HEH HEH HEH
I WON'T LET ANYONE HAVE HIM!
HE IS MINE!
NA... NANAMI?
ふわり
FLAP
I SEE.
I UNDER-STAND. NOW
!
I'LL EASE YOUR SUFFERING NOW...

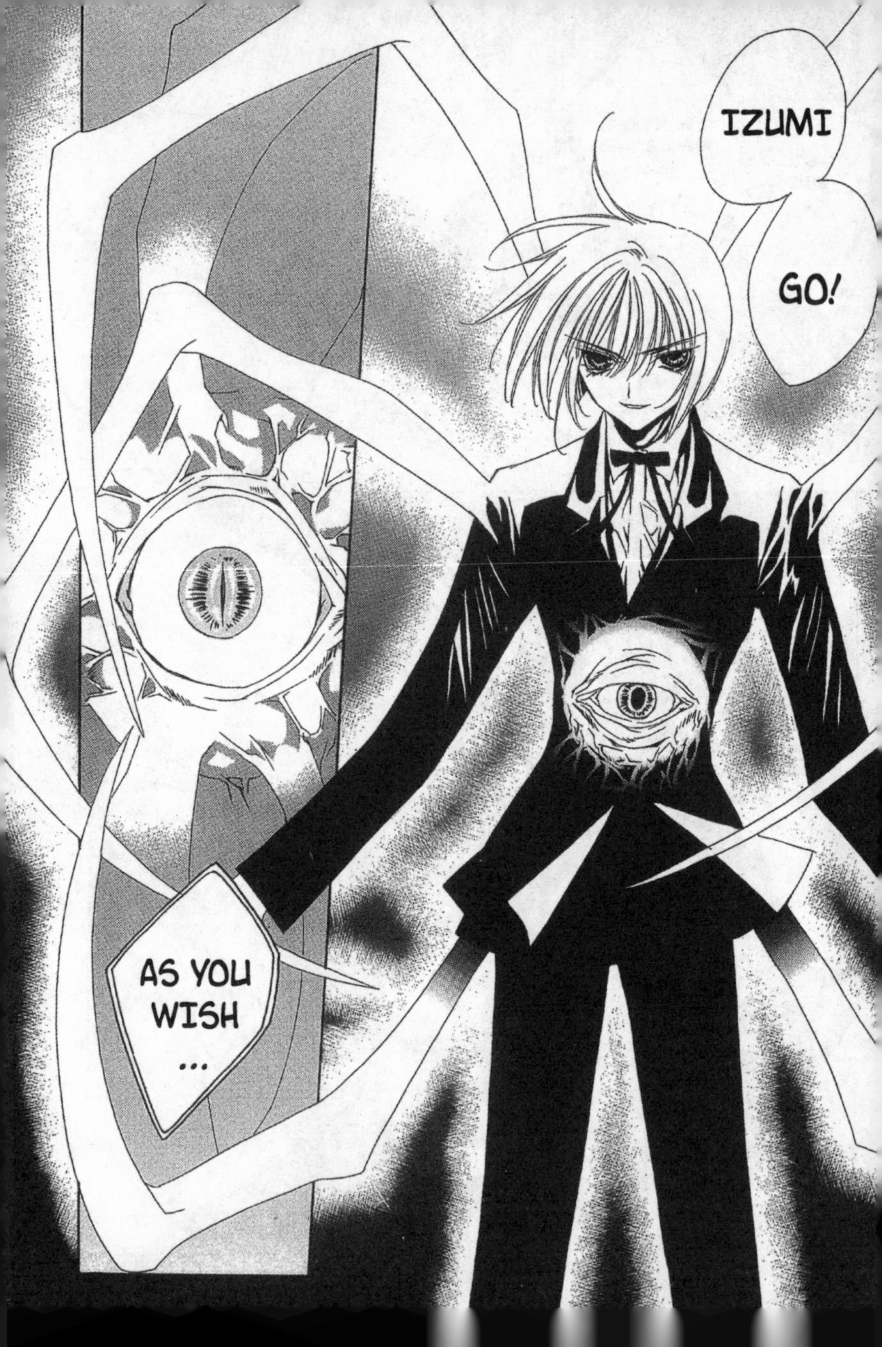
IZUMI
GO!
AS YOU WISH ...

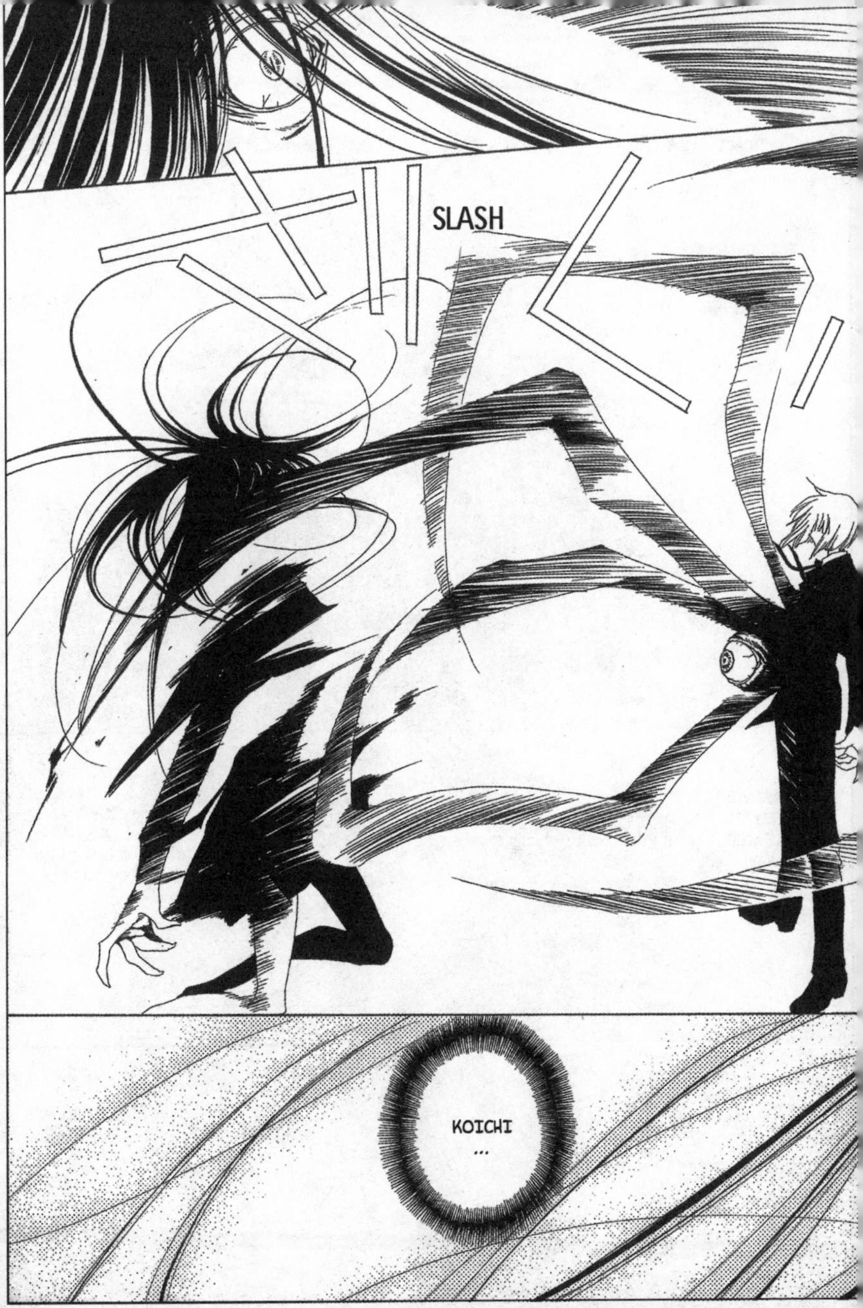
SLASH
KOICHI
...

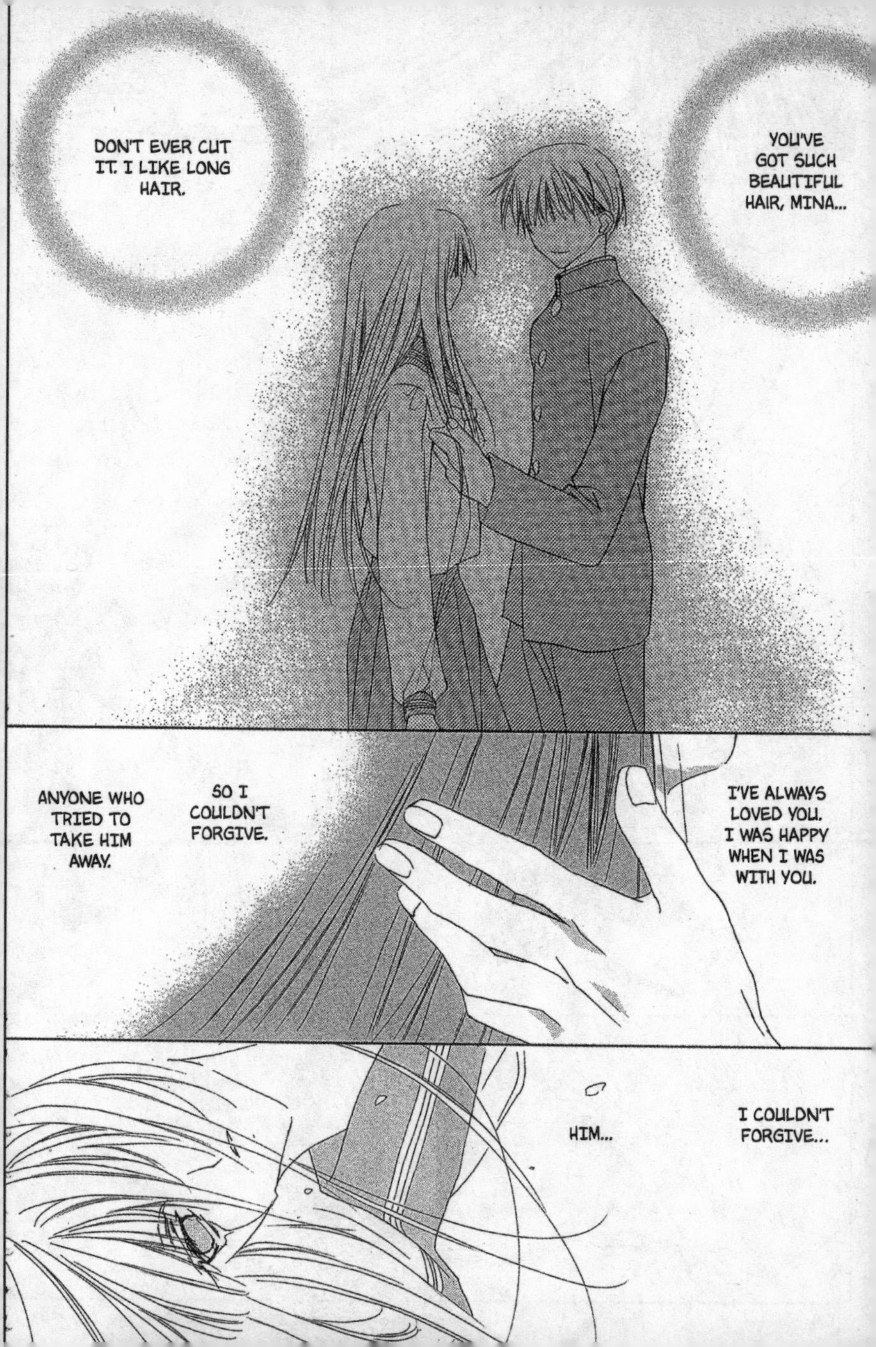
YOU'VE GOT SUCH BEAUTIFUL HAIR, MINA...
DON'T EVER CUT IT. I LIKE LONG HAIR.
I'VE ALWAYS LOVED YOU. I WAS HAPPY WHEN I WAS WITH YOU.
SO I COULDN'T FORGIVE.
ANYONE WHO TRIED TO TAKE HIM AWAY.
I COULDN'T FORGIVE...
HIM...

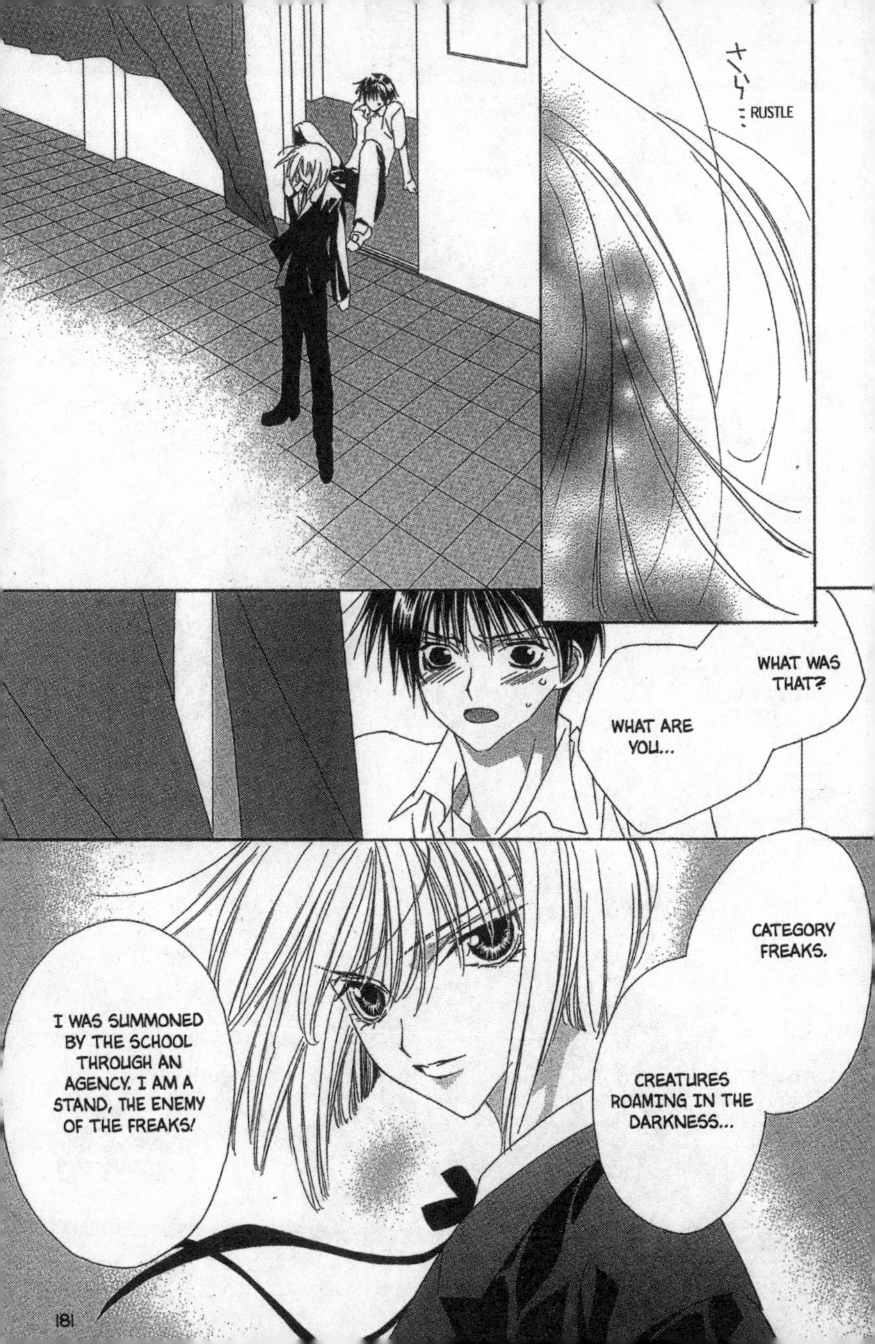
RUSTLE
WHAT WAS THAT?
WHAT ARE YOU...
CATEGORY FREAKS.
CREATURES ROAMING IN THE DARKNESS...
I WAS SUMMONED BY THE SCHOOL THROUGH AN AGENCY. I AM A STAND, THE ENEMY OF THE FREAKS!

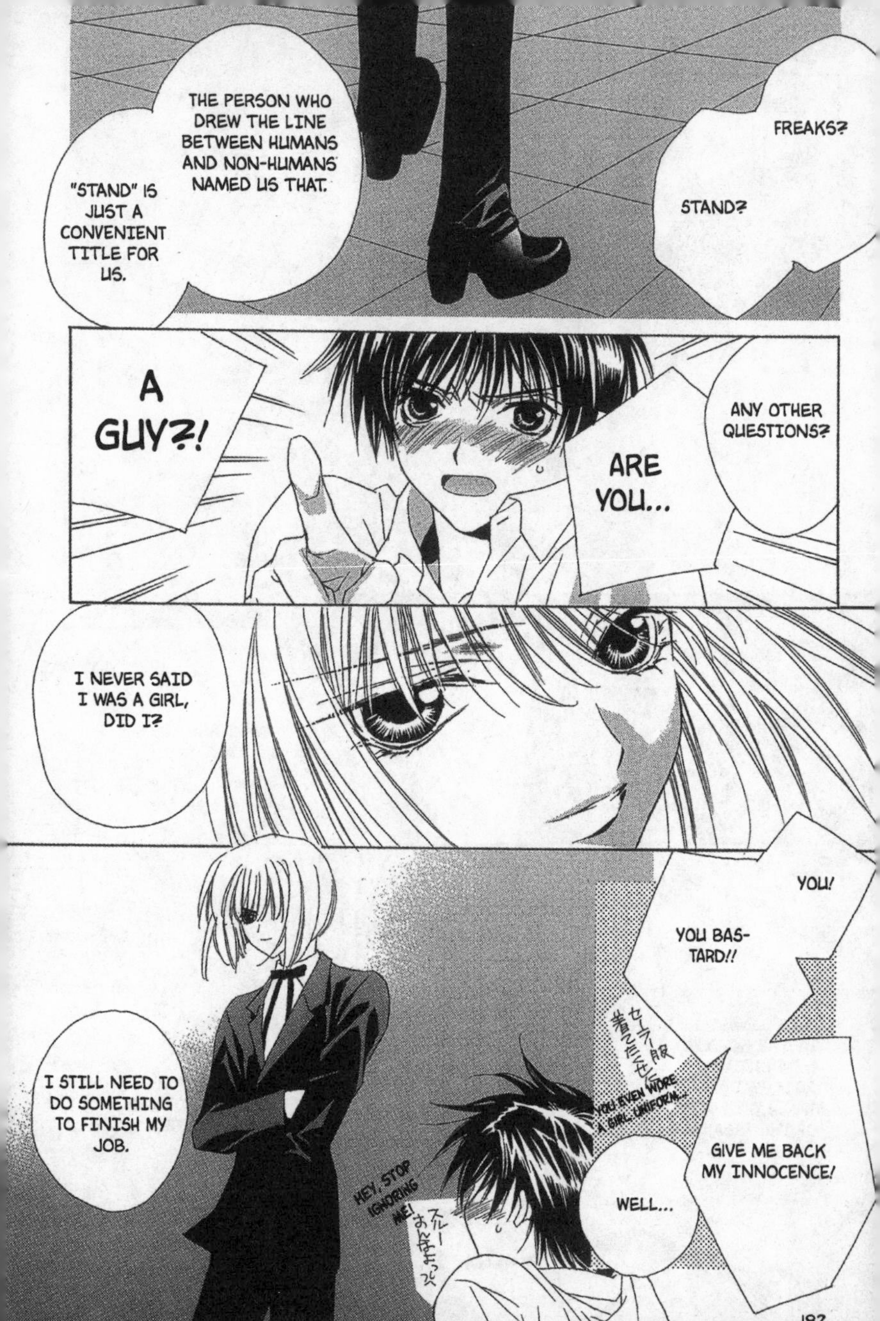

FREAKS?
STAND?
THE PERSON WHO DREW THE LINE BETWEEN HUMANS AND NON-HUMANS NAMED US THAT.
"STAND" IS JUST A CONVENIENT TITLE FOR US.
ANY OTHER QUESTIONS?
ARE YOU...
A GUY?!
I NEVER SAID I WAS A GIRL, DID I?
YOU!
YOU BAS-TARD!!
GIVE ME BACK MY INNOCENCE!
セーラー服着てたくせに
YOU EVEN WORE A GIRL UNIFORM...
WELL...
I STILL NEED TO DO SOMETHING TO FINISH MY JOB.
HEY, STOP IGNORING ME!

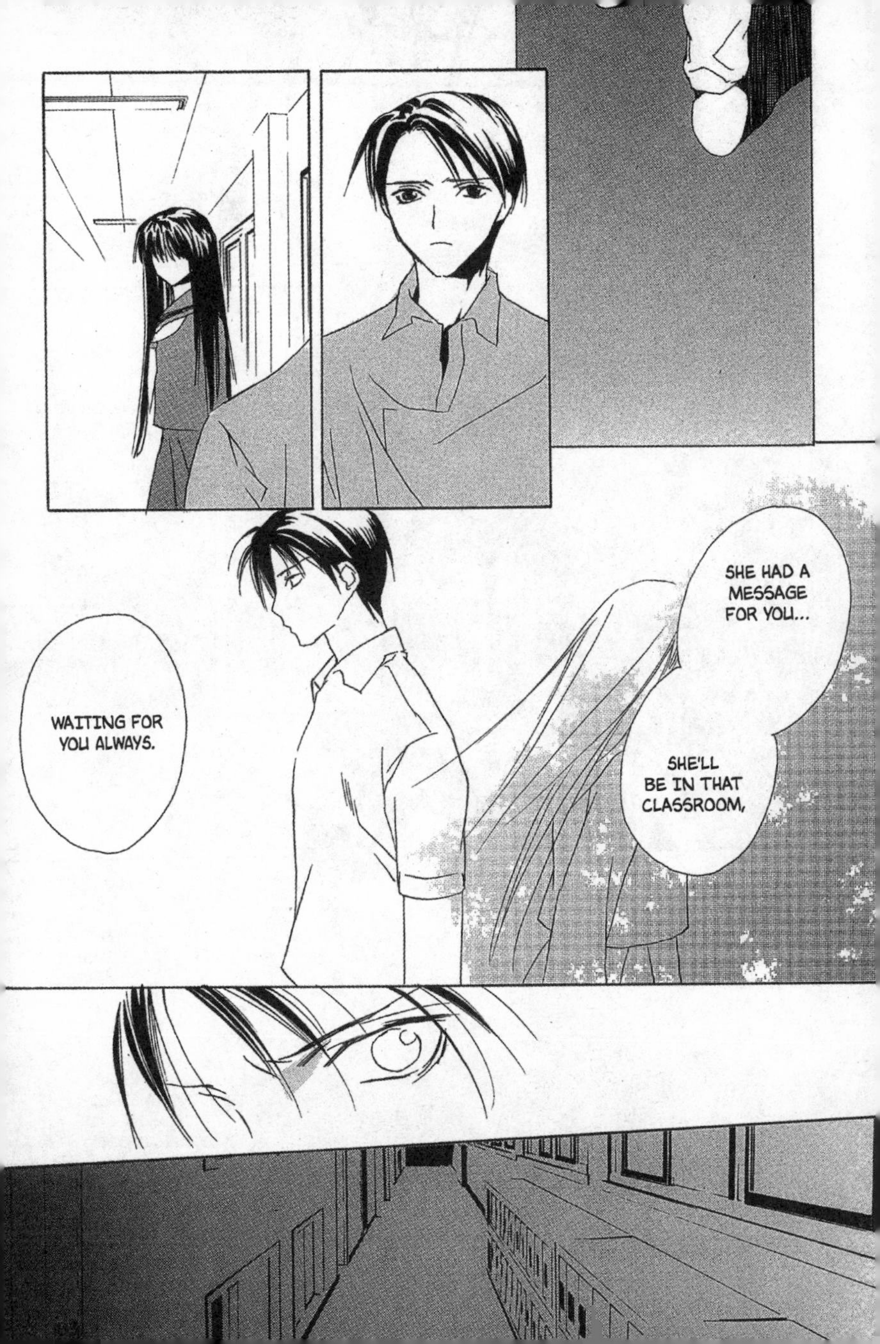
SHE HAD A MESSAGE FOR YOU...
SHE'LL BE IN THAT CLASSROOM,
WAITING FOR YOU ALWAYS.

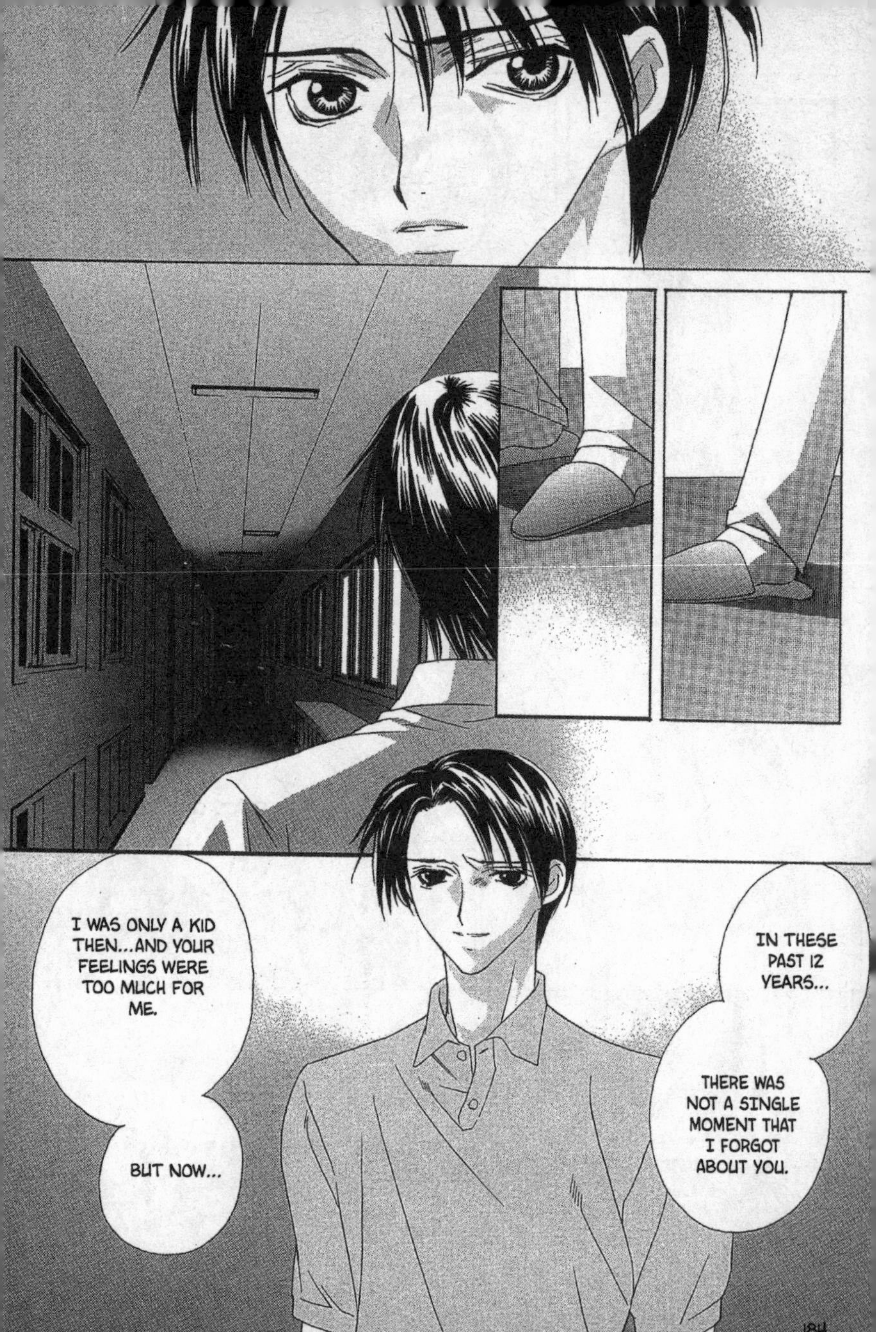
IN THESE PAST 12 YEARS...
THERE WAS NOT A SINGLE MOMENT THAT I FORGOT ABOUT YOU.
I WAS ONLY A KID THEN...AND YOUR FEELINGS WERE TOO MUCH FOR ME.
BUT NOW...

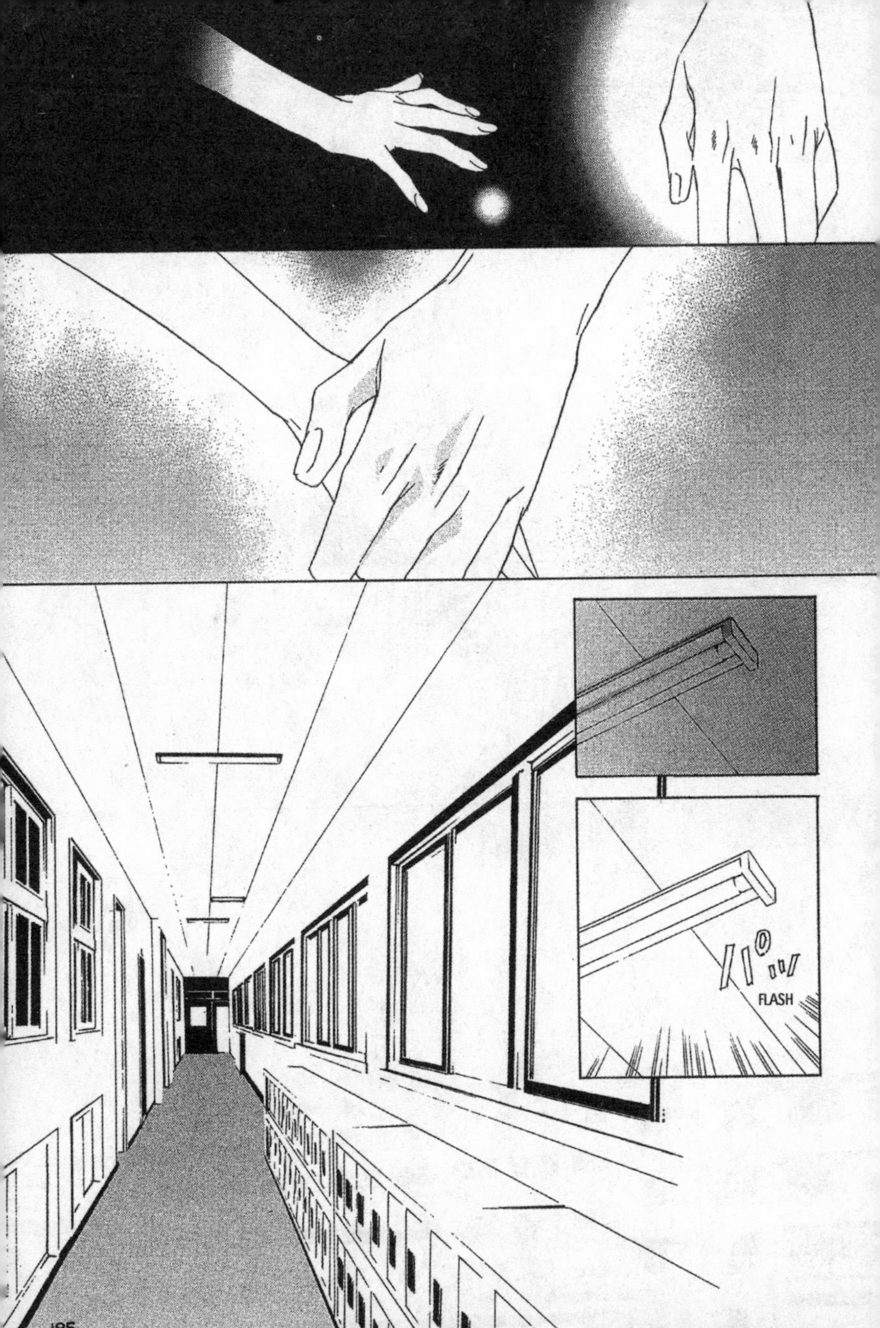
FLASH

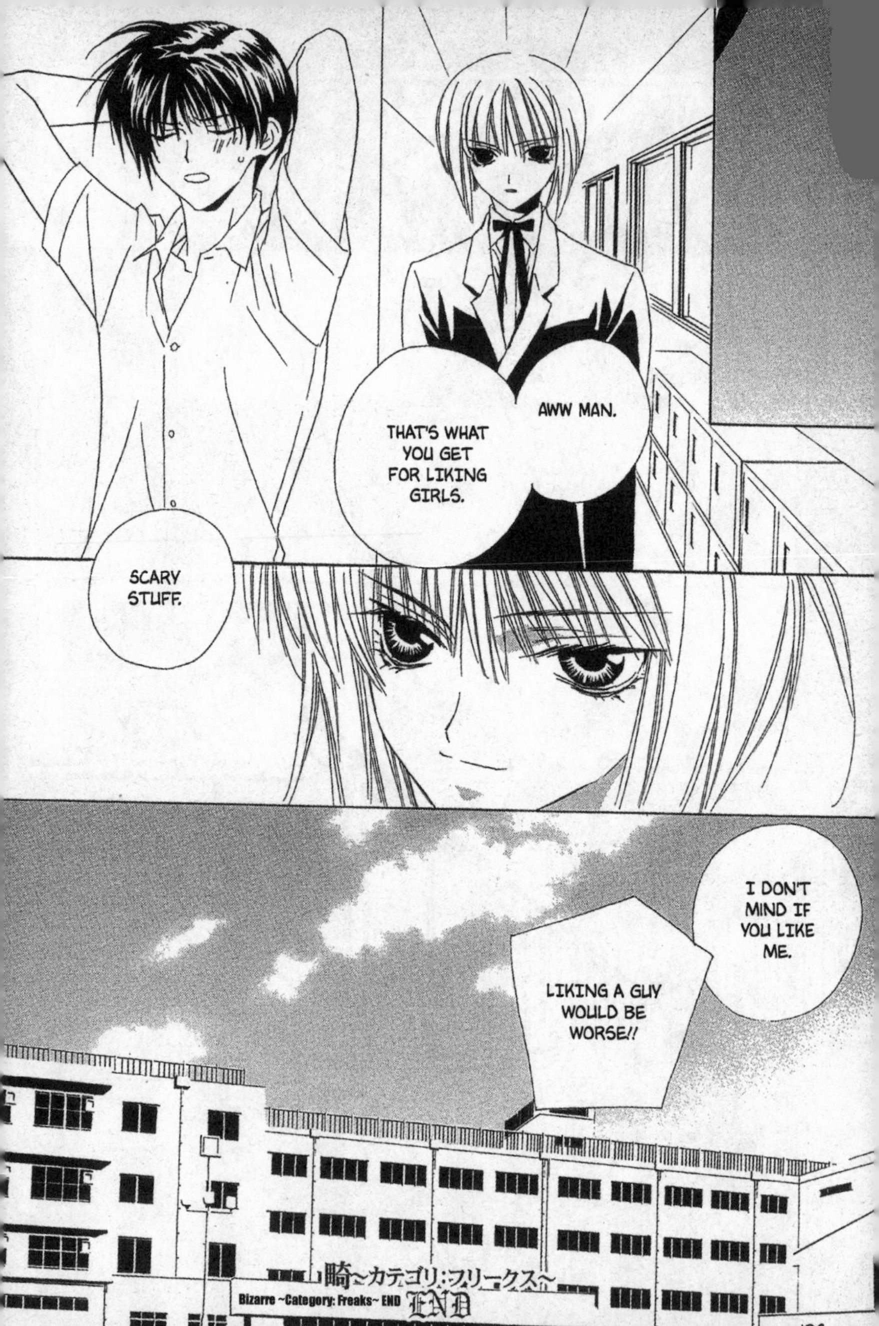
AWW MAN.
THAT'S WHAT YOU GET FOR LIKING GIRLS.
SCARY STUFF.
I DON'T MIND IF YOU LIKE ME.
LIKING A GUY WOULD BE WORSE!!
畸～カテゴリ：フリークス～
Bizarre ~Category: Freaks~ END
END

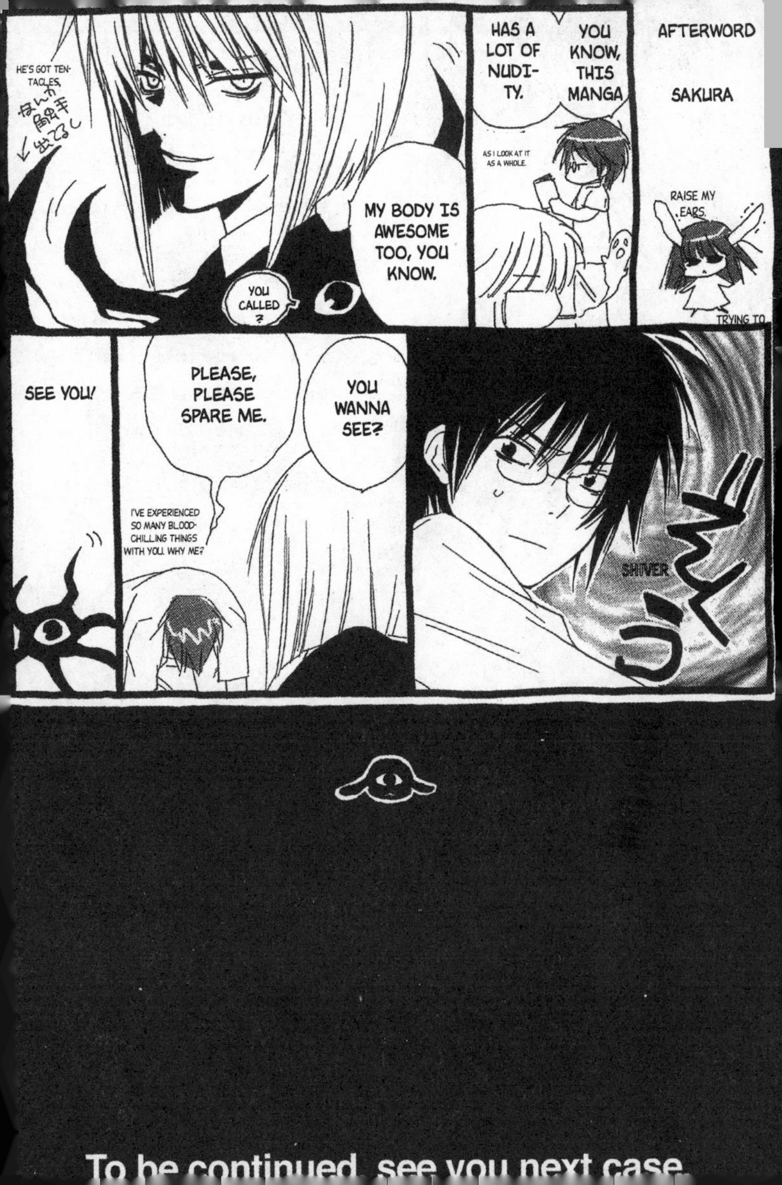
AFTERWORD
SAKURA
TRYING TO RAISE MY EARS.
YOU KNOW, THIS MANGA
HAS A LOT OF NUDI-TY.
AS I LOOK AT IT AS A WHOLE.
MY BODY IS AWESOME TOO, YOU KNOW.
YOU CALLED?
HE'S GOT TEN-TACLES,
なんか触手出てるし
SHIVER
YOU WANNA SEE?
PLEASE, PLEASE SPARE ME.
I'VE EXPERIENCED SO MANY BLOOD-CHILLING THINGS WITH YOU. WHY ME?
SEE YOU!
To be continued, see you next case.

High School Girls

By: Towa Oshima

A hilariously hip account of life at an all-girl private high school. As the student body comes of age we witness their search for love, sexual controversy and the rivalry between cliques. Based on the authors own real life experiences this is one manga you don't want to miss. If you enjoyed the drama in "Heathers" and "Clueless" you'll love High school Girls!

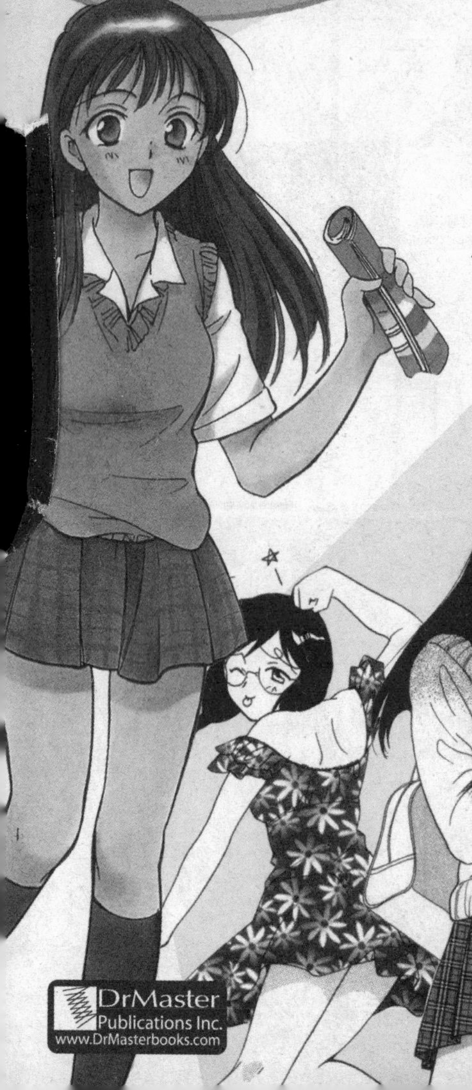

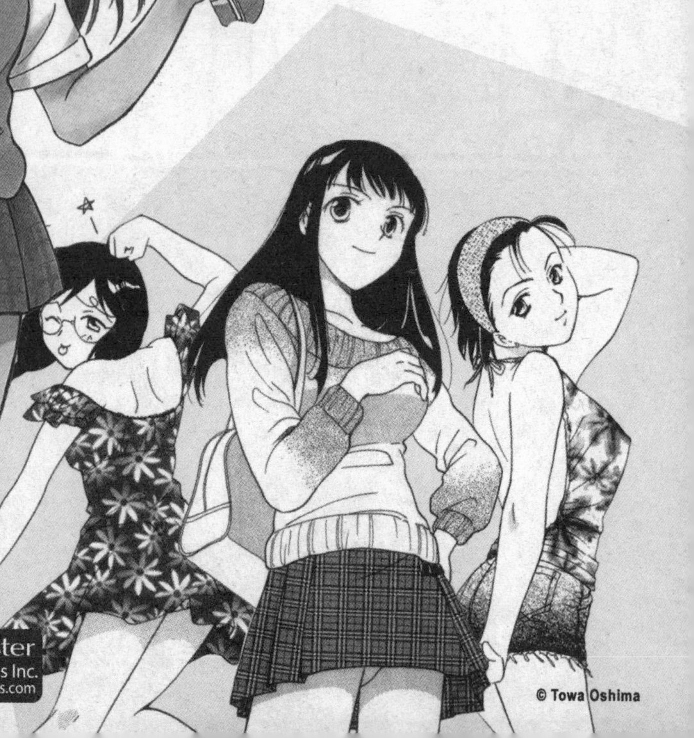

DrMaster
Publications Inc.
www.DrMasterbooks.com

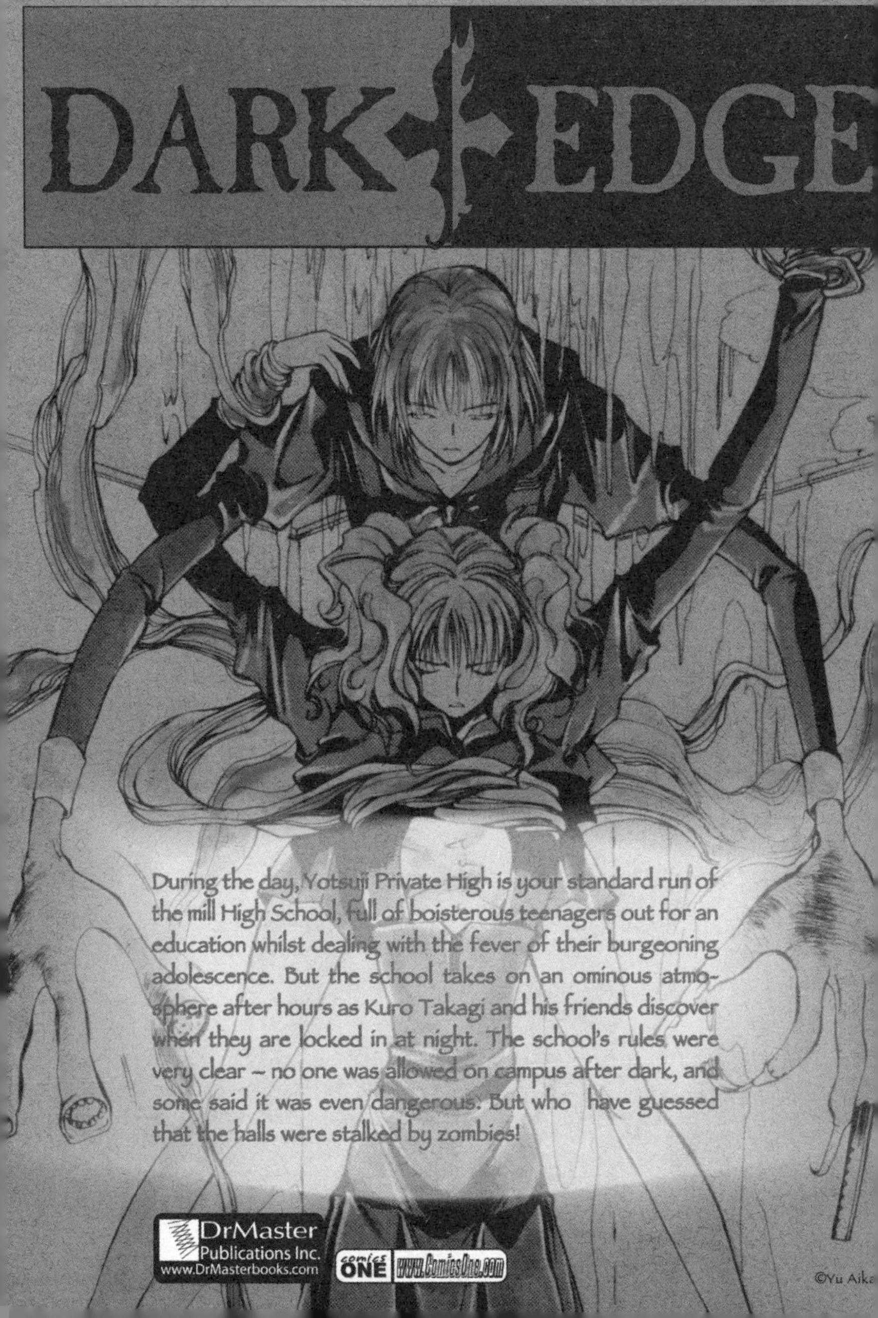

DARK ✝ EDGE

During the day, Yotsuji Private High is your standard run of
the mill High School, full of boisterous teenagers out for an
education whilst dealing with the fever of their burgeoning
adolescence. But the school takes on an ominous atmo-
sphere after hours as Kuro Takagi and his friends discover
when they are locked in at night. The school's rules were
very clear ~ no one was allowed on campus after dark, and
some said it was even dangerous. But who have guessed
that the halls were stalked by zombies!

DrMaster
Publications Inc.
www.DrMasterbooks.com

comics ONE   www.ComicsOne.com

©Yu Aikawa

LUNAR LEGEND
TSUKIHIME

月姫

DrMaster
Publications Inc.
www.DrMasterbooks.com

comics
ONE | www.ComicsOne.com

BLUE BLUE GLASS MOON, UNDER THE CRIMSON AIR

A CHILDHOOD ACCIDENT HAS LEFT YOUNG SHIKI TOHNO WITH A VERY SPECIAL ABILITY.
HE CAN NOW SEE THE HIDDEN LINES OR WEAK POINTS IN ALL THINGS -- BE THEY
ORGANIC OR INANIMATE. BY STRIKING OR CUTTING ALONG THESE LINES SHIKI CAN SLICE
THROUGH VIRTUALLY ANYTHING LIKE A HOT KNIFE THROUGH BUTTER. UNFORTUNATELY
THE GIFT COMES PACKAGED WITH A NEARLY IRRESISTIBLE URGE TO KILL USING HIS
NEW ABILITY. A YOUNG GIRL FALLS VICTIM TO SHIKI'S KILLING LUST. YET SHE IS
APPARENTLY REBORN UNHARMED AND DEMANDING SHIKI'S AID. WHO IS SHE AND WHAT
COULD SHE WANT?

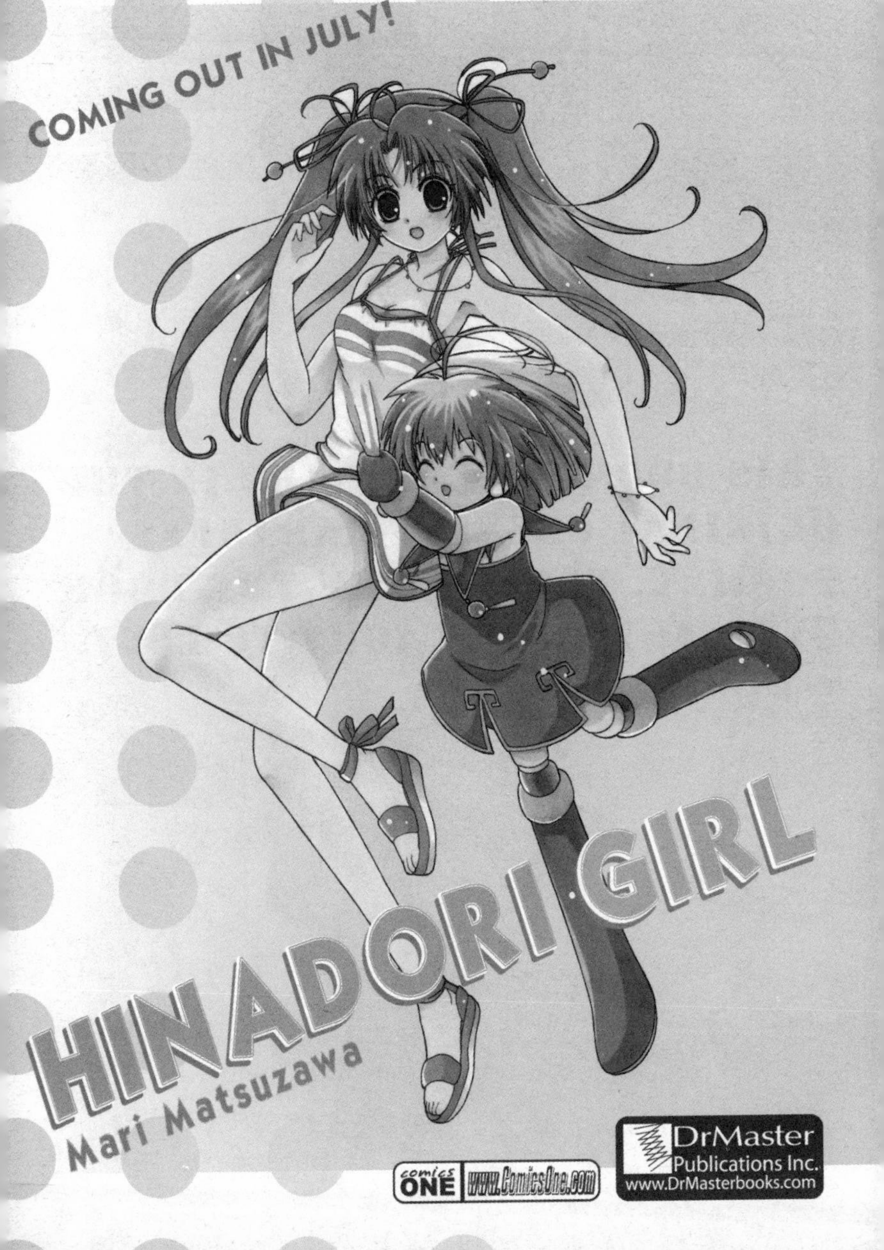
COMING OUT IN JULY!
HINADORI GIRL
Mari Matsuzawa
comics ONE
www.ComicsOne.com
DrMaster Publications Inc.
www.DrMasterbooks.com

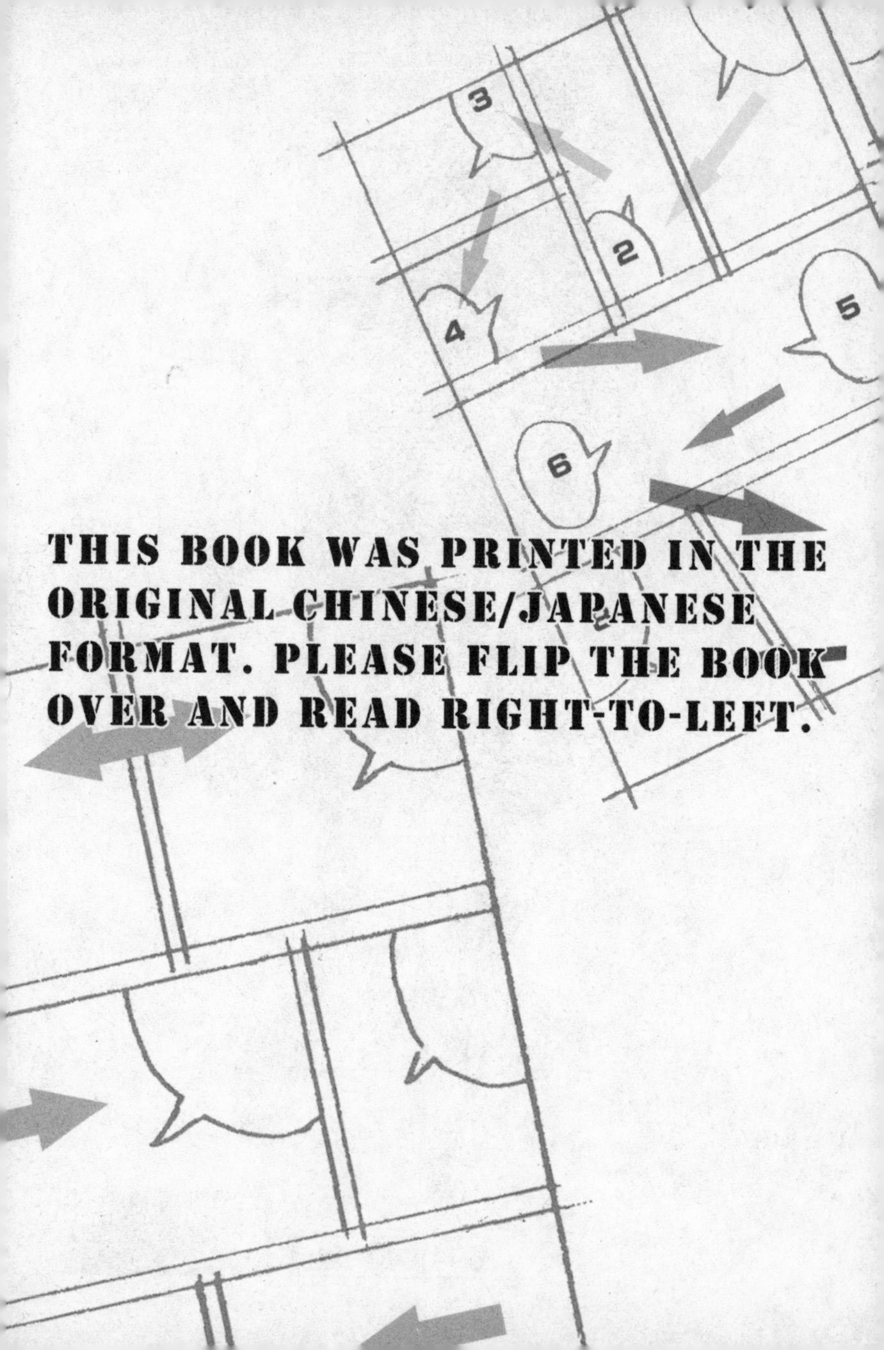
3
2
4
5
6

THIS BOOK WAS PRINTED IN THE ORIGINAL CHINESE/JAPANESE FORMAT. PLEASE FLIP THE BOOK OVER AND READ RIGHT-TO-LEFT.